Society of the Dead

Society of the Dead

Quita Manaquita and Palo Praise in Cuba

TODD RAMÓN OCHOA

University of California Press

BERKELEY   LOS ANGELES   LONDON

University of California Press, one of the most distinguished university presses in the United States, enriches lives around the world by advancing scholarship in the humanities, social sciences, and natural sciences. Its activities are supported by the UC Press Foundation and by philanthropic contributions from individuals and institutions. For more information, visit www.ucpress.edu.

Parts of chapters 1 and 2 were originally published as "Versions of the Dead: Kalunga, Cuban-Congo Materiality, and Ethnography," in *Cultural Anthropology* 22, no. 4 (November 2007): 473–500.

University of California Press
Berkeley and Los Angeles, California

University of California Press, Ltd.
London, England

Library of Congress Cataloging-in-Publication Data

Ochoa, Todd Ramón, 1969–.
    Society of the dead : Quita Manaquita and Palo praise in Cuba / Todd Ramón Ochoa.
        p.   cm.
    Includes bibliographical references and index.
    ISBN 978–0-520-25683-5 (cloth : alk. paper)
    ISBN 978–0-520-25684-2 (pbk. : alk. paper)
    1. Palo.   2. Afro-Caribbean cults—Cuba.   3. Cuba—Religious life and customs.   4. Cuba—Religion—20th century.   I. Title.
    BL2532.P35O24   2010
    299.6'7—dc22
                                                        2010002017

19   18   17   16   15   14   13   12   11   10
10   9   8   7   6   5   4   3   2   1

For Christiana Mutzl Zilke, David Zilke, and Raúl R. Ochoa

Contents

Acknowledgments

This book is nearly twelve years in the writing, if one includes as writing the marking one undergoes in the process of fieldwork. It would never have been finished without the help of innumerable people, many of whom must go unmentioned because they would never recognize themselves as contributors to the work of a stranger. These are the many who have listened in conversation, commented on a question I might have had, then disappeared into the crowd; the many who agreed with a tentative hypothesis or simply stepped aside to see what would become of me; the many authors—ethnographers, philosophers, writers, poets—who have inspired this writing directly or imperceptibly. How many cannot be named in these words of thanks?

In Havana, I could not have taken a step without Margarita Saéz Saéz, the healer and teacher of Palo and Ocha/Santo who guided me through the complex worlds of African-inspired praise in the capital. Sergio Rajiv Gomez Saéz accompanied me through much of what is unwritten here and through restrained humor offered comfort when field situations seemed most difficult. Rodolfo Herrera O'Farril brought me into Palo with confidence and joy, despite the many obstacles that stood in his way. The gathered membership of the Quita Manaquita praise house of Guanabacoa has always been generous with its energy, time, and intellectual resources. The uninterrupted eighteen-month stay in Havana between 1999 and 2000, during which the fieldwork for this project was conducted, was made possible with the logistical support of the Fundación Fernando Ortiz, under the direction of Miguel Barnet.

Also in Havana, Caridad Acosta Acosta housed me and cared for me in innumerable ways during those eighteen months and lent a keen eye to my tentative observations of Cuban social, economic, and political life. Carlos

Alberto Aguilera Chang and Carmen Paula Bermúdez, along with Pedro Marqués de Armas, involved me in Cuban literature and the politics of art in Havana. They brought a depth to my understanding of Cuban life in the 1990s that is implicit in every page that follows. Dannys Montes de Oca y Moreda immersed me in these depths through her singular intelligence, good humor, and generosity in moments of impossible hardship. If a tone of delight rises from time to time in these lines, I owe it to her. Many others have hosted me and cared for me in my nearly two decades of fieldwork on the island, and to this generous and quiet multitude I am deeply grateful.

This project was born in the Department of Anthropology at Columbia University in the second half of the 1990s. Michael Taussig, who oversaw my work, gave it a rigorous intellectual orientation and a writer's attention. More important, despite reservations he affirmed it through the great latitude he gave me in assembling ideas and fieldwork into the doctoral dissertation that became the prototype for this book. Steven Gregory and Neni Panourgia were indispensable interlocutors and steadfast supporters during treacherous stretches of writing. To Richard Kernaghan and Daniella Gandolfo I express my everlasting admiration for their discipline, curiosity, and razor-sharp intelligence. Without them there would be no intensity to the ideas that underlie this book. Drew Alan Walker introduced me to the starry night of ideas and to the solar limits that lie on the other side. Dora King, Karina Rosenborg, Olga González Castañeda, Nicole Ridgeway, Eleni Myravili, Paulina Palacios, Lance Lattig, Paul Mendelson, Stuart Mclean, and Emilio Spadola, among many others, have marked the intellectual matrix in which this book is embedded.

This writing became a book during three years I spent as a President's Postdoctoral Fellow, then as a Chancellor's Postdoctoral Fellow, in the Department of Anthropology at the University of California, Berkeley. I am grateful to Shiela O'Rourke in the Office of the President for her unwavering support during those years. William Hanks was an unrivaled mentor and superb friend at Berkeley. The example provided by his combination of passion and discipline made the revision of this text a pleasure to undertake. Any subtlety this writing might have is owed in large part to colleagues at Berkeley who generously provided their critique and also their friendship to this itinerant scholar briefly in their midst. My warm gratitude goes to Cori Hayden, Stefania Pandolfo, Saba Mahmood, Charles Hirschkind, Lawrence Cohen, Mariane Ferme, Donald Moore, Alexei Yurchak, and Xin Liu. Thanks are due as well to Peter Skafish, Mark MacGrath, and Sean DeHaas at Berkeley for their time and generosity as interlocutors on many aspects of this project. My editors at UC Press have been exceptional, beginning with Stan Holwitz and including Reed Malcom, Marilyn Schwartz, and my superb copyeditor Susan Silver. Two anonymous reviewers for UC Press made comments on the manuscript that greatly improved it. I am grateful to the editors of *Cultural Anthropology* for permission to reprint significant portions of an article that first appeared in that journal.

I have been warmly embraced by my colleagues in the Department of Religious Studies at the University of North Carolina, Chapel Hill. Their generosity, collegiality, and optimism have made finishing this project easy, and for that I cannot thank them enough. I am especially grateful to Jonathan Boyarin for his thoughts on things Jewish in Cuban-Kongo praise and for his joyful embrace of the recombinant powers of diaspora.

My mother, Christiana Mutzl Zilke, and my siblings Christiana Ochoa and Max Ochoa have been unflagging supporters in every aspect of this project. I thank each of them for reading the manuscript at various moments and offering me their honest criticism. Erika Samoff, my partner since before Cuba was ever on my horizon, has accompanied me through every moment in the writing of this book. It would not have been finished without her steady, patient support and her enviably sharp intellect. Our children, Gabo and Marcos, have joined us during a period of professional itinerancy with the fluidity and openness that only children bring to life, and for that I thank them so much.

Introduction

This book is about insignificant experiences, fleeting events, and minor intimacies felt at the limits of our reason. It is about registering such experiences, which are of no consequence until they are collected, agglomerated, and allowed to become forceful, which is to say influential, in our lives. It is about respecting the inconsequential and finding in insignificance a turbulence that makes all the difference, that lends direction—to perceptions, substances, and lives. In short, it is about instabilities at the limits of awareness and relation, or sociality, such as the tremble of an eyelid or the tiny catch in a person's voice when telling a version of events.

It is a book about the Kongo-inspired society of affliction called *Palo* and its practitioner-teachers in Havana.[1] It is about the education these men and women impart to their initiates, whom they instruct in forms of thinking that celebrate the fleetingly visceral apprehension of the dead as the basis for knowledge and action. It is also about the collections of healing-harming substances cared for at the heart of Palo practice. These are called *prendas*, *ngangas*, or *enquisos*, and they take the shape of cauldrons or urns packed with soil, sticks, and entities called *nfumbe*. This is also an account of being befriended by two teachers of Palo who for the past decade, but especially for eighteen months between 1999 and 2000, have guided my research under the rubric of a Palo apprenticeship.

Put simply, Palo is a craft of working with the dead to transform the fates of the living. The works *[trabajos, obras]* that Palo effects both heal and harm. For this reason, Palo is widely feared in Cuba as a form of witchcraft *[brujería]*—a tag practitioners of Palo do not reject. Palo craft includes rites of cleansing, the making of protective bundles, the crafting of dangerous strikes of fate meant to frighten or kill rivals, and, ultimately, the manufacture of the prendas-ngangas-enquisos that teachers of Palo keep at the center of their craft and from which all other works emerge. Each work engages the dead where these are found: in materials such as dirt, sticks, feathers, and the remains of animals and people. Those highly knowledgeable in Palo craft also work the dead in less palpable, but no less concrete, registers, such as allusions and rumors. Palo is as much the art of crafting matter into fatefully powerful substances as it is a narrative art that creates shapes of hope and fear from the silences that pervade our everyday lives. Despite the considerable air of dread that surrounds it, Cubans of all sorts are drawn to Palo when their immediate prospects seem to sour and despair enters their lives.

1990s

I first traveled to Cuba in 1992 to gather an experience of the Cuban Revolution, which I was sure would soon disappear along with the rest of the Soviet Bloc. From Ann Arbor, where I had just finished my undergraduate degree in political science at the University of Michigan, the Cuban Revolution appeared to be teetering on the brink of collapse without the aid it had for decades enjoyed from the Soviet Union. On that first visit, which I made independently, I had only a marginal interest in Cuba's African-inspired forms of thought and practice. I had no knowledge of Palo and only vague understandings about Ocha/Santo [Santería], by far the most public form of African-inspired association in Cuba.[2] My interest in Marxist political economy led me to study the national generation of wealth, income distribution, political power, and social justice during the economic crisis. I was there for four months.

Havana in 1992 was unreal to my eyes. Basic markers of a large city were missing—the streets were empty of taxis, buses, and cars; there were no signs designating storefronts, no window displays, no shoppers on the sidewalks. Those places where jeans or televisions might be bought were hidden behind mirrored glass and impassive attendants. Without cars or buses, the city's formidable columned thoroughfares—Malecón, Calle 23, Carlos III–Reina, Infanta, Ayestarán, Belascoaín, and the winding Calzada del Cerro—were silent. The movement of people was minimal, and the lines for public buses wound in baroque entanglements seeking shade under trees and covered sidewalks. The collapse of the transportation infrastructure was so grave that getting to the countryside beyond Havana was impossible. The standstill was near total, and except for an occasional heavy truck, only bicycles plied Havana's wide avenues as people covered tremendous distances in search of food and cooking fuel. Money and food seemed impossible to come by, but, with the economy at a stall, time was plentiful and there was always enough to resolve [*resolver*] the scarcity.

At night, with the foraging and gleaning behind them, entire sections of Havana went without a single light, and in their gloom and stillness the streets were eerily alive with the faint sounds of thousands of people going about their evenings at home. Silverware clinked against china as tables were cleared, doors closed quietly, discussions waned. These sounds haunted public space and betrayed a hidden, or hiding, population. Occasionally, more exuberant sounds would unstill the night—laughter, brawling, and crying.

In 1992 I lived against the terms of my tourist visa by taking up with a family near the intersection of Águila and Monte, which marks the boundary between the neighborhoods of Jesus María, in La Habana Vieja, and Los Citios, in the more modern part of the city called Centro Habana. This was the family of the woman who made my bed in the hotel behind Havana's interstate bus terminal to the west, on the Plaza de la Revolución. Milagro, who along with her husband lived with her parents and her older brother, ran significant risks by taking me in. She could have lost her job for plucking me out of one of the Revolution's hotels, and though I did not understand why Cubans weren't allowed to take in a traveler, or how exactly she calculated her risk, I believed her when she said that she wouldn't be caught. Over the next two decades I would time and again defer to Cubans in calculating political and legal risk. Milagro's neighborhood was among Havana's poorest, and the poverty and despondency of her family and neighbors made evident the violence of the U.S. embargo on the faltering Revolution.

Living in Jesus María and Los Citios in the early nineties was a crash course in Cuba's arcane centralized economy and, more important, a tough introduction to its yet more inscrutable underground markets. Despite crushing shortages at state-run distribution depots that left ration cards unfilled for months, there was hardly a necessary product or service that wasn't somehow available illicitly. It was a matter of having the time to find things and the money to buy them. The same functionaries who provided state-rationed goods and services (such as rice, refrigerator repair, or oral surgery) sourced the illicit markets for each, so people knew where to start looking for their food, their condenser motors, their antibiotics. Goods that disappeared from behind counters where they should have been available at subsidized prices reappeared under those very counters at ten to a hundred times the price. There was rarely bread at the corner bakery, but for twenty times the subsidized price the baker would bake all the bread anyone wanted. Until the midnineties, much of the centralized economy collapsed while neighbors and friends kept from going hungry by devising their own schemes on the vast underground channels that keep Havana alive to this day.

Milagro's husband, Pedro Pastor, was a garbage collector on extended work leave due to a stab he received in a street fight, or so he said. While Milagro worked at the hotel, Pedro introduced me to their life in Havana. He was gifted at maintaining an argument and explaining economic and social chains of cause and effect that were invisible to me, not least because I sustained illusions about Cuban socialism. At the time, he made money from the tiny commissions he received as a numbers runner for Havana's immensely popular and illegal numbers game *[la bolita, la charada china]*. We spent the mornings walking the streets of Los Citios, hailing his clients in the balconies above and taking bets in code—ten cents on "butterfly," a peso on "dog shit," three on "the cemetery." Afternoons were spent chasing the family's dinner across Pedro's formidable illicit networks, which would yield a few eggs, some bread, whatever, just enough to get by. Electricity and natural gas were two utilities that could not be resolved at all in the early 1990s, and without them the most mundane aspects of life could be unbearable. Many afternoons were spent with Pedro doing nothing but carrying water up several flights of steps to fill a barrel in their apartment because the pump for their building was never on. The refrigerator was useless, so there was no way to store food like milk or meat. In fact, without electricity the refrigerator was more like a locker, not so much for food as for despair born of hunger. Milagro's mother, Ydolydia, cooked on an improvised kerosene burner that regularly flared to burn her and tainted our hard-fought meals with soot. We ate dinner in turns around the light of a single smudgy lamp.

I returned to Havana a year later, still traveling alone, and again lived with Pedro, Milagro, and their family during the autumn of 1993. Economic dissolution had spread, and the political discontent of people during that visit was palpable. My emerging understandings of Havana's formal and informal economies allowed me to appreciate social suffering more subtly, and I was touched deeply by the economic hardship and political disenfranchisement of everyday people. On one occasion, for example, the dentist about to remove an impacted wisdom tooth from Milagro's brother, Oswaldo, claimed he had no Novocain until we offered him hard currency.

I was introduced to Palo on that second visit to Havana. Pedro and I were on a run for one thing or another when he unexpectedly popped into the house of a woman he knew. Pedro was facing two court dates, one of them a criminal case against the man who had stabbed him. The other was a charge against Pedro himself for an attempt to leave Cuba in an improvised raft in the months before we had met. His mother had encouraged him to see her cousin, Celia, who practiced Palo in the neighborhood and could help him with his situation. The conversation between Pedro and Celia was impossible for me to understand, except that he was dubious about the long list of materials the healer requested to revalue his fate. It took us many days to gather those materials using all of Pedro's contacts and calling in many debts he could have saved for another day.

That day came the following summer, during the excruciatingly hot month of August 1994, when Pedro again tried to flee Cuba along with tens of thousands of other rafters who joined in a mass exodus. Those with excellent underground networks were the ones who got the best tractor inner tubes, wooden planks, and electrical cable to lash the rafts together, not to mention the plastic jugs to carry fresh water, or the hardboiled eggs and grapefruits the makeshift argonauts would need on the open sea. Trustworthy illicit markets were a matter of life and death as people cobbled together precarious launchings with what their friends and neighbors delivered. I later learned that it took Pedro less than a week to put together a vessel for his second attempt to flee Cuba, and then, with two friends from the block and his new teenage lover, he was gone. I also learned from his mother that Pedro went to see Celia for Palo craft during that frantic week. That Pedro would have added anything to the already urgent tasks of gathering materials to construct a raft, breaking up with his wife, and saying good-bye to his mother and family still impresses me. Unbeknownst to me, the realization that Pedro spent the week hunting not only for parts to build the raft that would carry his life but also for countless insignificant materials Celia needed to transform the fate of his crossing became the seed of this book. Pedro disappeared not into the depths of the Florida Straits, as did so many on that occasion of mass flight, but into a new life in the heavily Cuban comings and goings of Miami's Hialeah section. Last I heard, he was in Tennessee.

UNDERGROUND MARKETS RELEASED

The exquisitely intricate social and economic situations I experienced in early 1990s Cuba led me to anthropology. During the first years of my graduate studies in the midnineties, Cuba began to experience unimaginable changes, many of them decreed by the Revolution's leadership to bring its illegal markets under control. Many illicit forms of making money—from shoemaking to sandwich peddling to welding—became licensed forms of self-employment, which under Cuba's centralized economy had not existed on the island for thirty years. In 1994 the U.S. dollar was decriminalized [de-spenalizado], and Cubans were encouraged to make contacts with exiles. The previously despised "maggots" [gusanos] and "scum" [escoria] of Miami, Union City, and Barcelona became overnight, in the new official language, "the Cuban community abroad." Not surprisingly, dollars in the form of re-mittances started flowing in enormous amounts from family outside of Cuba. State-run stores that accepted *only* U.S. dollars soon opened ostensi-bly to carry luxury goods, the sale of which the Cuban state has used since then to recover [recuperar] the remittances. By 2000 the "shopping" stores—Cubans had dubbed them with the English word—had mutated into socialist-capitalist monstrosities selling staples such as cooking oil, milk, and chicken, at prices wholly incommensurate not only with the average Cuban wage, but also with the currency in which the Cuban state pays its people. To this day, the shopping stores are among the Revolution's principal means of netting hard currency, though with significant overhead. More recently, fees on U.S. dollars changed into "convertible currency" are netting the Cuban state a handsome return. These state-mandated exchange rates and fees, along with adjustments in prices at the shopping stores and cigarette price fluctuations, are among the primary mechanisms used to regulate the value of the U.S. dollar in Cuba's slowly decentralizing domestic economy.

Over the past twenty years, these changes had marked effects on do-mestic underground markets but did not eliminate them. Since the mid-1990s, the Revolution has made massive capital investments in tourism that have yielded yet new underground economies, while supercharging the existing ones. Within a couple of years, prostitution and tourist hus-tling, which hardly existed between 1961 and the early 1990s, became im-portant means for snaring foreign currency to buy cooking oil and milk in the hard currency–only stores.

It was during these intense years of economic and social change in Havana that I started thinking more about Palo. The Revolution's tourism strategy began to take on a life of its own. Young women and men offered themselves to tourists for sale in dollars; artists and artisans of all sorts did too, as did anyone with a craft or knowledge that could be sold for a tip or "donation." Cuba's African-inspired societies were no different: Ocha/Santo, Palo, and the Abakuá men's societies have each engaged in some form of commodifi-cation in the new exhibition-for-dollars arrangement. Of these societies it is Ocha/Santo that has most efficiently adjusted to the new trade. Palo and the Abakuá men's societies have approached tourism with more circumspection, but with no less interest in finding a way to earn the tourist dollar.

PETRIFIED THOUGHT, THE OBJECT

Tourism and its influence on Cuba's African-inspired societies interested me, but not as much as other anthropological concerns, such as how to understand hierarchy and subordination in a highly urbanized, economically complex, and politically vertical social situation. The beginnings of my work in Palo were marked by my abiding concern with how *force* emerges and spreads from even the tiniest pores of political and economic hierarchies, and especially how it is deployed at the faintest limits of social interaction to constitute control. Such limits are largely those of language, and I was interested in how power is exercised and felt, "sensed," in Gilles Deleuze's terms, where matter and language touch in a fold.[3] In short, I wanted to know how authority over another person was crafted through absolutely subtle uses of force. My study of Palo addresses this concern through my emphasis on the art of insinuation, which is so important to Palo craft.

My interests in the subtle force of domination echoed in an intellectual register for me, and I connected it to the problem of *reification* as posed in critical theory, which points to forms of social organization whereby conscious thought becomes petrified and remote. To paraphrase Hegel, what is apparently closest to one is in truth most removed.[4] My sense was that such alienation of a person from his or her consciousness had to be imposed on the individual, but to be sustainable such force had to be imperceptible, pleasurable when felt, and nearly inscrutable. There are strong intimations by Hegel, assertions by Karl Marx, and emphatic appeals by Georg Lukács that the principal device used in the transfer of this subtle social force is *the object*, which, like a gleaming jewel, seems forever to embody more social potential than its simple matter can possibly hold.[5]

But the object is not only a "mechanism" of control; it is also an agent of transformation capable of inspiring entirely captivating landscapes of desire, as later interpreters of Marx and Hegel, such as Walter Benjamin and Theodor Adorno, insist.[6] This insight lies implicit in Hegel, whose own fascination with the object is often overlooked, as is the role he accords it in the constitution of human consciousness. It is the object—in Hegel's famous narrative that thing of beauty fashioned by the slave that makes the master feel desire—that is responsible for lifting human consciousness out of a consuming immediacy characterized by absolute vulnerability, or in Hegel's understanding, infinite receptivity.[7]

Hegel's lesson, which I sought to explore in my study of Palo, is that properly manipulated the object can transfer forces that solidify one version of reality, just as it can create a tear in the screens of petrified, fated thought and for an instant make fluid thinking possible. The object, as I understand it, is a daunting point of control and enchantment, just as it holds tremendous potential for change—of thought, of fates, and of lives. From what I learned, Palo practiced and taught a form of craft that cultivated at the center of its labors exquisitely complex "objects"—prendas-ngangas-enquisos—through which marvelously ambivalent transfers of social and conceptual force occurred.

"INSPIRATION"—THE NEW

I use the words "inspiration" and "inspired" when writing about the African-inspired societies of Palo and Ocha/Santo. Palo is central African, specifically, Kongo-inspired. I use the term instead of "African-derived," which is common among researchers but implies that the topic under discussion is in some way a degraded form of an immutable African essence to which it is beholden. I also choose it because of my discomfort with the term "Afro-Cuban," also popular among researchers, but which binds people and the materials they engage to an originary and inescapable African past. Neither of these commonly used formulations necessarily acknowledges "the new" that is so crucial a part of diaspora and Creole culture.[8] "Inspiration," as I use it here, functions as a hinge between the past and the future, inspiration being the active, forward-looking, creative spark linking past forms with objects, powers, and rules born anew. Inspiration implies a playful attitude toward past and future, as opposed to a perspective marked only by the trauma of dislocation and impossible recovery. Inspiration is a force of the moment that arrives unannounced and has little time to recognize its debts before being swept up in the currents of its own prodigious, and often unexpected, creation.

I also ask "inspiration" to do the work of the term "religion," which I try to avoid in this text. Religion is, for me, overladen with European assumptions of form, doctrine, and homogeneity, in short, with a static sense of belief and practice. Inspiration seems less defined; it is a more mobile term that has nonreligious usages important to my description of Palo's overflowing creativity. In the ambiguities of this term I find a space for Palo, which is best understood as a fluid mode of engaging the dead *in matter* to transform fate in a flash.

Palo, then, is Kongo-inspired. It is a form of inspiration capable of sovereignty and equal in its fate-transforming capacities to west African–inspired Ocha/Santo. Despite the presence of central African slaves in Cuba nearly since the beginning of the Spanish colony, Palo dates to the late nineteenth or early twentieth century, when it emerged from a cauldron of myriad Kongo inspirations. Important among these were the healing rites Victor W. Turner has called "drums of affliction," the central African form of which John M. Janzen has treated under the name of Ngoma.[9] Of these, one inspiration was Lemba, the long-lived trading and healing society that developed on the north bank of the lower Congo River in the mid-seventeenth century and thrived until early in the twentieth century. Lemba was a response to disruptions caused by the trade in slaves and goods initiated by contact with the Portuguese; like so much of Kongo sacred life, Lemba survived the Middle Passage.[10] Another Kongo society that made the passage before becoming an inspiration for new associations in Cuba was Nkita. Among the people of the lower Congo River, who in the nineteenth century were ravaged by slavery, Nkita addressed ruptures in lineage succession. Through initiation Nkita reaffiliated members of the society, in Janzen's terms, "with the ancestral source of their collective authority."[11] Given the defining role integrated kinship networks played in determining freedom and slavery in Kongo life prior to and after contact with Europeans, this reaffiliation in the Caribbean can be seen as fate transforming indeed.[12] Both Lemba and Nkita are directly cited in Palo today, as are their practices of keeping socially potent substances for revaluing the fates of their members.

During the century and a half between 1725 and 1875, more slaves were delivered to Cuba than in all years prior.[13] These inspirations and others from diverse central African peoples were nurtured in Havana's Kongo-organized mutual aid societies [cabildos].[14] Lemba and Nkita were but two among what must have been many inspirations that recombined fortuitously and creatively, just as surely as they struggled against one another for the hearts of people seeking counteragents for the misfortunes of slavery. These inspirations fused into newly relevant forms within the crucible of the cabildo structure, and when they emerged in discrete form from the ruin of Spanish colonialism at the turn of the twentieth century they did so as Palo, which in Havana is referred to as La Regla de Congo, translated as "Kongo Rule" or "Kongo Law."

Palo has four branches [ramas], each of which is ritually, musically, and perhaps linguistically distinct from the others. These branches are Palo Mayombe, Palo Briyumba (Villumba, Vriyumba, or Biyumba), Palo Monte, and Palo Kimbisa. This book is largely, though not exclusively, about Palo Briyumba. Each branch proliferates into smaller communities called *munansos*, which I call "praise houses" because they coalesce in the home of practitioner-teachers and around the prendas-ngangas-enquisos they keep and feast there.[15] In the mid- to late 1990s Palo Briyumba and Palo Monte praise houses were predominant in Havana, with the latter apparently more pervasive than the former. Perhaps this explains why La Regla de Congo is often referred to in scholarly and popular literature as "Palo Monte."[16] In keeping with popular usage among people who practice Kongo Law in Havana, I have adopted "Palo" as more accurate, if generic, shorthand for La Regla de Congo.

In Havana, Palo is considered a "left hand" to Ocha/Santo.[17] When Kongo inspirations emerged as La Regla de Congo sometime near the beginning of the twentieth century they did so in conjunction with, or perhaps in response to, the emergence of a similar code that established the rules for teaching west African traditions of inspiration, known as La Regla de Ocha. I translate this term literally as "The Law [or Rule] of the Oricha" but refer to it throughout my text as "Ocha/Santo."[18] The relationship between Palo and Ocha/Santo is exquisitely complex and is superficially characterized by a division of labor wherein Ocha/Santo does the healing and Palo does the harming. Though not entirely false, this distinction is overly simplistic. My approach to treating this relationship has been to recognize Palo's conceptual, ritual, and organizational autonomy from Ocha/Santo and to accept that the two laws—Kongo-inspired and west African–inspired—exist within mutually productive relations of influence and contention. I think of Palo and Ocha/Santo as independent "sovereignties of fate," each with its internal laws geared toward transforming the fates of those over whom they rule, and each related to the other through mutually accepted, nearly diplomatic, protocols of contact. Relations between Palo and Ocha/Santo are made yet more complex by the separate postures of subordination and insubordination each law maintains with Spanish Catholicism, which despite fifty years of socialist revolution remains a critical referent for each African-inspired society. A single individual can practice Palo and Ocha/Santo, and be Catholic as well, and though each form of inspiration is sufficiently complex to require that its great teachers specialize, many people benefit from a productive, and conflictive, multiplicity of practice.

PRENDAS-NGANGAS-ENQUISOS

Popular discourse about Palo focuses on its purported hierarchy, exaggerated masculine aesthetics including explicit homophobia, and supposedly violent initiations. Before I became familiar with Palo practice I postulated these features were intimately bound-up with healing-harming substances teachers of Palo gathered and cared for at the heart of their praise houses. I also assumed that the webs of insinuation that cast Palo as the principal mode of African-inspired sorcery in Cuba were somehow spun out of these agglomerations of earth, sticks, animal remains, and labored substances packed into iron cauldrons and clay urns. Throughout this text, I refer to these collections as prendas-ngangas-enquisos but mostly use the profoundly Creole and popular term *prenda*, a word with a remarkable proliferation of meanings and translations from Spanish, of which "pawn" or "collateral" and, by extension, "jewel" or "gem" are the most common. *Nganga* is nineteenth-century Kikongo (the language of the BaKongo people) for "sorcerer" or "healer."[19] Prenda nganga is thus a healer's jewel, his or her guarantee against the afflictions of economic, political, and fated indebtedness. As such, the term *prenda* comprises an explicit understanding of revaluation in the trading of its forces for concrete transformations of fates and lives. *Enquiso* refers to Kongo *minkisi* (*nkisi,* sing.), which are turns of the dead shaped into powerful substances that from the nineteenth century to today define Kongo notions of causality and property. Kongo minkisi, like prendas, are powerful versions of the dead, synonymous with curing *and* affliction, that were drummed up at the heart of Kongo-inspired healing societies to revalue the fates of those gathered.[20] This is not to say that prendas are essentially Kongo forms, but rather that they are Creole entities specific to the encounter between Kongo-inspired forces and Cuban Catholic and Yoruba-inspired forces, encounters that are yet unreconciled.

Before beginning my long-term study of Palo I had no illusions about the difficulty of working with prendas-ngangas-enquisos—Palo is as strict a discipline as any doctoral program in anthropology could invent. I did, however, fancy that my ideas about hierarchy, social power, and the status of "the object" as a relay for imperceptible transfers of force that both petrify reality and render it fluidly immediate, might be nourished by contact with prendas-ngangas-enquisos. Yet I quickly found the Hegelian premises of my ideas about objects ineffective in formulating reiterations and paraphrases of practice that my teachers of Palo could recognize. I eventually found *negation itself*—that most powerful of Hegel's elements of thought—to be an obstacle in my comprehension of Palo. Prendas-ngangas-enquisos, it turns out, do not conform to a Hegelian logic that would limit their social capaciousness to the dialectic of object and subject. Far from being an "object," isolated and determined by a subject as Hegel would have this, prendas-ngangas-enquisos are indivisibly connected with immanent materiality; they emerge from material connection and refuse logical reduction thereby. As such, prendas-ngangas-enquisos are not "objects" and definitely not "fetishes," which is what European enlightenment discourse calls matter that won't conform to the designs of a rational subject. They are better thought of as agents, entities, or actors concatenated in asymmetrically realized networks we call "societies."[21]

ISIDRA AND TEODORO

I met Isidra Sáez in the summer of 1999. I was carrying a letter for her from an anthropologist friend who had taken a rumba lesson from her, and when I dropped by her house Isidra invited me in. She was a practitioner [*practicante*] of both Palo and Ocha/Santo and we began preliminary conversations about her helping me with my fieldwork. Isidra wasn't her first name but rather her grandmother's. She asked me to use it in my writing, not so much to buffer herself and her son from any unintended consequences arising from my publishing our work together (of which she was very conscious), but more to honor her grandmother, whom she credited for her knowledge and whom she wanted to memorialize. Isidra soon became my teacher [*madrina*, literally, godmother] and principal interlocutor throughout my fieldwork.

I was an apprentice [*ahijado*, literally, godchild] of Isidra's, though not exclusively. She introduced me to Teodoro Herrera and the Kongo-inspired community he presided over, the Munanso Quita Manaquita Briyumba Congo praise house of Guanabacoa, on the outskirts of Havana. Though Isidra was ever at my side, it was my apprenticeship with Teodoro and the care I learned for the prendas-ngangas-enquisos (Teodoro also called them *kandangos*) of the Quita Manaquita house that taught me much of what I know about Palo craft. Teodoro, who was much more impulsive than Isidra, insisted that I use his full name and the name of his praise house in my work—to honor the dead, specifically his late father, Emilio O'Farril. I have not used his name because in his brash style I don't think he understood the possible repercussions of this, but I have used the actual name of his praise house at his emphatic insistence. Together, Isidra and Teodoro taught me what they could about Palo. At times they struggled against one another with differing interpretations of Palo craft and practice, and in such moments I have tried to make their disagreements evident. This work, and especially the understandings of the dead that ground it, would have been entirely different, if not impossible, without their teachings or their singular rivalry.

THE DEAD

Isidra and Teodoro agreed on one point in their teachings and this was that the most basic sense of African inspirations in Cuba could be had only by drawing close to the dead. This precept applied to both Palo and Santo, but in particular to Palo for those trying to understand the prendas-ngangas-enquisos Palo healers keep. Isidra made it clear that if prendas are complicated, then the dead are more so. I agree with Isidra that one must have a sense of the dead before attempting to write about Palo and its prendas. Isidra and Teodoro taught me the dead through typical Palo pedagogy, which involves stories, songs, and specific styles of talk and recollection, all modes of its singular practice. Importantly, they also taught the dead as a type of visceral apprehension, especially when engaging a prenda-nganga-enquiso.

In each instance, they taught the dead as contiguous and immediate to the living, and argued for a materiality of the dead that was coterminous with that of the living. I want to stress this point because it introduces an argument important to much of what follows, which is that Palo's understandings of the dead are not only elaborate conceptual affairs that revel in the mutual and indivisible affirmation of matter and the dead, but primarily visceral ones felt in the bodies of the living and discerned in the world around. In this, Palo's definitions of the dead reside simultaneously in categories that are generally considered mutually exclusive by scholars inspired by the Hegelian tradition: concept and matter, and immediacy and the object.[22]

I attempt to communicate and interpret Palo's dead in every page that follows. My characterization of Palo depends on describing the dead as having many versions, mutually coexisting and simultaneously affirmed. My approach asks the reader to sustain multiple (and at times apparently exclusive) definitions of the dead simultaneously. The reader might find this confusing at times, but this method helps portray the baffling proliferation of the dead in Palo's teaching and craft. When contradictions arise between mutually acknowledged definitions of the dead I do not attempt to resolve them by means of dialectical negation, which is very good at clarifying. Rather, what I propose is a description of the dead that makes good use of conceptual concatenation and entangled implication by affirming each turn of the dead. This method is in keeping with the way my teachers of Palo discussed the dead. In one moment the dead were discrete responsive entities such as a deceased parent or sibling, and in the same moment the dead was an undefined and pressing mass made up of infinite numbers of unrecognizable dead. This mass simultaneously suffused and constituted the living. The difficulty in characterizing the dead with such variety is that instead of narrowing an understanding of the dead to a single established identity, the logic of affirmation, concatenation, or implication I pursue here leads to a proliferation of definitions.[23] If Palo can "identify" the dead at all, it is as an ambient mass, immanently turning out versions of itself.[24]

To help describe the proliferation of Palo's dead and the mode of understanding it implies—wherein something can be itself and its apparent opposite without contradiction—I employ the term "version." A version is a rendering of a given form that is made unique through an exercise of force that changes its direction, which turns its shape or meaning, and thus its appearance. The crucial element here is the physical relationship between force, direction, and meaning. In Palo the dead have countless versions, each a sense of the other. As this book proceeds, the reader will find these versions of the dead spreading through the text, so that before long the dead will be revealed as a feeling of unattributable apprehension and as a bit of sawdust from a powerful tree; the dead will be a song and also a skillful allusion in a fate-changing encounter. The dead are the words of others that return to echo in our minds with uncanny poignancy, and they are bones exhumed from forgotten graves; they are blood and stones. The dead in Palo are best imagined as an uncontainable spreading, each version becoming yet another until the multitude that accumulates overtakes and saturates the very imagination that attributes to the dead presence and volition. One can seek to understand Palo by approaching it through any one of these turns.

Some may rightly point out that a version suggests a grounding in an original form, which generates and authorizes its representation in other forms. The Cuban-Kongo dead, Palo's dead, however, has no dominant entity or idea to authorize its proliferating shapes.[25] Rather, what was described to me by Isidra and Teodoro was an anonymous mass of the dead [Kalunga, *el muerto*] to which no discrete identity is ascribed, and in which most other forms of the dead are immanent before they emerge in discrete form. I describe this anonymous mass of the dead as an "ambiance" immediate to matter and life. Following my teachers and other practitioners of Palo, I seek recourse in metaphors of fluids, flows, tides, and waves to depict this ambiance. Metaphors will take me only so far, however, because the principal characteristic of this ambient dead is to evade determination, become unstable, remain strange, and forever exceed dominant languages that seek to inscribe it. In Palo thought, the ambient dead, Kalunga, resides nowhere specifically, yet saturates discrete forms, like bodies. Most often, when it was evident, Kalunga was a vague sense in the wake of an insinuation or a clever imputation. The dead are a studied and refined discourse on the part of the practitioners of Palo, a discourse not only of words, but also of pauses, creative omissions, clever puns, unverifiable implications, and allusions born forever anew, as it were, from the overlap where concept and matter, the felt and the thought, the immediate and the object, touch.

AESTHETICS OF PALO, AESTHETICS OF WRITING

Unstable as this multifarious discourse of the dead may be, it makes possible a reflection on the sentiments that Palo prizes and educates. These are feelings at the edges of immediate sensation and thus at the limits of attribution and identification—like intuition, inspiration, and creeping fear. Palo loves the implicit and the "given," which it seeks to turn into something new through a clever play of force. This playing, this turning of substances and situations, this making something new out of fixed arrangements—this is Palo craft. The discourse of the dead in multiplicity reveals the aesthetic values Palo instructs and through which its craft is exercised: the volatility of substances, speed of decision, the use of force against adversaries, and unsentimental action taken to transform fate. A teacher of Palo will say that what is fated has no heart, so neither must Palo when revaluing it. The refinement of these values is what Palo reveres and considers beautiful. These values are cultivated by teachers of Palo, who instruct their initiates to seek them among the ambient dead as affective lines of approach and escape running through a series of the dead, often without apparent affinity or resemblance between them.

To convey this education, which is the shaping of an apprentice's volition, I have made stylistic decisions that I hope are consistent with Palo aesthetics. I expect that my choices will also engage important critiques of ethnographic authority developed in the discipline of anthropology over the last thirty years. I have sought a language that is self-conscious without centering myself in the text and that values description and considers it important enough to make it the bearer of interpretation, rather than have it forever subordinated to the authoritative voice of explanation.

I have been inspired in my stylistic choices by the philosophical conviction that explanation in writing must value the object of interpretation and insist that thought be lost to the object, rather than the object lost to thought. In this I am aided by the fact that both Palo's dead and its healing-harming substances, prendas-ngangas-enquisos, elude dominant forms of rational explanation because of their complexity, or their proliferation into variant and unstable definitions that neither negate nor transcend one another. In fact, their definitions insist on forever becoming minor to one another, as minor as a handful of dirt and a murmured whisper, as minor as a little cut and a bit of ash. Confronted with such materiality, as an ethnographer I have sought to simply be conscious of my *will-to-explanation* and resist elevating minor definitions to the status of answers, or keys, or transcendent principles, thus negating their brute materiality, baseness, or simple minority. I have tried to convey inconsequential elements like murmurs and ashes in their unimportance and indeterminacy. I ask these minor definitions of the dead to gather haphazardly and accrete slowly so that explanation, when it emerges, does so not under a beam of light but rather in descriptive folds where meager definitions gather, one upon the other. Explanation in the text, then, appears as an unexpected assemblage of prior minor descriptions. One result is that the scenes of Palo practice rendered in this text are necessarily incomplete and despite an air of comprehension they are irremediably impure, not only because a complete revelation of Palo would be impossible—it is infinitely recombinant—but also because incomplete description is one of Palo's pedagogical values. Impure description is taught as an intentional strategy to protect Palo knowledge and ensure creative, speculative, inventive extensions on the part of those learning.

The creative extension I bring to Palo in this text is to value the turns of Palo's dead, each in its basic materiality, while allowing each to be spoken for by other versions, in its own irreducible particularity. This choice requires a writing practice that handles matter such that it survives its encounter with system-integrating thought. Attempting to follow Theodor Adorno's advice, which is to surrender the logic of identity and systematicity of thought, I instead enter into the vertiginousness of a writing that loses itself in its object, *à fond perdu*.[26] In other words, I venture to record an immanent critique of Palo from within Palo's substances and forces.[27]

Writing, like all practical forms, is experimental. My approach when confronted with this experiment has been to choose a narrative style. In contrast to the style of dominant social science, which seeks to restrict and limit definition ever in the service of clarity, narrative allows for Palo and its dead to be described in perpetual indeterminacy. Narrative is best when awash in the tension inherent to a series of events or statements that portend more than they clarify. Explanations in this text are permitted to proceed out of contradictory definitions and the paradoxes of mutual affirmation, which arise as the meaning pleats up on itself. This stylistic choice has analytical consequences, such as the deferral of clear explanation, but I believe it is consistent with the spirit of empiricism that defines ethnography. The reader is left with a text that has a tenuous relationship with resolution, for the life of narrative, like that of Palo, rides on the *unresolved.*

PART I

The Dead

Isidra was attentive to events in her body and on its surface, like the fluttering of her heart, breathlessness, goose bumps, and chills across her neck. In these sensations, and others, she sought the dead (chapter 1). My apprenticeship with Isidra and the years that have transpired since have been spent trying to understand what Isidra found there, in her gut and on her skin. She ascribed these feelings in a most general sense to Kalunga—which she also called *el muerto*—the vast and ever-proliferating sea *[mar]* of the dead (chapter 2). Kalunga is ambient: Kalunga surrounds, Kalunga saturates, Kalunga generates, and Kalunga dissipates. This teaching allowed her to communicate yet another aspect of the dead crucial to Palo thought and craft: the dead subsists in matter, where it assumes countless aspects (chapter 3). Trees, their branches and twigs, the sticks we pick up, water, the earth in which trees grow, the animals these sustain in turn—in countless expressions the dead spread through matter. And Isidra maintained that the living and the dead they recognize (who recognize the living in return) subsist as equal forces suspended in Kalunga's protean flows (chapter 4). Fruitful relations with these responsive dead demanded a consciousness of Kalunga's expansive mass—permeating and sustaining the living, the dead, and their exchanges. These perceptions about the dead, which were not explicitly taught but rather imparted through subtle intimation in the wake of practice, were Isidra's way to understanding Palo, its culture, and its craft.

1. Isidra

There was hardly an exchange between us that didn't turn to the dead. As Isidra and I got to know one another, the dead appeared more often. She was pleased that a scholar from New York would take an interest in her reflections, which she considered outside the notice of academic inquiry. It's not that Isidra was unfamiliar with researchers and universities. She was sixteen when the Cuban Revolution triumphed in 1959, and among the children in her tiny town she was chosen to become part of the Revolution's first university class. She was proud to have a degree, and she considered herself more than conversant with university people like me.

Isidra was also familiar with social science and anthropology. In her understanding, however, anthropology had little to do with African-inspired life and practice in Cuba. As she understood it, African inspirations like Palo and Ocha/Santo were in the realm of folklore studies. The Soviet-style anthropology she had learned in college, with its counting and charting, had little room for what she had to say, so she was very interested that I would take time to listen to her interpretations of Palo and Ocha/Santo. Isidra was retired from her longtime job as a dance instructor and when I met her was a part-time volunteer organizer for the Union of Retired Employees of the Ministry of Culture. She seemed to thrive on the hours I spent with her and the slow pace of our conversations.

Isidra was soon an active interlocutor in my research, driven as much by her own curiosity and keen intellect as by my many questions. I was disoriented by the complexity of Palo and Ocha/Santo, by their productive cross-pollinations as much as by their obvious differences, and by the fact that a person can practice both Palo and Ocha/Santo (as Isidra did). In such cases, which are hardly rare, those who practice both take care to sustain the hierarchy that divides them and insists on the exclusivity of their feasts,

23

initiations, and ritual languages. Having lived her whole life within Cuba's African inspirations, Isidra felt that to understand the conjunctions and incongruities of Palo and Ocha/Santo one had better understand the dead. The dead were terribly important to her, yet they seemed to have such a faint influence on Palo and Ocha/Santo that they were altogether unrecognizable to a novice.

What she said about the dead was often contradictory or confusing. She had several names for the dead, and the most important were Kalunga, el muerto, and *eggun*. At times she spoke about the dead in terms that were familiar to me, like when she attributed to the dead the individuality of an ancestor she had known. "It can be your teachers and friends," she said. "It doesn't have to be a relative." But she would just as often refer to the dead as something else, something akin to a writhing, boundless mass, impersonal and anonymous. Isidra's interpretations also attributed to the dead material forms, and she refused most of my attempts to classify and distinguish them. In fact, for weeks it was difficult for me to attribute to such an incongruous theme the importance Isidra did. Compared to Palo's crafts of sorcery and prenda-keeping, the dead seemed inconsequential. In this I annoyed and frustrated her greatly. Yet Isidra was forever referring back to the dead and many of her comments about Palo seemed to rest on what was for me an elusive understanding of the dead. I tried to delineate an image of the dead from what Isidra had to say but she was hardly straightforward, and I was left to cull her thoughts on this topic from anecdotes, comments in passing, and childhood yarns, which I would pursue into subsequent conversations, always referring back, looking for clarification.

On any normal day I would arrive at Isidra's house, which occupied half of the first floor of a five-story apartment building in the El Cerro district of Havana. El Cerro is an enormous section of Havana, like Brooklyn is to New York City, or East LA to Los Angeles. Her neighborhood was, in her words, behind the bus station, away from the print shops, and just around the corner from the *pre de economía*—the preparatory secondary school for economics.

El Cerro has lived many lives, and its neighborhoods are unique reflections of its history. Some of its neighborhoods are famous, like those painted by René Portocarrero along the Calzada del Cerro. The Calzada is the principal avenue running from Habana Vieja to the Cuatro Caminos market, then beyond through the neglected sections of El Pilar, Atarés, El Carraguau, and El Canal, which meet at the famous corner known as *la esquina de tejas*. From there it snakes toward the outlying sections of Nuevo Vedado, Pogolotti, and La Lisa. It is lined by giant neocolonial houses dating to the nineteenth century, when much of Havana's petite bourgeoisie hungered for out-of-the-way retreats near running water and high ground. Today the Calzada is plied by resurrected Chevrolets, Dodges, and Oldsmobiles that coast and creak their hard-winding way along the Capitolio–La Lisa corridor, carrying those who can pay the hefty fare.

Isidra's neighborhood was neither high-end nor destitute—although these days the two are the same. Her section dated to after the Second World War, when El Cerro expanded north and west toward the avenues of Carlos III and Ayestarán. Hers was a section defined not by dilapidated columns and disintegrating neocolonial balconies and portals but by hardscrabble modern industrial buildings, service garages, delivery ramps, and the backsides of uninspired office buildings built by the Communist Party. Her building was like so many others on her street and in the surrounding blocks—a streamlined modern design built in the fifties of cement and lots of glass. She was not too far from the Plaza de la Revolución, where the Cuban state has arranged its principal bureaucracies around the concentrated trio of state power: the headquarters of the Revolutionary Armed Forces, the offices of the state newspaper *Granma,* and the Central Committee of the Communist Party of Cuba. Sharing the plaza with these, albeit in a peripheral position, was Cuba's decidedly modernist national library, named after the inspired poet and independence leader José Martí. A few blocks from her house in another direction was Havana's beloved baseball stadium, the Latinoamericano.

Knocking on Isidra's door was a matter of making oneself heard down the long hall of her apartment, where most of the sound from the street died on its way to the back. She was usually at the rear of the house working in the kitchen or the tiny outside patio. During blackouts, which were common day and night, there was no way for a caller to know the bell wasn't ringing at the back of the house. In the beginning we missed one another many times because of this, until her son, who was fourteen at the time, showed me the trick of rapping on the glass panes of the front door with a key or a coin. The severe strikes rang rudely through the apartment, but their stridence was made softer by the fact that anyone knocking thus was a friend.

Isidra would come forward, and we would talk in the sunroom that acted as a parlor at the front of her house, up the hall from the dining and sleeping rooms. Its high walls of opaque glass set into a painted iron grid were the modernist ideal for Havana's modest winters, but in the summer it became unbearably hot with the afternoon trapped inside. There were windows, but her years of healing people through Palo made her wary of them. Her work, like the work of healers in many places, had earned her the enmity of many and she preferred not to leave her house open to sorcery or other ill will. The shades, with their twisted slats, frayed cords, and covering of dust, didn't appear to have been lowered in years. Isidra disliked the heat and knew her guests did too; she was always ready with a glass of cold water or a clean cloth to wipe away the sweat.

In the bright, diffuse light of this room her brown face showed burned orange and took on dandelion hues. She had a smile of bright teeth that captivated most people with its ready generosity. The rest of her face spiraled around her mouth, coming forth and fading back, one feature more prominent than the next depending on the emotion she evoked or the stress she sought to lend a point. Her face was her principal device for creating an atmosphere of consequence in which her ever-repeating words weighed with self-evident importance. Her eyes were attentive just as they were unyielding in their scrutiny and concentration, and she was practiced at breaking the back of a lie with her stare. These eyes were distorted as she blinked past gold-framed glasses that magnified them as she looked around her into a world she saw clearly but that evaded me altogether. That was the world of the dead, which she inhabited in forms I would be long in learning.

Isidra was an athletic woman for her age. Lithe muscles defined her slender arms, and she was likely to jump to her feet to stress a thought or to take off down the hall to rescue a pressure cooker she had forgotten amid the turns of conversation. She usually wore donation jeans and a tattered T-shirt, and sandals out of which curled her bony toes. She kept her head covered with a light blue scarf. This was obeisance paid to Yemayá, the Ocha/Santo sovereign of maternity and of the sea, to whom she was pledged. She wrapped the scarf haphazardly, and corners of it were forever poking out at angles never quite settled. As we talked she would sit on the very edge of her blue sofa, her elbows on her knees with her head sunk between her shoulders, her whole body supporting her words and in ready state to receive whatever might be my reply.

With her powerful attention and physical strength fully engaged, Isidra came to the conclusion that I was not paying enough attention to the dead in my research. Much of her energy in our first conversations was spent trying to get me to focus on the topic. She was quick to notice when lines of conversation departed from the dead or didn't refer to the dead with sufficient acumen. She considered such tangents indicative of ignorance in matters of African inspiration. Her insistence could be tedious, and I wondered early in my work if I would continue with Isidra as my principal interlocutor in matters of Palo.

Isidra discerned the dead around her constantly. She saw the dead as synonymous with what was noteworthy in the everyday. To her the dead was the series of never-ending happenings that emerged out of life's routines, prosaic though these could be. All through the first decade following the collapse of the Soviet Union, the dead were to be found inhabiting moments of grace and despair as the food and electricity shortages drew ever longer and more severe. The dead were behind much of the creativity the crisis spurred; the dead were the genius behind the new tricks for getting by in the shattered economy. As people caught on to each trick, the dead permeated the gossip on the block. And as the gossip spread, the dead infused her work as a healer of people forlorn and anxious because of the economic collapse.

About her doubts concerning the role of the Revolution in the economic crisis, Isidra had little to say. Where others were accustomed to complaining unrelentingly about the corruption of the Communist Party, Isidra chose indifference and preferred to spend her thinking time otherwise. She took for granted the dishonesty of the butchers, bakers, and ration distributors [bodegueros], as well as the shameless malfeasance of the middle managers in Cuba's extraordinary commodity distribution apparatus. She did not share in the irritated chatter most people spent the better part of their day in. Neither did Isidra think much of the network of illicit contacts she cultivated for her acquisition of everything from rice to toothpaste, to sugar and coffee. She lived in apparent immediacy with this network, in the same way consumers in market economies live in reified relation to their commodities and social lives. These micro-networks of wandering, clandestine salespeople whom Isidra had known for years supplied her with what the state failed to provide, either on time or at all. The underground runners in her neighborhood were mostly men and women her age, walking from house to house in their flip-flops with unassuming bags loaded with powdered milk, cheese, sweets, and bread made secretly at home, as well as with medicines, including drugs such as Valium, chlordiazepoxide, and painkillers like codeine. Isidra esteemed these people greatly and was forever detaining them from their rounds with questions about their lives and their families.

It was not surprising, then, that some of the pensioners and homemakers who supplied her were also her clients. So were some of her neighbors. As I would meet them Isidra would include me in conversations with them, and as we gained confidence she would share worries specific to cases of affliction she was attending. There was a lot Isidra knew about the problems of her clients that she kept from me, and she tended to limit what she said about her healing to personal doubts she was having about her approach to a case. More importantly, Isidra sought as often as she could to turn conversations about her healing practices into lessons about the dead, because it was the dead that did the bulk of the work in her attempts to revalue lives and fates.

.   .   .

I arrived one morning at Isidra's and she drew me immediately through the door. She was agitated and thinking fast and she sat me down to listen. This was not rare, and I settled in to follow her and listened carefully to her words.

"There is little I can do," she said. "Everything I try either doesn't work, or the dead [Kalunga] warns me off. I promised Lucy that I would have a solution to her problems at work at the Ministry of Agriculture, the maneuverings of her enemies; they're working Palo against her, but I'm frozen. I've tried a couple of things, but they haven't given her the result she's looking for, and she's dissatisfied and losing confidence. I told her to come by this afternoon, and you can imagine, I couldn't sleep last night. I was up in the middle of the night; you should have seen me, sitting on the edge of my bed and pacing up and down the hall. It was one of those nights where I just move through the house, without thinking. I can't sleep, so I get out of bed and wander around. But it's not me that chooses to get up. It is my dead [mis muertos] that have me, they who pull me. Then I was sitting on the edge of this couch, here in the sunroom. The dead [Kalunga] led me here last night, where the only light was from the blue streetlight outside. You know my lamp burned out a week ago, don't you? You said you'd bring a bulb. It doesn't matter. I'm never on this couch at night, lamp or not, you know that; you know I like to be in the kitchen, but to this couch they brought me in the darkness and the streetlight, and I sat here. Everything was blue from the light outside, blue like shadows in the sea. Did you hear that? Like shadows in the sea. And you know what? The solution came to me. It did, suddenly, just like that. It was the dead [Kalunga], the dead that woke me and brought me here to think, and my dead [mis muertos] that hinted at the answer to Lucy's problem, so that she would be convinced."

Isidra paused for a second, looking at me sternly to make sure she had my complete attention. For such a stare there was no response except a hurried nod of assent, after which she continued. "You know, I don't choose to get up. It is my dead [mis muertos] that have me, they who pull me. Then I was sitting on the edge of this couch, here in the sunroom. The dead [Kalunga] led me here last night, where the only light was from the blue streetlight outside. You know my lamp burned out a week ago, don't you?

I'm never on this couch at night, lamp or not, you know that; you know I like to be in the kitchen, but to this couch they brought me in the darkness and the streetlight, and I sat here. Everything was blue from the light outside, blue like shadows in the sea [Kalunga]. Did you hear that? Like the shadows of Kalunga. And you know what? The solution came to me. It did, suddenly, just like that. It was the dead [Kalunga], the dead [Kalunga] that woke me and brought me here to think, and my dead [mis muertos] that hinted at the answer to Lucy's problem, so that she will be convinced."

When she was excited Isidra often spoke by repeating herself. In response to my clarifying queries, she tended not to paraphrase herself, but rather provided quotations of herself from previous talk and statements, sometimes within the same conversation, just sentences apart. This was one of her modes of emphasis, and of making sure that in future conversations there would be no doubt about what she said and that she was understood according to her interpretation. In this mode she was more impatient than usual as a listener and often interrupted replies in midsentence, assuming she knew where others were taking their responses. Often it was best to just listen silently. Her anecdotes tended to become monologues in which she would repeat momentary thoughts before finishing her statements, tarrying with them just a second to make sure they didn't contain some unexpected truth before she went on. Disquiet and delight marked her voice.

"The dead led me here last night, where the only light was from the streetlight outside. You know my lamp burned out a couple of weeks ago. I'm never on this couch at night, lamp or not; you know I like to be in the kitchen or down the hall, but here they brought me in the darkness and the blue shadows of Kalunga, and I sat here. And the solution came to me. It did, just like that. It was Kalunga that woke me and brought me here to think, and my dead that hinted at the answer. I heard, felt [sentí], my mother, Cucusa, you know her, telling me what is hurting Lucy. Cucusa said to me, 'The guinea hen thought she knew everything so she slept on the ground.' That is what Cucusa said. And that is the answer, you see? Lucy isn't seeing things clearly; her rivals are taking advantage of a blind spot. She thinks she knows everything, but someone is betraying her. She doesn't know it; she doesn't know it. She isn't looking around; her weakness is obvious to everyone but her, and she is going to lose her job at MinAg because of it. They're pushing her out, retiring her, betraying her. She has trusted the younger people, trained them, but they're turning. All her years in the party for nothing. So I ask Cucusa, I ask, 'Who is it? Who is it? Who is working Palo against Lucy?' And Cucusa is gone, nothing, and I sit here on the couch in the darkness and I wait in silence, because I can't go back to sleep; Kalunga won't let me sleep. I can feel Kalunga right here, in my gut. It's keeping me awake, you see, so I wait. I wait here on the couch, in the darkness except for the streetlight through the glass; you know I never come down the hall at night. Then I hear them *[los siento]* again, my dead [mis muertos], and they say, 'It won't be your enemy that kills you, but rather a friend.' And then I recognize her, and it is Old Chacha, my great aunt Chacha, *la vieja*. And she said to me, Chacha said, 'It won't be your enemy that kills you, but rather a friend.' That was one of Chacha's parables, her terrible wisdom. Hard as it might be, it is just like Old Chacha to make you look where you least want to for the person who is hurting you, to make you look among your friends. Chacha said this to me last night—that among the people hurting Lucy is someone she confides in; this is what Chacha said, what my dead [mis muertos], said to me."

Isidra smiled broadly when she got to this point in her story, the point where the dead arrived in the conversation to explain so much. It was her broad, familiar smile, the one that said she was speaking the most obvious truth, which said I was a fool if I didn't understand her. And I didn't. What did Isidra mean when she said the dead dragged her out of bed and to her living room to give her answers to pressing concerns? Isidra did not stop to let me ask my question but continued in this mode for a long time with nothing from me but nods and little sounds of acknowledgment.

·   ·   ·

Such was the appearance of Kalunga in Isidra, as this actualized in her very sleeplessness, as it inhabited her body. Such were her dead as they came to populate her anecdotes and stories with instances of tension in her body and with voices and words she recognized as responses to her moments of despair. And such was Isidra's mode of conversation, her overwhelming presence in an exchange, her insistence that one receive her meaning in the way she intended. Such was Isidra's insistence on the dead.

2. Kalunga, the Ambient Dead

There are important definitions to gather in Isidra's words, and before writing further about Palo craft and its arts of healing and harming I insist on exploring the topic of the dead, as she did. To say that Isidra pushed me to focus on the dead is an understatement, and when I finally began to do so I was still not convinced hers was the research path to pursue. But at some level we struck a deal, and in a very deep way I trusted that Isidra's emphasis on the dead would bring me to Palo eventually, if by a less transcendent path than is normally taken. Accounts of the craft usually focus on the prendas-ngangas-enquisos at the heart of Palo, and I, too, end with them, but I hope that my version of these formidable social entities will be a revaluing one because of the attention paid here to the dead. Whether or not such revaluation is novel or interesting will depend greatly on communicating, in a felt way, what Isidra meant by Kalunga.

A felt sense of the dead was first made real for me in Isidra's retellings, such as the account of her encounters with the dead the night she sought a solution to Lucy's problems. In fact, Lucy's healing began with the dead, as the dead manifested in Isidra's body. I was slow in gathering this understanding, wanting always to uncover some symbolic content in Isidra's invocation of the dead. At her insistence, it took an epistemological leap to realize that grasping the value Isidra placed on the dead would require taking her *literally* when she said the dead were in her gut. Isidra considered everyday experiences such as sleeplessness and pangs of anxiety not as "signs" of the dead in her body but as versions of the dead in themselves.

It's not that Isidra didn't attribute to the body a signifying capacity—at times she did—but rather that certain experiences neutralized the transcendent qualities of both corporeality and its signifying potential, rendering both fluid and strange. Her sense of the body allowed for its transformation

31

into a material form of the dead. It would take yet more epistemological stretching on my part to come to the realization that this was possible only because Isidra considered the body itself a version of the dead, literally brought into being by those who had birthed her and then made to ring in intense material agreement with the strange, indifferent tones the dead had taught her to hear. Other versions of the dead would appear as our work together continued, perhaps more influential versions such as the prendas-ngangas-enquisos she kept or the bones they contained. But realizing that a twinge of suspicion, a chill, and the turns of the stomach that accompany astonishment *were* the dead was crucial if I was to understand the ubiquity of the dead in Palo and thus Palo's importance overall.

In some part, my difficulty in grasping Isidra's experience of the dead was grounded in habits of thought ancient to my learning, bad habits left by the dead and assumed as original or essential by the living. Of these, the most vexing was the one that told me an experience could not be visceral and intellectual at once. This lesson was as old in me as learning itself, absorbed in the interminable series of the yes-and-no questions of first language. Language's secret content is equivalent to the basic premises of dualist thought as laid down by Plato and affirmed again and again in the rote responses of the Enlightenment tradition. A dualist mode of being posits a relation between viscera and intellect that is mutually exclusive because these are related to one another only through negation. In Isidra's explanations, viscera and intellect were mutually affirmed without contradiction. Such effusive, paradoxical affirmation made Isidra's dead akin to what Gilles Deleuze and Felix Guattari have called an "event"—a moment churning with "singularities," singular eruptions of meaning not yet reduced to dominant codes of signification.[1] For Isidra, the experience of events on the surface of the skin and in the depths of the viscera presaged moments of transformation in her fate, or the fate of the afflicted she sought to help. Her task as a healer was to recognize such events as they occurred, effectively lingering with the dead in a zone of change until she recognized figures—her mother, her aunts—that would inspire creative interventions into the all-too-given realm of fate.

Viewing the dead as a felt overlap of visceral and conceptual sensation is critical to understanding the overall spread and ubiquity of the dead in Cuban-Kongo thought. This overlapping is the dead prior to the identification of a source to which the experience of the dead might be attributed. Though she described the dead to me as people dear to her who had died and who continued to exist with her, Isidra maintained that the dead was "more than individuals," more than the appearance in her body of her mother or aunts. These appearances were vitally important to her but were only brief moments of what I call "condensation" or "precipitation" within a much broader sense of the dead. At its most basic level, this sense of the dead was "felt" [*sentido*] as a ubiquitous and ambiguous force at the limit where reason and bodily sense are mutually affirmed.

Pursuing this notion of the dead as a sense prior to individuation or identification, Isidra described for me a ubiquitous dead she said was "more than central" [*más que central*] to Palo. The distinction she made between the ubiquitous and the central suggested that the dead she sought to teach me was not to be apprehended as an elevated and central power like a divinity. Neither was this ubiquitous dead to be confused with the discrete individualities she identified in responsive figures like her mother or aunts. Isidra's notion of a dead that was ubiquitous seemed to abandon the elevation, centrality, and individuation normally associated with the divine in favor of a multiplicity of tenebrous visceral apprehension. In insisting on the dead as the very basis for understanding Palo, Isidra went to lengths to distinguish a notion of the dead that in its spread was very different from the divine powers revered in Ocha/Santo or Catholicism. Using a term from Cuban communist discourse, she would say, "The dead is not centralized [*el muerto no esta centralizado*]! It is not centralized in any normal manner! Not unless you would say water is central to the sea. Do you see what I mean? Water isn't at the center of the sea; it *is* the sea. When you talk about something being central, other things must revolve around it, like the sun and the planets, or the Party and the masses. There is a difference here. The sea doesn't revolve around water, it *is* the water!"

To Isidra, the dead at its most basic was neither height nor center, but an indifferent and infinite event seething with yet uncodified potentials. Isidra used another water metaphor in trying to make this understanding clear to me. Using one of the tight phrases common to Palo sacred speech, a mix of Spanish and Palo Kikongo often condensed into three or four words riddled with allusion, she said, "Kalunga *sube*, Kalunga *baja*—the Sea rises, the Sea falls."

It is no coincidence that she would equate the dead with the sea. This is a distinctly central African motif that Isidra often used, the realm of the dead residing in the depths of Kalunga, the sea, for BaKongo people.[2] Kongo cosmology emphasizes the dead as an important force in the world of the living, and its explanations situate the dead not only as residing beyond the sea, but as prolific and excessive, much like the sea in its vastness.[3] The dead were in Palo cosmology and in Isidra's teachings much as they were in Kongo thought: immanent to the living, infusing and surrounding them. The dead were to the living, in Georges Bataille's words, "like water is in water," dependent on no object and belonging to no subject, rather everywhere within these at once.[4]

This sea, Kalunga—Isidra sometimes called it "el muerto" [the dead]—comprises all the dead that could possibly exist or have existed. It is ancient beyond memory, and within it the dead exceed plurality and become instead a dense and indistinguishable mass.[5] This dispassionate mass of the dead is felt pressing close in Palo; one is educated to discern it filling space and rising in moments of indeterminate poignancy. Then it appears to recede. Isidra felt Kalunga as a range of visceral and ineffable feelings that took form in an uncanny metonymy of liquids. Isidra said that Kalunga, the sea, should be thought of as a broth [*caldo*] where the dead float and drift among countless other dead. The undulating mass of Kalunga is a plane along which other versions of the dead emerge and become themselves, where they teem and proliferate to infinity, then dissolve again.

Feeling Kalunga, el muerto, so close—in her body and on her skin—Isidra insisted that the living and the dead float together. Growing voluminous, the fluid sea that is the dead rises—a tide surrounds the head and body. Her elaboration of Kalunga dissolved the expected opposition of living and dead, so that not only did these two great ordering categories of Enlightenment thought no longer stand in opposition to one another, but at the limit of her characterization became an indivisible coupling, mutually becoming one another like the surfaces of a Möbius strip. Placed within the context of Kalunga's saturating immanence, the living are best understood as singular densities of the dead precipitating in a fluid at its saturation point. Kalunga is a plane of immanence from which subjects and objects emerge and into which they are lost.[6]

Isidra's notion of Kalunga as a fluid immanence that permeates and saturates life helped her advance the idea that the body is something shared with the dead. Within the immanence that is Kalunga, the body is less fixed, more like a membranous peel constituted in any depth it might have only by the hydraulic fluctuations and rearrangements of the dead across and through its surface. This was the status of the body in Isidra's formulation of Kalunga, the body being a form of the dead, material insofar as matter was understood as a momentary condensation, precipitation, or coagulation of the fluid immanence of the dead.[7] The importance of this formulation becomes evident in later sections on Palo craft, where healing and harming are understood as the transformation of the fluid broth of the dead saturating the body of a client or a victim.

By way of another metonym, Isidra described the dead as a tide rising to surround our heads and fill them. This is an apt amalgam of west and central African motifs, with the dead inhabiting the head being west African and the metaphors of fluid ubiquity being Kongo inspired.[8] The use of liquid metaphors extends to Miami's authorities on questions of African inspiration in their community, who write that Palo and Ocha/Santo healers "live totally immersed in a dense 'spirit' reality formed out of supernatural beings with whom they maintain intimate and permanent contact."[9]

It is noteworthy that when dualist thought has been pushed to its limits in the philosophical cannon of the West, when the inviolable line between fluid immediacy and the concrete object has been blurred and immanence been allowed a moment to swim free, water metaphors abound. Friedrich Nietzsche used them to describe the vertiginous quality of a thinking life uprooted from both Platonic idealism and a Hegelian philosophy of negation. His sea and his waves speak of an overflowing life made so by taking to heart the Heraclitean suspicion that the "true" world is but a lie added onto the all-too-truthful testimony of the senses.[10] Bataille, an idiosyncratic thinker in that he allowed himself to ponder Nietzsche and Hegel simultaneously, wrote of water explicitly when he struggled with the problem of immediacy as posed by Hegel. And Deleuze, who tried to contemplate immediacy directly, said that it is like a giant wave, rolling and unrolling smaller waves of concepts across its surface.[11]

But Isidra's water metaphors hardly exhausted her references to the dead. Her language was suffused by a shifting terminology of the dead, which not surprisingly had many synonyms. Kalunga was synonymous to "el muerto," from Spanish, which can mean both "the dead [one]" and "the dead [mass]." *Lango*, from Kongo, means "water" and she used it interchangeably with Kalunga. Other times Isidra used the word *eggun*, from Yoruba, which in the original tongue means "the dead," "the ancestors," or "the bone [of a corpse]."[12] An ambiguity of number pervades el muerto and eggun in that either can be singular or plural, depending on usage. When Isidra spoke of el muerto and eggun she was using a plural-singular, like "crowd" or "multitude," and whether she was referring to a mass of anonymous multitudes or to a single responsive dead person depended entirely on her intention. Understanding her was a matter of context. Isidra believed the variety of forms of the dead to be independent of one another, yet emergent from a common plane of immanence—Kalunga. On rare occasions Isidra used the word *iku* to refer to the dead, which from Yoruba meant "death."

Isidra's multiplicity of terms for the dead could be a wholly subjective catalog, comprising nothing but a purely idiosyncratic interpretation within Cuba's African inspirations. But Isidra was not alone in assigning many names and forms in her efforts to explain the considerable, if diffuse, influence of the dead in Palo and Ocha/Santo. Lydia Cabrera learned a similar lesson about the proliferation of names for the dead relative to their influence. In her studies during the forties and fifties with Cuban practitioners of Palo and Ocha/Santo, the inimitable Cuban ethnographer and folklorist lived, worked, and learned in close proximity to the black people around her, especially elderly women. Cabrera appreciated their wisdom and willingness to teach.[13] In a paragraph that could easily be overlooked in *El Monte,* her monumental book describing the African inspirations of Palo and Ocha/Santo, Cabrera makes clear that these informants were emphatic about the dead: "The cult, it would be more precise to say the reverence for the ancestors, is one of the foundations of their religion. This is what my black teachers are going out of their way to explain to me when they affirm categorically and repeat with so much insistence that 'the Dead, in all the Laws [of African inspiration], give birth to the Saints.' 'Before you pay homage to the Saints you must greet the Dead.'"[14]

"Without the dead there is no Ocha" is one version of a translation from Old Yoruba and Spanish of a phrase Cabrera's informants must have spoken to her countless times. They said to her, like Isidra said to me again and again: "*Iku lobi ocha.*"[15] This old proverb is spoken in broken, antique Yoruba and repeated as the most basic and popular knowledge about Ocha/Santo. It is meant to carry knowledge like rhyme carries memory. In Palo and Ocha/Santo, where knowing often depends on indescribable intimation and intuition, proverbs like this one are like fleeting flashes of truth. For this reason they are often cast as riddles.

An interpretation of this phrase adds dimension to the fluid immanence of the dead, or Kalunga. It can help us understand the influence of the dead on African inspiration in Cuba, in part because the saying is as pervasive today among those who practice Palo [*paleras, paleros*] and Ocha/Santo [*santeras, santeros*] as it was sixty years ago. The wisdom of this phrase lies in its gesturing to the generative force of the dead. The term *iku* is recognized as "death" or "mortality." *Bi-*, as a part of *lobi*, is "to give birth, beget."[16] *Ocha* is short for La Regla de Ocha, which is synonymous with Ocha/Santo. Isidra translated "Iku lobi Ocha" into Spanish as *El muerto pare Santo,* or "The dead give birth to Oricha, the saint [*santo*]." The Spanish she used for *iku* was *el muerto,* and the verb she used for *lobi* was *parir,* which is not easily rendered into English. It means to give birth, with a reference first to production. The production of fruit and cattle is described with the verb *parir.* But *parir* derives from the Latin *parere,* which is also the root of the Spanish word for "appearance" [*aparencia*]. What is being acted upon is Ocha: the dead produces the saints, the Orichas, by giving them appearance. To make something appear is not to create it, but rather to bring forth what is already in the process of becoming present. By this rendering, the fluid immanence of the dead does not create the divine of Ocha/Santo but rather brings an animate, apparent, quality to them.

Morphogenesis (conceptual or narrative), then, happens at the interface of the dead and the subject or object in which it is actualized. If the dead can be said to be generative of the divine Orichas of Ocha/Santo, or the prendas-ngangas-enquisos of Palo, it is only because the dead are divinity's verb, or potential—not existing prior to it, but generating life in Divinity itself. The dead are an immanence "carrying within it the events or singularities that are actualized in subjects or objects."[17] Such singularities include practitioners of Palo and their prendas and the Orichas of Ocha/Santo. For those who would study only the divine saints that dwell in Ocha/Santo practice or Palo's prendas-ngangas-enquisos, this phrase, *iku lobi Ocha*—el muerto pare el santo—is an imperative from practitioners to focus on the dead as a prolific inspiration, however negligible the dead may appear in practice. Ultimately, it is the dead that inspire action in Palo and Ocha/Santo, and the dead that are the generative spark behind all that is beautiful and emergent in them.

Kalunga, el muerto, iku—others in Palo will talk of *lango*—to this proliferating language of the dead I would like to add my own term. To better communicate Kalunga as a plane of immanence, I would like to speak of "the ambient dead." I do this because at times Kalunga, in its saturating yet barely discernable influence, was like an "atmosphere" or a "climate." I borrow from the vocabulary of meteorology and speak of a climate of the dead with zones of high or low pressure. Promise or dread are felt in these zones as lingering potentials. When the ambient dead is felt, which is not always (climate is so often in the background), it is felt as a pocket of high or low pressure, a tension inside one's gut that runs up the nape of the neck, becoming a moment of anticipation or fear.

Kalunga, the ambient dead, is the immediacy, or plane of immanence, of Palo inspiration. From it emerge objects and subjects, like clients and healers. The ambient dead is a climate of transformation, complete with zones of woe and marvel, flashes of inspired intuition, and thunderclaps of astonishment that echo in the cavities of our bodies to wake us from our petrified thoughts. The ambient dead is as likely to seize us as an interiority or an exteriority; its influence is as likely to be discerned in our "subjectivity" as in the world of objects around us. Palo teaches that Kalunga takes form and exerts influence in objects exterior to the self, suggesting that Kalunga and its powers of creation and decomposition are found in seemingly countless forms. In substances and objects (including the body), as well as in the mysterious fastness of a life, the ambient dead is felt as a force—anonymous, vague, and inscrutable. By these qualities its "sense," as Deleuze might understand this term, is made.[18]

As much as being the plane of immanence from which subjects and objects emerge in inspired moments of tension and grace, Kalunga is also the sea into which objects and subjects recede, to be formed anew. Being prior to valuation, Kalunga is indifferent to the subjects and objects it conceives and is as likely to generate something new out of its flows as to consume what is diminishing. This propensity to receive and transform what has form but is fading lends a future quality to Kalunga, the ambient dead. Forms will not find stasis but will continue to change. What the ambient dead gives rise to will not persist or transcend. The new and the singular, like bodies, selves, subjects, and objects, born of the events that happen in the immanent plane of the dead will likely begin to diminish just as they have taken shape. To dissipate and destroy what is given is not beyond Kalunga's potentials. Kalunga is, in Nietzsche's sense, beyond good and evil—Kalunga sube, Kalunga baja— the sea rises, the sea falls.

Isidra's point for months was that Kalunga is a sheen of shifting textures across the surface of Palo valuation. The order of explanation it suggests is thus far from total; it is full of gaps and desolate lacunae. The ambient dead as an epistemological or cosmological ground does not come close to the absolute understanding of the world offered by a divinity or by Western philosophical notions such as Plato's Idea or Hegel's *geist*, though it may be possible to locate the ambient dead within Hegel's movements. Somewhere in Hegel's story of coming to consciousness, perhaps in the folds of sense certainty's negation, are the dead as Isidra lived them and became them every day.[19]

The dead as generic ambiance, insinuated into ubiquity by Isidra, offers only a contingent coherence of explanation for Palo thought and teaching. In the same moment one begins to ground Palo in the dead, as it should be, the dead then denies itself as ground because as a concept the dead glories in the paradox and contradiction of its multiple definitions. The dead is generically multiple, immaterial, *and* ubiquitous in the matter of our bodies—the dead is concept and experience at once.[20] Many of the outstanding features of African-inspired healing and harming in Cuba, including substantial powers that rule over life and fate, can be understood through concealed approaches that wind through the inconspicuous, ubiquitous, fluid potential of the dead. Trained healers in Palo and Ocha/Santo attribute their finest blessings to the raw potential of the pure immanence that is the ambient dead. They make a study and art out of feeling such potentials and therein seek clues into their fates and those of their clients.

Kalunga, el muerto, the ambient dead, as Isidra taught it, moiled between the living and their senses as an infinite yet barely evident kingdom of thinking and feeling that seized those who were attuned to it. As she described it, the dead permeates us as living individuals and saturates us with its frightening yet hopeful indeterminacy. The dead, as an unattributable, irreducible perception, renders the world and our experience of it comprehensible in its most utterly basic sense. Kalunga, el muerto, and lango were the words Isidra used to speak the experience of thinking without thinking, of feeling without feeling. The dead were the background against which elements of our experience of the world are perceived so faintly they seem no more than weak vibrations of themselves. Isidra was determined to teach me that Kalunga was the most premature understanding of the terrible immediacy of the world around us. This is what Isidra meant when she said that the dead get her out of bed when she can't sleep at night.

3. Little Corners

Kalunga, el muerto, the ambient dead, takes many turns and assumes multifarious shapes as it becomes influential. As a zone of indeterminacy prior to dominant signification, as a formless zone ambiguous and ineffable, Kalunga is forever churning forth versions of itself, which it generates spontaneously. These forms are the excess of possibility sparked by the mutual affirmation of immediate existence and objectified matter in the lives of those who practice Palo. Kalunga seizes subjects and places in their hands shapes of itself, which are material versions of the dead. These versions are ubiquitous to matter, like the immanent mass of the dead. Some material versions of the dead are so inconsequential that researchers easily overlook them, and even initiates in Palo do not often appreciate them. They include minor shapes such as ash, dirt, and the sawdust trails that stream down behind termites as they burrow into the trunks of majestic trees. What could easily be the most obvious of these minor material forms of Kalunga are the "little corners for the dead" [rinconcitos al muerto].

Kalunga has territories in matter. It creates versions of itself there, materializations of its excesses, shaped into inconspicuous assemblages of found objects kept and maintained by practitioners of both Palo and Ocha/Santo. Compared to the exquisite shrines kept for Ocha/Santo divinities such as Ochún, Yemayá, or Changó or to the caring for prendas-ngangas-enquisos, the practice of maintaining these aggregations seems insignificant and distant from all that is exciting and important in Cuba's codes of African inspiration.

The place of el muerto, the ambient dead, in the world of matter is but a sliver of floor here or there. Taking the form of a collection of household and found objects, the ambient dead occupies a secluded corner of the house, out of the way. The "little corners" as the assemblages are called, are routinely kept outdoors in a far corner of the patio or in an outhouse, as seen in the words of one of Cabrera's informants: "Me, as for my dead, I'm satisfied giving them the food they loved most in a little corner, in the outhouse, which is where they eat. That's how I keep them happy."[1] To say the little corners are shrines or altars to the ambient dead would be too much. They are unlikely places of deep respect, littered haphazardly as they are in many homes. The fragmentary collections of objects are, however, surrounded by simple, implicit restrictions.

Within Ocha/Santo, where glorious altars, or thrones *[tronos]*, are built in honor of Ocha/Santo divinities on feast days, the little corners are inconspicuous.[2] Within Palo, where an aggressive and creative engagement with the dead is taught, the little corners are surprisingly ignored. Palo and Ocha/Santo have exclusive material practices, except for the little corners, which each affirms yet keeps minor. In fact, Palo and Ocha/Santo each insist that before any feast their practitioners seek the dead in the little corners. In their marginality, the little corners, which is to say the ambient dead itself, are almost outside of Palo and Ocha/Santo, as if prior to or beyond these two Laws, yet paradoxically indispensable to them.

One of the most outstanding points about the little corners is that in their marginality to the Laws of Palo and Ocha/Santo they gain a unique autonomy. They are free from the social hierarchies that define ceremonies in Palo and Ocha/Santo because one does not have to be initiated to keep a rinconcito. Indeed, they are assembled by their keeper, unlike Santo sovereigns and prendas-ngangas-enquisos, which are given or awarded by ranking paleros and paleras, santeros and santeras, or *babalawos*, who are devoted to the Ocha/Santo sovereign Orula. Isidra's prendas-ngangas-enquisos, and the tureens that were her Ocha/Santo sovereigns, had been earned in initiations and ceremonies of investiture by Palo grandfathers *[tatas]* or by Ocha/Santo priests. For these she paid and sacrificed a great deal. By contrast, the rinconcito she kept was of her own making, awarded by no one, conceived of her own initiative. A rinconcito to the dead is too intimate, too personal, to be given or withheld by anyone. "The little corners are too special to pay for," she said. "A little corner to the dead comes from your past, from inside."

She kept her own rinconcito tucked into a niche made by a column running up her kitchen wall. Her little corner impressed me every time I was in her kitchen, where she rarely received anyone except family and close friends. In general, people in Havana are uncomfortable to let people near their stove, sink, or surfaces where food is prepared. The refrigerator is the secret of secrets in a Cuban house—never will casual guests be asked to help themselves to something in the fridge. This was certainly the case with

Isidra, whose kitchen lay down the long hall from her receiving room and beyond her living room. I had known Isidra for a while before she asked me to follow her there. Little by little, as we established confidence and our friendship developed, the prohibitions on her kitchen were dropped, and Isidra allowed it to become the place where we met, and she often fed me there. The back part of Isidra's house was dark because the windows there opened only onto her airshaft of a patio. She didn't have the hard currency to buy light bulbs. Her vision was poor, and when I could I would bring one in thanks of the many meals she shared with me. At least once I brought her a pair of eyeglasses.

Isidra's was a typical rinconcito. There must be thousands and thousands like hers in Havana. It had two principal elements, each a version of the dead that did not reach its plain potential unless assembled in a little corner. The first of these was an old red semicircular roof tile. "Like in colonial times," she said, "if it is broken even better." In teaching me she said, "Put the tile on the ground into the corner standing upright and facing out. Now mark it with white *cascarilla*, nine equilateral crosses—three rows of three equilateral white crosses. A rinconcito is incomplete without this, without the marks of the dead, which number nine."[3]

The other element is a tall staff or stick that is nestled into the curve of the tile and leaned into the corner. It could be an old broomstick, usually cut a bit shorter, or the straight slender limb from a special tree. In Havana Isidra used an old mop handle, though in her hometown of Sierra Morena her little corner sheltered a walking stick that had belonged to her mother, Cucusa. The stick usually extends well above the tile.

The stick in Isidra's corner was topped with an old doll's head. This is not unusual, but neither is it the rule in the rinconcitos. The heads are usually missing eyes. They have patches where the hair has been yanked out or rubbed off by a child and are generally soiled a dusty pink into gray. They were once adored, then discarded, objects of affection now valued for their utter loss. Isidra's doll's head was of a little blond girl with disheveled hair, perfectly pursed lips and a child's dirty cheeks. The sight of the doll's head on the stick drew my eye indiscreetly, again and again. There are times when these stick-head assemblages impress one as funny, because the doll wears a comic expression. African-inspired healers in Cuba use dolls in other contexts, but they are quite different from those in the rinconcitos. In most other cases the dolls' bodies are usually whole with brown skin, and they are dressed in versions of the sumptuous robes worn by sovereigns such as Yemayá, Oyá, and Ochún. These dolls sit on a person's bed or in a prominent place such as the living room, where a small chair is sometimes made for them. They are guardians over a person's fortune in one or another realm of fate. Care is taken to keep their dresses from collecting dust. "However," said Isidra, "any old head will do for the little corners."

Isidra's little corner was likely to include broken plates, chipped glasses, and little bowls made of halved gourds, unwashed and soiled with decaying food and rotten milk. There was stale bread. Because they are tended to infrequently and their offerings are left to decay, the little corners can be repellent. If they are kept outdoors, these unassuming place settings are often tipped over by cats, rats, or pigs. A corner to the dead is precisely the kind of collection that should be displayed discreetly and courteously ignored because of its baseness. People's commitment to the dead, to feed the dead and attend to the complex ambiance of Kalunga without fault often keeps the unappealing corners out of sight.

The first time I saw Isidra's rinconcito it was in such a state, about five days past a modest sacrifice she offered to the Ocha/Santo sovereign Obatalá. The little bun of bread that was Isidra's daily ration from the Cuban state had been placed there direct from the bakery and was already covered in mold. State-rationed bread has improved since the worst days of the economic crisis in the early nineties, but sometimes it still comes sour. On dishes laid out in rings around the tile and the doll-head stick was the food she had offered. The dead have a special preference for little bits of coconut smothered in orange *manteca de corojo*, a buttery paste from the African palm, each piece topped with a tiny black pepper corn. Isidra had also prepared *ajiaco* without salt. Ajiaco is a stew of potatoes, chard, yuca, plantains, sweet potato, carrots, and so on, which is adored by the dead. Isidra had served this in a little chipped bowl that had been turned over by an intruding cat from the alley beyond her patio. She was without rest chasing the stray cats out of the house on feast days. In futile resignation Isidra maintained that her old ones, her great aunt Chacha and her aunt Kimbito, said that it was good if the stray animals ate from the dead's share. A cat should not be scolded, they said.

On the floor next to the spilled and molding ajiaco were several little glasses. Some had been knocked over and others remained upright, their contents undisturbed. There was a shot glass of cane liquor and a glass of black coffee that still had a cigarette laying across its rim. There was a glass of coffee with milk and a glass of warm milk with sugar. This last one, along with the glass of water and raw sugar, had been overturned. In the center of everything was a small dinner plate, more like a salad plate, on which meat had been presented. The only items remaining on the plate were some dried-out beans and an outline of discolored fat of what was surely a choice piece from a white rooster, one of Obatalá's choice animals. The whole display was going to waste. Puddles of hardened candle wax were here and there.

Of the many African-inspired assemblages in Cuba, the little corners are the most bound to the ambient dead. Isidra's little corner was but one form that Kalunga took in her life. Each material element—the tile, the stick, the doll's head, and the offerings—was an unimportant expression of the dead, a becoming material of excesses and singularities amid Kalunga's churning. Condensed by her obeisance and self-sacrifice, these pieces together became a poignant site for Isidra's engagement with the dead in all of its multiplicity—including the responsive dead that spoke to Isidra in her moments of emergency.

4. Responsive Dead

Isidra's interpretation of the dead, while being profoundly intimate in that it radiated from folds of sensory and conceptual apprehension, also speaks to the order of knowledge shared to some degree by Palo and Ocha/Santo. Her practice of locating the dead at the faint limits of sensation and her emphasis on the ubiquity and indeterminacy of the dead is consistent with historical accounts of Palo and Ocha/Santo practice, as well as with contemporary treatments of Kongo religion. By my account, the dead in Palo are conceived as an immediacy that seizes people in the double affirmation of visceral-intellectual couplings, such as pangs of doubt and anticipation. The fact that this immediacy seizes practitioners of Palo rather than being controlled by them reveals the dead as a plane of immanence that teems with potentials and events. These in turn become countless versions of the dead actualized in subjects and in objects, such as the rinconcitos, the little corners for the dead. This chapter is about the responsive dead, or those dead that emerge from the immediacy of Kalunga to be actualized in the self, in the interiority of one's mind and memory, and which have strong influence on those in whom they manifest.

I would like, then, to write about spirits for a moment—a term more familiar to anthropology than the ones I have been using until now. I have carefully avoided the terms "spirit" or "spirits of the dead" for a variety of reasons; most importantly, few times if ever in my work with Isidra and other practitioners of Palo (or Ocha/Santo for that matter) did I hear the word "spirit" [espíritu] uttered to describe the dead.[1] Following Marx's example, I have chosen as literal a translation of the dead as possible, thus exiling "spirit" to a marginal position. Displacing the word "spirit," essentially prohibiting myself its use when writing of the dead in Palo, has made me painfully aware of the Christian and Western philosophical influences, especially Platonic and Hegelian, in most thinking and writing about the dead in the lives of people in the world. Such a conception of spirit is limited, constrained within a Western episteme that adheres to a logic that does not admit affirmation unto excess as a valid ground for logic. Negation must always accompany excess as its Apollinian minder.[2] This is the step that distances many of those writing about the dead in terms of spirit from the people who live the dead in the materiality of their lives each day. For just this reason I have sought to write about the dead in a language that seeks routes around spirits.

Isidra's discourse of the dead often included talk of versions, or aspects, of the dead to whom she could call and from whom she would receive a response; these I call the "responsive dead." Isidra spoke about such responsive dead in the possessive, referring to them as "my dead" [mis muertos]. "They are mine," she would say, "because they respond to me *[porque me responden]*." They were figures that inhabited her life intimately and whom she adored. In Isidra's retelling of her sleepless night trying to find a cause for the affliction of her client Lucy, these dead emerged from faint sensations to take the forms of her mother and her Aunt Chacha. Responsive figures such as these, individualized figures of the more diffuse and ubiquitous churning of Kalunga, are important in all forms of African inspiration in Cuba today.

When Isidra spoke about "her" dead she referred principally to her parental ancestors and also to specific dead, such as teachers and friends, who had come before her and who had touched her and changed her and who now established a privileged, responsive intimacy with her. She guarded a list of these dead in her memory, and she called to them regularly. Paramount was her mother, Vicenta Petrona Sáez, who those back home in Sierra Morena called Cucusa. Also among her responsive dead were her grandmother, Isidra Sáez; her aunt Chacha, *la vieja;* and her great-grandmother, remembered only as Kimbito. These were the principal dead that accompanied Isidra from her childhood in the countryside of central Cuba where she grew up. Cucusa, Isidra, Chacha, and Kimbito were pervasive figures in Isidra's anecdotes of the past and the authorities that grounded many of her interpretations of Kalunga and Palo. They were the sources of her proverbs and wisdom and also of much of what she knew about the dead and the crafts of Palo and Ocha/Santo.

Cucusa, her mother, was the one Isidra most sought, and who most responded. Cucusa had been highly regarded as a healer in Sierra Morena until 1995, when she died a very old woman. Throughout the Revolution, but especially before, people came to Cucusa with their fear and their worry, and she was generous and skillful in helping to straighten their crooked fates. She was especially revered for treating illnesses and she was widely beloved for her devotion to Babalu Ayé (San Lázaro or Lazarus the beggar), an old Dahomey and Catholic—now Ocha/Santo—sovereign of healing, illness, and death. Cucusa kept an altar to Babalu Ayé–San Lázaro in her house, which is still used by people in town. She was known to practice Kongo-inspired crafts in her healing as well. When the Revolution came to power Cucusa became a member of the party and was the first head of Sierra Morena's Committee for the Defense of the Revolution [CDR]. In most of Cuba the committees were important for policing African-inspired celebrations and gatherings throughout the sixties, seventies, and eighties.[3] Despite the demand that she curtail her practices and feasts, Cucusa never gave up her healing consultations, not even during the most Stalinist days of the Revolution in the seventies, and people kept coming to her for help.

In her list of responsive dead, which Isidra recited every morning when she divined, were some of Cuba's renown paleros and santeros, great diviners and Kongo-inspired healers such as Nicolás Angarika, Ta' Gaitán, Vejuco Finda, Emilio O'Farril, and others. The great singer, santera, and rumba dancer Mercedita Valdéz, whom Isidra had cared for in her last days in Centro Habana, was also among the responsive dead Isidra received. Like the dead of her family, these dead, individuals among the singularities forever emergent in the ambient dead, were close to Isidra and could be called on to respond to her in moments of anticipation.[4] At the same time, these dead were fragile and needed attending to if they were to keep from disappearing into the vast anonymity of Kalunga, which she cohabited with them. Individual responsive dead were at best momentary condensations of Kalunga and appeared as if silhouettes, suddenly emerged and backlit by the affective glow of its anonymous ambiance. These dead "are easily offended and scared away," said Isidra. "They are easily forgotten."

There were yet other dead that watched over Isidra and whom she recognized as guides and sought out for a response in moments of danger. Like so many people involved in Palo and Ocha/Santo, Isidra claimed she was watched over by a Plains Indian chief, as well as by a little old woman "from colonial times [de la época de la colonia]." Such dead are recognizable and responsive but one must learn about them from Kardec-inspired *espiritistas,* who "see" them usually around the vicinity of a person's head. Espiritistas are important mediators of the dead for practitioners of Palo and Ocha/Santo. In "masses" [misas], which usually take the form of intimate gatherings held in a client's home, espiritistas see Plains Indians, seventeenth-century martyred nuns, austere Franciscan missionaries, Arab scholars, little old ladies with long gray braids, and slaves, among many others. Importantly, during their masses, espiritistas help the living engage these dead through a complex theater of possession, often involving the appearance of Kongo dead, usually runaway slaves.[5]

Interestingly, espiritista dead in Cuba do not include political leaders or figures from Cuba's struggle for national independence, unlike depictions of espiritismo-inflected practices in many Latin American countries, such as in Venezuela and in descriptions of Cuban espiritismo before the Revolution.[6] This absence is curious and one can only imagine it is a result of the strong prohibitions on political commentary since 1959. However, Isidra found this explanation absurd and took issue with the idea that the politics of the living could have an effect of any sort on the dead. She could not fathom, and took offense at, the suggestion that independence leaders like Maceo or Martí, let alone a revolutionary figure like Che Guevara, would be found in circulation around anyone's head or that espiritistas would engage them in possession. It was impossible to speak about it with her. At the same time, she and Teodoro had no doubts that the "supreme leader of the Revolution" is involved in sorcery and divination, or that he has such figures among his dead.[7]

Isidra kept a small table in the bedroom around which versions of her dead gathered. Hers was a typical espiritista-inspired collection and included a little plaster likeness of a Plains Indian chief, airbrushed in glowing pastels. Along with such figurines, espiritistas encourage people to keep photographs of their deceased on the little table. The photos should surround eight glasses of clear water and a vase of fresh-cut flowers. In the middle of the glasses should be a crystal chalice, into which a crucifix is leaned, half submerged. This chalice brings the number of glasses to nine, which in Cuba is the number that corresponds to the dead. The water and flowers are meant to cool or refresh [refrescar] the dead and must be changed regularly. Thus attended to, as Isidra did, the responsive dead watch over the living, take interest in them, and accompany them. To not maintain such a table would be to neglect these dead and risk their dissolution in the murky washes of Kalunga. One would hate to lose the protections of so fierce an ally as an Indian warrior, let alone the watchful eye of learned Arab scholars from centuries ago. When an espiritista mass is held, this table becomes the nucleus of invocation and possession.

Isidra lived with her responsive dead and observed them and struggled with them in the intimacy and monotony of everyday life in Havana. She was exceptionally devoted to her dead, was drawn to them, and lived among them in her body and in her thoughts. She sought the dead regularly, especially in moments of apprehension and dread. She had the dead near in her memories of them and in the unexpected recollections of their sayings and wisdom that lived in her in the form of unforgettable proverbs like the ones recited by Cucusa and Chacha. Isidra's mode of living with the dead was hardly an eccentricity. She had learned it from her mother and others in Sierra Morena, and she taught it as an ethical, mutual engagement with the dead. The responsive dead have influence; this is the evidence of their vitality and force and what they share with the living. With *influence* as the standard of existence, there was no doubt in Isidra's mind that the dead existed, sometimes with more force than the living themselves. Such a mode of engaging the dead wasn't simply a function of Isidra's imaginary or a simple exercise in memory but also a will to listen to and relate viscerally and personally to the voices and images emerging always from the immediacy of our inner experience. These voices and scenes, sometimes visages, sometimes vague feelings, are lodged within us and within our relationships to objects and situations in the world, and in moments of special clarity they are felt and heard.

PART II

Palo Society

• • • • •

The dead in its multiple and compossible forms—Kalunga, el muerto and the dead ubiquitously spread through matter, the responsive dead (part 1)—inspires Cuban Kongo social life, which might better be referred to as Palo society, a community of the living in the service of the dead, which are cultivated as a force against the vagaries of fate. In this way, Palo is alike to healing associations already of ancient lineage for the BaKongo in the nineteenth century, societies that gathered the dead in substances much like the prendas-ngangas-enquisos kept at the heart of Palo houses today. Palo society breaks down into branches and then individual praise houses; the one Isidra belonged to was the Quita Manaquita Briyumba Congo society of Guanabacoa, a city important as an enclave of freed slaves in colonial times and now engulfed by Havana (chapter 5). She was a matriarch within the Quita Manaquita house and in that capacity introduced me to Teodoro Herrera, who presided over it (chapter 6). Like all Palo praise houses, his was marked by closed initiations and a strict hierarchy that privileged men within the society, but not so much that knowledgeable women could not rise to prominence within it, as Isidra had (chapter 7). As a leader among Quita Manaquita members, Isidra challenged Teodoro, whose direction had brought a shadow over the house (chapter 8). She believed the course of Teodoro's life was dangerous for him and his praise house and wanted Teodoro to practice a more disciplined service to the dead. She dreamed the house might again be a resource for the community, drawing new members to feasts of initiation, as did other houses in Guanabacoa (chapters 9 and 10). What Isidra sought more than anything was the welfare of the prendas-ngangas-enquisos kept by Teodoro, which when properly cared for, would inspire gatherings where living and dead meet in feasts of mutual regeneration.

5. Emilio O'Farril

Isidra met Teodoro in the early sixties, when she was newly arrived from the countryside and the capital was still new to her. She was a teenager from the central Cuban town of Sierra Morena, come to study with the first university class sponsored by the Revolution, and during her first couple of years in Havana she kept a proper materialist distance from the capital's versions of African inspiration. They were alien to her, in any case, because back home in Sierra Morena she was used to a fluid form of inspiration she called Bembé, which allows central African (Kongo) and west African elements to braid together at feasts.[1] In Havana, Palo (Kongo-inspired) and Ocha/Santo (Yoruba-inspired) Rules keep exclusive distance from one another. Havana Palo and Ocha/Santo, with their elaborate initiations, are also more hierarchical than Bembé, which does not initiate.

So, Isidra's early reticence regarding Palo and Ocha/Santo was naturally circumspect. She was cautious about associating with Havana teachers and healers, and not only because she was wary of their authoritarian influence and artful cosmopolitanism. She also kept her distance because in her first years in Havana the Revolution marginalized religion in general. If one had ambitions within the Communist Party, which Isidra did and which was rapidly becoming the sole arbiter of social and institutional power in Cuba, it was best to keep one's distance from religious inspiration, be it African or European Catholic.

Isidra met Teodoro through Cuba's Conjunto Folklórico Nacional.[2] As Isidra finished her university degree in physical education as an instructor of dance, she was drawn to the recently formed dance company, which was perhaps the only official institution in those years where African inspirations could be invoked without risk to one's standing in the party. In retrospect, the Conjunto appears to have been the Revolution's attempt to sublimate

African inspirations into its great modern edifice (in a classic Hegelian manner), elevating antithetical religious practices into aesthetic forms in the same instant it divested them of social and civic standing. By the time Isidra was associated with it in the mid- to late sixties, the Conjunto sheltered a group of respected practitioners of Palo and Ocha/Santo, gathered as informants around the director of the company, the talented anthropologist Argeliers León.[3] Isidra never performed with the Conjunto, but it was there she met the men and women who would become her teachers of Havana's interpretations of central and west African forms. Among them was Teodoro's father, Emilio O'Farril.[4]

From the mid-1940s until he died in 1995, Emilio O'Farril maintained a Kongo praise house in Guanabacoa, a section in the extreme east of Havana. It was a house founded on the teachings of his mother who, according to Isidra, came from the central Cuban countryside not far from where she grew up. Emilio maintained his mother was African, brought to Cuba as a slave. As proof of that he said, and Teodoro repeated, she kept a Congo charm in the form of a large bundle wrapped in a sack that hung from her ceiling, which she called *mboumba,* and which she would lower to the ground to work her craft.[5] Following his mother's wishes, Emilio disposed of the mboumba when she died, something he later regretted. Drawing on his mother's inspirations, which were rural and formed outside the influence of Havana Palo, Emilio soon became a master of the urban form of Kongo Law. His praise house, the Munanso Quita Manaquita Briyumba Congo was a refinement of this form and by all accounts dominant in Guanabacoa prior to the Revolution.[6] Even later, after Emilio had become an adviser to the Conjunto Folklórico and the Revolution's hostility toward unintegrated African-inspired praise houses became clear, his house was widely influential among Guanabacoa paleros. Emilio's son, Teodoro, grew up in the praise house and was its most privileged initiate, reaching its highest degree, tata nganga, when he was ten years old.

When Emilio's mother first moved there, sometime in the 1920s, Guanabacoa reclined on a couple of hillsides across the port from Havana. The capital grew after the Second World War, spreading around the harbor's backwaters until it swallowed its outlying communities; today Guanabacoa is indisputably a part of greater Havana. Guanabacoa's many sections follow the elevations of slopes and the winding lines of creeks. Footbridges over streams connect neighborhoods where streets do not, and when it rains the creek beds swell with sewage and garbage. As Guanabacoa's numerous plazas, cathedrals, and built-up neighborhoods dissipate into the countryside, its outlying parts take on a rural feeling, an important characteristic for practitioners of Palo who rely on plants and materials from the countryside or the forest *[el monte]* for their healing craft. Guanabacoa and its sister city, Regla, immediately to the northwest, make up two of Havana's largest predominantly black communities.[7] Both towns have been seeped since colonial times in the prestige and fear that surround African inspiration in Cuba. In the popular imagination, Regla is famous for its knowledgeable santeras and no-frills Ocha/Santo rituals, while Guanabacoa is feared as a place of poverty and witchcraft, a zone of Palo power over the dead. The Revolution has been unable to change those reputations despite fifty years of efforts to control Palo and Ocha/Santo. Of this Teodoro was proud, proud of the Revolution's failure to erase what he called "La Regla de Congo" in Guanabacoa.

The Quita Manaquita house was perched on a hill in Guanabacoa, in a neighborhood a little distance from the center of town. It was a steep walk up from the avenue Independencia, along a broken street and past a once-touted organic gardening project. Like in many other neighborhoods in Guanabacoa and Regla, the houses were cobbled-together affairs—shanties of broken boards tacked to termite-eaten posts, doors sagging on hinges, and roofs made of mismatched rafters covered by sheets of tar paper pinned by bricks and rocks to flattened leafs of corrugated metal. Families, often three generations and siblings with spouses and children, go about their lives inside.

However poor, the houses could be beautiful. This was never more so than when they crouched under the extended branches of giant gray ceibas, enormous cottonwood trees, some of which date hundreds of years. It is not uncommon to have the tumbledown rooms of the houses built to surround the trees, creating an inner courtyard. The robust trees wholly dominated such compounds, their powerful roots extending from the trunk in graceful arcs descending into the ground. The shade from a ceiba can cover several buildings, protecting them as much from the merciless sun of August as from October's torrential rains. Those who live under them hardly miss a chance to compliment the grace with which ceibas resist hurricane-force winds. Not surprisingly, African-inspired knowledge in Cuba sets these trees apart as powerful versions of the dead.

The Quita Manaquita house was a variant of such an arrangement, with a ceiba in the back patio that reached nearly to the street with its branches. Teodoro would come out from under the roof of his four-post, clapboard house, which leaned precariously to one side, and on his way to or from the outhouse would praise the tree with a hard slap on its trunk. "Ndundo dame tu sombra Manaquita cara'o!" he would say. "Ceiba, give me some shade. Manaquita says so, damn it!" Then he would laugh at himself because such a command could only be a joke, as if the ceiba didn't already cover his house, as if it would possibly respond out of its gray silence. In Teo's opinion, the tree had done more for the house over forty years than had the Revolution, which for decades had been the only source for construction materials of the kind the house now needed. Gaps in the clapboard walls of the house let in light, along with drafts that were especially hard in winter. Teodoro did nothing to keep up the house, and the dilapidation inside was considerable. He lived there alone, Emilio having died five years earlier.

The fortunes of the society mirrored those of the physical structure it was indivisible from. Emilio was the widely admired founder of the house and, until his death, the presiding authority *[tata diambola]*. Along with his half brother, Pedro, Emilio had been building and maintaining his circle of initiates for more than forty years. It is well established that Palo, like Ocha/Santo, is organized in Havana around praise houses led by knowledgeable, prestigious healers.[8] Teodoro's neighbors, many of whom were Quita Manaquita themselves, said that Emilio could heal terrible misfortune, including disease. Myth surrounded the memory of Emilio, and neighbors retold stories about him curing mad children and epilepsy. He was rarely suspected of witchcraft, despite the fact that many, if not all, of his neighbors probably had Emilio work aggressive sorcery on their behalf.

Until the 1960s the Quita Manaquita praise house was registered officially as a Catholic social club—La Sociedad "Hijos de San Juan de Dios" [The Society of the Children of Saint John of the Divine]. Since at least the eighteenth century, black praise societies in Cuba used the simulacra of Catholic civic societies to shield themselves from widespread racism and white fear.[9] Teodoro was only ten when the Revolution triumphed in 1959 and he hardly knew any reality other than the Revolution's, but was terribly nostalgic for the society. He painted a scene in which the Quita Manaquita house was never hassled by the authorities in the 1950s, something that changed with the triumph of the Revolution. Isidra felt such assertions to be little more than efforts to rehabilitate the fifties and read considerable disregard toward the Revolution in such statements. When she pushed back, he would concede that police interfered with Quita Manaquita feasts since the day it was founded, but then turned the accusations of harassment back on the Revolution, which were undeniable.[10]

By Teodoro's account, with which I largely agree, throughout the sixties the Revolution systematically eliminated organizations that were autonomous from state control. As the Revolution came to regulate civil society in the wake of its complete control of economic life—not too long after the middle of 1968—Palo and Ocha/Santo praise houses lost their civic facades as Catholic social circles and were left without civil or juridical proxies to buffer them from centralized state rule. La Sociedad "Hijos de San Juan de Dios" was dissolved then, but the praise community Quita Manaquita Briyumba Congo lived on, albeit more discreetly than before, always working out of Emilio's house.

Despite hostility on the part of the Revolution, Emilio managed to maintain the Quita Manaquita Briyumba Congo praise house as a vibrant hierarchy of the living in the service of the dead. "There were years when no drums were heard on the sidewalks of Havana," said Teodoro, "but they sounded at the Quita Manaquita house, at its feast for Zarabanda, Emilio's beloved prenda."[11] Only during a short spell in the seventies, the so-called *década negra* [black decade] of Soviet orthodoxy, did the drums of the Quita Manaquita praise house fall wholly silent. By Teodoro's account and those of many others, praise house members throughout Havana took to playing percussion on their thighs and chests to keep the sounds of their praise subdued. According to Teodoro, the Manaquitas numbered more than fifteen hundred initiates by Emilio's, Pedro's, and his hands when Emilio died. Today the house survives, but hardly anyone comes around and this is something that shamed Teodoro deeply. This shame, said Isidra, was proportional to what had been lost. "All that is left is a shadow."

6. Teodoro

Teodoro and I met at Isidra's, in El Cerro. He was an irregular visitor to her house. He usually appeared uninvited, at the end of some errand that brought him across the harbor from Guanabacoa. This was always by bus around the backwater, and I never knew Teodoro to take the ferry from Regla, where he had lots of family. Sometimes he came running to let Isidra know of a feast he desperately wanted her to attend, and sometimes he needed her help with an initiation. Other times he would come by just wanting to talk Palo. A lot of times he would show up drunk and spend his time complaining about the betrayals in the Manaquita house. Listening to him it was hardly clear who was responsible for them. Then he would insist on dinner. Isidra received him on these occasions only because of her memory of Emilio. Teodoro's visits always troubled Isidra; he was a privileged antagonist of hers and an unwelcome affliction whom she tolerated more than she might have liked.

It didn't take Isidra long to notice that she could bear Teodoro better when I was there; and because she herself learned a lot about Palo from him, soon she was arranging meetings for the three of us to talk at her place. When she fell into a good conversation with him she loved reminiscing about Emilio and Manaquita feasts, sharing with us her memories of specific singers and versions of dead that appeared from out of the flows of Kalunga to test their force against the living. Among these feasts was the scene of Emilio's funeral, where his corpse was "danced" among a gathering of Manaquita members, and which seemed to mark Isidra and Teodoro's last great moment in the Manaquita house together.

Isidra appreciated Teodoro's knowledge but felt that sometimes his interpretations of Palo were crass, and she would often try to supplement his teachings. He bristled at her correctives, and tense exchanges would ensue.

Teodoro felt Isidra's takes on Palo were too often biased toward an Ocha/Santo perspective, which Isidra practiced but Teodoro did not. Teodoro was not very good at expressing his divergences from her and would sometimes imply that Isidra lacked allegiance to the Manaquita house. She vehemently defended her loyalty, especially as it bore on her authority within the society. Few things riled her more than Teodoro's questioning her commitment. Contention marked every one of their visits. It was hard to get caught in their sharp exchanges, but their habit of arguing about Palo interpretation often led to more carefully defined questions or problems for all of us.

It didn't take long to notice that Teodoro was jarring. The shadow hanging over the Manaquita house clung to him and from the first it was possible to feel the fateful pall that surrounded him. He was an incongruous jumble of anger, tenderness, and helpless vulnerability, held together by some force unknown perhaps even to him. Self-doubt was his dominant mode, and his lack of confidence was so acute that he barely trusted himself on any question other than those having to do with Palo. Regarding this, he could be plainly authoritative to the point of being boorish. He seemed determined to avoid the self-reflection that might have made him easier to be with, and the swings he suffered between this arrogance and his various states of uncertainty were hard to behold.

Teodoro could be deceptive and shameless. He was erratic with commitments, which he was loath to make because he knew from experience how poorly he kept them. Nevertheless, his unrelenting sense of guilt compelled him to offer what he knew he did not have, and he was forever caught up in promises he could not keep. Then he would vanish rather than admit he hadn't kept his part of a deal. He would lie to get his way, though he wasn't especially skilled at manipulating others. His deceptions were conspicuous, such that it hurt to watch him getting into dead-end situations, even when he had lied his way into them. His lies were ultimately harmless because he was too uncertain of himself to possibly hold great sway over anyone. Teodoro seemed aware of his shortcomings, but he also seemed powerless to change. Instead he chose to be pitied and in the end disrespected.

In spite of all this, there was an unexpected charm to Teodoro. He could be funny and often hid frank assessments of Isidra or the Revolution in facetious wit. He was an entertaining storyteller with a sense of humor that made light of his shortfalls and troubles. He was most honest about himself when he was joking. He loved to give his time if he could be telling a story—that was on his terms. In his conversation he fused the living and the dead in such a way that new realities appeared woven in his tales of everyday life. He could hold forth with gusto about his work and travels

with Emilio, and he liked nothing more than to recall over a bit of aguardiente, cane liquor, his adventures with his father. Listening to Teodoro re-
count his life with Emilio, it was clear that his love of stories was at once
his love for the dead and that the two, stories and the dead, were but different forms of the same atmosphere of possibility and becoming that is
Kalunga. Working through a bottle, he would begin to exaggerate and
eventually fall into mumbled bouts of self-loathing.

But Teodoro was ultimately buoyed by his good humor, which lifted
him out of his otherwise despondent self. When he wasn't telling some
story, Teodoro was a good listener in conversation. This redeemed him
greatly and must have come from some secret store of generosity hidden
within him. His skill as a listener had to do with the fact that under much
of his persona as a raconteur and cheery drinker was a quiet, even shy, person. Around strangers he was timid, unless he was drunk. His shyness had
to do with his inability to keep at bay the casual jabs and everyday exer-
cises of power others tend to deploy thoughtlessly. He appeared to have
none of the witty defenses people normally develop that make them so
seamlessly sociable, like chatter, and he preferred to stay out of conversations with people he didn't know. To me it seemed as if what was intolerable about him—his lying, his drinking, his guilt—were direct extensions
of his irremediable self-doubt. He was so resigned to his everyday despondence that with people he trusted he would do little to hide himself, and his
humor usually betrayed feelings he might rather have kept concealed. This
made him paradoxically vulnerable.

As a teacher of Palo, Teodoro was very much like Emilio who, despite
Palo's ethos of secrecy, was disposed to teaching it broadly. Emilio's participation with the Conjunto Folklórico in the early sixties went against the
better advice of many in the Quita Manaquita house, like his half brother
Pedro, who wanted to keep Palo secret. Like Emilio, Teodoro understood that
Palo could be taught to noninitiates so that its prestige would be heightened
rather than diminished, and to some degree Teodoro saw his involvement
with me as akin to his father's involvement with the Conjunto, if on a much
smaller scale.

Teodoro clearly enjoyed teaching, and he was good at conveying his
love of Palo. The craft of revaluing fates, even if another must be harmed to
do so, was his life, and he was at times a teacher of startling clarity. But in
general, he preferred to push his apprentices by unfolding the plane of
knowledge well ahead of their understanding, to the extent that it seemed
as if disorientation was something he purposefully employed in his teaching. Teodoro veiled much of what he taught in riddles and cosmological

conundrums built on a prior teaching, and his skill at concentrating a lesson into a mysterious three- or four-word proverb was extraordinary.[1] Like with blues lyrics—and Palo has the blues—he preferred to say a lot by saying very little, all of it deep. Patience as a teacher was not Teodoro's strong suit, but perhaps this was because of the urgency with which he felt an apprentice, once initiated, must learn.

Maybe this was why his pedagogue's toolbox included among its instruments degradation and fear. These are regrettably common in all forms of teaching, and in a case where fate-changing knowledge is taught it is not surprising to find them in common use. Teaching is among those activities with a special proximity to love, and it is among love's unfortunate possibilities to be hidden under turbid aggression. Teodoro no doubt learned his craft and his passion with considerable doses of each from Emilio. This is some of what made Teodoro so powerful and at the same time so unbearable a teacher.

"Teo," as Isidra sometimes called him, was average size, and his skin was darker than Isidra's. Skin tone, despite fifty years of Revolution, is an important determinant of social prestige in Cuba, and she teased him about his darkness relative to her. She would often drive home a barb by nailing him with the exclamation: "Congo Africano!" This comment was meant to highlight what she perceived as his relative slowness in conversation. His hands were scarred and callused from years of hard work, and his fingers overlapped one another, so that his hands were bent like claws. He lodged his filterless Populares cigarettes at the very base of his index and middle fingers, so that when he smoked, which was always, his whole hand would lift in a cup to cover his mouth and chin. His hands were in the same bowed position when he rested while playing during a Palo feast, and I imagined that the only time his fingers opened was in the flash of striking the drum. A white beard and moustache tinted yellow by cigarettes framed a handsome set of teeth, while a high forehead of white hair cut across the upper lines of his brow. The eyes locked inside this hedge of white were boyish and smart, with a beguiling light. The seductive resources of this face were at his full disposal, and when the story was on his side he could make his features jump their borders to take on appearances that were not his own.

Despite being as poor as anyone I ever met in Cuba, Teodoro liked to look good. He spent a lot of time on the street and kept in touch with young people in his neighborhood. His look was unaffected, but he had a penchant for wearing out-of-style donation clothes combined so as to achieve a youthful edge. His clothes might sometimes be meager, but Teodoro was meticulous about them. Whatever he wore, regardless of how outdated, or "Soviet,"

Teo would update it with a subtle, unique strut. The one part of his look that shamed him was his shoes, which over the years have been everything from ruined vinyl tennies to wrecked flip-flops stitched together in countless places. Great importance is placed on clean and polished shoes in Havana, especially in poor communities, and Teo was self-conscious about his feet. Decent shoes were available *only* in U.S. dollars at the hard currency "shopping" stores. Prostitution, theft, and con jobs, usually from a trip to a hotel lobby, or remittances from family in Miami, are the everyday source of almost all quality shoes in Cuba. Teo dared no such trip; he was too afraid to join the hustlers in touristy Habana Vieja and had no family or initiates in Miami that cared enough.

Scrounging for dollars on the fringes of Cuba's tourist trade invariably carried its risks, but there was more that frightened Teodoro. He feared the Cuban state, which was most obvious in the care he took when he talked about it. He was forever scared of being arrested because he didn't work. His unemployment, combined with a criminal record from many years past, was enough justification for the Revolution to charge him with the crime of "dangerousness."[2] Teodoro could earn a subsistence working Palo, which hardly lifted him out of poverty and certainly didn't count as gainful employment as far as the Revolution was concerned. Life under the Revolution had been terrible for making a living from Palo until the late nineties, and Teodoro had been a dockhand and truck driver during his younger years. But his Palo craft afforded him a precious autonomy from a state-supervised job and the pressures of party integration. In 1999 he felt the risks of working Palo were equal to the risks of unemployment, especially since the generalized liberalization of religion in the wake of the Pope's visit in 1998. Teo's choices did not please the authorities, who on more than one occasion while I worked with him between 1999 and 2000 visited him to try to get him to accept employment. But Teodoro had given up on the state, and at moments this simple decision led him to hard times Isidra could never imagine.

It should have hardly been a surprise to me that Teodoro abhorred the Revolution. He had dark skin; he was poor, unemployed, from Guanabacoa, and on top of everything a palero before all else. As far as he was concerned, party militants, let alone the Revolutionary elite, had never looked upon any of these favorably. Teodoro felt that for forty years Palo had been accorded no room under the Revolution, and even at the end of the nineties the space granted by implicit decree to African-inspired practices in the wake of the Pope's visit was hardly respected. He hated having to get a permit to hold a feast at his house, and he was resentful of the years of pressure the Revolution had brought against African inspirations. He was unable to forgive the regime its ideological excesses, especially those of the 1970's.

Teodoro had a fixed rant on the Revolution. "The Manaquitas were at the top before the Revolution! Palo was strong. Look at Palo now; look at it! I can introduce you to one, two, a hundred paleros and take you to countless feasts, but it is nothing compared to what it was. The old ones have died, and too little has been taught. The Revolution has ruined Palo and Ocha/Santo; anyone will tell you that. First the persecutions, for thirty-five years persecution! You couldn't get a raise if you were a palero, or santero, or even Catholic. No moving up! You couldn't be a member of the party, and being a member of the party here is like being a capitalist in the United States! I worked for thirty years at the waterfront, thirty years! And I'm nowhere because the Revolution has always hated Palo. Countless abuses! And now tourism, the way the Revolution sells religion. You are seeing the strangest things on the street these days, people who spent the Revolution running away from Palo now making things up to earn a dollar!"

Teodoro would get started, but he would just as quickly quiet down, afraid of being overheard. He preferred not to share his malice with Isidra. Though he had a case against the Revolution, by his own fault his arguments were unconvincing. He was often incoherent in his critiques, jumping from allegation to anecdote and eschewing historical precision. Such was hardly the way to win a quarrel against someone as sharp as Isidra, who even if she could be made to hear his point would never agree with such shoddy argumentation. When he got going she would derail him by critiquing his form, and hardly ever had to take the substance of his complaints seriously. But what Teo's critique lacked in intellectual arrangement it made up for in visceral intensity, which only made his disdain of the Revolution all the more real to him. He carried this on his forehead and under his shoulder blades. I trusted him on questions about the street, poverty, and the police. From his hilltop slum in Guanabacoa, middle-class neighborhoods in Havana like El Vedado and Playa were the same to him as the elite sections of Miramar and Siboney, where the party leadership lives in its gated homes. Many of the visitors seeking help from Teo were from his neighborhood, poor people like himself, younger, with dark skin, and sometimes facing prison or a criminal charge. He and his clients, many of them initiates of Emilio's, shared an assessment of the Revolution that began in powerless resentment.

My own experience in the early nineties in Havana had taught me that there was little of the Revolution left to defend dogmatically, and doing so only led to distance, if not ridicule, from everyday Cubans. I had long ago adopted a posture of listening openly to tirades like Teodoro's and we soon developed a confidence on political matters that excluded Isidra. At first I thought that Teodoro mistrusted her; that he was afraid that as a vanguard militant of the party *[militante de vanguardia]* she would inform on him. That was hardly the case. Teodoro knew that other forces bound Isidra and determined her loyalties, and he was confident that Isidra's ultimate allegiances lay with the Manaquita house and Emilio's prendas, which were kept there.

What Teodoro *did* fear was Isidra's harangues. That they shared the leadership of a once prominent Palo praise house did not preclude them from vociferous disagreements. She knew his critique by heart and when he intimated it she was overwhelming in her defense of the regime. Teodoro didn't have the rhetorical skills to keep him from being railroaded by her, and he was nearly powerless to deflect her arguments and reason. Oblique jokes and tiny gestures that highlighted the corruption of the state were his way of speaking his political mind to Isidra. He was a master of the dry observation and the acid comment spoken into the tension of a social encounter, and he could sometimes disgust Isidra into not responding. This was Teo's privileged zone of action, at the limits of reason, style, and taste, and he could be devious in his barbs. He knew her love of Palo and Ocha/Santo and he could make comments which, placed into a joke or a one-word reply, made the abuses of the regime against African-inspired praise houses emerge in self-evidence from the flow of routine conversation. There were many points she could not argue against when he brought them forth in his snipes, such as the fact that people had been denied party membership or promotions for being paleros or santeros or the fact that permits were necessary to hold Palo and Santo gatherings. But she disdained it when he cited the regime's efforts against Cuban traditions of inspiration within a larger assumption about the overall social validity of the Revolution, and if she could not correct or limit the commentary she simply changed the topic.

But mostly we worked hard to keep the conversation away from politics and on Palo. Even then, it wasn't easy to follow Teodoro. He had a deep voice and spoke from the back of his mouth in gargled tones. He spoke fast and stuttered. Stuttering embarrassed him and he tried to conceal it, and when he couldn't he blamed the dead for his blocks. He also blamed his bouts of drinking on the dead, especially on the dead condensed in his principal Palo cauldron, which he called Lucero Mundo Saca Empeño. I remember seeing him after an especially bad stutter bow his head in defeat and pinch his eyes across the bridge of his nose. Rubbing his forehead with the back of his hand, he then flicked it away from his face, and shook his head to clear it. People sometimes make that combination of gestures during Palo and Ocha/Santo feasts, when they feel the dead or an Ocha/Santo sovereign taking them and seek to stave off the possession. Teodoro mumbled, as if surprised by the power that moved him, "Eh! What's going on here, now? Eh! Fuck! Who's there? Enough of that! Go on, get out of here!"

Besides his rumble of a voice and his stutter, Teodoro wore dentures that didn't fit and made his speech imprecise. They were the artifice of his perfect smile and in their imperfection disarticulated his speech. It took effort to hear through Teodoro's fog of a voice and, even deciphered, it was no easier to understand him. He spoke a language of his own, a mix of Spanish and Palo Kikongo learned from Emilio that was baffling to my ear, even as a native Spanish speaker. Isidra would laugh at Teo's impassable vocabulary, at the same time that she admired it. When he didn't, or wouldn't, translate for me she would try to offer her own translations for Teodoro's Palo *lengua* [tongue], which I call Palo Kikongo.[3] There were times when she didn't understand a word of what he said. On such occasions she would tease him with good-humored exasperation that combined a nod of respect with a malicious barb, "Congo bozal, Africano de verdad!" "A true African," she said, using the term *Congo bozal*, borrowed from the vocabulary of slavery. Bozal is Spanish for "muzzle," and Isidra said the word was used in the colony to describe the heavily accented, drawled, muzzled Spanish of slaves newly arrived from Congo and other African lands.[4] She seemed oblivious to the crudeness of the term.

Palo Kikongo is an uncommon tongue, sourced in the nineteenth century and continuously elaborated and transformed through repetition, song, and improvisation. In helping me make sense of Teodoro's Palo Kikongo I had the indisputable aid of my native Spanish, and Teodoro was usually willing to provide translations—once. After that he insisted not only that I remember Palo Kikongo definitions but also that I use Palo Kikongo in our discussions. Failing to do so resulted in playful but relentless scolding.

Teo routinely used words from Palo Kikongo for parts of the body, plants, animals, kinship relations, and the dead. Much of Cuban slang, not by chance the language of poor urban youth, comes from the ritual languages of Palo and Ocha/Santo and the Abakuá men's societies.[5] But Teodoro's Palo Kikongo wasn't slang. Rather, it sprang from people like him, older, accustomed to the workings of the dead, improvising along Kalunga's protean flows. Younger folks in Havana draw words from Palo Kikongo to put into circulation as the semisecret codes of prestige and belonging people love to participate in. Both Spanish and Palo Kikongo are in constant play in poor neighborhoods of Havana, where Palo Kikongo stretches across the surface of fluid Spanish as a tenuous web of foreign terms suspended aloft by unimagined couplings and prescient retranslations. Occasionally, a Palo Kikongo word at the fringe of this structure arrives too soon and too fast across the face of Spanish, breaks off, and plunges through common understanding, leaving behind it a trail of new meaning. Along with much patient listening and many requests for clarifications, learning Teodoro's speech involved becoming aware of these fragments in everyday Cuban Spanish, picking them up, and bringing them back to him for comment.

One example from my early years in Cuba was the word *fula,* which was in popular circulation after the collapse of the Soviet Union. In the early nineties fula meant "money," particularly U.S. dollars, which were illegal to possess in Cuba until 1993 and precious on the underground market. Not surprisingly, fula also meant "hot," as in both "heat" and "stolen," much the same way these two words combine in English slang. Fula had circulated as slang in Cuba in the 1970s, but with a different meaning, "dirty" or "not allowed." In present-day Palo Kikongo fula has none of these meanings, but rather "gunpowder," which is important in Palo craft.[6] Not only is gunpowder hot in terms of temperature when lit, it is also hot because Cuban law prohibits its sale or possession and it must be acquired by means of theft. Teodoro used fula to mean gunpowder and U.S. dollars both.

As our conversations took us beyond words and into the actuality of understandings, Teodoro provided more obstacles. Rarely did he follow a theme across more than four or five sentences, and he tended to stray in his thought. He was attracted by those glowing nodes of meaning where knowledge and prestige condense. These bubble-like bonds radiating genius coalesce constantly out of the generic and indeterminate flows of the Kalunga, sometimes many at a time, and could lead Teodoro on a meandering course of conversation. Sometimes he managed to connect several nodes—to constellate words, meanings, and the impression of force they conveyed—and an image of Palo would suddenly appear. Teodoro was unable to hold these constellations for long; they would just as suddenly be lost to the indifference of Kalunga, and the image of Palo I discerned would disappear. My take on Palo was honed over countless conversations with him and Isidra, where meanings changed and definitions shifted.

"Palo is truth!" Teodoro emphasized, "Eh, kandango! Palo Tengue, Palo Yaya. Palo is what you can trust! Look at me standing here. The things I've seen! The things I've gone through, the hard times! Palo is the reason I am standing here now. Eh, Palo! Blessings Briyumba Congo, Nzambi, Nzambi Mpungu. Palo's blessings! Nzambi's blessings. Eh, Palo! What do I trust? Palo is my confidence. Palo is my truth. Palo Briyumba Kongo is what I trust. Eh! *Palo kindiambo lucena baceche, mi pangñame.* Palo cares for your head, my friend."[7]

He continued, "The grief I have suffered to learn—the punishments! You don't learn without a scolding, without confusion in your heart. A prenda has no heart. The fear. The restlessness I've endured. The lessons my prendas have taught me. Anything can take your life: a hurricane, *mbele*— the knife—an accident, disease.[8] Only Palo can guarantee your life! *¡Que lindo es el brujo!* Palo is beautiful! Sorcery is beautiful! The beauty of kandango Palo! Briyumba Congo! You don't fool around with kandango Palo. Do you hear me? You don't get into this for fun or to take care of a minor problem. No! You bow before a kandango when you're lost, when your life is at *nsila ngoya*—at a crossroads and your options are gone. Palo is fire and storms: *prenda nganga fula va Ndoki!*—Ndoki's on the loose!"

"You cannot be a true healer," he said, "if you don't have a prenda nganga." He would ask, "Where does harm come from? Who is hurting you? That is the question. How are they hurting you? With Palo, of course! Illness and misfortune do not come from nowhere. People harm people! They use Palo to do it—that's Palo! How can you defend yourself from Palo, except with Palo? Why be initiated? There is only one thing strong enough— *nganga kindembo siete nkunia.* A prenda with seven sticks. You can't expect to heal someone if you don't know how to handle Palo, if you haven't got a prenda in your hands. If someone comes to you afflicted, imagine, afflicted with a failing life, how are you going to cure that? Palo Tengue, Palo Yaya! Palo works the fastest, it doesn't fail. Great Santo healers, babalawos, each and every one of them, has a prenda nganga. They talk trash about paleros and paleras, but when their back is against the wall they would be fools not to come to Palo, to save their lives while they can. Palo works here, in the world. Results are plain to see! There is no waiting. If things aren't worked out immediately you are being swindled. Palo isn't about waiting weeks and months to see if you've had a result. Palo acts in fractions of a second. The blessings! Kandango Palo!"

Such was Teodoro's way of speaking—fast—between topics, on the verge of making himself understood but then taking off in a new direction. For me to get him, every word had to be slowed down and captured, turned, rephrased, and sent back to him to give him another chance to convey his meanings. Through the haze of his anger, his fear, his authoritarianism, and his disdain for the Revolution, through the complexity of his everyday use of Palo Kikongo terms, an outline of the Quita Manaquita house came into view and along with it the contours of Palo society.

7. Palo Society

Once I was able to piece together some of Teodoro's Palo Kikongo and begin to understand Palo as he lived it, I was surprised by the degree to which Palo society and the entities it serves, the assembled substances called prendas-ngangas-enquisos, were inseparable for him. He was reluctant to recognize a distinction between the two, just as I might be reluctant to recognize a distinction between the words on this page and the larger document they compose. Palo society and prendas-ngangas-enquisos were distinct events emerging from Kalunga, which was the vast, immediate, and indifferent substrate of unspecified sensation underlying both. For Teodoro, talking Palo while not simultaneously talking prendas-ngangas-enquisos was strange, if not ridiculous. To separate the drumming, song, and dance of Palo from prendas-ngangas-enquisos made no sense—they gave rise to one another, as did the hierarchies, the formalities of initiation, and the codes of patriarchy that arise from, and give rise to, prendas-ngangas-enquisos. Both are versions, or turns, of the dead that fire imaginations and saturate life. Palo society and prendas-ngangas-enquisos are in a feedback loop of mutual affirmation, what Deleuze would call a "Palo-prenda-nganga-enquiso machine," because each part validates the other without negation. The machine is itself emergent in the plane of transformation that is Kalunga.

Community, friendship, trust, song, dance, drums, knowledge, and, most of all, confidence in the realm of the dead—those qualities that define Palo society and make it beautiful—churn around prendas-ngangas-enquisos. Prestige and confidence collect in and around them and can be felt when one handles them with skill. Competence with prendas-ngangas-enquisos means competence in transforming fate—this is Kongo Rule in Cuba. Such is the reward for the sufferings one bears in order to receive and keep such entities. Teodoro said, as if offering a cipher to all of Palo society, "*prenda manda muerto, y el muerto es mi confianza."* He said, "prenda rules the dead, and the dead is my confidence."

Like Teodoro, it now seems difficult for me to talk Palo without including prendas-ngangas-enquisos. But I do so for the sake of clarity, for the prendas-ngangas-enquisos by themselves are confounding in their resilience before any simple explanation.[1] My aim has been to begin an analysis of prendas-ngangas-enquisos through studying the dead and to describe the societies of affliction that maintain them. Only thus, it seems to me, will approaching prendas-ngangas-enquisos in their inassimilable materiality make sense.

Palo society surrounds prendas-ngangas-enquisos. It sustains their powers in the hearts of people and gives them life.[2] Palo society is knowledge and sociability knotted into a lace of power and prestige capable of determining life and death. Palo society teaches deference to teachers, elders, and the dead, who are all praised.

The Quita Manaquita house was hardly a stellar example of a Palo praise house; its once multitudinous membership was now scattered and frayed. When its remaining associates gathered perhaps eighty people could be counted on, which is very good by today's standards. But what for others would have been a successful house was for the Manaquitas a state of unconscionable disrepair. Still, discipline was enforced and when the tatas and yayis gathered, with the padres, madres, and the ngueyos too, then its hierarchy was still very much intact. As with all Palo houses the senior men were called tata nganga, the senior women yayi nganga. These were the authorities of Kongo Law in the house, second only in the hierarchy of Palo value to the prendas-ngangas-enquisos they served. As in all Palo praise communities—and there are hundreds if not more in Cuba today—the tatas and yayis in the Quita Manaquita house initiated people into the service of their prendas-ngangas-enquisos. They also possessed the knowledge to fabricate these powerful agglomerations of fate-changing substances for advanced initiates. The Quita Manaquita tatas and yayis were the leading teachers of the house and foremost arbiters of its direction.

House members praise these seniors when they are alive and present at feasts and remember them in song when they are dead. Palo feasts routinely begin by invoking dead tatas and yayis and asking them for permission to proceed. Even though Emilio had been dead for years, Manaquita feasts happened only with his consent, which was ascertained through Palo divination and espiritista mediumship. Teodoro headed the Manaquita house, but to some degree Tata Emilio still ruled it. He was deeply missed by those who remained.

Teodoro, like his father, was tata nganga among the Quita Manaquitas, and Isidra was yayi nganga. Beneath their level in the hierarchy of Palo society were those called padre nganga and madre nganga, who occupy the second tier of prestige and authority in any Palo house. They are students of a tata or yayi and members of long standing, distinguished by initiations that elevate them above the most junior members. The initiation usually bestows on a padre or madre their own prenda-nganga-enquiso, which is given to them by a tata with the help of a yayi. The prenda-nganga-enquiso padres and madres receive are said to be "born" or "sprung" [*nacer*] from the prenda-nganga-enquiso that rules a Palo house, and for the Quita Manaquitas this was Emilio's formidable Zarabanda. To this ruling prenda-nganga-enquiso, padres and madres have greater access and liberty than lesser members, and even after they receive their own prenda-nganga-enquiso they must still pay obeisance to it.

The new prenda-nganga-enquiso has power over its keeper, power the new padre or madre seeks to wrest from it. At this level of initiation, it is padres and madres that become the privileged pupils to tatas or yayis, from whom they seek to learn the intricacies of Palo, which are prenda care and craft. A new padre or madre is excluded from the making of the prenda-nganga-enquiso they receive and are thus largely ignorant of its contents and thus of how to employ it in healing-harming work. Tatas and yayis will often "make" a new padre or madre and then hide what the new prenda-nganga-enquiso contains, or even how to care for it. To neglect a prenda-nganga-enquiso under one's keeping is to risk drawing its ire. No one wants an angry prenda-nganga-enquiso generating misfortune, illness, and death. By limiting their teaching about how to care for prendas, tatas and yayis thus keep new madres and padres under their command until the latter can learn enough to work their own craft.

But many times a padre or madre will learn only enough to care for their prenda-nganga-enquiso and never enough to engage a prenda-nganga-enquiso in works [*trabajos*] of force that heal and harm. It is by means of these works that clients are healed and persuaded to commit themselves to serving a prenda, that their confidence and obligation are won. A padre or madre able to craft Palo will soon have a following and soon be initiating by their own hand. A new praise house will be born. Tatas and yayis are reluctant to teach because, once so empowered, a padre or madre will have the basic elements in place to cut loose.

Tatas and yayis will teach padres and madres dear to them, and those who are allowed to learn Palo craft are fortunate. Little by little these initiates slowly learn the practical basis of Palo works of turbulence and how these are used in healing and harming. On rare occasions, a madre or padre may be asked to help a tata put together a prenda-nganga-enquiso, considered by many to be one of the great privileges of Palo society. Those fortunate enough to partake in this task are people of confidence to a tata, people whom the tata trusts wholly and also entrusts with the teaching of others. If a tata has a padre who assists him regularly in this task, that person is considered *bakofula* to the tata, *mayordomo* in Spanish—an aide, literally, a steward. The position of bakofula in Palo hierarchy exists only between men. Yayis at times preside over prenda making, as Isidra sometimes did. In such cases, because madres do not serve in the role of bakofula, she would appropriate a tata and his bakofula to do most of the physical labor involved in gathering materials and assembling a prenda-nganga-enquiso.

Another factor that separates padres and madres from tatas and yayis is that they have no initiates of their own. It is possible to go many years, or even a lifetime in the rank of padre or madre, without ever initiating a member by one's own hand. In fact, the presiding tatas or yayis of a house will be very reluctant to allow a padre or madre into their rank and will do everything in their power to be the ones who initiate any new members a padre or madre may bring to the house. Great tatas and yayis have many padres and madres in their houses, and with their help attract newer initiates, who are called ngueyos.

A new member of a Palo praise house is usually a person who has been casually consulting with a palero or palera and seeking aid. There are many reasons to consult African-inspired healers in Havana, and among the common issues are health, love, property, and money. When a person's misfortune regarding any of these becomes so acute that it gives rise to the fear of witchcraft being at work, one goes to see a palera or palero. A cure in the form of a revaluation of fate is effected and, according to Palo's renown, a solution should be immediate. When it is not and a client's problems persist, the consulting palero or palera will usually suggest undergoing a *rayamiento*, which is the first initiation into Palo society, whereby an ngueyo is made. To rayar means "to cut" or "shred" in Spanish. It also means "to draw a line." A rayamiento is a "cutting," where initiates are made by offering their blood to the prenda-nganga-enquiso they are appealing to for aid. If at this point the client has been consulting with a padre or madre who belongs to a larger praise house and pays obeisance to its tatas and yayis, it is common for the padre or madre to present the new prospect for initiation at the house. This was the case with the Quita Manaquitas, and accounts for the number of initiates Emilio and Teodoro claimed. A powerful tata like Emilio will craft his knowledge and the prestige of his prendas into a vast community of service and tribute.

Once a person is cut he or she becomes a ngueyo, which means "child" in Palo Kikongo. Ngueyos occupy the lowest rank in Palo society and are known as much in Palo Briyumba as in Palo Monte as *pinos nuevos* [saplings]. The reference to "Palo," to sticks and trees, should be obvious. Ngueyos are allowed to participate in the feasts and rites of a Palo house, as their rank allows this, but they are excluded from all initiations ranked above those that make other ngueyos. They are expected to attend the annual feasts in honor of the house's presiding prenda-nganga-enquiso and to contribute to these gatherings with offerings of food, drink, or hard work. Ngueyos with a special debt or charge offer animals to feed the prenda-nganga-enquiso that has protected them. Gifts of aguardiente, cigars, candles, flowers, and money are also common. These offerings are always presented directly to the prenda-nganga-enquiso that rules over the house and never to the tata or yayi who maintains it. I was initiated first as a ngueyo several months after meeting Teodoro and later as a padre.

Kneeling or squatting at the foot of a prenda-nganga-enquiso, the tatas, yayis, madres, and padres teach ngueyos the correct forms of address a prenda requires. They teach the bodily posture one must assume when in the presence of prendas-ngangas-enquisos, the kind of bench one should use to sit when not kneeling, and how far to keep one's body from a prenda. They teach ngueyos how one should smoke a cigar and drink aguardiente, the rum that prendas-ngangas-enquisos prefer. Palo society teaches the etiquette of contact a prenda-nganga-enquiso demands—how it should be spoken to, touched (if ever), and deferred to. It teaches care for prendas-ngangas-enquisos: how they should be cooled and heated before they are engaged, sacrificed to, and left to rest. It teaches the types of animals different prendas-ngangas-enquisos prefer in sacrifice and the combination of animals necessary to fully appease them under various circumstances, for they each have special tastes. The combinations of sacrificial animals for all prendas-ngangas-enquisos are not so many, and just as important as knowing these is learning how to care for an animal before it is offered.

In Palo the animal is sung to when it is prepared; it is touched and held and its feet are washed, and it is given water to drink. Ngueyos learn the songs of praise animals receive before they are killed, and they sing them in chorus as the animals pass out of their hands and into those of their seniors, who are authorized to sacrifice them. This is about the limit of a ngueyo's knowledge, which is taught over months and years. To learn more, ngueyos must spend inordinate amounts of time tagging along with their initiating tata or yayi, learning by watching and listening to songs and deciphering riddles, always in practice, never prematurely. To become padre or madre and receive their own prenda-nganga-enquiso, ngueyos must accept or pursue further initiations. There is a widely held sentiment in the higher echelons of Palo society that ngueyos should be excluded from much Palo lore because their commitments are binding only to a certain point. The ultimate commitment to Palo is to receive and keep a prenda-nganga-enquiso and until then, says Baró, one of Cabrera's great Palo informants, ngueyos "don't need to learn."

Just who learns in Palo society is tangled in sexual politics. Patriarchy dominates Palo society in Havana. It is rare that a yayi has her own praise house, though this is not unheard of, as shown by the Guinda Vela society of Guanabacoa before the death of its presiding yayi. Isidra made much of the fact that even Tata Emilio of the Manaquitas had received his Zarabanda from his mother, who was a great *ngangulera* from the central Cuban countryside.[3] Today, most Havana Palo praise houses are presided over by men, though not without significant challenges from the ranks of women that make up the madres and yayis of the house.

Women are not allowed to receive a prenda-nganga-enquiso during their menstruating years, though this is contested.[4] Menstrual blood is said variously to weaken a prenda-nganga-enquiso and to spoil a prenda-nganga-enquiso for the blood of its keeper. Menstruating women are asked not to go near a prenda-nganga-enquiso for fear they will contaminate it to the point of its destruction. It is said that a prenda-nganga-enquiso will kill a menstruating woman because when it senses her blood it then desires more of it, which it receives by leading the woman to a bloody death. Senior women in Palo society uphold this prohibition on receiving a prenda-nganga-enquiso, because once they do receive one of their own their power over other menstruating women is unquestionable. Isidra was of this school and maintained the importance of withholding a prenda-nganga-enquiso until after menstruation has ceased. She maintained this position even as she recognized the patriarchal edifice it established, where women were ten to twenty years behind some of their male counterparts in receiving a prenda-nganga-enquiso. At the same time she was nonplussed by this, reminding me that many men receive prendas-ngangas-enquisos when they are in their teens, twenties, or thirties, only to be denied the knowledge to use them. Isidra argued that what was important was being taught by a tata or yayi, and that by the time she received her prenda-nganga-enquiso from Tata Emilio she had received more wisdom from him than most men did in a lifetime, with the exception of Teodoro.

Nonetheless, Isidra recognized that throughout Palo society in general, in different praise houses, men kept much of the knowledge that madres and yayis were entitled to. She was adamant on this point and argued vehemently for the equality of yayis and tatas, madres and padres. She maintained that her mother, Cucusa, had taught her that in Africa, Palo began as the rule of seven women among the Kongo, who wielded seven batons of power. The men stole these batons in the chaos of slavery, and when Kongo Law was reborn in the Americas, it was the men who held the power. She would argue Teodoro into a corner when he refused to teach her on the basis of her being a woman and refused to accept any intimation that she could be excluded from the innermost circles of the Manaquita house. When Emilio lived she was allowed total access to Manaquita gatherings, feasts, initiations, and funerals.

All the same, Isidra maintained one tenet above all: that Palo was about service and submission to a prenda-nganga-enquiso. Regardless of one's status or hierarchy in the society or house, the benefits of discipline and obedience were worth the subjugation of one's will. As the presiding yayi in the Quita Manaquita house, she maintained many padres, madres, and ngueyos in her service and argued that their benefits in exchange were many.

Palo society is discipline and subordination, security and prestige, taught in praise and song. It involves collective drumming and singing and dancing, and prendas-ngangas-enquisos are never so pleased as when their keepers and devotees gather to grace them with energetic and prodigious performances. Distinct from those of Ocha/Santo, which are two-headed *batá*, Palo's three drums are played upright and called *tumbadoras*, not surprisingly referred to also, and especially in English, as congas. Tumbadora refers to the drum's power to knock things over *[tumbar]* and most likely speaks to the first movement in the act of Palo possession where practitioners are "dropped" or "knocked over" by the Palo dead. The drums call the dead, and the dead knock people down. Goatskin is the preferred membrane to serve as the striking head. Different tension systems are used to give the drum its voice, but none in any way resemble the specialized system used by Ocha/Santo's batá. These days, tumbadoras are hard to find and drum makers are more interested in the production of batá. Often there are no tumbadoras at a Palo feast. The Manaquita house had only one drum left. Under such circumstances Palo is played on plywood boxes *[cajones]*, built and sanded for their resonance. The boxes are easier to make than tumbadoras and are precise musical instruments despite their humble appearance.

Much of Palo lore exists in the form of music, which is sung almost at all times when one engages a prenda-nganga-enquiso. They like to be sung to; they like to be addressed in song and have drums played for them. Each prenda-nganga-enquiso has songs that "belong" to it, praise it, and rouse it. They are warmed up with song, stirred to awareness by it. Palo drums drive Palo song, sometimes ahead of the beat, sometimes behind. Teo insisted that the difference between the four branches of Palo society could be discerned in the relationship between the song and the beat. Each branch of Palo knowledge plays differently, distinct beats at various speeds relative to the sung voice. "Palo Mayombe is the fastest, African," he said. "Listen. Palo Briyumba comes next; listen to the Manaquita drums, not much different, but slower than Mayombe. Briyumba and Mayombe are the African ones; listen to the drum, how it dominates. It pushes the voice ahead, like an animal through a chute; it's fast, unforgiving. Some songs are shared by Briyumba and Mayombe. Palo Kimbisa and Palo Monte are slower—listen to the drum; listen how the voice lags behind; listen how slow the voice and drum are, sounds like a hymn, like a church hymn, slow, high. Kimbisa and Palo Monte are pretty. Emilio liked them a lot; he loved matching up in Palo Monte, especially. As a Briyumbero he could hold his own at a Palo Monte feast." During my time with Teodoro I never saw Mayombe or Kimbisa played in a praise house proper to them; rather, they were sung by Mayombe and Kimbisa guests at Briyumba and Palo Monte feasts.

During feasts, after the sacrifices and the formalities, the drums sound and paleros and paleras match up or play Palo *[juegan Palo]*. They compete in song, calling riddles as tests of knowledge against one another to determine hierarchy and rank. The matches—Teodoro called them nkisi malongo—are mostly good spirited, with guests from other praise societies deferring to their hosts and singing in time with the rhythm of the praise house they are visiting. The chorus backs the callers, supports their struggles for prestige. When a feast comes together, when the initiations of ngueyos are done, if there are ngueyos to be made, and when the sacrifices are complete, the song moves out of the sealed room where the prendas-ngangas-enquisos are kept, and the match begins. The Quita Manaquitas matched up at Teodoro's house, in the patio under the ceiba's leafy embrace.

A beat is established and the tatas and yayis sing back and forth between themselves, singing call and response with the gathered chorus and struggling to take the song *[tumbar el canto]* from one another, to become the caller *[gallo]* and rule the chorus. They throw riddles and barbs *[puyas]* at one another in Palo Kikongo to test both knowledge and one's will to remain in the match. Callers within a house and between houses know one another, and know the strengths of their adversaries. Elaborate strategies of conceptual charge and retreat are devised on the occasion of feasts. New riddles are formulated, and for this a singer must be well versed in Palo Kikongo and ritual lore, for nothing betrays an inexperienced padre or ngueyo entering a Palo match more than a poorly formulated riddle or garbled speech. There can be only one winner in a match of nkisi malongo. Winners establish their dominance by stumping opponents on riddles, or getting them to break understood protocols of composure and respect for one's adversary by forcing them, through skillful gibes, to lose their cool and resort to personal insult in their sung responses. There are verses and songs that recognize such falls out of sacred knowledge, which humiliate the loser. Sometimes, feasts begin to degenerate into general insult, especially if there are not tatas or yayis or knowledgeable singers present to maintain discipline. Then there is no chance the dead will come, and those seniors present will complain with feigned indignation, "*Ya, nos cambiaron de Palo pa' rumba, ya no sirve la fiesta!*" "That's it," they say, "They've gone from Palo to rumba and now the feast is ruined!" The reference is to rumba, one of Cuba's great forms of secular, largely Congo-inspired music, which is famous for its back-and-forth use of personal insult and veiled disrespect in song.[5]

Drummers also vie with one another, taking turns playing and chiding one another. Callers sing, stripping one another of the song, and either drop out or advance in the match. All the while, the chorus dances "Kongo," slightly bent at the waist, kicking their legs back at the knee and swinging their arms. The better dancers kick and swing and spin in place, moving their head from side to side as they sink into the charge of the feast. Dancers do not compete, though exceptional dancers are recognized implicitly by a sense of prestige that surrounds them, evident in the space the gathered crowd gives them to move. These great dancers are often recognized bearers of the dead that frequent the feasts of a particular praise house. Unlike Ocha/Santo feasts, where dancers form a line and dance before the trio of batá drums as a chorus, Palo dancers move through the gathering as individual vectors of speed and force without a fixed line. Any moment is propitious for possession by Palo powers during a gathering of nkisi malongo, but none so much as when a dancer lets him or herself be transformed by the drum into a version of the dead. It is then that the house's dead arrive, drawn through Kalunga, the ambient condition for their becoming, by the joyful praise and service of their gathered devotees.

Just what force takes hold of the living and crafts their body into the designs of grace and strength we call possession is not entirely clear. My contention is that this force is the potential of the dead gathered around a prenda-nganga-enquiso at each particular feast, a potential that actualizes in the living to turn them into versions of the dead. In Palo, *the living* are condensations of Kalunga, the ambient dead, and are easily transformed. In possession, the living pass from being a version of the ambient dead to being a version of responsive dead, and back again. A single Palo feast can include many of the living taking on the form of one of the dead, which validates the idea that a prenda-nganga-enquiso, and the dead it collects, can become many versions of itself simultaneously. Each form is an event along the surface of the sea of the dead that is Kalunga. When the members of a praise house like the Manaquitas manage to call one or more of these dead forth from their ambient flows, they are effecting transformations of the dead according to their bidding, and the bidding of their tatas and yayis. The tatas and yayis cannot do this alone, only the society together can.

The initiations, sacrifices, feasts, gatherings, and matches of song and dance, along with the gradual accumulation of knowledge through listening to elders and watching them repeatedly match fate-transforming strength, begin to sediment a sense of certainty in the prestige of one's teachers and the power of prendas-ngangas-enquisos. Practice, time after time, involving all of one's senses, establishes confidence in Kongo Law, just as one submits to it. Practice not in terms of rehearsal—though Palo isn't devoid of rehearsal or performance—but in terms of labor, of having to do something over and over, is how Palo is learned. It is like any craft, in the old sense of the word, watching and learning and trying, for all of one's life. With time, confidence in the skill to stand on one's own in Palo is established. Eventually, one learns what one must do to defend against misfortune and the enemies that sent it, and then Palo can be felt in all of its beauty and strength. This is another of Palo's gifts, earned through struggle, sacrifice, and surrender of oneself to a prenda-nganga-enquiso. Isidra possessed this confidence in her prendas to a greater degree than Teodoro, who should have enjoyed all of Palo Briyumba's many blessings but for his inability to find stillness in himself. Whatever goodness or grandness of being he might have felt as a tata of great standing at Guanabacoa Palo feasts was lost the moment the feast dispersed.

For myself, I caught on quickly that the abstract knowledge one can receive about Palo must always follow commitment and action. One watches yayis and tatas in their work, in their relationships with their prendas-ngangas-enquisos, in their healing and sorcery, and in their singing and drumming and riddle-making. One plays the drum and listens and learns to change the beat and rhythm according to the lead drummer and the caller. One dances and learns to step correctly and to mouth the words of Palo Kikongo with the gathered chorus. One listens to the words of songs and tries to unravel their innovations, which are Palo's future. One watches those gathered be overcome by the dead, watches them move and learns to move like them, inviting the dead to consider this new member. One feels admiration for sacrifices and the animals slaughtered, with extraordinary regard for their blood. One assists in transforming generic materials into powerful substances with song and verse, appreciates—without detesting—fear and force, and nurtures prendas-ngangas-enquisos to keep the dead from dissipating. One is drawn to all of this and puts oneself to the task of learning these lessons. This wisdom is in a Palo verse that is sung first person in a prenda-nganga-enquiso's voice, which summarizes the value of learning first by practice and only later by questions:

> *¿Por qué tú me buscas si tú no me conoces?*
> *¡Eh! ¡¡Por qué tú me buscas si tú no me conoces?!*

> [Why are you looking for me if you don't know me?
> Hey! Why are you looking for me if you don't know me?!]

8. Decay

The Manaquita house was hardly a thriving munanso congo. Only a fraction of the feasts that were held in years when Emilio presided were held now, and initiations were few. Still, when the Quita Manaquitas gathered there were more people present than could fit in the house, and the patio was full. Tasks and privileges were assigned according to the initiation hierarchy, and sacrifices were thorough, with four-legged as well as plumed animals offered. The singing and dancing afterward was likewise good, but energy seemed to lack. Most of the longtime Manaquita tatas and yayis were in their fifties or older, and a youthful cadre of padres from other houses tended to dominate the drumming and the calling matches.

Once I began to spend time with Teodoro at the Manaquita house, and certainly after I was initiated into it, I began to wonder about the apparent decline of the house. Though Teodoro was extraordinarily gifted at Palo, he was seemingly unable to draw from Palo its most precious rewards. He simply didn't have the strength of self-understanding to hold the house together. Isidra agreed with my diagnosis of the situation, but believed that what I called a cause was in fact a symptom.

Teodoro soon became my principal teacher of Palo, but Isidra was forever at my side. She did not entirely trust him as a teacher though he taught Palo with devotion, as if it were the only truth in the world. He believed in practicing and working together, as did Isidra. Both held to the ethic of service on the part of the initiate to his or her educator. But Teodoro had a fast and casual manner she found annoying, and she was always adding to and rephrasing what he said. Though I would have liked a little more autonomy in my work with Teodoro, I was nonetheless grateful for her presence. She was a huge help in reiterating Teodoro's speech and teachings, and without her I would have moved much more slowly. Her take on things did tend to favor a santera's view of the world, something she recognized and justified by saying that where she came from in the countryside Congo and Santo were mixed anyway. She also maintained that Ocha/Santo was a more moderate practice of fate shaping and that it did us well to go slowly when getting involved with Palo.

Isidra was moved by west African influences much more than Teodoro, whose passion was for urban Palo. This was their principal and ultimately irreducible difference, though it took me months to see it clearly. Isidra united the west African and Kongo influences of central Cuban Bembé, which she had received as a child in Sierra Morena, with urban Palo and the rules of Havana-based Ocha/Santo. Her combinations, which were re-worked and recombined every day, were generally coherent and when they weren't she was clear about the paradoxes she sustained. Through her vig-orous remix of Bembé, Palo, and Ocha/Santo I was also better able to make sense of Teodoro, whose tendency when talking about Cuban traditions of inspiration was to call Ocha/Santo sovereigns by their Palo names and to transform objects around him into, in his words, "the dead." Teodoro and Isidra would spar if he felt she was giving Palo short shrift in an interpre-tation, and he would try to signal how her Ocha/Santo influence was dis-torting his teaching. The chemistry between the three of us was at times tense. After I was initiated as ngueyo, Teodoro and I became closer and meetings at Isidra's home became less frequent. She started complaining that she didn't feel at ease with him in her house and started to make ex-cuses to keep us from gathering there. At the same time, she started dread-ing our trips to Guanabacoa and the Manaquita house.

"He is undisciplined," she would start. "He's not serious, can't take on his responsibilities. He's self-interested. Teo knows so much, but he wastes his knowledge. No one with his knowledge and abilities should be in the situation he's in. He is too talented to be squandering Emilio's knowledge. So much wisdom in his hands, and such a miserable life. If you had his knowledge, if you knew, you would live in peace and be respected, like Emilio. Look at his situation, look at his house. Look at his drinking. Emilio had so many initiates; Teo has so many, and look how he is losing them. Emilio taught him everything and all he does is offend people. Offensive! You've seen his house; you've seen it; you know his house. That house was beautiful when Emilio lived there; it was immaculate, and the people that came and went from there were decent people. Now look at the mess. Your initiation was the first interesting thing to happen at the Manaquita house this year. There is no society to speak of any longer, Emilio's society, his house. No community, the group is scattered. They come around only when something big is going to happen. Thousands of initiates and a praise house that was the envy of Guanabacoa . . . irresponsible."

I would defend Teodoro, because I thought she was unfair and because defending Teo was a good place to begin asserting my autonomy from her. But she would continue, "Do not trust Teodoro; he doesn't respect you. He doesn't respect me or himself or the knowledge he carries. Look at his house, the society, the situation; look at it. It is a crime. Nothing compares with his disrespect. The community should be whole, robust. The feasts should be big and never should his prendas be without offerings. The initiates. Think about Emilio's initiates, how willing they would be to lend a hand with the house, with the feasts and animals, if only Teodoro would show some respect! Emilio had more than a thousand initiates. How can he have let things degrade? It's irresponsible. His prendas have no offerings."

In her emphatic way she continued, not just one time, but day after day: "Nothing compares with his disrespect. Look at the community; look at the Manaquitas—you know them. They were alone among Havana's great munansos. On the feast day for Zarabanda the *only* drums to sound in all of Guanabacoa were Emilio's. That was respect. That was a feast! Can you imagine that? No, you can't imagine the act of deference. To have only the Manaquita drums sound for Zarabanda in all of Guanabacoa! Bless Tata Emilio! Kalunga! Only the Manaquita drums played; people came from all over to praise Zarabanda and match force at Emilio's. There must have been a dozen Kongo praise houses in Guanabacoa, and during Emilio's day not one of them held a feast for Zarabanda. Emilio's house was the only place to be. Now look at it. How many feasts each June for Zarabanda in Guanabacoa? Every house has a feast! Who doesn't have a Zarabanda? Most of them were born from Emilio's prenda. It's a complete lack of respect. Teodoro! Teodoro! He has all of Emilio's knowledge; he's a walking encyclopedia, but none of Emilio's discipline, which is respect. He lacks dignity, and you can see it in how he treats his father's prendas. Look at the prendas!"

It is a truism that *madrinas* and *padrinos*, godmothers and godfathers, the people who initiate "godchildren" into Palo and Ocha/Santo practice, are possessive of their initiates. To see initiates spending time in another Palo house, to hear them come with other teachers' knowledge on their lips, to fear losing their confidence and loyalty and therefore the secrets you have taught, nothing petrified Isidra more. Though she denied it when I fought her possessiveness, she feared that Teodoro would persuade me with the status and power that came from male-only revelations of Palo craft. She feared I would be drawn into circles of power that would change my loyalties within the house. When she got especially depressed her worries would spread and she started to fear that Teodoro would use Palo craft against her to weaken her grasp on me. She had suspected him of sorcery against her before, and the thought of it troubled her deeply. She was no match for him under the rules of Palo, and Ocha/Santo could do very little to protect her from his works. His trabajos would be intricate and involve combinations of prendas-ngangas-enquisos. In a struggle of Palo works, she would have to count on those of her dead that populated the flows of Kalunga around her for protection. Her relationship with these responsive dead was sound, and they were steadfast; if anything protected her in a match with Teodoro it was this. Her dead would act only in her defense, so there would be no stopping his attacks, only deflecting them. At best she would be left weak and exhausted from such a conflict and vulnerable to other attacks, from other enemies. Only once while I worked with her did I see the toll a battle of Palo could take on her, when she sparred with an old friend who betrayed her, a palero who was much more powerful than she was. A war of sorcery has very real consequences and can leave a practitioner sleepless, penniless, and with considerably frayed nerves after weeks of hostilities. In Isidra's case the attack, and the healing she worked against it, lasted one week. Her physical recovery from hardly having slept or eaten during that time took much longer. Her sensitivities and her sense of visceral apprehension, her relationship with the ambient dead, were also transformed. She changed as a person, if only slightly. The thought of going at it with Teodoro was too troubling to contemplate. She preferred instead to worry about other matters, like why he was being more secretive in his dealings with her.

In fact, what troubled her more, and what drove her against him, was the thought of being left out of one of his teachings. The possibility drove her to distraction, made her say and do things she later regretted. To be left out of teachings was something she had suffered her whole life. She often mentioned, when lecturing on secrecy, that her mother went to her grave with a hundred secrets. "Kimbito did the same. The old nganguleras were the most reserved, the most secretive. They taught us, but they left many things unsaid. Cucusa would turn her back on me to do things she wanted to hide. There are a hundred secrets she never revealed. Today it is the men. They are intolerable. Emilio taught me, and Teodoro teaches me, but he leaves me out. If I figure out he is hiding something I can force him to give it up. But he is a liar and it is not easy."

Isidra believed she had a right to those secrets held by men in Havana's Regla de Congo. She said, "I became madre nganga when my menstruation dried up. I have a prenda. I have the highest category of initiation—yayi nganga. There should be no secrets kept from women. In Santo yes, of course

Ifá is closed to me. But in Palo women are equal to men once their menstruation ends and they receive a prenda nganga. Yayi nganga are equal to tatas, and above any padre or madre. It is a Spanish imposition, something Creole, that men in Palo hide secrets from yayi nganga. It wasn't like this in Africa. In Africa the women had the secrets. Look at my mother. There were no secrets Cucusa didn't control."

"He's a liar," she said. "He is a liar and he doesn't know any better. He doesn't know any better. I watch him and I learn from him, like you do. He tells you things because he wants you to put them in your book, and I learn. But don't trust him. He is immature. Irresponsible. Teo and I work together; it's true. We know *how* to work together. I have my reasons, just like you do. He can be great; it's true. He has knowledge; he has Emilio's knowledge. But he is sloppy. Don't forget that. Teodoro is not Emilio; he is a vessel for Emilio's knowledge. Nothing more. He gave up being a person long ago. You should expect nothing from him. Do not venture off with him and not have me with you. He can't be trusted. You will be too far over your head before you know it, and then what?"

In the course of one of these bouts, because she demanded it but also because I thought it was correct, I promised Isidra I would tell her everything I learned from Teodoro. Several times after my initiations Teodoro made me promise the exact opposite. In the end, I kept my word to her.

Her doubts about Teodoro led Isidra's feelings about him, though she also felt admiration for him. When she was working with a client and he would arrive, she would cede the little bench on which she squatted in front of her prendas-ngangas-enquisos and allow him to conduct the divination and craft the work. He was much better at using the four coconut disks to query the dead [chamalongo] than she was, more creative and flexible in his conversations with the dead, and more sensitively tuned into Kalunga, el muerto, such that he was able to make more favorable sense of its intimations and suggestions. She trusted his throws and readings despite his crassness at times with her clients, who were usually older professional women like herself. She would follow him in the making of packets of substances and charms, sometimes writing down in a notebook the things he told her while they worked. Isidra had a notebook full of jottings, an old date book from the eighties. Other notebooks, her Ocha/Santo ones, she kept hidden elsewhere, but this one she kept locked in the closet given over to her prendas-ngangas-enquisos.

Something else troubled Isidra, something undeniable, and when I learned it the seed of doubt was planted in my own relationship with Teodoro. She mentioned it one afternoon as we rode the bus home from Guanabacoa.

"Look at his prendas," she said. "Look at his prendas. What do you see? You don't see, because you haven't been around. He isn't strong enough. It was Emilio's great mistake to imagine Teodoro would be strong enough. Teodoro struggles with his own burdens, let alone having to take on Emilio's. No one can handle Emilio's charge. It is too much. The prendas—Zarabanda! His family doesn't help. The initiates don't. Who would expect them to? Quita Manaquita Briyumba Kongo! His uncle Pedro is too old. Emilio's initiates know their fate rests with those prendas. Emilio's Zarabanda! Think about Emilio's initiates who are counting on those prendas to protect them and answer for them, and they know that Teodoro mistreats them. Teodoro doesn't respect himself, or his father or his prendas, which is worst of all."

There were many prendas in Teodoro's house, more than a dozen, including smaller ones that were aides to the larger, older assemblages. They rested in a corner of the back room under a large triangular shelf, chest high, which acted as a roof above them. They sat on two low steps of earth that had been built up for them, with Teodoro's prendas on the lower, nearer step and Emilio's resting higher and deeper into the corner, obscured by shadows and gray dust. Most of the prendas-ngangas-enquisos were knee-high, though some were taller. The majority were three-footed iron cauldrons overflowing with dirt and packed with sticks, bones, animal skulls, and railroad spikes. The protruding materials were covered in dry feathers that clung to the sticks and spikes. Emilio's Zarabanda was typical in this regard, and its brimming contents were bound in heavy iron chains. In the interstices of sticks and stuffed into the links of chain were bits of paper and little bundles of substances.

Atop it all goat skulls rested on what looked like a bed of packets and charms. Zarabanda was tall, waist high, including the broad pair of bull's horns that ultimately crowned it. Isidra said it required four men to lift, but not since Emilio's death had anyone knelt beneath it to be initiated. Teodoro initiated ngueyos under his Lucero, which he used more than all the other prendas combined. Though all of them seemed dry and dusty, Emilio's Zarabanda was the focus of Isidra's lament. This was because it was to this prenda that she and the rest of Emilio's initiates belonged. Their fate was bound up with it, revalued time and again by sacrifice and loss. After his father died, Teodoro inherited Zarabanda. Little by little the prenda diminished, and eventually Teodoro moved it back into the corner. Of its past glory the only thing that remained was the array of other prendas-ngangas-enquisos around it, which now rested a step below Zarabanda and radiated outward from it. They were the evidence of a once great society of affliction able to care for so many entities and able to cultivate so much power. Teodoro also inherited Emilio's Lucero, and his Tiembla Tierra, along with three prendas gendered feminine—Mama Chola, Ma're Lango, and Centella Ndoki. Teodoro had his own version of Zarabanda, born from Emilio's, but smaller, and kept off to the left. He also had a Siete Rayos. There were also several aides and allies, powerful objects in themselves, built into smaller iron vessels and gourds. These had names like Pluma Sucia, Brazo Fuerte, and Cuatro Vientos Vira Mundo; the latter was a small wooden statue with four faces. There were other allies whose names and stories I never learned.

For Teodoro all of it was secondary to his beautiful Lucero Mundo, a small prenda-nganga-enquiso that stood jutting forth from the rest, almost in the center of the room. It was also built into a three-footed cauldron and was distinguished by a low row of evenly cut sticks running around the mouth of the cauldron. Protruding from the center of this ring was an enormous conch shell plastered with dry feathers. The mouth of the shell was sealed with some substance, perhaps soil mixed with wax and blood. In the middle of this plug was lodged a little mirror that stared like an eye from the depths of the shell. It was through this eye that Teodoro peered into cause and fate and effected all divination and initiation in the Manaquita house.

When I knelt to greet Teodoro's Lucero the first time I visited the Manaquita house, I had the benefit of several weeks' exposure to Isidra's prendas-ngangas-enquisos. This helped settle the grave sense of apprehension that overtook me the first few months of my work, when prendas-ngangas-enquisos were new to me. They are viscerally intimidating to confront, especially when in groups as they were at Isidra's and Teodoro's. The jumble of vessels sprouting sticks, bones, animal remains, and feathers is overpowering. With the aide of a skillful Palo healer, these entities begin to churn values and soon congregate around them the lives and work of hundreds of initiates. To greet them is to greet the gravitational heart of a society of affliction. Not until I spent much more time working with Isidra and Teodoro, and eventually helped build a prenda, did this feeling subside. Until then, my limited experience praising Isidra's prendas-ngangas-enquisos helped to lessen the impact of kneeling in utter ignorance before so many of them at the Quita Manaquita house.

It is common to see closets given over to prendas-ngangas-enquisos, but in the case of Emilio and Teodoro the prendas had long ago overrun the closets of their simple two-bedroom house. When Teodoro was too young to remember, his bedroom was given over to them and he took to sleeping with his father. Now they took up nearly half the room, bisecting it at an angle from corner to corner. That a whole room is taken over, or even that a separate enclosure is built outside to shelter a group of them, is not unusual to see in Havana. Prendas-ngangas-enquisos grow and overflow their kettles; soon materials used in crafting Palo works, including fallen bundles, begin occupying the floor around a prenda's feet. Prendas-ngangas-enquisos do not like to rest on wood and they forbid a tile floor, so bricks and dirt are brought in, and a low shelf of earth is built for them. Before long a zone of dedication is established around them that engulfs the entire room, which cannot be entered without first asking the prendas-ngangas-enquisos for permission, and when this is granted then kneeling before them in greeting. At a feast held at a prominent Ocha/Santo praise house in the little town of Palmira outside the provincial capital of Cienfuegos, Isidra and I greeted and praised a prenda-nganga-enquiso set off by a line of bricks stacked two high that had taken over half the kitchen. It belonged to the head of the Cabildo de Cristo, and we praised it in his house the year before he died. It was well cared for, with its surface, as well as the surface of outlying objects and the floor around it, glistening with new blood.

There was hardly a part of Teodoro's faltering house that was not given over to his craft. In the living room, at the entrance of the house, another corner altar dominated the scene. On this one stood two damaged plaster sculptures of San Lazaro—Lazarus the Beggar—set against a mural that took up large parts of the walls and depicted people in a forest, near running water and with snakes at their feet. The sky above them reflected the yellow of the setting sun with blue clouds. A leak above this altar had caused the paint on half the wall to peel. In fact, the whole house was slowly collapsing, with broken furniture and provisional repairs to walls, windows, and doors. The last time I was there the entire altar had come down, the statues had been destroyed or sold, and the corner was swept clean.

Directly across the living room from the front door was a passageway leading to the back of the house. Above the opening to this hallway hung a hand-painted sign of an open eye, staring. From the blackness of the pupil emerged a bleeding red tongue pierced by a dagger. The caption below this image stated, "*Te estoy cazando* [I am hunting you]." Images like this are common in the homes of people involved in Cuban practices of sacred command. They are warnings against envy, gossip, and glances that bear ill will. They advise those who may turn against the house that their actions are observed, and in exchange for any harm there will be bitter punishment.

Beyond this sign, the Manaquita house was off-limits except to those invited. The single hallway led down the side of the house, where it emptied

into the back patio. The hallway also acted as the kitchen, with a squat refrigerator from the fifties next to a simple enameled washbasin set into a
tiled countertop. There was no running water, but a large water barrel he
was forever filling from a neighbor's tap. Teodoro cooked his meals on a
converted gas burner that spewed kerosene and painted the entire hallway
black with soot. Along the left wall were the two bedrooms, Teodoro's and
the one belonging to the prendas-ngangas-enquisos, which was larger. At
the end of the hallway out the back, a collapsing fence of barbed wire
and rusting sheet metal marked off the surrounding lot. The winter I met
Teodoro, the ceiba in his patio, which was young but already enormous,
shed its leaves, as the great cottonwoods do every few years. After the annual October hurricanes, light in Havana is oblique and yielding. We spent
that autumn and winter talking Palo in Teodoro's quiet patio, under the yel-
lowing, gently falling leaves of the glowing ceiba.

"Look at his house, the disrepair, the mess, the lack of respect," reminded
Isidra. "There are reasons why. He isn't alone to blame. It was Emilio's great
mistake! He overestimated Teodoro, his strength, endurance. Now he is losing, and Emilio should have known. His prendas are too strong. They are
too strong, and Teo's gotten lost. His prendas have the upper hand. They are
punishing him. Can't you see that? Can't you see his life—his poverty,
drinking, and desperation? It is his prendas that are doing that to him. No
one with his coverage, with his security, with the *trust* of those prendas,
should have a life in such terrible shape. His prendas should be protecting
him. Are they? Emilio's prendas are more than enough to protect anyone. I
will tell you, because you don't know, but very few people have prendas like
those, very few. And he disrespects them. Disrespect for a prenda is disrespect for the Quita Manaquita house; they cannot be separated. Without
those prendas there is no Quita Manaquita Briyumba Kongo. Look at them:
they are dry and covered in dust. It hurts one to look at them. I lose my
breath when I'm there. The Quita Manaquitas have sunk with them—
pathetic. Nothing compares with his disrespect. Zarabanda, Lucero, Siete
Rayos, Ma're Lango, Mama Chola, Centellita, Tiembla Tierra, they should
be healthy, moist, well fed. Nothing compares with his disrespect."

One of Palo's first lessons, learned before one is ever initiated, is that
prendas-ngangas-enquisos protect from misfortune, ill will, and grief. They
should not be betrayed. I remember Isidra telling me, warning me, that a
deal made with a prenda-nganga-enquiso is a deal for life. Ocha/Santo has
similar understandings about its initiations and the sovereigns it connects
its initiates to. It is a source of great fear and anxiety to think about losing
their protection once they have been entrusted. Prendas-ngangas-enquisos

are sought because life is bigger than one individual, and fate and chance are hard to change. To lose the protection of the collected capacities of a prenda-nganga-enquiso is to lose the grace of the dead in serious matters; it is to face the hazards and unexpected turns of life's course alone.

Palo heightens this sense of fate-shaping capacity by investing prendas-ngangas-enquisos with the power to harm or kill not only the enemies of their keepers but the keepers themselves. Prendas-ngangas-enquisos are considered beautiful in their force and potential, just as they are considered dangerous. Unless one knows a prenda-nganga-enquiso well, one approaches it with respect based on fear. Such were the prendas-ngangas-enquisos kept at Teodoro's house, which, crouching in the shadows of the back room, brooding in their abandon, were disquieting indeed. Isidra approached them with confidence, because she knew them well. At the same time, she recognized the danger in letting them go so long without being feasted. She didn't take their complacence for granted and always approached them with the greatest respect. We would never arrive at Teodoro's without offerings of aguardiente, cigars, candles, and cascarilla chalk. Supplicants should never approach prendas-ngangas-enquisos without their head, hands, and feet marked with cascarilla to demonstrate the thoughtfulness of cooling their body. The cascarilla protects against any heat the prendas-ngangas-enquisos may have in the atmosphere around them. Taking precautions honors prendas-ngangas-enquisos and the person who keeps them with a show of humble regard in anticipation of their force. Once basic conditions are met—a candle lit, the body marked with cascarilla, the prenda cooled with aspirations of aguardiente and clouds of cigar smoke—it is a privilege to sit in their presence, to bathe in the strength of confidence they collect and inspire.

With the Manaquitas disillusioned with the treatment of Emilio's Zarabanda, few were the initiates who would come with gifts of aguardiente and candles, let alone the animal sacrifices, necessary to keep the prendas-ngangas-enquisos fed and moist. Isidra routinely scolded Teodoro for not having these items on hand. "They are essential," she told me. "You can't care for a prenda without these things. Can you see why they are against him? Every day they should be bathed in candlelight and cooled with aguardiente and cigar smoke. Do you begin to see the depth of his irresponsibility, of his disrespect? He must be crazy to take the risk."

Isidra was convinced Teodoro's prendas-ngangas-enquisos had devised elaborate and lengthy punishments to coax him back into subjection. Some time ago, she also said, they began to draw their sustenance directly from him; that was the deal. Little by little they sapped his strength and, as the struggle intensified, began leading him down blind paths sure to weaken or endanger him. If he would not feast them, they would feast off of him. This was Isidra's interpretation, and she saw little hope for a resolution that would spare him. "Eventually they will get what they need," she said. "They will prove to him that he must care for them by teaching him some terrible lesson, of which I want no part. Or they will take him, they will feast on him, and someone who will do right by them will replace him. It is a matter of time, and they will win."

The experience I had with Isidra's prendas-ngangas-enquisos should have alerted me to the fact that the Manaquita prendas were in bad shape. But the first several times I was asked to greet Teodoro's prendas-ngangas-enquisos I was too overwhelmed to see how they differed from hers. Only after she pointed it out did I notice their condition, and there was no question about what she said. Teodoro's prendas-ngangas-enquisos were parched and monochrome gray, bone dry. They had none of the black gloss of prendas that are routinely feasted with blood. They had none of the bright sheen of new feathers covering their bodies. They had none of the brassy, bloody smell of prendas that feast regularly. In fact, Teodoro's prendas-ngangas-enquisos were so desiccated and uniformly gray that I soon began to wonder if he hadn't covered them in ash, or some other powder, so thick was the covering of dust on them. Ash is important to Palo craft, used to cool, and it looked as if maybe Teodoro had tried to seal them off or smother them.

Isidra had seven prendas-ngangas-enquisos of her own, gathered around her magnificent Siete Rayos. These prendas were well tended and fed. They were covered in glossy feathers kept moist with aspirations of aguardiente and dry white wine. She kept them in a closet, resting on earth she had hauled back from the countryside of Sierra Morena. A large deposit of melted wax on the bricks that made-up the low retaining wall showed that she lit them regularly. Kept damp by her daily libations, her prendas smelled like the earth, dank, like soil that clings to the roots of plants, like a wet hollow in the bones of the earth. Their smell was deep and sure, dense and humid.

The locked closet where she kept them was halfway down the long hall of her apartment. There they were deposited as sentinels against anyone or any ill will that would come near her bedroom. She would open up the closet door and we would often sit there, on low benches, singing to them and talking, then sitting there in silence for a long time. They were black with feathers and blood and submerged in shadows and candlelight. Her principal prenda was a Siete Rayos, a kettle painted red with tall sticks bound tightly together by an iron chain. She had her own Lucero, a Ma're

Lango, and a Centella Ndoki. She also had several aides and allies, including a piece of rock coral from Sierra Morena about the size of an orange that sat in a gourd bowl on the ground. It had been given to her by an old ngangulera from a town down the highway from Sierra Morena who called it Batalla [Battle] and said that if cared for it would bring Isidra more power and protection than any prenda in Havana. Around these prendas, tucked into the corners and out of sight, were bottles containing aguardiente, honey, and molasses. Isidra kept a proper jug of *chamba,* an infusion made with ginger, tiny hot peppers called *aji guauguau,* green onions, plenty of pepper, ground bones, and sawdust from the branches of "hot" trees. Aspirated, chamba is used to heat prendas-ngangas-enquisos and rouse them from slumber or to clear a room when things get too heavy during a Palo feast. Properly made and blown, chamba provokes tearing and coughing. Chamba is also used to test Kongo dead when they appear; it is blown square into the eyes and face of the possessed. That Isidra kept chamba was evidence of her commitment to her prendas-ngangas-enquisos, because it is difficult and costly to make in Havana today.

When she sat with her collection of prendas-ngangas-enquisos Isidra felt sure. She was confident in her divination, though she knew only a fraction of the Palo Kikongo Teodoro used. She also sang to her prendas every day and would stand and dance for them, slapping her chest and thighs in moments where the songs portended conflict. She kept a long baton in a corner of the closet, wrapped in many-colored ribbons and hung with jingle bells at the hooked neck. She would dance and cleanse people with the baton in hand, hitting it against the floor, and the pitched jingle added emphasis that was becoming of her. Mostly, though, after the initial greetings and aspirations and any work that had to be done with her prendas, Isidra sat quietly with them in the candlelight, thinking and holding still.

This is why she loathed Teodoro's house and hated to see its condition. Though she found no peace or confidence there, she still went periodically to greet and pay her respects to Emilio's Zarabanda. She was among the handful of Emilio's initiates who came around when a feast wasn't in the works. When Teodoro and I became closer she went with me often, though she was uncomfortable presenting herself before Zarabanda with it in such dismal condition. Her security was bound to it, and she would get scared or irritated when she thought too much about what was at stake in this neglect. She would berate Teodoro in the very room where the prendas-ngangas-enquisos were kept. "They are dry, dry and thirsty," she would begin. "You've got no aguardiente for them, no candles, no chamba, no *menga* [blood].[1] Look at mine! Mine are healthy, alive, while yours suffer. You are irresponsible, Teodoro, and defeated. They were always too much for you—Emilio's mistake. Emilio should have initiated you into Santo as a boy. There was no other hope for you. Your prendas are too hot—Palo is too hot—to be bearing the load on your own. You can't handle it. Can't you see? Can't you see your indiscipline? No one can maintain the prendas you have without Santo. You need Santo to refresh. Santo could have saved you. It could still."

Teodoro bowed his head, made excuses, rubbed his forehead, and eventually demand she stop. He despised her moralizing and her certainty that she had a cure for his predicament. Teodoro recognized that Ocha/Santo would help cool him, that having a Santo sovereign claim his head would be a tremendous help. But he refused it as had Emilio until the end of his life, when suddenly he took it on before he died.

Following through on her explanation for Teodoro's misfortune, Isidra turned to an understanding that hinted at the graceful ways in which Palo and Ocha/Santo complement one another. Teodoro was mistreating his prendas-ngangas-enquisos and slowly losing their confidence. A terrible struggle was under way, and he was losing against them. But he also had options and precautions against the powers of Zarabanda and the others that he could have taken. It was in this that Isidra believed Emilio had erred.

"When you work with Palo," she said, "when you match-up with Palo, you play for keeps. It's too hot, too hot. You'll end up charred. You need to be able to step back from it and refresh yourself, recover your energies. That is what Ocha is for. Palo is hot and Ocha is cool, refreshes.[2] One thing leads to another. When you enter Palo, you go in deep; you become entangled with Kalunga. That is why they call it Palo! Certain ceremonies, and there is no going back. If you get into this, you get *into it*. If not, stay out. That's why you need Ocha, because there's no getting out, just cooling off. You will eventually have to turn to Ocha for refreshment. Otherwise you end up like Teodoro, or worse. Prendas play for keeps. No one should have known this better than Emilio. That is where he failed; he let rivalries and pride keep him from initiating Teodoro. He thought his little boy would be more of a man if he handled his prendas alone without Santo. Now look at him. Even Emilio was initiated into Ocha at the end. Why would Guanabacoa's great tata diambola, Emilio O'Farril, get into Santo at the end of his life? Answer me that!" Before I could think it through she gave the answer, as usual. "Because Santo is cool; it brings you together, helps you collect your wits and find equilibrium in your head. This is about your head. Ocha *refreshes* the head, makes it steady. That is what Emilio sought at the end, and the same would come kindly to Teo if he put his stubbornness aside."

Teodoro disdained Isidra's interpretation. Ocha/Santo didn't interest him, though he knew a lot about it. When pressed he could perform the role of a Ocha/Santo priest, an *obá*, or an *oriaté*. His sister, Cándida, was a celebrated santera in Regla, but he would not be initiated. He said Emilio was initiated because others had manipulated him, that as a young man Emilio had rejected it. Emilio's half brother, Pedro, with whom the Quita Manaquita house was built, kept his distance from Ocha/Santo too. Pedro was an old man now, in his eighties, and was often told by his children, all involved with Ocha/Santo, that he would extend his life if he received the initiations of Ocha/Santo. He refused, saying time and again that Zarabanda was all he needed. Teo respected Ocha/Santo but disregarded Ifá, the male-only code of Yoruba-inspired divination that ultimately rules over Havana Ocha/Santo. And he disagreed with Ocha/Santo elements being imported into Palo, which is why he rejected Isidra's suggestion as a kind of bad evangelism.

Teodoro saw his predicament rooted in Palo and considered his situation unchangeable. Like Isidra, he sought the cause for his predicament with the prendas-ngangas-enquisos. He said, "Manipulation! To say I should become a santero only then to have a babalawo tell me what to do. Where is the peace in that? Ifá is a scam, the way they control you. And it's not cheap! Isidra should drop it. I've got what I need here, with kandango palo. ¡*Bendición Briyumba Congo confianza mía!* I have confidence in Palo's blessings! What else do I need? If there is any problem, if there is anything that distracts me from my work and my responsibilities, it is my Lucero Mundo. You see, Palo is complicated. You don't just receive a prenda like that, without suffering. That's a lie. Palo changes you. Changing hurts. You begin to act like your enquiso. That is why it is so important to get a good one. Among the dead, even the good can have bad qualities, and in my case my Lucero is wild. That is the way it goes."

Teodoro referred to his prenda-nganga-enquiso, Lucero Mundo Saca Empeño, which, with its little mirrored eye looking back at him, now ruled Emilio's house. The enquiso, as he called it, was a *prenda cristiana*. This ultimately meant that he could not kill with it; it was meant to heal. It also meant that the bones of the dead that resided in it were baptized, not the bones of a criminal or a mad person that are sought for some prendas. The problem was that Lucero prendas are often rambunctious and hard to handle. They are considered playful and mischievous and sure to bring unexpected twists and turns to their owner's fate in exchange for their aid. Teo considered his transgressions linked to his affinity with his unruly Lucero. He also said that the dead in his Lucero loved aguardiente, and that when he drank he was honoring the enquiso.

It is a common notion in Palo that a keeper becomes like his or her prenda-nganga-enquiso, that a relation of becoming exists between the dead condensed in a prenda and the person sworn to care for it. Teo held to this, as did his uncle, Pedro. I heard it from time to time among other paleros when they spoke about their prendas-ngangas-enquisos and told anecdotes about them. A Lucero has deep affinities with Eleguá, the Ocha/Santo sovereign of thresholds, crossings, and paths. Like Eleguá, Lucero dead are said to be playful but naughty, powerful but at the same time arbitrary and childlike in their actions. Teo keyed to this, making light of his troubles and woes as being part of the fate assigned to those who served Lucero. That was a generous interpretation, one that Isidra shared only in part and did not consider sufficient to explain his predicaments.

I heard Teodoro's explanations only once or twice. He preferred to run from Isidra's accusations and attacks. Privately, it was hard to get very deep with Teodoro; too much pained him. He grappled with the basic truth of the situation of the Manaquitas and his prendas alone, which spoke to me of a terrible shame he carried. He disdained having it brought up at all; he wanted his prendas to be none of Isidra's business. But he could not deny that she had a right to speak, because her fate was bound to Emilio's Zarabanda. Those who knew Teodoro understood his burden. Teo mostly remained silent in the face of his predicament, except when Isidra and a few others would draw it out. Were it not for them the silence would have consumed him and his prendas long ago.

9. A Feast Awry

Teodoro cursed himself for being late, then tried to explain it away, mumbling excuses as if rehearsing for his hosts. Isidra kept quiet, muted by her apprehension. We were on our way to a rayamiento, an initiation into a Palo house.[1] The hosts, the Palo Monte Mundo Nuevo Guinda Vela praise house of Guanabacoa, was known for its strictures.[2] "They don't like stragglers," said Teodoro, again and again. "You should never be late to a feast. If we don't make it to the rayamiento, then I'm not staying for the match [juego] afterward, no point. It's no good to match up if you've been left out of the sacrifice [matanza]. You miss the charge [carga]; you miss the virtue of the offering. You'd be at a disadvantage against those who shouldn't be able to touch you. Humiliating."

Isidra and I had come from Havana at the invitation of the tata who headed the Mundo Nuevo Guinda Vela house. Initiations in Palo can build over months, or they can come together suddenly to heal a person from a moment of unexpected danger. Tata Anselmo was a longtime friend of Teodoro's and had extended an invitation to this rayamiento. He had heard from Teodoro that I had been initiated as a ngueyo and wanted me to visit his munanso, his praise house. As my initiating godmother, Isidra welcomed the invitation because it would give me a chance to witness the ceremony I myself had undergone. Palo neophytes are blindfolded when they are brought into Palo society and the first step for an ngueyo who is going to receive a prenda as padre or madre is to witness the full initiation of another ngueyo. Isidra would have preferred that I do this in the Quita Manaquita house, because the Manaquitas were Palo Briyumba, whereas the Guinda Velas were Palo Monte. But she also knew that any Manaquita initiations would be long in coming. She was apprehensive that I would become confused by witnessing a Palo Monte celebration before a Palo Briyumba one but wanted me to move forward in my learning. Teodoro, who was now my godfather in Palo, didn't see any danger of confusion at all. "They are totally different," he said.

We were running late because when we arrived at Teodoro's he was engrossed in the *King of Cattle*, the Brazilian *telenovela* the Revolution was beaming daily to its masses. On Saturdays a long summary of the previous week's episodes was broadcast. It was a rags-to-riches story of a beautiful peasant girl from the North of Brazil who falls in love with Bruno Metzinga, a powerful landholder known in the São Paulo countryside as the "King of Cattle." Like the rest of Cuba watching along, Teodoro and Isidra were awed by the luxury they saw in the episodes of the *King of Cattle*, something they were unused to after decades of Soviet-style programs that disparaged the ostentation of the bourgeoisie. They loved to see the exquisite interiors of Bruno Metzinga's houses and to watch him board his private plane. The vistas over the city of São Paulo, with its mirrored skyscrapers and terraced apartment towers, were inspiring. Brazilian and Colombian telenovelas are by far the most popular programs broadcast on Cuban television. If that wasn't reason enough to watch, then the fact that most of the new political jokes that circulate in Cuba play off the characters and situations in the novellas was. In a land where political speech is rare and precious, and a good joke makes brilliant political satire, it was best to tune in.

Now we were huffing through Guanabacoa's neighborhoods, which cling to hillsides or crown hill ridges. Little ravines, dry riverbeds, and crumbled bridges set neighborhoods apart—Los Cocos from Cruz Verde from La Delicia. We were dashing from one side of Guanabacoa to the other, from Teo's to El Mata Siete, a neighborhood across town, downhill and then up to the far highway. Around us the streets lights were out, and the path was dark. Without the streetlights the blue light throbbing from the television in each house became a string of beacons we followed, each of them tuned to the only signal, the state news that followed the *King of Cattle*.

As we entered El Mata Siete, Teodoro began to know more people. Some came floating down the hill on shadows; others we overtook on our climb. Friends of Teo's made swift comments, greeted us, and waved us on. Many in Guanabacoa knew Teodoro as a restive but undemanding character, in many respects failed and unredeemable, but generous in his empty heart. Strangers shouted greetings and two-word jokes and took an interest in us as they pointed us ahead—the ceremony started just now, they said, go on, hurry. Palo gatherings are formally secret, yet one would think by the way we were hailed that everyone in town knew about the feast that evening.

Crowning the hill, our path opened to a row of low houses on our left and the empty blackness of the old cemetery on our right. It was a clear night in March, and the stars filled the sky down to the horizon, sinking into the cemetery. "Campo Lemba," Teodoro said, pointing to it as if across an open sea.[3] Against the dim glow of starlight the hulking shapes of mausoleums and the broken tops of obelisks could be discerned. Drums could be heard. The moon was not yet up in the east, but it would be near full when it appeared. Palo initiations are timed with the waxing moon and are best performed as the moon reaches its fullest light. As the moon grows so does the potential of the dead; the moon and the dead reach their brightest in tandem. The dead press close, like the tide. Kalunga rises—with the moon, like the sea—then Kalunga falls. Isidra took to the long sidewalk opposite the crumbling cemetery wall. Halfway down the block the cemetery gate rose up, tall and closed.

The drums sounded from a house that faced the gate, and a white-blue light from its entryway shone into the street, setting off the crowd of people in the door. The closer we got the more we were drawn—by the thud of the drum, by the shifting heads of people moving in and out of the house, and by the effervescence of the gathered crowd. The drums were going strong; festivities inside were well underway. Just before we reached the entrance Teodoro turned to me and said cryptically, "You'll be hunted; don't doubt that. Never assume you're safe at a gathering of nkisi malongo. Just when you think you're in, you're out. Just when you think you're safe, someone works Palo against you. Isidra? Right now we're covering you, but someday you'll have to do this on your own, so pay attention. Don't cross anyone; keep to yourself." He seemed tense and I took Isidra's continued silence as an endorsement of his warning. Then, in a characteristic about-face, Teo recognized someone at the door, summoned a broad smile and lunged forth, eyes shimmering with delight, a cool hand extended at his waist. "¡Hecha! ¡Carajo!" "Hey!" he said, "Fuck!" followed by laughter, smiles, and the banter of acquaintances. Isidra, however, remained withdrawn.

With each greeting came another step into the low house, slowly through the front door, pressed on by the rising mass of heat and sound, of people talking in excited tones. We were pulled into a small living room sunk in an atmosphere of humid vapor, cigarette smoke, and voices; it was the breath of the house itself. The density of the bodies in the living room had me feeling closeness itself, as if it had pushed inside me. Teo was continually greeted; Isidra looked around for people she might know and seemed anxious to get along to the room where the initiation was happening, where she would at least know the tata of the house. Teo was conscious of this and did his best to fend off friends, finally guiding us to a shifting section of the crowd. Soon we were moving through the crush of people along a slow-cutting flow that wound through the living room and out a hallway leading toward the back. People greeted us but did not detain us. "Teodoro!" they said. "Hey! You made it! Teo, hey, we thought you were going to sit this one out! Teo! You've come; hurry to the room!"

We glided through the living room, with its dim light and faded orange paint. The walls were spare, a small metal plant hanger attached to one wall, plastic flowers hung from another. A large Soviet-era television filled one corner, but it was off. There was barely room for the furniture: a couch and two knock-offs of modern European armchairs upholstered in vinyl. Children playing and uninitiated men and women sitting patiently, waiting for the party to spill into the living room and include them, could be seen below the standing people. On the couch along one wall was the mother of the young woman being initiated tonight. She sat straight-backed in a dull green dress, her small purse on her lap, with friends on either side of her.

She was present at her daughter's rayamiento but she wasn't participating in the ceremony. She must be a child of the Revolution, I thought to myself. Judging by her age she was probably born with it and brought up during its early years. And her daughter must have been born late in the seventies or the early eighties, the end of the Revolution's aggressively Stalinist era. Drawing from other people her age I met at Palo and Ocha/Santo feasts, I imagined this woman was the child of a family where Palo and Ocha/Santo had been part of the lifeblood of the household before the Revolution. Yet in the years of her childhood and youth she was encouraged away from them. Or she may have given up Palo and Ocha/Santo without much thought. The social upheaval in the course of forging a national revolutionary culture was tremendous in the first half of the sixties, and like many in her generation she probably chose paths opened to her by the Revolution—toward secularism and scientific rationality, the nominal abolition of economic classes, equality between men and women and among people of all skin tones, a progressive family code, universal health care, and education: socialism's modernity. If these ideas weren't attractive enough, which for many they were, she would have faced discrimination by identifying too closely with Palo or Ocha/Santo, or Catholicism for that matter, and her parents probably protected her from the Revolution's fervor by channeling her childhood toward what opportunities the Revolution offered. The woman's twenty-year-old daughter, Virtudes, had come of age in a time when these practices were no

longer persecuted outright, a time when the Revolution had ceded much social control to powers rivaling its orthodoxy and fervor: tourism and multi-
national capitalist investment. Today Palo and Ocha/Santo ride the coattails
of these, pleased to step into the bare outlines of civil society such investments demand, while maintaining a wary eye on new trends. As her mother
had drawn away, Virtudes had drawn close.

Before I had time to think more, the current we were following led us into
a dark hallway and directly to what is called, in Palo as well as in Ocha/Santo,
el Cuarto de religión, or, more simply, *el Cuarto* [the Room]. The door to the
Room was bright orange and made of the thinnest particleboard—sawdust
pressed into a solid sheet, ready to crumble. A curtain would have been better,
and in fact, in the Cuban countryside, curtains are preferred to mark off such
rooms. It was not the door, or its matter or construction, that kept people out,
nor what kept secrets in. That was something else, understood by everyone in
the house and ultimately unspoken. To knock at the door would bring nothing but misery and grief to the unaffiliated.

Our first knock was unheard. Three sharp blows as proscribed, each alone
in its own resonance. But inside the drums and singing overtook and turned
all other sound. People streamed past us in the dark hall, coming and going
from the patio as we waited impatiently. Teo knocked again and not until he
pushed at the door was the boundary man inside alerted. The door moved.
"Kinani!?" An eye and mouth split by the door narrowed in suspicion. The
lindero, the boundary man, is usually a recent initiate into the code of padre
nganga. Among initiates at the level of padre, being a lindero is the least of
tasks, yet the most important. This lindero was an old man, probably a member of the Guinda Vela house grown tired of attending to the prendas-
ngangas-enquisos at feasts like this and preferring instead a bit of distance
from the intensity of facing them. In his old age he could hardly be bested at
his work, knowing as he probably did the names of most of Guanabacoa's
Palo societies and the possible combinations of paleros who might arrive at
the door.

"Kinani!?" He shouted again, insisting, "Who's there?"[4] He and Teo knew
one another, but Teo replied with his initiation name nonetheless, as required:
Tata Nganga Lucero Saca Empeño Mundo Nuevo Carile Quita Manaquita
Briyumba Congo.[5] He said it with self-importance and a flair I couldn't have
reproduced. Isidra went next, speaking for the first time since we had set out
from Teodoro's house. Clutching her black purse she gave her initiation
name. When my turn came and I hesitated Teodoro spoke for me. I was unable to say my name with the certainty and decoration the delivery seemed

to require: ¡Ngueyo Mprenda Siete Rayos Ngo Batalla Quita Manaquita Briyumba Congo, *hasta que tango ya lemba* [until the sun sinks into the cemetery]!

A pause, and the elderly lindero slowly stepped aside. He took a step back into a crowd that hardly left him room to swing the door as they moved and sang with their backs to us. His face relaxed, and though he smiled he didn't erase completely the expression of disapproval at seeing Teodoro arrive with such unexpected company. "Shoes off," he said.

The Room was tiny, a cinderblock cube without windows, packed with people. The atmosphere was dense with sweat and moving bodies, tense with anticipation inspired by the drums, which filled the space beyond capacity with their reverberations. People were packed together and swamped by heat and sweat. Perhaps the elderly lindero took the door because he could get an occasional draft of cool air. Women in tank tops and bare-chested men fought the heat by sheer force of will. We couldn't see the drummers; they were facing the prendas-ngangas-enquisos, squatting on the ground near the front of the crowd, their tumbadoras braced between their thighs, striking with all the strength in their arms. The scene was lit by a green bulb screwed into the ceiling in the center of the room, hanging just above our heads. The feast appeared to be well under way and the expectation of sacrifice, bloodletting, and the hoped-for appearance of the Kongo dead coursed through the gathering. Thick cigar smoke clouded the room. A woman slipped between the bodies, sending a plume of smoke into the air around the heads of those near her by inverting a lit cigar in her mouth and blowing through it. "*¡Hecha humo!*" The first day I had visited Teodoro and sat with him next to his father's prendas he demanded that I blow smoke, too. He put a cigar in my hand and had me puffing smoke into the air. "It cools," he said.

Sweat ran down the necks and backs and into the pants and shorts of the people around us. Their clothing was plain, consisting of simple pants, dresses, work clothes, and many homemade pieces cut from way out-of-fashion Soviet-era ochre-tint polyesters. Crossing their chests and tank tops, the men and women wore strands of colored beads hung with bundles and charms to protect them from unexpected discharges of force in the Room—from the prendas, the sacrifices, or the pervasive ambiance of the dead of which we were all a part. Those not wearing the necklaces were likewise protected, discreetly, by charms in their pockets or brassieres. Teo kept a charm in his pocket, a big bullet brought back from the Angola conflict that he had "loaded" with his own mix of fluids and powders. Isidra also kept charms on her body. I wore the long strand of beads [*collar bandera*]

I had been presented during my initiation. In brushed whispers the bare feet of the gathering graced the floor with the energetic kicking and movements that define Palo dance. The singing was in tense unison, and the drums ached with sound. This was the Palo Monte Mundo Nuevo Guinda Vela house, gathered to bring a new member into its world.

Closing behind us, the door revealed a stack of shoes against the back wall. For me this was exceptional. To go barefoot in Cuba is so socially and habitually prohibited that it is one of the few broad practices I encountered in Cuba I would call a "taboo," in that it was absolutely uncontestable. From the time a child is lifted out of its crib, it is wearing shoes. A Cuban may lie to the police, critique the state, ignore an elder, steal from work, betray a friend, or not keep her part of a bargain with the dead, but will *never* go barefoot, except at the beach and in bed. Perhaps while bathing there will be some bare footedness, but even in the shower the pervasive *chancleta*, the rubber flip-flop, separates the feet from the floor, as it does throughout the house. Here, a roomful of people danced and shifted in dense proximity *wholly* barefoot. This was Palo practice, different from celebrations and drums of exaltation for Ocha/Santo sovereigns, where those gathered come wearing the most glorious shoes they can afford. In this little room, the crowd shifted and slid and shuffled and twisted on their dusty bare feet. I was impressed and mentioned it with goodhearted interest to Isidra, whose answer was unexpectedly defensive. "Did *cimarrones* wear shoes? Did runaway slaves have shoes? Did masters provide their slaves with shoes?"

The pile of shoes and shirts and purses behind the door was also astonishing because of the confidence in the house it communicated. The poverty of people in Havana, and especially in Guanabacoa, is such that shoes are the most precious of clothing, being not only the most expensive, but also the most distinctive element of dress. In the dollars/pesos economy, where the only shoes available in the national currency were Soviet-era throwbacks so stylistically appalling that only desperate pensioners would wear them, a nice pair of shoes was an investment and a first-order determinant of social status. Fear of thievery was, in the 1990s, nearly as sure a "social fact" as the taboo on going barefoot and to see the shoes stacked up all together spoke to the prestige of the Guinda Vela community. Proof of their reputation in that moment rested on the integrity of the pile of shoes and purses behind the door. Isidra, not one to always assume the best of people, took her sandals off without a second thought and put them on the pile, along with her purse.

As the old lindero settled back into his spot, we were engulfed by those in the room singing in greeting for the prendas-ngangas-enquisos. Their melody was sad and high:

Caller:	¡Buena noche la santa noche, amilé	Good evening, holy evening,
	Buena noche la santa noche, Palo!	Good evening, holy evening, Palo!
Chorus:	¡Buena noche la santa noche, amilé,	Good evening, holy evening,
	Buena noche la santa noche, Palo!	Good evening, holy evening, Palo!
Caller:	¡Buena noche la santa noche, amilé,	Good evening, holy evening,
	Buena noche la santa noche, Palo!	Good evening, holy evening, Palo!
Chorus:	¡Buena noche la santa noche, amilé,	Good evening, holy evening,
	Buena noche la santa noche, Palo!	Good evening, holy evening, Palo!

A young padre nganga led the chorus. His song rang with all the brass in his chest and reached into the drums and the night. He hung on the last word of each line, drawing out the final vowel until it died in the last wisps of his breath; then the words of the next line followed in swift succession. His voice was clear and by its plain confidence brought the chorus along with him. He changed songs at will, the chorus behind him:

Padre:	¡Buenas noches, mi lemba,	Good evening, my dead,
	Buenas noches, mi lemba!	Good evening, my dead![6]
	¡Mundo nuevo carile,	The world is new, carile,
	Mundo nuevo carile!	The world is new, carile![7]
Chorus:	¡Buenas noches, mi lemba,	Good evening, my dead,
	Buenas noches, mi lemba!	Good evening, my dead!
	¡Mundo nuevo carile,	The world is new, carile,
	Mundo nuevo carile!	The world is new, carile!
Padre:	¡O, las buenas noches, mi lemba!	Oh, good evening, my dead!
	¡Yo sienta ngoma, mi lemba!	I hear the drum, my dead!
	¡La siete legua, mi lemba!	At seven leagues, my dead!
	¡Campana Luisa, mi lemba,	Like Luisa's Bell, my dead,
	la mundo nuevo carile,	The world is new, carile,
	la mundo nuevo carile!	The world is new, carile![8]

Chorus:	¡Buenas noches, mi lemba,	Good evening, my dead,
	Buenas noches, mi lemba!	Good evening, my dead!
	¡Mundo nuevo carile,	The world is new, carile,
	Mundo nuevo carile!	The world is new, carile!
Padre:	¡Eh, la buenas noches, mi lemba!	Ah, good evening, my dead!
	¡La buena ntoto, mi lemba!	This is good earth, my dead!
	¡Chichi bilongo, mi lemba!	Maggots, my dead!
	¡Ya Zarabanda, mi lemba!	Zarabanda is here, my dead!
	¡La Tiembla Tierra, mi lemba,	Tiembla Tierra is here, my dead,
	La mundo nuevo carile,	The world is new, carile,
	La mundo nuevo carile!	The world is new, carile!
Chorus:	¡Buenas noches, mi lemba,	Good evening, my dead,
	Buenas noches, mi lemba!	good evening, my dead!
	¡Mundo nuevo carile,	The world is new, carile,
	Mundo nuevo carile!	The world is new, carile!

We had arrived in the middle of a greeting song used in many Kongo praise houses. The padre leading would continue, improvising, adding, returning to a previous stanza, establishing lines for the ever-ready chorus at the outset of each verse. They seemed to still be working through greetings and this reassured us we weren't too late. Still, the energy in the room was a little off, too intense for such an early point in the feast. Isidra noticed it and signaled me with a miniscule twist of her mouth.

As the greeting came to a close—and the song lasted several minutes after we entered—we moved forward. It was inconceivable that we would arrive and not approach the prendas-ngangas-enquisos to beg their permission to participate in the initiation. Though Tata Anselmo had invited us, it was the prendas that reigned in the room and to them we were obliged to show obeisance. Tata Anselmo waved us forward.

The crowd was four or five people deep. Their skin tones ran from *blanco* to *prieto*, to *mulato, trigueño, amarillado,* and *jaba'o,* terms Cubans use to describe a person's skin. True to the Creole quality of Palo society at the turn of the twentieth century, there was not a shade of skin that was not represented among the Guinda Vela house. Older men and women were gathered closer to the prendas-ngangas-enquisos at the front of the room, opposite where we had entered. With the exception of the lindero behind us, those closer to the door were younger, more raucous in their singing and praise. We twisted our way through the stiff lines, bumping into the backs of those closest to the prendas.

Tata Anselmo had followed us with his eyes from the time we entered. He stopped the young padre from beginning yet another song, so that we might greet the prendas without having to get around the drummers while they played. Anselmo seemed pleased to see us; Teodoro brought with him the memory of the Manaquita House and the blessings of Tata Emilio. Though they belonged to different branches of Palo practice, Teo and Anselmo were longtime friends, Teodoro being the older. Anselmo was the grandson of the elderly yayi who headed the Guinda Vela house back when they would plan feasts together with the Manaquitas. Anselmo and Teodoro also belonged to the same Abakuá society. With a stern but satisfied smile on his reddish round face, his heavily lidded eyes downcast, and a nod of his head, Anselmo motioned toward the floor.

The prendas were sitting on a large piece of plywood. The prohibition on prendas-ngangas-enquisos resting on tile or cement was thus observed. Prendas-ngangas-enquisos draw force from the earth and from wood. Their true home is the secret fastness of the wilderness [el monte], and if they could have their way they would nestle half-buried in the earth under the roots of ancient trees lost in the forest. That being impossible in Havana, most prendas find themselves resting in closets on built-up beds of dirt brought from the countryside. Anything is better than tile or cement, and when there is no other option *playwo* [plywood] is the best resort.

Things around the prendas were ordered to their wishes. This was not their usual resting place, so they needed much coddling and attending to. They had been brought from near Teodoro's house across town to be close to the cemetery, which was considered auspicious for the initiation. They were much smaller than those of the Manaquita house; compared to Emilio's and Teodoro's prendas set in their iron cauldrons standing two and three feet tall, these were a fraction of the size. They looked like the smaller aides and allies Isidra and Teodoro kept around their larger prendas-ngangas-enquisos. I was surprised to see them, but then again my experience was solely with Palo Briyumba, and the Guinda Velas were a Palo Monte house. The practical differences between Palo Briyumba and other branches of Palo that Teodoro had explained in terms of their music were evident as well as in the form their prendas-ngangas-enquisos took.

There were maybe five or six of the little prendas, some set in miniature iron kettles tinted black, others in what looked like little terra-cotta vessels, none any larger than a gallon volume. Lying around the prendas, half hidden in the shadows and nooks created by the crowding of so many objects in so tight a space, were little terra-cotta dishes holding beaded necklaces and bundles of substances being vitalized as protective charms. The plywood on which they rested was covered with *hierba fina*, which is plain lawn grass, pulled up by hand and strewn thick around the prendas to connect them with the outdoors. A curtain of *cun de amor* was hung along the wall behind the prendas. Cun de amor is a gentle vine with wide, heart-shaped leaves, not too different from morning glory but with smaller orange papery flowers lobed like teardrops. Cun de amor is good luck to those who bring it into their home because it cools the dead and purges ill-boding condensations from the surrounding ambiance of Kalunga. It is common to see lengths of it wrapped fresh around prendas-ngangas-enquisos. On either side of the prendas sugarcane stalks leaned in from the corners of the Room, rising in an arc that framed the scene. In the center, hung on the wall behind the veil of cun de amor, was a cloth banner that read, in black letters stitched on red satin: Palo Monte Mundo Nuevo Guinda Vela. Under the society's name was stitched a *firma*, the house's signature made up of arrows, equilateral crosses, circles, and other shapes used to condense, contain, and discharge the potentials of the dead.[9]

The prendas were black; everything in them was black. Little sticks and jagged edges poked out of them. They shimmered black under a viscid patina of blackness that confused the eye. When we were able to approach them unobstructed, we could see they were covered in glistening new blood. This stood out iridescent against the blackness of the prendas, glowing almost orange. The sacrifice had been made. Just before he knelt to greet the center prenda Teo shot a look of surprise and warning our way that seemed to say, "Hey!" His furrowed brow said, "Be careful!" Isidra took it further, unconcerned about being overheard in her caution and commanded me, as if I didn't already feel it, "Don't touch!"

There was blood everywhere. Blood on the hierba fina, on its bright green leaves. Some was already thickening, losing its glow, turning toward the blackness it was fated to become. Blood overflowed the mouths of the little cauldrons and collected in pools in the plates and vessels at their feet. There were offerings of fruit lying at their feet, covered in blood. To the side of the center prenda a machete rested on its handle pointing up, a trickle of blood down its blade. A crude homemade sword was propped on the other side, dripping with blood. In front of the prendas a single candle burned in a small crystal holder in the shape of a star, drawing the dead with its light. A low glass of water sat next to the candle to help cool the dead churning around the place. Near the glass of water, to the side of the candle and on the edges of the whole scene, were little flowers, colored daisies and white *azucenas* [lilies] and mariposas. These had been stepped on and were stained by the same drops clinging to everything else. Recycled soda bottles full of aguardiente stood here and there, offerings to the prendas from those gathered. Teodoro presented them with a bottle on our behalf, a delicious aguardiente made by a chemist turned illegal distiller in his back yard in El Vedado, back in the center of Havana.

Blood from a sacrificial animal is considered to be exceptionally hot. It is dangerous in the extreme because it actualizes the very potential of the ambient dead; it is a prized version of Kalunga, el muerto, immanent to each of us. Blood, in its warm, gelatinous heft, was the dead drawn out of its ambiance to be folded back on itself.

I had serious misgivings about getting any closer, but there was nothing I could do to withdraw. There was barely room for the three of us to kneel between the Guinda Vela drummers and it was almost impossible to get down without being pushed into the prendas, let alone into the field of force and prohibition that surrounded each drop of blood.

Atop the center-most prenda, nestled in its ring of protruding sticks and railroad spikes, was the head of a goat, the blood of which adorned everything. Its eyes were closed and its large black ears hung limp on either side. Its short horns arched back toward the orange flowers of the cun de amor. In its mouth was a handful of grass. The animal's mouth was tied shut with a fiber cord wound several times around its snout. Out of sight inside the mouth there was probably a charge of substances that had been used in discerning the conditions of Kalunga earlier in the night.

Much had happened before we arrived. The goat had been sacrificed by Tata Anselmo and his assistants. Roosters had followed, offered with little pomp. It takes two people to offer a rooster, because they are strong and often break free. One person restrains the animal's feet and wings while the other holds the head, extending the neck. With caller and chorus praising the animal's life and anticipating its blood, the presiding tata will pet the rooster and speak to it, pry open its mouth and mumble to it in a low voice for a few seconds. What commands or invocations are spoken to the animal in this moment are known only to the speaker and the bird. The rooster's head is then quickly cut off, and its blood covers the prendas with its freshness. When both roosters have been offered—it takes two to freshen or cool [levantar, refrescar] the blood of a goat or a ram—they are then plucked by those nearby for their ornamental tail and wing feathers, which are stuck into a prenda and used to cover it as it sinks into repose. When the roosters are spent they are thrown to the ground to join the carcass of the offered goat. With little ceremony the animal mass—goat and rooster carcasses together—is gathered up by junior members of the house and abruptly flung from the Room. Prospective initiates of the house wait outside to cut up the bodies for a collective stew.

We came late and saw none of the killing, but evidence of this course of events was everywhere. The goat's black-and-white hind legs and its front legs, severed at the animal's knees, rested crossed in sets of hind and front on either side of the center prenda. Out of the mouth of the prenda, from under the goat's head, the black and brown-green, gold-flecked, iridescent feathers of a colored rooster fanned out in a necklace for the goat's head. All around, the other prendas were likewise bathed and decorated—blood collecting in rivulets ending in coagulated beads, and rooster feathers poking out and covering the prendas and adhering to any spot of blood. They had feasted and now they rested and cooled. It had been a generous offer for a rayamiento. Initiation into Palo society requires an offering of just two cocks.

From what we could see the principal prenda was a Zarabanda, but those of Palo Monte were different enough from Briyumba ones that the only hint I had was the disproportionately thick chain wrapped around the diminutive kettle's potbelly. Zarabanda loves goat followed by a mature colored rooster for its feast meal. Zarabanda is a fighting prenda, one made to concentrate the properties of iron and metal like the Ocha/Santo sovereign Ogún, into whose territory of fate-changing potential Zarabanda incurs. This prenda had an inordinate amount of metal pieces jagging out from it. Along with the others, Zarabanda was now in repose and basking in the afterglow of the offering, and I was loathe to disturb them. As in so many times in my fieldwork, I surrendered to the judgments of my teachers and followed Teodoro and Isidra. She too deferred to Teo that night and let him pass first. He rapped his knuckles three times on the floor before Zarabanda where his fingers would touch no blood and then spoke in Palo Kikongo Creole to Zarabanda. Isidra followed suit.

I was the last to greet them. Where Teodoro and Isidra spoke to the prendas in whispers, my greetings were mute and awkward. I was dumb when faced with them. Only later and with much practice was I at all able to overcome my reluctance to speak to them. As I rose from greeting the prendas, Anselmo released the drummers and the young padre broke into a song for the honored prenda:

Padre:	¡Zará, Zará, Zarabanda!
	¡Zará, Zará, Zarabanda ayé!
Chorus:	¡Zará, Zará, Zarabanda!
	¡Zará, Zará, Zarabanda ayé!

Padre: ¡Zará, Zará, Zarabanda!
            ¡Zará, Zará, Zarabanda ayé!

Chorus: ¡Zará, Zará, Zarabanda!
            ¡Zará, Zará, Zarabanda ayé!

We sank back through the crowded little room singing, becoming part of the chorus as we headed for the spot where we had entered. As we took in the animals' spent blood and their death, the air seemed to coagulate into a brassy, viscous slurry that felt substantial and impenetrable. The whole place was reeling, the singing now louder, and the movement of bodies more agitated. The room exploded with delight and excitement.

The heat, the moisture, the singing and the drums, created an atmosphere that gave the cinderblock walls, placed and stacked not quite square, the appearance of veering and bulging. This sense of distortion was coming in waves that settled into a throb, which matched long undulations in the patterns of the drums. The dancing and singing would sometimes come into cycle, and the whole room would appear to shift from left to right, opposite the collective sway of shoulders. The voices shouting the song, and the drums hammering rhythms straight into the dead, created a pulse felt as if it was crossing my skin, pushing a current of the dead straight into my head and abdomen.

10. Virtudes

Things were amiss and Isidra's growing discomfort was obvious. The sacrifices were done, which meant we had missed the rayamiento. In my limited experience—my own rayamiento as ngueyo—the animals were offered after I was cut. I looked around the room for the initiate, who would be obvious because of her bloody shirt. Also, the greeting song in the air when we entered is usually sung at the beginning of ceremonies, not after the killing. And the energy of the crowd, despite being intense and rousing, was likewise off; coming after the sacrifices it should have been more coherent, intact, in unison. I had doubts about where exactly in the ceremony we were and was disappointed to have come so late. Isidra's tensed shoulders and the bowed angle of her head said she was skeptical. Teo was steady, however, and he somehow recognized the initiation had yet to happen.

In the midst of the next song, into which the caller had shifted seamlessly, the door opened. Those gathered pressed closely together, making room and clearing a path forward. First came the candle floating, then the hands of the woman who held it, who was dressed in white. In her fifties, she was stocky and walked in short steps as she swayed back and forth to the beat of the drums in "Congo" fashion. A young woman followed her, swaying also, with her head bowed and her hands on the older woman's shoulders. She was blindfolded. This was Virtudes being led by her madrina, the woman who would become her godmother in Palo.

Virtudes was in her teens, small and sturdy. She was dressed in white and she was barefoot. The broad white piece of cloth that covered her eyes set off the burnished luster of her hair, which was iridescent like the rooster feathers now crowning Zarabanda. She seemed calm. Against the bronze of her skin little bits of green leaves stuck to her shoulders, arms, and neck. Those were from the bath of herbs godmothers give initiates to cool them before they face the prenda of their rayamiento. The smell of hierba buena, *albahaca* [basil], and *bledo blanco* on her body were unmistakable as she passed by. Only weeks before I had been similarly bathed, attired, and constrained.

Her blind walk very much exemplified the path to initiation faced by all ngueyos—one enters Palo ignorant and approaches its forces in a position of exquisite vulnerability. Through the parting crowd she was led to stand on a Palo firma, or signature, which Anselmo had been drawing on the ground in white chalk since we had retreated. It was impossible for us to see what he was writing, but he had been kneeling for almost the whole time it took for Virtudes to be led forward. It has to have been a firma for Zarabanda, though its exact form remained a mystery to me. She came to stand atop it.[1] She faced Zarabanda and Tata Anselmo, who with a simple gesture stopped the din of chatter that had risen up when Virtudes entered. He called Nzambi Mpungu, a commanding version of the Kongo dead:

Tata Anselmo:	¡Nzambi!
Chorus:	¡Dios!
Tata Anselmo:	¡Nzambi!
Chorus:	¡Dios!
Tata Anselmo:	¡Nzambi!
Chorus:	¡Dios!
Tata Anselmo:	¡Nzambi!
Chorus:	¡Dios![2]

Some of the men in the room, younger ones, ngueyos, began to make comments about how the last initiate fainted with pain. Another man joked about a dull machete. Anselmo called it all to an abrupt stop. The older tatas and yayis said nothing, and there was silence.

Anselmo did not speak to her. He seemed pleased with her preparation and the form with which she had been brought into the gathering. He then turned to her madrina and began by asking her to identify the person she had brought to the Guinda Vela house. "Who is this person? Why has she come here? What is the purpose of her visit? Why have we gathered? Why does she seek?" The madrina's response was straightforward: "Her name is Virtudes Salazár Mendoza, and we are here because she is in danger. Because enemies surround her, because of envy they hunt her."[3] Anselmo looked at the madrina with scrutiny. There was more theater to his stare than anyone might have wished to admit. He knew this woman and knew

Virtudes; he had consulted with both of them before. But it was important that admittance to the society not be de facto.

Without a signal, the drums jerked the crowd into swaying motion just as Tata Anselmo "took" the song from the young padre who had been calling, beginning the first of what would be four or five songs of initiation. The first of these was not the rocketing and jolting that define most Palo rhythms but rather a soft touching of the fingers and palms over the drum head. The result was a low roll played out of synch on three drums of different pitch. It was indistinguishable from distant thunder.

The first part of the initiation took place to this sound. A long initiation song asked the initiate to pledge to items she couldn't see. Tata Anselmo placed each in her hand as he sang:

Tata Anselmo:	¡Jure, mbele bobo, Jure, mbele bobo!	Swear, razor blade, Swear, razor blade!
Chorus:	¡Jure, mbele bobo, Jure, mbele bobo!	Swear, razor blade, Swear, razor blade!
Tata Anselmo:	¡Jure, makondo, jure, Jure, makondo, jure!	Swear, plantain, swear, Swear, plantain, swear!
Chorus:	¡Jure, makondo, jure, Jure, makondo, jure!	Swear, plantain, swear, Swear, plantain, swear![4]

Each item had a verse, and the barber's blade was first. It was followed by a plantain, a machete, and other items. The song continued for a long time as the initiate promised blindly, and it was doubtful that she understood the language in which the objects were being named. With each new verse, the singing grew more agitated, and the prenda to which the entire gathering was devoted began to reveal its power. Zarabanda desired this initiate, and it called her; to that end it had called together the Guinda Vela house. They moved in unison around the prenda, sang its songs, and played the drums for it. It reveled in this attention and waited for the initiate's blood. Virtudes could not see it. It was squat on the ground, practically at her feet. In her consultations with Anselmo she had not seen it, as she might have never seen her godmother's prenda. Many paleras and paleros consult uninitiated clients without ever revealing to them the prendas-ngangas-enquisos with which they effect their transformations of fate. Zarabanda Guinda Vela now reposed silently before her, and she knew nothing about it except that it could help her. Virtudes could have reached down to hold or lift it or could have easily kicked it over, but instead she stood helpless before it, unsure even of what it was. I marveled at this gesture of surrender, the trust and willingness in the act of offering oneself to a prenda-nganga-enquiso while

largely ignorant of its powers. One thing had been made clear to her, however, as it had been made to me when I was in her position: the prenda called
her, and she needed it.

Prendas-ngangas-enquisos revel in the homage paid them in such gestures. More than anything else, they seek to grow in size and prestige. Those
who question the ontological status of prendas-ngangas-enquisos as actors
or entities sometimes ask "What's in it for the prenda?" or "What do prendas want?" The one certainty is that prendas-ngangas-enquisos want to
grow.[5] To this end, a prenda's keeper builds elaborate networks of aid and tribute to guarantee it will be fed. Ngueyos are brought before prendas-ngangas-
enquisos, ready to pledge themselves, beginning with the gift of their blood.
This is requisite of all ngueyos. As far as a compact was being sealed between
them, Virtudes's blood was the matter on which her contract with Zarabanda
would be based.

I learned a lot from Virtudes's rayamiento, not so much because of what
I saw or witnessed, but because Teodoro and Isidra were willing to talk
about another's initiation more than my own. This is Kongo Law, and for
that reason I don't write about my rayamiento here. But the outline of
Virtudes's agreement with Zarabanda Guinda Velo is the following. In exchange for her service and surrender the prenda would protect her from
her enemies and retaliate should they try to hurt her with Palo. She must
in return serve Zarabanda Guinda Vela, coming with offerings to its birthday feast each year and to other Guinda Vela celebrations. She must offer
to it on the anniversary of her initiation, too. She must not contravene this
arrangement, for once her blood is absorbed by Zarabanda a path through
the blind reaches of Kalunga is established between them, drawn in blood
through the wilderness of the dead. This path magnifies Zarabanda's power
to heal or harm her.

I would like to pause and think about this path *[camino]*, the one drawn
in blood, and how it is understood in Palo. Like most everything in Palo,
when confronted with initiation and sacrifice one must consider the dead.
Images used to describe the dead in Palo are keen to fluids, densities, coagu-
lations, condensations, and immanent transfers of force—such is Kalunga,
the vast, indifferent sea of the dead. Kalunga is the horizon where reason
cedes to immanent perception and from which arise a multiplicity of versions of the dead. Blood is such a version. Though the ambient dead in its
indifference cannot recognize a hierarchy among the versions of itself generated in its flows, the living consider blood a privileged form of the dead.
Blood is foremost a fluid, alike to Kalunga in its turbid, shifting form. It is
also overflowing with force—flowing, coagulating, and bonding. Blood is

energy, warmth, and life-giving vitality. It is intimate to life, just as its cooling is intimate to death. Blood saturates the living as does Kalunga; it is one form Kalunga assumes as it passes through the porous body. In that moment of passing, it can be captured and transformed. It would be a mistake to assume that blood is a sign or symbol of the dead in Palo thought. It is not. Blood is a material turn of the dead, valued by the living for its concrete properties, for its visceral, nonrepresentational force, which unfailingly remands the living to the dead enfolding us.

Substance is the operative word in this figuration, encompassing both matter and ephemera simultaneously, mutually affirming each, refusing contradiction. By means of their craft, paleros and paleras create substance by making evident the dead already inherent in the matter they are working, thus revealing matter as a version of the dead. This is the basis of all Palo craft, and paleras and paleros know how to craft blood into densities they deem useful in healing and harming. Their craft begins with drawing blood, as in the cutting of an initiate in a rayamiento.

One of Palo's treasures is its knowledge and practice of working with blood. Palo sacrifice, with its strictures and style, is an accomplished discourse on the appreciation, capture, and transformation of blood. Songs are written about blood; two in particular, which I include below, are sung during sacrifices. Blood is handled and worked creatively to produce structural effects, especially when mixed with earth into an indurate cake that holds fast the contents of a prenda-nganga-enquiso. Blood is also fashioned into visual and textual effects across the surface of prendas and other objects, the most striking of which is the black, glistening coating a cared-for prenda-nganga-enquiso achieves. Blood is kept bottled, where it putrefies. Its stench is valued, and it is mixed with other labored substances to intensify the force of a charm or harming bundle. Of all the matter Palo routinely fashions into fate-transforming forms of the dead, blood is first. It is most alive, most potent, most versatile, and only bones compare with its capacity to generate social force. Lydia Cabrera, in a little-known posthumous publication, comments on blood: "Blood was life and . . . the soul. Blood, like the voice, is the person itself. If one's blood is spilled one has to be careful that a witch not use it to dominate the person. It is correct to clean up the floor or soil where it has fallen. Blood, which gives life and resilience, is an insuperable medicine. Bathing the ill in blood, one can cure leprosy. With blood one can resurrect the dead."[6]

Virtudes's offering was called for because in being drawn out of her, the blood became a version of Kalunga, to be filtered back into the dead through Zarabanda, which would then exist in explicit continuum with her. Once it ingested her blood, the prenda-nganga-enquiso would thenceforth be able to find her among the countless other densities of the dead, "like a hound," said Isidra. By this means, the prenda would be able to aid her at any given moment, regardless of the physical distance that separated them. It would also be able to harm her or kill her, by following the trace of her blood back through the ambient dead to rejoin her body as hazardous forms of the dead, such as spiders and scorpions. The promise of expedited protection and healing, as well as the threat of immanent attack, helps guarantee loyalty to a prenda-nganga-enquiso. The path established provides the certainty that the house will prosper and that the prenda-nganga-enquiso will be served and will continue to grow.

The chorus was agitated in its song. Virtudes was the next initiate to join this bond, to give of herself so that she might become stronger and more integrated with the dead that churned around Zarabanda Guinda Vela. It was with the dead, ultimately, that her fate would be revalued and where she wished to strengthen her presence. Anselmo called the chorus down: Nzambi!

Chorus:	¡Dios!
Tata Anselmo:	¡Nzambi!
Chorus:	¡Dios!
Tata Anselmo:	¡Nzambi!
Chorus:	¡Dios!
Tata Anselmo:	¡Nzambi!
Chorus:	¡Dios!

Anselmo then turned to his bakofula, his steward, who had been prominent at his side since we entered. A bakofula is a tata's principal assistant and presides over the ceremony when the tata is otherwise occupied. In this case the bakofula had anticipated his tata's request and handed Anselmo a straight razor.

Other means of cutting initiates come from the stories told by old folks and others. As we watched Virtudes prepared to be cut, Teodoro remarked that Emilio used to cut with *espuela 'e gallo*. He said, "You were marked with a 'rooster's spur.'" For a long time afterward I imagined that he referred to the long, nail-like growth that extends from the back of a rooster's lower leg, called its "spur." This growth is filed in cockfights and is quite sharp. But Teodoro could also have referred to the long, extremely sharp thorns from a bush of the same name, espuela de gallo, which grows throughout the Cuban countryside. In my initiation I was cut with a Sputnik disposable razor blade left over from the Soviet days. None of these options could be as elegant or smooth as the instrument Anselmo now held in his hand. It looked like an East German blade and Virtudes could be grateful for his choice.

Anselmo held it in a neatly folded kerchief. He poured a little rubbing alcohol over it and carefully cleaned the blade, studying its edge with his thumb. The bakofula then reached into his back pocket from where he produced a small case, out of which he drew a pair of eyeglasses. They were narrow reading glasses, which are rarely seen in Havana except among party bureaucrats who have had the privilege to travel abroad. They were unheard of among the poor of Guanabacoa that filled the room, and in their uniqueness they spoke to the possibility that Tata Anselmo had initiates who were powerful party members or who lived abroad. Without direct signal, the young padre who had been singing when we entered the room broke into one of Palo's songs of blood, bringing the drums with him:

Padre:	¡Mbele mbele,	Knife, knife,
	Mama quiere menga!	Mama wants blood!
	¡Mama quiere menga,	Mama wants blood,
	Mama quiere menga!	Mama wants blood!
Chorus:	¡Mbele mbele,	Knife, knife,
	Mama quiere menga!	Mama wants blood!
	¡Mama quiere menga,	Mama wants blood,
	Mama quiere menga!	Mama wants blood!
Padre:	¡Mbele mbele,	Knife, knife,
	Mama quiere menga!	Mama wants blood!
	¡Mama quiere menga,	Mama wants blood,
	Mama quiere menga!	Mama wants blood!
Chorus:	¡Mbele mbele,	Knife, knife,
	Mama quiere menga!	Mama wants blood!
	¡Mama quiere menga,	Mama wants blood,
	Mama quiere menga!	Mama wants blood![7]

This song, an enduring homage to the desire for blood in Palo, is also sung at the moment animals are sacrificed to prendas-ngangas-enquisos. It is a praise song for the knife, perhaps speaking in the knife's first-person voice, demanding blood. The song could also have been speaking in the prenda's voice, demanding blood from the knife. In either case, the knife was set apart from objectified reality by distinguishing it through song, which is Palo's sovereign speech par excellence. The song focused those gathered into the role of the knife and its power to deliver blood. The chorus repeated the lines over and over, and the crowd thickened. Virtudes was the only person in the room not initiated, and those who were reveled in the anticipation of her cutting. We sang: "Knife, knife, mama wants blood, mama wants blood!"

Something about sacrifice deserves mention here, something confounding, thrilling, but in the same moment obscene. The combination of emotions at times resembles the feeling one gets when confronted with the erotic. It is excitement based as much in anticipation as in fear and attraction, strong and incontrovertible, with palpable disgust felt from the violation of standing prohibitions. The whole of it is infused with that troublesome and inextricable devilishness that confuses moments of suffering and pleasure. In initiations, as the moment of cutting draws near and the ngueyo surrenders to the knife, those gathered push forward, extending their bodies in the direction of the wound. The crowd condenses, presses together, and increases its contact. Ossified potentials inherent in matter and relations begin to stir.

I had seen this condensation of bodies many times before, in sacrifices during Palo and Ocha/Santo rites. It could happen with only two or three people present, as when Isidra made offerings to her prenda Siete Rayos. Those offerings were always very private. With Teodoro's help and mine, an animal—in the case of Isidra's prendas-ngangas-enquisos a rooster or a duck—was chosen. The knife was fixed. As yayi she would draw the animal close to her, holding its head in one hand and the knife in the other, as one of us held the body. At this point tension would overtake us, as it does in any gathering where animals are given, drawing us into a bunched fist. It begins with the person wielding the sacrificial weapon and spreads to those present. The killer is tense and nervous when faced with the gravity of her task. She is intimately within the influence of her prenda's will and is working to increase it with volatile substances, such that if mistakes are made she could face unpredictable danger. Between the tension surrounding the letting of a victim's blood, and the tension surrounding the prenda awaiting it, stands a person, inconsequential and tiny when compared to the fields of force she seeks to unite with her knife and her creative will. Those gathered take up this strain; they understand the considerable risks involved in sacrificial killing and, unable to resist, draw closer.

When tatas and yayis have readied the animal, the electric freeze overtakes the killer and spreads to those present. The crowd sinks into stillness and slowly pushes forward; it gathers round. The lack of discretion as the moment draws near is disconcerting. Those who have not gotten their vantage point, who have not been able to find a way around the heads and backs and shoulders of the others, press closer yet. Hands reach forward and rest gently on the shoulders of others, who accept the touch. People stand on their tiptoes. The whole group creaks forward on its joints. Weight shifts on to others, who in turn have shifted. What was impossible a second before is suddenly permitted, desired. Bodies touch, heat transfers. We must see the knife, the blood, if possible get a look into the animal's eyes, to see the seizures that overtake its struggle against its killers. We must see its blood, bright red and warm, run over the prenda, make sure it is soaked, and lament the drops wasted on the floor. The goat kicks; roosters fight by trying to free their wings; the men holding them tense against their strength. We love to see this struggle, the sinews in the forearms of those fighting the animal's will to life. This struggle, which is a struggle for life and beautiful because of that, is praise to the dead and honors them as raw perseverance and the will to live exuberantly and free when faced with insurmountable adversity. When the animal finally relaxes in its killer's hands, the killers, too, relax. The animal ceases to move, and the blood stops flowing. The group relaxes, pivoting back onto its heels, released from the hold to which it had momentarily surrendered. Slowly the group draws back from the precipice it reached when witnessing the killing and the giving. There is a sigh of relief at the end of a sacrifice that can be felt as a withdrawal back into the conscience of expected bodies and relations, away from the trembling and boundless community of the collective effervescence that is Kalunga, the ambient dead. It is a return to the prosaic, the given, and the fateful.

This pressing, reaching, tensing, and touching is all the more urgent and automatic when the offering is the blood of a person. Normally, because of the heat and potential held in blood, animals are offered after people. Palo orders blood according to its force and potential, or, better said, its "heat." A person's blood is said to be the hottest, followed in order by that of turtles, sheep, ducks, and goats. Feathered animals, such as roosters, chickens, and pigeons, are of a different order. The blood of these animals is considered cooler and is used to "freshen" or "lift" the sacrifice after the giving of the hotter animals. Dogs, cats, nutrias, and other animals from the wilderness figure toward the hot end of this hierarchy. It is important, in Palo as in Ocha/Santo, that the cooler blood follow the hotter blood. Palo Briyumba holds that a prenda-nganga-enquiso that tastes the blood of an initiate without it being washed down by cooler blood will develop a taste for it, eventually hunting the initiate to a bloody death, unable to control its hunger. For this reason we were left dumbfounded to see the sacrifices already performed before Virtudes was led in. Later, Teodoro speculated that there was some purpose in this, that maybe Anselmo was trying to leave the taste of the young woman with Zarabanda Guinda Vela, so that its path to her might be clear. Isidra considered this extremely dangerous and foresaw nothing but ill coming from it.

No one restrained the initiate. Virtudes stood alone amid the Guinda Vela house, her soon-to-be sisters and brothers in Palo society. Her madrina led her another few inches forward, positioning her atop the firma Anselmo had made on the floor. Her madrina now stood behind her steadying the young woman by putting her hands on her shoulders. The rest of the crowd shrank back enough to give Tata Anselmo ample room to move around the young woman, such that a circle of exclusion soon surrounded her. I can remember feeling impressed by Virtudes, the way she stood, arms at her side, head slightly back, blindfolded in a room she had never seen, surrounded by people she could not see, soon to be cut and have her blood offered to a prenda she did not know.

It is at the point of being cut that new initiates are taken by the dead, if they are to be possessed at all. Isidra and Teo both said that fainting was not uncommon at this moment. The prenda takes to the initiate in a manner of its choosing. Value is placed on fainting and possession during initiation, because it portends a strong affinity between the prenda and the initiate. It is an honor to become the bearer of its force, its dog *[perro de prenda]*.[8] As a prenda-nganga-enquiso receives animal offerings with either more or less approval, so it receives initiates.

Tata Anselmo asked Virtudes to kneel, which she did with the help of her madrina. The madrina now held the candle with which she had led Virtudes into the room behind her initiate as Anselmo finally addressed the girl:

"What is your name?"
"Virtudes Salazár Mendosa."
"Who brings you here?"
"My godmother."
"What do you seek here, in the Mundo Nuevo Guinda Vela Kongo House?"
"Protection from my enemies. I seek knowledge, force, and peace."

Anselmo said nothing in reply and asked no further questions; he then bid Virtudes to stand again, which she did, holding her godmother's hand. Anselmo moved the razor close to her skin, contemplating the best place to begin. She was wearing a white top, low cut with thin straps, so the upper part of her chest and back and her shoulders were bare. Anselmo seemed almost bashful about touching her, as if he were extremely self-conscious about putting his hand on someone so vulnerable. The crowd tensed, expecting the cut. During my initiation I felt the same breathless pressure of the crowd around me, the presence of an enormous weight bearing down on the back of my neck as everyone gathered leaned forward to see the cutting. Like Virtudes, I had been blindfolded, and Isidra was determined that I not miss the cutting. She had designs on me becoming padre nganga in yet another initiation, and she thought it was essential that I see with my own eyes how the cutting is done. She pulled me to her, where she had a good vantage on the scene, just to the side of Virtudes, peeking past several heads.

Tata Anselmo motioned the candle near, and the madrina brought its glow close to Virtudes's skin. No two materials seem to share so little likeness as sharpened steel and a person's flesh, but with the glimmering of candlelight there was an affinity. The blade picked up the gold hues and the warm glow of her skin, and for a second there was an unexpected kinship between the two surfaces. Anselmo seemed to recognize this and respect it, as he appreciated the exquisite privilege of being allowed to wound another. The instant was illuminated in unstable blinking light, and the gathering was frozen in anticipation when the bakofula called out:

Bakofula:	¡Menga va correr!	Blood will run!
	¡Como tintorera,	Like dye,
	Menga va correr!	Blood will run!
	¡Eh! ¡Menga va correr!	Ah! Blood will run!
	¡Como guarilanga,	Like dye,
	Menga va correr!	Blood will run![9]
Chorus:	¡Menga va correr!	Blood will run!
	¡Como tintorera,	Like dye,
	Menga va correr!	Blood will run!
	¡Eh! ¡Menga va correr!	Ah! Blood will run!
	¡Como guarilanga,	Like dye,
	Menga va correr!	Blood will run!
Bakofula:	¡Menga va correr!	Blood will run!
	¡Como tintorera,	Like dye,
	Menga va correr!	Blood will run!
	¡Eh! ¡Menga va correr!	Ah! Blood will run!
	¡Como guarilanga,	Like dye,
	Menga va correr!	Blood will run!
Chorus:	¡Menga va correr!	Blood will run!
	¡Como tintorera,	Like dye,
	Menga va correr!	Blood will run!
	¡Eh! ¡Menga va correr!	Ah! Blood will run!
	¡Como guarilanga,	Like dye,
	Menga va correr!	Blood will run![10]

As we sang, verse after same verse, Anselmo made his initial cut. The first mark was on Virtudes's chest, below her collarbone on the right side. Where he needed the straps of her top drawn to the side, Tata Anselmo had her godmother do it so that his hands would be free to steady the knife. His first cut and the ones thereafter were unexpected in their motion.

There was not a drawing of the knife, and there was not a cutting movement, slice nor stab nor poke. To my surprise Anselmo placed the rounded corner of the straight blade near Virtudes and just touched the surface of her skin. It was nearly impossible to see the contact. He pulled the blade back and examined the wound, pinching Virtudes's skin and asking the madrina to hold the candle closer. We stared in dumbfounded fascination, the entire room still singing, calling for blood, frozen in tension, as we watched Anselmo's eyes for confirmation of the blood. As a tiny drop began to form, Anselmo's and the madrina's eyes were fixed to the spot, and he asked the madrina for her approval so that he could continue cutting. The singing rose in proportion to the wounds made, and the charge in the room redoubled. Inspired dread took the room by force, gripping us.

Having made the first wound, Anselmo now went about his work more quickly, but not with less care or skill. He cut her three more times on her right side, a hand's width below her collarbone on the broad plain of her chest. The wounds were vertical lines in a compact row, like slash marks in children's counting games, except that in this case the little cuts, none longer than a centimeter, were barely visible against her skin. Only when the blood began to flow was it possible to discern her wounds.

Anselmo moved to her left side then, to mark her chest again below the collarbone, followed by the madrina whose candle lit the rite. After making similar incisions there, he rounded her left shoulder where he pressed the razor first vertically, then horizontally, to make a simple equilateral cross, tiny. It is the crosses that are the most painful and if any scar is left from a rayamiento it would be the tiny points where the two lines of a cross intersect and a double cutting occurs. Moving around her left side, to her back, Tata Anselmo marked each shoulder blade in a manner similar to her chest, except with one horizontal cut under the row of vertical ones. Her right shoulder received a simple cross; it was the one wound we were able to see perfectly from where we stood. Small equilateral crosses were cut on the back of each hand, in the fleshy point between the index finger and the thumb. Her feet were cut with tiny equilateral crosses, as were the backs of her knees.

Some Palo houses mark more elaborate designs, and harsher, as I knew from my own experience, though it is rare for anyone to be permanently scarred from their initiation. I have seen scars from initiation markings on the shoulder blades and hands of some people, but they were the exception. After I was initiated, once I knew where to look for them, I studied the shoulders and upper backs of people around me at Palo feasts and I am still surprised with how few people showed any initiation marks. Once, on a bus back to Havana from Guanabacoa, I saw two santeras, godmother and god-daughter perhaps, with bold scars in the form of equilateral crosses on the backs of their hands, just where one is marked in Palo initiation. This was one of the few times I saw scars from a rayamiento. Among the Guinda Velas gathered for Virtudes's cutting no one had scars that I could see, a testament to Tata Anselmo's gentle hand.

They say that in the past the markings were deeper, meant to scar. Slaves brought from Africa sometimes bore scarifications on their chests, shoulders, and faces, which slave owners often used to identify them.[11] That Palo seeks a bond of similarity with slave ancestors by marking the body—and that some initiation cuttings and Palo firmas resemble scarifications— is worth probing. This is especially interesting if we keep in mind the idea that blood is a privileged substance because it establishes a loop of continuity linking the living and the dead. By the end of the twentieth century, however, the point in initiation cuttings was no longer to mark, except temporarily. If the idea before was to establish a link of sympathy between the living and the dead by scarring the body of the initiate, the point now was to gesture politely to that tradition and then establish a material link, one of contagion with the prenda-nganga-enquiso. Felt as ambiance and materialized as blood, cutting in Palo is meant to draw the fluid dead forward to pass it back through the prenda-nganga-enquiso, itself a multiplicity of the dead.

Once Anselmo had rounded Virtudes's back and began cutting there, with the madrina following immediately with the candle, the bakofula went to work, waiting by each wound for the little drops of blood to form, so that he could collect them on a small square of brown paper. This task was delicate, and one that required some dexterity, as the blood soon flowed faster than the bakofula could collect it. It would have been unspeakable to let a drop of it go to waste on the floor. As the little scoop made by the paper filled with blood, the bakofula would transfer it into a small gourd bowl. When Anselmo finished with the markings, he exchanged the knife for a similar piece of paper, to keep up with the flowing blood. At the height of the rite the three of them circled the candlelit Virtudes with respectful distance and deference, tending to her surrender as the chorus sang in praise of her running blood. When they finished, and their work was done quickly, the bakofula handed the gourd back to

Anselmo, who held it underneath the blade of the knife as he washed it clean with cane liquor. He let no blood go to waste. He did the same with the little scraps of paper, pouring aguardiente over their surfaces. He then crumpled the scraps and tucked them in the edges of Zarabanda Guinda Vela. Collecting the blood and washing the knife took a matter of seconds.

Anselmo packed the wounds. For this he used a combination of chamba and *ntufa*. Chamba, the ritual brew Isidra made and kept at home, heats and burns. It is used to rouse and lift the dead from idleness and lethargic repose. In people it provokes coughing, sneezing, and watering eyes. The concoction of cane alcohol, hot *guau-guau* peppers, ginger, cinnamon-like *palo malambo*, ground black and white pepper, garlic, animal remains and bones, among other ingredients, is used to agitate the dead and the living into becomings of one another. Tata Anselmo circled Virtudes, aspirating chamba onto her wounds. Chamba mixed with blood dripped down her chest, back, and arms. She did not flinch or cough, despite the considerable discomfort the blasts of chamba caused in the room. He circled her again, this time aspirating little sips of aguardiente onto her body and face, cooling her. Her madrina surrounded her in cigar smoke. Then, from another little gourd, Anselmo drew a pinch of ntufa, which he pressed onto each cut. Ntufa is a powder made primarily from ashes, cascarilla chalk, sawdust from powerful trees, and earth from an open grave, among other substances. As Anselmo moved around Virtudes with the ntufa her madrina followed, this time dripping candle wax over the cuts, smudging it with her fingers, and sealing the ntufa in her wounds. The packing of powdered substances into the cavities of objects is exemplar of most Palo craft, and in pressing the ntufa into her wounds Virtudes began to resemble charms and healing packets, and even the prendas themselves. Her white tank top and her white shorts were now stained in broad streaks of rust and gray where her clothes touched her wounds and muddy streams of ntufa and candle wax dripped down her chest and back. But she stood still and seemed calm. She didn't falter once, a testament to her resolve. But neither had Zarabanda claimed her in possession, not even a little bit. When he finished with the ntufa, Anselmo took the straight razor and without ceremony lifted a curl of hair from the crown of Virtudes's head and cut it at the base. Anselmo folded this into his hand. I did not see it again.

Virtudes was asked to kneel again. Time passes in bursts and starts, then lags, when one is blindfolded for any period of time. I was blindfolded for three quarters of an hour, which seemed double that under the circumstances. I remember feeling impatient with my handlers, wondering if their rite wasn't slipping into an unnecessary exercise of power. This is Palo, always pushing the edge of one's domination over another, testing submission and resistance to learn the limits of another's will. Palo loves the moment of insurrection and seeks it and studies it by pressing the subjugated. In my case, the ritual came to an end soon enough, as it did for Virtudes. She knelt. The cement ground beneath her feet was wet with spilled chamba and aguardiente, muddy with spilled ntufa. The chalk firma on which she stood was smudged and blurred, but its overall integrity remained.

Now Anselmo bent over and lifted the little Zarabanda in his hands. It was heavier than it appeared and quickly his bakofula came to his aid. Between them they raised it high above Virtudes's head. A young padre took that as his cue and broke into song:

Padre:	¡Levántalo, que no se te cae!	Lift it; don't let it fall!
	¡Levántalo, que no se te cae!	Lift it; don't let it fall!
Chorus:	¡Levántalo, que no se te cae!	Lift it; don't let it fall!
	¡Levántalo, que no se te cae!	Lift it; don't let it fall!
Padre:	¡Levántalo, que no se te cae!	Lift it; don't let it fall!
	¡Levántalo, que no se te cae!	Lift it; don't let it fall!
Chorus:	¡Levántalo, que no se te cae!	Lift it; don't let it fall!
	¡Levántalo, que no se te cae!	Lift it; don't let it fall!

Slowly Anselmo and his bakofula brought the prenda down level with Virtudes's face. She must have been able to smell its sour, meaty smell. It was less than an inch from her face. They knelt there momentarily, the Zarabanda immediately in front of her. She moved her head slightly from side to side, smelling, trying to get a fix on what was in front of her. After a few moments Anselmo asked her to extend her hands, where she found the prenda waiting. Slowly they let it come to rest in her palms. The two men spotted her, for it couldn't have been an easy weight for her to bear, kneeling with that awkward, sticky prenda in her hands.

Again, from what I knew, this made little sense. A prenda-nganga-enquiso should not be handled after it has been bathed in blood and left to cool with the offering of the roosters. Its repose must be inviolate. This is another reason the cutting of the ngueyo and the lifting of the prenda should happen before the animal sacrifices. It seemed out of order from the start.

As she held Zarabanda in her hand the song changed slightly:

Padre:	¡Aguántalo bien, que no se te cae!	Hold it now; don't let it fall!
	¡Aguántalo bien, Pa' que mañana no te pese!	Hold it now, So it won't weigh on you tomorrow!

Chorus:	¡Aguántalo bien, que no se te cae!	Hold it now; don't let it fall!
	¡Aguántalo bien,	Hold it now,
	Pa' que mañana no te pese!	So it won't weigh on you tomorrow!
Padre:	¡Aguántalo bien, que no se te cae!	Hold it now; don't let it fall!
	¡Aguántalo bien,	Hold it now,
	Pa' que mañana no te pese!	So it won't weigh on you tomorrow!
Chorus:	¡Aguántalo bien, que no se te cae!	Hold it now; don't let it fall!
	¡Aguántalo bien,	Hold it now,
	Pa' que mañana no te pese!	So it won't weigh on you tomorrow!

Little by little they brought its full weight to rest in her hands and she held it alone for a moment. Anselmo and his bakofula then brought the prenda right up to Virtudes's face for her to kiss. She did this, kissing Zarabanda Guinda Vela's bloody potbelly before they tilted it yet further and had her kiss the forehead of the sacrificed goat, which rested atop Zarabanda, its eyes clouded and cold. This final kiss, completely generous in its surrender and goodwill, was praise of the highest form for the dead animal.

Then they lifted Zarabanda and brought it to rest gently on the top of her head, where Anselmo had taken the tuft of hair. Again, they slowly released their grip and let the full weight of the little prenda rest on her head, holding it steady. This couldn't have been without discomfort, but at last she was relieved of this weight, and the prenda was brought back to face level. With no signal at all the lead padre changed again and the chorus followed:

Padre:	¡Jure, nganga, jure,	Swear to the nganga; swear,
	Jure, nganga, jure!	Swear to it; swear!
	¡Jure, nganga, jure,	Swear to the nganga; swear,
	Jure, nganga, jure!	Swear to it; swear!
	¡Como Nzambi a mi me manda,	Like Nzambi commands me,
	Jure, nganga, jure!	Swear to it; swear!
Chorus:	¡Jure, nganga, jure,	Swear to the nganga; swear
	Jure, nganga, jure!	Swear to it; swear!
	¡Jure, nganga, jure,	Swear to the nganga; swear,
	Jure, nganga, jure!	Swear to it, swear!

	¡Como Nzambi a mi me manda,	Like Nzambi commands me,
	¡Jure, nganga, jure!	Swear to it, swear!

They now received her as ngueyo, a sister of the house Munanso Congo Palo Monte Mundo Nuevo Guinda Vela. As she stood, the song changed to a celebratory high note:

Padre:	¡Semillero Congo,	From the Kongo nursery,
	Nace un gajo nuevo!	A new sapling is born!
	¡Semillero Congo,	From the Kongo nursery,
	Nace un gajo nani!	A twig is born!
Chorus:	¡Semillero Congo,	From the Kongo nursery,
	Nace un gajo nuevo!	A new sapling is born!
	¡Semillero Congo,	From the Kongo nursery,
	Nace un gajo nani!	A twig is born!
Padre:	¡Semillero Congo,	From the Kongo nursery,
	Nace un gajo nuevo!	A new sapling is born!
	¡Semillero Congo,	From the Kongo nursery,
	Nace un gajo nani!	A twig is born!
Chorus:	¡Semillero Congo,	From the Kongo nursery,
	Nace un gajo nuevo!	A new sapling is born!
	¡Semillero Congo,	From the Kongo nursery,
	Nace un gajo nani!	A twig is born!

Virtudes was back on her feet and we sang to her new status, her arrival into the light and confidence of Palo society. Anselmo asked her to remove her blindfold herself. What Virtudes saw as she pulled off the wrap was the brightness of a candle's flame very close to her face. Her madrina had the candle there, centimeters from her eyes. Behind the candle's flame Anselmo held a crucifix, pulled from one of the prendas on the floor. In my own initiation it was hard to look at both at once, with the plane of focus shifting back and forth between the flame and the blood-sprinkled Christ. With that sight to behold, confusing to me to this day, Anselmo said to her, as Teodoro had said to me: "*Acabas de jurar diablo.*" He said, "You've just sworn to the devil."

I hadn't known what to say either; I was simply relieved the initiation was over. Virtudes was embraced by her madrina and then by Anselmo and was then given the task of offering a drink of aguardiente to all present, which she did with grace. The little half gourd which had held her blood was put in one hand and a bottle of aguardiente in the other. Slowly she moved among us, handing us the gourd with hands crossed one over the other and we received it with crossed hands, too. As she approached we greeted her ritually, now receiving her as an initiate: "Sala, Malekun!" And she replied, "Malekun, Sala!"[12] It was humbling to be faced with her: tired, shaken, dirty, yet confident in her new relationship to Zarabanda Guinda Vela, the dead, and all of us. She moved through the society unassumingly, yet sure of herself. It was hard to look into her eyes, into her grace under duress, her dignity after the abjection of her ordeal. And so she went through the crowd, bloody, dirty, and disoriented, but all the same surprisingly steady.

We didn't stay long after the rayamiento was finished. The Room quickly emptied as we all sought the freshness of the night outside. Virtudes was led out of The Room to the patio, where she ritually greeted the growing moon, which had risen while we were inside. She was then led by Tata Anslemo and her madrina through the living room and past her gathered well wishers, across the street where she greeted the cemetery at its gate. She was then free to mingle with the others, who had moved the drums into the living room and were dancing and singing Palo there. Others who were not allowed into The Room now joined the rest, and a celebration of Virtudes's addition to the house was soon under way. Isidra, not having shaken her displeasure with the ceremony, was sure there would be no possession come from the celebration, evidence, she said, that the dead were displeased.

Before we left I talked with Virtudes and learned what brought her to be initiated. She worked in a hotel, in the low ranks of management, but was somehow in contact with dollars. Others in the hotel resented her for her good fortune, and webs of intrigue and ill will soon surrounded her. She was on the verge of losing her job, accused of stealing money and sharing it with a superior, with whom she was rumored to be having an affair. Her madrina had advised her that the only way to counter the coming misfortune was to enter Ocha/Santo, but first through Palo. Ocha/Santo would steady her, and Palo would counter her enemies. It is best to join a Palo society of affliction before committing one's fate to an Ocha/Santo sovereign. I would have liked to talk to her longer, but Virtudes was the party's guest of honor, being urged to dance and greet those who didn't witness her rayamiento. She invited us back for the last phase of her initiation the next day, when the sacrificed animals would be served for lunch and perhaps she would be taken by the Kongo dead.

PART III

Prendas-Ngangas-Enquisos

．　　．　　．　　．　　．

The Quita Manaquita Briyumba Congo house of Guanabacoa was, until Emilio O'Farril died in 1995, a thriving society of affliction. Like Nkita healing societies in nineteenth-century Kongo, it successfully integrated the dead and the living to address crises of fate experienced by its members. At the heart of the Quita Manaquita Briyumba Congo praise house were Emilio and Teodoro's prendas-ngangas-enquisos, which effectively, and literally, grounded encounters with the dead through their astonishing capacity to condense and direct the ever-fluid potential of Kalunga, el muerto, the ambient dead. The dead and the living circulate through prendas-ngangas-enquisos, which collect social force to dissipate it and make anew what is fixed and given. Even as the house declined, the prendas-ngangas-enquisos exerted forceful influence on Teodoro and, by extension, on its members.

Despite what can only be described as their agency within a Palo house, prendas-ngangas-enquisos are the most elaborate production of Palo craft, and the pages that follow concern the art of their making (chapters 11 and 12). Like others who have treated their composition, I have focused considerable attention on the matter collected in a Cuban-Kongo cauldron. Still, what I have attempted to narrate in the pages that follow is how this matter is transformed into fatefully influential substances by means of strategic and necessarily contentious turnings of the dead in seemingly insignificant allusions and insinuations (chapters 13 and 14).

Prendas-ngangas-enquisos are inspired elaborations of matter—they are complex and singular efforts to actualize Kalunga, el muerto, the ambient dead (chapter 15). Their inspiration, like most everything in Palo, owes to the creative spark that crossed the Atlantic with BaKongo and other central African peoples. Prendas-ngangas-enquisos are uniquely Cuban forms of Kongo minkisi, which are materializations of the influence of the dead that defined, in the nineteenth century and today, Kongo notions of clair-voyance, causality, and self-definition. Kongo minkisi are powerful forms of the dead, synonymous with curing *and* affliction, and traditionally occupy the heart of Kongo healing societies. Significant aesthetic, material, and conceptual affinities shared by prendas-ngangas-enquisos and Kongo minkisi will become evident throughout the chapters that follow, just as will the recombinant, distinctly Cuban shape of Palo itself.

11. Lucero Mundo

Early 2000 saw an initiation into the hierarchy of padre nganga on the horizon. At first it was a suggestion, then in February a possibility. Initiations into the hierarchy of madre or padre are rare and happen with much more deliberation than rayamientos like Virtudes' as ngueyo. This is not to say that initiations into the code of padre or madre do not happen without urgency; they can, but they are generally more negotiable in their time frame. Among other reasons, an initiation as madre or padre nganga means a person will be receiving her or his own prenda-nganga-enquiso, and gathering the materials is no easy task. The man who was to be initiated was a longtime ngueyo in the Quita Manaquita society, and a friend of Teodoro's. His name, too, was Teodoro, but we knew him by Tocayo, which in Spanish designates a friend or acquaintance with whom one shares a proper name. Teodoro Tocayo had almost been initiated at the beginning of the year, when I went from ngueyo to padre nganga, but hesitated at the last minute because he was unable to gather some of the materials for what would be his first prenda, a Zarabanda. Since then, many things in his life had gone wrong, and it was understood by everyone that Emilio's Zarabanda had grown impatient with his hesitation to become one of the Manaquita padres. The prenda had begun to withdraw its protection and was slowly leaving him to a threatening fate. Ill-meaning dead sent by his enemies gathered near Tocayo, and until he received his own Zarabanda he would face open peril.

Teodoro Tocayo knew that Isidra had a good collection of materials to make prendas-ngangas-enquisos left over from my own initiation as padre. Almost immediately from that day, where he was present but did not participate, he began to suggest that she have Teodoro make her one of several prendas-ngangas-enquisos she felt she needed and that afterward she should give him what remained of her materials. She was skeptical at first, but

Tocayo had impressed her with his discipline and hard work for Teodoro in the Manaquita house. For quite a while Tocayo had apprenticed himself to Teodoro to learn what he could about handling prendas-ngangas-enquisos and about Palo craft. I liked Tocayo and knew that without Isidra's help he would not manage to have his Zarabanda made for a long time. What he mostly needed were animal remains and feathers that were difficult to obtain, either because they involved traveling to the countryside or were rare and expensive in Palo underground markets. Since most of Isidra's materials had been gathered in her hometown of Sierra Morena a few months back in preparation for my own initiation, a trip I had financed, I felt I had some say over the use of the materials.

Eventually, Tocayo's pleas convinced Isidra, and she contracted Teodoro to help her make not one, but two prendas-ngangas-enquisos: a Lucero Mundo, which she felt I needed in addition to the Siete Rayos I had received as padre, and a Mama Chola Nkengue, for herself. In the midst of her negotiation with Teodoro over exactly what his role would be in making the prendas-ngangas-enquisos, they decided to also refurbish two of her existing ones.

For the work Isidra promised the standard rights [derechos] of the Manaquita house. Derechos are fees paid to those who teach and perform Palo and Ocha/Santo work, and it is common wisdom that derechos in Palo are more reasonable than those charged in Ocha/Santo. Isidra knew very well what Emilio's derechos had been, and when Teodoro insisted on inflating the price she talked him down. She probably could have badgered him to do the work for free, but Isidra understood that one *must* pay a derecho by virtue of Palo and Ocha/Santo rules. Teo, for his part, saw that around him healers were asking exorbitant fees for their services and he wanted to join the trend. He eventually accepted the established Manaquita derechos.

A tremendous amount of work had now been agreed to, because making a single prenda-nganga-enquiso can take many days. To do the job well, it should be done with all the materials on hand, and with good help. Some of the materials used in making prendas-ngangas-enquisos are extremely volatile and unpredictable versions of the dead, so it is better if one does not sit around half made for days. It should be "fed" (sacrificed to) within a day of its completion. Isidra had grave doubts about Teodoro doing so much work with conscientious discipline, and she doubted that she or I would be able to keep him focused as his endurance flagged. In due course, she decided to approach Teodoro's uncle, Pedro, who was Emilio's half brother who had helped build the Manaquita praise house. Pedro was Isidra's friend independent of her relationship with Teodoro. He harbored not a little resentment against Teodoro for what had become of the Quita Manaquita house, and except for certain rites having specifically to do with caring for Emilio's Zarabanda he no longer worked Palo with his nephew. He decided to join us nonetheless, because he liked Isidra a lot and agreed with her that too many things could go wrong with a project that involved so many prendas. He knew that careless mistakes with materials, and slips of the tongue, could have ill-fated, irremediable consequences. His derecho as Quita Manaquita tata, of course, would be paid. At eighty years old, Pedro called himself *la garantía*, the guarantee. When we finally started working he said, "When the dead are brought into your hands, you must know the way— that is what old people are for."

A week later the four of us—Isidra, Teodoro, Pedro and I—were squatting on low benches in the spare room by Isidra's living room. In preparation for our work she had emptied the room of all its furniture and had cleansed it with a simple rite she knew from Sierra Morena. Teodoro Tocayo was absent. Until one is initiated as madre or padre, Kongo Law prohibits participation in making prendas-ngangas-enquisos. It is one of the great agonies of Palo that madres and padres can wait years to see, or never know, how their prenda-nganga-enquiso was made. To know many of the secrets of his prenda-nganga-enquiso, Tocayo would have to continue in Teo's service until he was invited to participate in the making of a prenda-nganga-enquiso for another initiate or could afford to have another made for himself.

Our backs already ached from bending over the floor. We were barefoot; Palo must be worked barefoot. High above us flickered a single florescent bulb that spent its last hours giving a dim blue light to our work. The still hour of the night threatened to swallow the glow of the fading lamp, and its light went only as far as the green walls before fading passively into the gloom of the corners. As our work advanced and the floor became muddy with earth and water our little gathering acquired a submerged feeling, as if our work were taking place at the bottom of a murky water hole.

We were up to our knees in the countless materials that go into a prenda-nganga-enquiso: stakes of wood cut from trees and different bushes; dirt of many textures, colors, and provenance; and a wide array of water samples of varied origins—a river, the ocean, pools in streams, and the tap. The whole floor was a slurry of water and other materials. Colored powders, spilled here and there, streaked the muddy floor with splotches of yellow, red, and blue. Little stones from a riverbed in Sierra Morena, railroad spikes, horseshoes, mosses of different sorts, seaweed, loose cotton, and little bottles of mercury added to the confusion. Around us were feathers and skulls from different birds and animals, bunches of herbs and weeds, coins, minute pieces of silver and gold. There were other marvelous ingredients, including a humming-bird's nest complete with the desiccated bird and its blue eggs. Yet more items crowded our feet, too many to mention. They were organized into countless plastic shopping bags we bought a few weeks back from the pensioners who sell odds and ends on the sidewalk market around Cuatro Caminos. The pensioners fence the bags for employees who steal them from the hard-currency "shopping" stores. Though most of the materials had come from Sierra Morena, many things we had found along with the bags in the underground market. These white bags now spilled their contents haphazardly across the room, or reached up from the floor with mouths agape, like blooming, dying calla lilies.

Between our bare feet we found room for a candle, and we thanked our dead that it burned as long as it did. It was tall and caramel-colored, made from beeswax by an elderly santera who lived down the block from Pedro in Santo Suarez. Pedro had brought four of them for our work, and because Isidra prized them so much I had also pedaled out to Santo Suarez one after-noon so that we would have many more. The woman who made them was welcoming to strangers like me. Her candles were clean and smelled sweet and had a thick flat wick made from finely braided twine. Other candles on the illicit market—and there were few other candles available in Havana—were infamous little sticks of paraffin loaded with pockets of water from sloppy craftsmanship. They were sure to burn quickly, or worse, sputter and go out when they were most needed.

We welcomed that candle's certain light, because we needed it to illumi-nate our work, as much in the room where we were working as among the dead that surrounded and saturated us. It helped us see around our feet, but the candle's principal task was to flicker into the darkness of the dead, to light our way. Its flame lit a halo around us that pushed into Kalunga with all of the sweet will and industrious consistency of the bees and of the san-tera that had produced it. As it pushed back the anonymous, ambient dead, its ring of light called our responsive dead and let them near us unhin-dered.

Many hostile powers among the dead are drawn to prenda making, in which large amounts of matter suffused by the dead are collected. Making them is about preventing these densities from dissipating, then extracting their force and concentrating them in different combinations. Kalunga condenses and knots in substances agglutinated into a prenda-nganga-enquiso, which becomes a point of attraction for the responsive dead amid the otherwise generic flows of Kalunga. In this, otherwise unknown or indeterminate forces among the dead insinuate themselves around those making prendas-ngangas-enquisos, and they are feared.

The little candle was indispensable against such insinuation. Palo should never be worked without a candle burning. As we began our work we sang to the candle, and when our singing flagged, days into our work, which it should never do, we sang to the candle, again. It's always correct to praise the candle that lights your work in Palo, so we took turns, late into the night:

Pedro:	Pemba carile, 'lumbra yo,	I light the realm of the dead,
	Pemba carile, 'lumbra yo-o,	I light the devil's realm,
	'Lumbra pemba la buena nfinda.	Light the good fields of the dead.
	¡'Lumbra yo!	I light!
Chorus:	Pemba carile, 'lumbra yo,	I light the realm of the dead,
	Pemba carile, 'lumbra yo-o,	I light the devil's realm,
	'Lumbra pemba la buena nfinda.	Light the good fields of the dead.
	¡'Lumbra yo!	I light!
Pedro:	Pemba carile, 'lumbra yo,	I light the realm of the dead,
	Pemba carile, 'lumbra yo-o,	I light the devil's realm,
	'Lumbra pemba to' lo nfumbe.	Light all the dead.
	¡'Lumbra yo!	I light!
Chorus:	Pemba carile, 'lumbra yo,	I light the realm of the dead,
	Pemba carile, 'lumbra yo-o,	I light the devil's realm,
	'Lumbra pemba to' lo nfumbe.	Light all the dead.
	¡'Lumbra yo!	I light!

The song went on for seemingly infinite verses, the third line being subject to improvisation. We passed the song back and forth in call and response, switching leads. Sometimes ten or more minutes could pass with only slight variations in the words, depending on the improvisational energy of each caller. Our voices were raw from singing without rest, and when we faltered and would go a minute or two in silence, Pedro would insist and sing again, starting a verse and then signaling us to carry on.

Pedro, Teodoro, and Isidra agreed the first prenda-nganga-enquiso should be the Lucero Mundo for me. Shadows of the dead pressed near us and, in keeping with its name, Lucero would help us in our passage through Kalunga's abyssal expanse. Lucero is Spanish for morning star, astral light, bright and blue. Lucero hangs on the horizon, a companion through the night, and the promise of a new day waiting. Lucero is gendered masculine, though this is the attenuated masculinity of a rambunctious kid, with whom he is often compared. An intrepid and tricky child, bright as a star, shines its lantern into the opaque flows of Kalunga and goes ahead. Venturing forth to work Palo among the dead without first securing Lucero's escort is so reckless an enterprise that it is hardly ever done. The nameless, unsigned flows of Kalunga can lead to indecipherable reaches of fear and despair. Kalunga is an unlimited mass, ever fading into anonymous planes that intersect without signal. It is a liquid forest without known routes, and those that are discerned shift suddenly and change direction, or disappear, leaving those working Palo craft lost among unrecognizable dead. Lucero is a skilled navigator of such daunting reaches, and it would help us to see and move through them.

There were other reasons for starting with Lucero, not the least of which was that this prenda-nganga-enquiso likes to be first in receiving the care of its keepers. Lucero can be capricious and vengeful if he does not feel that his claims to being first are respected. The project of making two prendas-ngangas-enquisos from scratch and refurbishing two others involved a prolonged dissolution of the lines that distinguished us from Kalunga. Such an intimacy with the dead, felt as immersion, would eventually overcome our bodies and wills. To spurn Lucero by not having him be the first to emerge made us vulnerable to Lucero's attack once he did emerge to find himself second, or third, among our creations.

In many ways, Lucero is like the Ocha/Santo sovereign Eleguá, with whom the prenda-nganga-enquiso shares a fellowship and potential in the Laws of Palo and Ocha/Santo. Eleguá insists on being paid homage first among Ocha/Santo's sovereigns. Eleguá claims this tribute by virtue of being a sovereign of the forest and especially for having exclusive power and presence over its roads, paths, routes, and crossings. Without him, there is no getting anywhere in the many kingdoms of Ocha/Santo. Eleguá, furthermore, rules over chance and fortune, just like Lucero mitigates debt. Both Lucero and Eleguá are perceived as children, full of caprice, tricks, and playful ill will if spurned. They both like to fool around and can be aggressive.

Appeals are made to Lucero when one's fate seems to be veering into uncertain terrain or when one is having trouble moving from one place to another. The cases of misfortune that come before Lucero are myriad. People hoping to leave Cuba, or to trade apartments, or to be promoted, come to Lucero for a cure to their misfortune. They are the same ones who go to Eleguá. Teo, whose Lucero was famous in his neighborhood and around Guanabacoa for getting people unstuck and moving, was the person to help get them out of Cuba, freed from the interminable condition of stasis and the imposed political climate. Lucero also kept people from the hands of the police or got them out of legal trouble.

This means that Lucero must be handled cautiously. Lucero loves a trick, and his interpretation of any deal will always be in his favor. Lucero likes to twist arrangements around a pun, or a possible misunderstanding of words, and delights in distorting sounds and connotations. Lucero defends these interpretations with severe certainty, and it is always best to settle in his terms. This the keeper of a Lucero knows, for such lessons are learned the hard way. When dealing with Lucero, one should always plan on unforeseen contingencies, for clauses in a deal that reveal themselves only days or weeks later. It is only then that some inexplicable event prompts one to return to Lucero and seek his aid once more. Like all prendas-ngangas-enquisos, Lucero likes to wrap his keeper in knots of obligation, especially when feeling neglected. Pedro said that a disrespected Lucero can kill its keeper—with an accident at a street crossing, for example. Lucero sends warnings, too, if he is upset, causing a brick or chunk of wood to fall as one passes below or by breaking a bone in his keeper's body by causing her to trip in the forest or on the street. Lucero, like a child with a strong will, is powerful and capricious and must be satisfied in excess for fear that he will act out. Pedro hardly distinguished Lucero from a rowdy goat, which not by coincidence is Lucero's choice feast animal. Lucero is just as stubborn, strong, and likely to escape from its handler's grasp.

Lucero, like all prendas-ngangas-enquisos, emerges from the indifferent flows of Kalunga. Lucero's version of this indifference takes the shape of paradoxical yet well-established couplings: gatekeeper and trickster, indispensable guide and temperamental ally. This is consistent with Palo aesthetics, to link the opening of fate and the very possibility of transformation to an inconsistent and pernicious power, which is valued precisely because of its indeterminate outcomes. In our work to bring Lucero out of Kalunga and into our hands, we would never lose sight of this.

12.   The Cauldron

We found the cauldron for Lucero by a circuitous route, though hardly an unexpected one, considering we were looking for Palo materials. Good cauldrons were hard to find, and the dingy craft fairs that clung to the empty storefronts along Havana's old commercial strips—Monte, Belascoaín, Galeano—sold shoddy ones, like all the Palo and Ocha/Santo wares at such venues.

Containers for prendas-ngangas-enquisos are of two types: steel cauldrons and clay urns. Pedro said that Siete Rayos, which uses a steel cauldron, used to be made with a clay pot, but because it is so sought after this prenda-nganga-enquiso grows quickly and often burst its sides.[1] Today in Havana, the prendas-ngangas-enquisos built into clay are Tiembla Tierra, Madre Lango, Mama Chola, and Centella Ndoki. What distinguishes this group is that although each has different powers and realms of action, each is gendered feminine. This does not make them any less powerful or reliable than Siete Rayos, Zarabanda, or Lucero, which are masculine and built into iron. The division is rather a comment on the frequency of their use and the impression of force they impose on those who confront them. Palo, which is patriarchal, does not accord the feminine prendas-ngangas-enquisos any less power. Clay, despite its fragility, is accorded great regard because of its kinship with the earth and therefore with the dead.

The vessel that receives and holds a prenda-nganga-enquiso's contents is also its limit among the living. Once constituted, the charge of indeterminacy and unspecified transformation that is the heart of all prendas-ngangas-enquisos seeks to flow and spread, and a sound cauldron is the only protection against this potentially dangerous agglomeration of the dead. No less important, the vessel chosen becomes the aesthetic base of what will soon be exquisitely intimidating and beautiful. Paleros and paleras are sensitive to the appearance of their prendas-ngangas-enquisos. A good part of Palo craft involves deliberate, if spontaneous, fashioning to achieve specific visual effects. The work of creating such effects with additions of blood, feathers, animal skulls, and packets of powerful substances goes on for years, for the life of a palera or palero, and a good cauldron or urn is the anchor of one's work in blood, bones, earth, and sticks. The finest materials should go into it, and stories of how they are acquired, from where and from whom, become part of each prenda-nganga-enquiso's history and prestige. It's not unusual to hear of paleros and paleras traveling distances to collect pieces and materials for their prendas, or of placing things dear to them in the cauldrons, never to be recovered. The fact that there are so few items with any grace on Havana's meager Palo markets makes the effort to acquire a good vessel, whether a cauldron or an urn, noteworthy and poignant.

The problem of poor wares available for working Palo in Havana was a problem at the turn of the century and parallels the domestic boom in Ocha/Santo and Palo participation. To address it, Isidra tapped a web of underground merchants who practiced Palo, unlike vendors in the craft markets or around the Cuatro Caminos market. The underground traders have no permit from the government to peddle their goods, nor do they seek one. They work out of their houses and specialize in the materials of Palo craft, many of which are compatible with those of Ocha/Santo. These practitioner/merchants buy their goods from intermediaries or directly from producers who specialize in items made or gathered in the countryside. The practitioner merchants keep irregular hours and are prone to close without notice due to inspections by the police, who are always on the lookout for those trafficking in contraband such as animal remains, gunpowder, and mercury. Isidra's labors with the dead were made more difficult because she relied on these sellers and producers exclusively, but her Palo ethic determined that she use only items made and gathered by hand, one by one.

Isidra's most trusted merchant was Juan, and when we found the cauldron for Lucero he was the conduit. One night a friend of Isidra's came calling with an urgent problem, and I was dispatched on my bike to find herbs and candles. The Cuatro Caminos market, which was close to Isidra's, was closed, and going as far as Santo Suarez to see the elderly santera with the beeswax candles was untenable. Isidra then sent me toward the port. Crossing Monte just where it becomes Calzada del Cerro, I ended up near Desamparados, where Juan had his shop. That evening his place was backlit in the dusk, his television antenna tangled up and listing along with the hulks of ships and cranes in the harbor's backwaters. The morning star, Lucero, was rising in the blue-black sky.

Juan was congenial and sweet, and always a little drunk. He was a young man who had taken over his mother's business and he prided himself on knowing his clients. He had good prices on plants and herbs, which were usually fresher than in other places. There is much concern these days among paleras and santeras about the price and quality of the materials that go into their craft. Juan's little place was recommended among serious folks, which meant he had good products and reasonable prices. But that evening chance had it that Juan had sold the last of his candles. Juan had seen me in his shop before and as I turned to leave asked me if I worked with Isidra. When I replied that I did he smiled softly as was his style, then gave me directions to another shop, in Atarés, where I should ask for Dagoberto.

Atarés is one of Havana's most neglected and notorious neighborhoods. Along with neighborhoods like Colón and Los Citios in Centro Habana, it is feared as a zone of irrepressible blackness and danger by those in more luxurious, predominantly white neighborhoods. I knew Atarés from attending Ocha/Santo feasts there with Isidra, but in the dark its broken streets were treacherous on a bike. Squeezed between the Calzada del Cerro and the port, Atarés is a bewildering collection of crumbling buildings, labyrinthine alleys, street-corner garbage piles, and abandoned lots. It stands out as a zone of neglect on the part of the Revolution. In the year 2000, all services lagged behind the more influential neighborhoods of the city.[2]

Dagoberto's place was tucked down a side street that nuzzled the depths of the port. Among the generalized dilapidation his stand hardly stood out. It occupied an empty lot strewn with countless materials that he kept fenced and locked. There were scattered piles of earth and bricks, stacks of wood, lengths of train rail, canvas bags filled with ash, scattered coconuts and their husks, pieces of rusting metal, and piles of horseshoes and railroad spikes. Coils of chain of different thickness, from sections of dog leash to links from a ship's anchor line, lay around his makeshift stand, which squatted near the front of the lot. The stand had a little roof over a table of herbs that he kept covered with moist burlap. From the rafters hung dried gourds, dried herbs, and countless lengths of string, like the beard of a Balinese demon. Along the back of the little stand was a set of cubbyholes where he organized his selection of sticks for Palo craft. In cabinets he kept the animal bones and carcasses that lend so much to prendas-ngangas-enquisos and other works of Palo manufacture. The feathers of hawks and vultures, owls and woodpeckers, were tucked here and there between posts and rafters.

Dagoberto could be reached at any hour of day or night. He had connected his ground-level apartment, which was contiguous to the lot where he kept his stand, by hammering a door through the wall. He was especially brazen in his trade, as his whole lot could have been confiscated by the state for countless contraband violations. To conduct his business in Palo wares in plain view of the street was a display of audacity unthinkable a decade earlier. But in Havana at the turn of the century little pockets of autonomous action managed to evade the overbearing will of the Revolution. Dagoberto could have kept inspectors and police for blocks around subdued with bribes and threats of sorcery. More likely, however, I expect he counted many among the police as his clients and discounted their wares and services.

Dagoberto was having a cigarette in the doorway of his apartment when I pedaled up. He was in his early fifties, a fit man, muscular, wearing only shorts and rubber sandals. As he came over I could see that the curly gray hair all over his body covered smudgy blue tattoos on his arms, chest, and back. He had a bold mustache, and under his bushy brows were smart attentive eyes. He unlocked the gate and let me pass under the shadow of his stand, where he lit a small oil lamp.

In the dim light I could see that his selection of materials, especially his collection of animal remains, showed Dagoberto to be knowledgeable about Palo. He sold only whole, desiccated animals with their organs intact. The prized brains, hearts, and other viscera are used in Palo for a variety of works to heal and harm. Dagoberto refused to sell anything that was preserved in formaldehyde, as bird carcasses often were in some of the shops near the Cuatro Caminos market. The chemistry tainted the animal's flesh, and Teodoro and Isidra considered such animals unsuitable for working Palo because the dead that infused them would be diminished or distorted. Dagoberto appeared to share their understandings of Kalunga as permeating the plants and animals of the forest, and he was skilled at handling materials such that their impression of force would only be enhanced.

He was short on candles, and went into his apartment for more. As I waited I spotted the little red cauldron at the very edge of the ring of light in which I stood. It was among five or six cauldrons that Dagoberto had in a pile. Most of his cauldrons were of the type cut from random steel tanks—air or fuel tanks taken from heavy trucks and other machinery, or stolen propane tanks that were newly in circulation in Havana at the time. As Soviet-era equipment continues its decline into ruin, its remains are recycled in ways imaginable only under the extreme economic duress of the Cuban economy in the 1990s. The air and fuel tanks from the underbelly of heavy trucks were never designed to become receptacles for intense condensations of the dead, but they are, in fact, ideal for this use. One fuel tank could be cut into two cauldrons, each about the size of a pail, or bigger. A little trio of legs of fine iron rebar was then welded to the bottom of each. This work requires some care, as the cauldron, packed with the contents of a prenda-nganga-enquiso, would weigh substantially. To have a prenda crush its improvised legs would be a disaster for its keeper.

Looking them over, even Dagoberto's bad cauldrons were good, of rare sizes and careful fashioning. But the little cauldron stood out. He returned with the candles, and I asked to put a small deposit on it, hoping he would hold it a few days. He looked me over, clearly wondering about my interest in the item. "*¡Ta linda la cazuelita!*" he said. "It is a lovely little cauldron." It weighed more than the others, though it was smaller. It had been cast rather than welded and its potentials seemed unbreakable because there was no seam and no doubt, therefore, that it could contain the powers of the dead. It had a little spout and three little rounded nubs for feet that emerged seamlessly from its bulging belly and on which it balanced nicely. "Balance is important," said Dagoberto. "Have you ever seen one tip over? I've been working on this one for a while. It used to belong to an old tata." When I asked him more about it he turned reticent.

I returned to Dagoberto's as soon as I could with Isidra, though it took several days. I didn't expect to see the cauldron again, but Dagoberto had set it aside. Isidra was an expert haggler, and as we came close to closing on a price a tall man emerged from the backdrop of materials that cluttered the lot. He had arrived as I was leaving Dagoberto's the night I spotted the cauldron, but on that occasion he kept to himself. I do not remember if he or Isidra first struck up the conversation.

"My name is Enrique Estévez Jiménez. I'm from Oriente." He said it with confidence, as if we should recognize his name. Oriente is Cuba's east and sometimes refers specifically to the city of Santiago, much like Havana often stands for Cuba's west. But Oriente is larger and comprises the provinces of Santiago, Holguín, Granma, and Guantanamo. It is a largely rural region and home of the Sierra Maestra, site of irremediable rural poverty and also the birthplace of the guerrilla insurrection that brought the Revolution to power. Oriente, in the imagination of the capital, figures as a region of backward rural life and untamed mountain forces. Fidel, for example, is from Oriente, and this fact is often cited as evidence of the unpredictable and life-altering forces that emerge from there.[3]

Isidra didn't answer Enrique and instead looked insistently at Dagoberto, looking to close the deal. But Enrique Estévez Jiménez went on, "I'm a *kimbisero,* and you?" Practitioners of Palo Kimbisa are rare these days in Havana and, other than from Lydia Cabrera's book on the topic, little is known about this branch of Palo practice.[4] Isidra held to the popular opinion that Palo Kimbisa was "made up," the invention of a man named Andres Petit, who wanted to craft a mode of contact with the dead that integrated the west African inspirations that underlie Ocha/Santo together with the central African inspirations that energize Palo. He wanted to achieve this combination by fusing these two forms of African knowledge with the spiritist doctrine of Alan Kardec, as well as with Catholic mysticism. The project became La Regla de Kimbisa Santo Cristo del Buen Viaje, or Palo Kimbisa. According to Teodoro, few kimbiseros remain except in Oriente, where Palo and Espiritismo mix intensely into what is called Palo Cruzado. Teodoro knew kimbiseros and he knew their music, but in general he distrusted them and considered them, in his words, "not Kongo enough."

Isidra reacted negatively to all but a very few people who were more powerful than her in terms of Palo or Ocha/Santo, Tata Emilio, perhaps, having been the last one to whom she submitted entirely. In encounters with strangers, Isidra relied on the dead for gathering an impression of a person, and in the case of the kimbisero from Oriente, the dead warned her off.

Enrique Estévez Jiménez could see her apprehension and grinned, then shifted his weight onto one of the poles of Dagoberto's stand. He fixed his eyes on the little kettle as he began to speak. "A cauldron like that is too much to give a new initiate, too strong. Madrina, you'll be setting him down the path alone. He'll lose control. It was used before. Prendas and paleros do not always get along, right? One mustn't get into things too quickly." Then he turned to me, "You know how to handle a prenda that gets out of control, right? Haven't you been told? There are dangers in this little pot. Hasn't your madrina pointed them out?"

He was a man of maybe fifty, but his eyes were mischievous and fast and gave the impression of a much younger person. He had cinnamon skin, angular features, and wavy black hair. His mouth was wide like a horse. Two golden front teeth were a gate for his unruly tongue, which whipped exaggeratedly about, bested only by his eyes as props for accenting his speech. He was sarcastic, but in a humorous way that let him get away with a good deal of disrespect. It was evident that he was practiced at creating around himself the impression of mystery.

What he suggested could have been true. It is not uncommon for prendas and those who keep them to have contentious, even violent, relationships.

This is among the many important lessons one learns before acceding to receive a prenda-nganga-enquiso and become madre or padre nganga. Teodoro's life was evidence of this, and Isidra often cited Teodoro as a lesson in the gravity of Palo commitments. In exposing me to Teodoro she had sought a very knowledgeable person who at the same time served to show the consequences of neglecting one's duties to a prenda in one's care: Teo showed that poor relations with one's prenda could bode badly and possibly be disastrous. And when Isidra talked about repercussions for revealing Palo's secrets, which she did from time to time, the consequences she referred to were directed not by members of a Palo house but by prendas themselves. She would say "They'll deal with you; they'll carry you to the grave. Don't betray them." It was not only the kimbisero from Oriente who implied that this cauldron might be too powerful.

He made much of the little cauldron and its potential for mischief. "The stronger the cauldron," he said, "the stronger the prenda, the more difficult it is to control. Look at this little cauldron, the weight of it! Its legs! What kind of enquiso was it before? Siete Rayos, Zarabanda, or Judía. . . ." His voice trailed off at the mention of things Jewish in Palo. "And once you charge it! Good materials seek replenishment and are costly these days." With that he shot his eyes at Dagoberto, then smiled and flicked his tongue in a grotesque barb about his prices. "And Dago won't be here forever. A powerful prenda nganga asks for many things and brings punishment when it is disappointed. What are you going to do then?"

Maybe Enrique Estévez Jiménez wanted the little cauldron; he surely didn't want us to buy it. Or maybe, Isidra said later, he wanted an initiate. It is common in Palo to see more experienced paleros and paleras vie for initiates, to see them try to steal them from one another. They do this by undermining an initiate's confidence in his or her tata or yayi. This can be done in a single word skillfully laden with allusions and doubts. The benefits of winning an initiate are great—especially ones entering into the code of padre or madre nganga, who already know much. It also establishes one's will over a peer in a definitive and terrible way. To steal a student is not only to establish dominance of knowledge and intellect but also to suggest a deficiency in one's rival. In a teaching like Palo, this can be a matter of life and death because a strayed initiate can reveal the secrets of one's power. It can be excruciating for a tata or yayi to lose an initiate. This had happened to Isidra before in her role of madrina in Ocha/Santo. It was something she spoke about rarely because it involved a member of her family in Sierra Morena.

Enrique Estévez Jiménez continued, "The prenda you make with that cauldron is going to be strong. How are you going to handle it?" Addressing Isidra he asked, "Madrina?" Isidra did not answer. She seemed flummoxed and slow to get out a reply, and her silence and hesitation were interpreted as ignorance. "A bit and bridle," he said. "How about a bit and a bridle? Have you thought about that madre nganga?" He called Isidra "madre nganga" and meant it as a barb. A person leading another to acquire their own prenda, especially someone Isidra's age, was surely yayi nganga, and the distinction means a great deal in the hierarchy that defines Palo society. She was not answering fast enough or keeping up with him, and Enrique Estévez Jiménez's suggestion was obvious. He piled challenge upon challenge in different registers of Palo discourse to torment her.

"So, how about a bit and a bridle?" he asked. Enrique Estévez Jiménez had the initiative and tried to turn even her facial expressions to his advantage. She remained silent. When Enrique Estévez Jiménez registered her inability to reply, he began to lift his eyebrows and smile theatrically, pursing his lips and looking aside as if in disbelief that she did not have an immediate response, that she could not, without pausing, explain how she intended to keep subdued the Lucero we sought to make. The glance he shot me suggested he was revealing Isidra to be a fraud for not having a ready answer to his challenges.

Her pause lasted an instant too long, and Enrique Estévez Jiménez went on, "A cauldron like that is going to need a brake, something to rein it in when things get tough, when it wants more blood than you can give it. I once had a prenda that slipped out of my hands. Death visited our munanso that year and many people died. I was sick and my wife was sick. That year I was hit by a car. I thought it was sorcery being worked against me. But everything I sent out to fight it came back at me, except worse. You know what? It was my prenda out of control causing mischief and trouble. You get my meaning? How are you going to stop that, madre nganga? And with a cauldron like that one!"

Isidra could not say the prenda should have a bit and a bridle lest she appear to have been schooled by her rival, and her inability in the next half second to come up with an alternative means to tame the irritated prenda of Enrique Estévez Jiménez's imagination established him as the winner of that little contest. As he continued his story he relented a little, "Don't think I didn't know how to handle my prenda nganga! Far from it. But it got crazy on me, wouldn't accept the animals I offered it and started making impossible demands. 'More, more!' it said, though I gave it everything. Imagine, in the middle of the Special Period! You couldn't find a farmer to sell you a chicken! And my prenda starts getting picky about the animals I bring it!" He smiled then, at last giving up his point. "You'll need a brake for it," he said. "By all means, don't put it together without one. It isn't easy to bring a prenda like that down, to subdue it by force. But that is something you are going to have to learn. A prenda will fight with all its might, and getting a bridle on it after it is used to attention and blood will be worse than any beast. Put one on when you build it—before you feed it—that will save you a lot of trouble."

His advice may not have been genuine, but his lesson had some wisdom. Even as he was losing our attention, Enrique Estévez Jiménez reveled in it. He started down another path of conversation; he could have gone on like that forever. He seemed to be enjoying himself, but Isidra wanted no more of it. With two words she let him know he was getting nowhere and that neither she nor I were interested in his stories. I personally would have liked to hear more, but it was impossible considering Isidra's growing dislike for the man. He was far too affected and theatrical and too eager to exercise power. In this the dead crawling along her skin and warning her were not wrong.

We bought the little red cauldron at a price Isidra felt fair, and Enrique Estévez Jiménez faded into the background of sticks, herbs, and Palo miscellany from which he had emerged. To Dagoberto's disappointment we left a lovely bridle hanging from the rafters where it was. By the time we were pedaling back to her place, Isidra clutching me as she rode sidesaddle on the rack, the kimbisero from Oriente was a shadow she chased in her mind. She was concerned he might have had some effect on me. She said, "He's trying to scare you. Don't think twice about what he said. Think about the little cauldron. It is a prize. There are many ways to handle a prenda nganga, and I'm going to teach you Tata Emilio's. A bridle is unnecessary if you've got a good relationship with the dead. You'll see. That was all nonsense to try to scare you into buying a bridle, and get a lot of money out of you. He would have split the money with Dagoberto and gone off drinking. Or maybe he wanted the cauldron. We've got it now." Then she laughed.

In fact, it was she who was spooked by the kimbisero from Oriente. When I would meet someone interesting like Enrique Estévez Jiménez, I would have doubts about her as a teacher, and I wondered if I couldn't do better work if I associated with more, or different, people. There were comments Enrique Estévez Jiménez made that would have been interesting to follow, paths into the dead he pointed toward. But Isidra's price for her guidance was jealous exclusivity, and I have no doubts this work was made both stronger and weaker for it.

13. Reckoning with the Dead

We began with Lucero Mundo sometime after dusk. In the green light of Isidra's back room we admired the excellent little cauldron. Teodoro, Pedro, Isidra, and I each held it in our hands and in turn commented on its weight and strength. Isidra was especially effusive. "This is a mighty thing," she said, "and it will be mighty again! Old Pedro says it has been years since he held anything like it." Pedro nodded, and looked it over again, then asked Isidra what she thought its previous uses might have been. He watched her for a moment, but before she could reply he spoke in his deep, rocky voice, sincere and steady, "This cauldron is small. It reminds me of the mortar Emilio used, which is now lost. I am sure this kettle has been used as a prenda nganga. Since the Revolution—I was more than forty years old when the Revolution came to power—I haven't seen anything like it. It comes from the time before, forged before the Russians. And it is in good shape. It has been hiding somewhere."

Pedro had taken hold of the little cauldron again. Neither Isidra nor I had repeated the story of its purchase. In fact, Isidra had purposefully left out details of its acquisition and implored me to say nothing about it. He was suspicious of her praises and of the absence of an anecdote. Isidra intimated that the cauldron was potent beyond the dead that turned the plain iron from which it was made. What Pedro discerned unsettled him and he began to seek the little cauldron's roots, which, he was right to guess, extended deep into the dead. He went looking, searching with his wisdom and not a little force of will, into the flows and densities of the ambient dead that surrounded us.

Pedro did not let go of the cauldron and continued to feel its weight in his hands. He seemed to tarry with something that pressed him. His whole life Pedro had spent in skilled labor, in contact with people who had made cauldrons like that one. In his old age he was a carpenter, and I trusted his appreciation and understanding of tools and materials like iron and wood. I further trusted that he had greeted and praised hundreds of prendas-ngangas-enquisos in his life and that he knew much about cauldrons and their use in Palo. Confronted with it, he seemed to pause and wonder. Beyond the world of what was apparent and into the dimension of omissions and thoughts unsaid, he went looking for insights into the cauldron's past. In the questions he asked Isidra, and especially in his paused consideration of her silence, he searched for the faintest traces of something that clung, tenaciously and quietly, around the little vessel.

"No story?" he asked again. Though his question was direct, his tone was curious, not suspicious. Still, Isidra didn't like it. To her, Pedro's questioning seemed aimed at the prestige of the vessel, and she avoided answering directly. Regardless of his tone, she sensed his suspicions and tried turning our attention back to our work. We had so much to do, and I thought she might succeed. Still, Pedro's question would not go away. A breach began to open in the air around us, and Pedro stepped into it with confidence.

At our feet, lost among the chaos of the countless ingredients on the floor, was a pail of herbal water, which Pedro called *agua ngongoro*.[1] This mix, which in Ocha/Santo is called *omiero*, is a bath of herbs, cascarilla, and holy water blessed by the Catholic Church, among other ingredients. Agua ngongoro should be mixed in a terra-cotta bowl or a large gourd, though more often a plastic pail is used. Herbs of many varieties are torn by hand in the holy water, until the pail is full of shredded matter. I have seen agua ngongoro made from well water and river water, each of which—because of their kinship with the dead as these churn in the earth and the forest—are held to be as good as holy water. I have also seen it made with tap water, though this clashes with formal Palo rules. Isidra let hers sit over night or longer, so that it took on the dank smell of rotting vegetation. Pedro and Teodoro approved of this, saying it was Emilio's practice. Pedro maintained that the more agua ngongoro stank, the more powerful it was at cooling, neutralizing, and keeping intact the potentials of the dead that inhered in matter. This is the sludge with which ngueyos-to-be are bathed just prior to their rayamientos. All elements hot and dangerous, or unknown, are washed in agua ngongoro before being allowed to come into contact with a prenda-nganga-enquiso. Palo Briyumba has a song for the herbal mix, which we sang while we worked with it. Pedro sank the little cauldron in the pail, and the water it displaced overflowed onto the floor. He sang,

Pedro:	Agua ngongoro sirve pa' remedio,	Cooling water is a cure,
	Agua ngongoro ¡¿cómo no cura yo?!	Cooling water will heal me, of course!
Chorus:	Agua ngongoro, sirve pa' remedio,	Cooling water is a cure,
	Agua ngongoro ¡¿cómo no cura yo?!	Cooling water will heal me, of course!
Pedro:	Agua ngongoro, sirve pa' remedio,	Cooling water is a cure,
	Agua ngongoro ¡¿cómo no cura yo?!	Cooling water will heal me, of course!
Chorus:	Agua ngongoro, sirve pa' remedio,	Cooling water is a cure,
	Agua ngongoro, ¡¿cómo no cura yo?!	Cooling water will heal me, of course![2]

He sang softly over the pail, and his aged voice sounded out the words in deep tones. He kept the little cauldron submerged. This bath marked its first step into the world of Palo craft, where the dead that infused it, and the dead it would contain and relay, would be available to us. Pedro considered this a propitious moment to study its secrets. Drawing it out, he put his face up next to it so that he was almost touching it and looked it over carefully, reading in the spaces between the little bits of crushed herbs that stuck to the cauldron's sides for clues about its concealed involvement with the dead. Any story he discerned would be relevant in the present, because the dead do not ever disappear. They linger and subsist as they permeate the materials of life waiting to be sought and mobilized. If there were responsive dead close to this cauldron it was Pedro's intention to find them and divest them of their claims.

Pushing the pail to the side with his foot, he took a sip of aguardiente from a small gourd. He refused to sip it directly from the bottle. Pedro aspirated the aguardiente over the little cauldron in a fine cloud, then followed with aspirations of dry white wine. Then he tapped the ash off the end of his cigar and inverted it, placing its glowing end in his mouth. He then blew through the cigar, sending forward a plume of smoke that filled the cauldron. When it was surrounded completely in a cloud, he took time to study at close range the smoke swirling in its depths. In the drafts and eddies of smoke he read much about the little cauldron and its involvement with Palo. With his head bowed between his shoulders, he sat with the cauldron cupped in his hands for a long time, staring until the last of the smoke dissipated.

Pedro did this twice, with aspirations of aguardiente and dry white wine, growing more pensive. He seemed, in these renderings of leaves and smoke, to discern many things. He paused and thought, and not one of us was willing to interrupt him in his handling of the cauldron. Then he asked for manteca de corojo, an African palm oil sold by herbalists as an orange paste, used in Palo and Ocha/Santo to settle and cool. Manteca de corojo has affinities with the dead and is fed in little bits to the dead in their little corners. Pedro slathered the cauldron with the paste. As he did, he proceeded to feel the cauldron's surface with his fingertips, massaging the paste into its sides. His poor eyesight made him nearly blind in the murk of the room, and he took his time studying the cauldron with his touch. He stroked the cauldron and sang to it:

Pedro:	Lucero primba,	Lucero first,
	No lumbra marugá,	Doesn't light the depths of night,
	Lucero primba,	Lucero first,
	No lumbra marugá,	Doesn't light the depths of night,
	Lumbra nkisi,	[Lucero] lights nkisi,
	¡No lumbra marugá!	Not the depths of night!
Chorus:	Lucero primba,	Lucero first,
	No lumbra marugá,	Doesn't light the depths of night,
	Lucero primba,	Lucero first,
	No lumbra marugá,	Doesn't light the depths of night,
	Lumbra nkisi,	[Lucero] lights nkisi,
	¡No lumbra marugá!	Not the depths of night![3]

We sang the chorus and he improvised over us, for the first time invoking the prenda we were making. We repeated the song in call and response as he rubbed the cauldron. Then he used his bare feet to clear a space for it on the floor and without looking laid it facing down.

Pedro said, "A dead one *[un muerto]* lingers here, with this cauldron. Things are wrong. There are many things I do not know about this dead one, and it is best to stop rather than risk working with this power in the room. It is a very pretty cauldron—this is true—but something dark among the dead *[un muerto oscuro]* lingers with it. I won't go on."

Isidra had brought Pedro into our work for his thoroughness. He was our guarantee, but now his caution threatened to derail the entire project. There was very little time to lose with so many prendas to make and all the sacrifices pending. Animals were on their way and they couldn't stand around for days in Isidra's apartment. She looked to Teo for his reaction, and he seemed to concur with his uncle. With this, the entire enterprise of prenda making was at a standstill, and in their hands.

There was silence, and after a moment Isidra spoke. "Of course it was a prenda! How could it not have been? It is too beautiful. Did you think it was just sitting around in a factory somewhere? You don't need me to tell you that." She could barely hide her impatience as she proceeded to tell the story of the kimbisero from Oriente. Both men listened intently.

Pedro put his finger on the bottom of the cauldron and pondered the situation. After a minute of silent consideration he seemed suddenly reconciled. "We'll go forward," he said. As he spoke, the atmosphere in the room lifted. Isidra was relieved, and it seemed that divulging her story had been a small price to pay for being able to proceed. However, the feeling of advantage in defining the future Lucero now rested with Pedro. Command over the powers of the dead inhering to the cauldron passed to him. This is what he had sought from the beginning, and now Pedro's authority over our gathering grew. Isidra's bid for control over the process of prenda making, in part riding on insinuating knowledge of the dead into the cauldron, had been lost.

By virtue of his seniority in the Quita Manaquita house, Pedro had the right to prepare the cauldron and he exploited this privilege skillfully with his cryptic readings into the cauldron's past. The next steps would be more intense and the risks would be greater, and Isidra seemed anxious that suddenly so much power rested alone in Pedro's hands. Surprisingly, she then turned to Teodoro to interrupt Pedro's monopoly on action. Pedro picked up the cauldron and asked to be handed the chalk-like cascarilla. He was about to begin marking the cauldron when Teodoro intervened. "With your permission, Tata, I am the one who must mark this cauldron," he said. "These are my initiates; this is my work. With your permission, Tata, it is my obligation."

Pedro looked up and stared at Teodoro. His eyes were gray in the dim light, and they stood out against the frame of his face. He had previously marked stark equilateral crosses on his forehead and cheeks with the white cascarilla, just as had he marked the top of his head with a circle inscribing a large equilateral cross. His face was grave, as if Teodoro had said the unspeakable. When I picture him today, I see his faded gray eyes staring elsewhere, into the dead or out from it, an apparition amid the shifting forms of Kalunga. Sweat drips from his temples, and his face is frozen into a vacant expression that condenses age and authority into an unquestionable access to the uncertain forces of the dead.

Without a word Teodoro shrank from his uncle. He turned to the side, as if afraid or ashamed. Knowing Teodoro, I had expected he would lose this particular struggle, but I was surprised at how easily. Great prestige accompanies the person who marks in Palo, be it a cauldron or a person's skin during a rayamiento, and I had expected him to defend his interests with more vigor. But this was something that was basic about Teodoro. Whether out of generosity or inability to counter another's bid for dominance, Teodoro was often giving up power. He was surprisingly ready to cede authority and when he wasn't, it was easy enough to strip him of it. Power was something Teodoro seemed utterly unable to maintain and quite prone to waste when he had it. In fact, the entire plight of the Quita Manaquita house sometimes seemed to me just that—a huge, profligate, squandering of power.

Pedro had introduced a disturbance into the flows of the dead that connected him to Teodoro, such that his nephew was made to tremble. Teo's surrender could be glossed only by the fact that there was something propitious in having Pedro do the marking on Lucero. His age and experience with the dead would help usher our first prenda-nganga-enquiso, and all of us, through the dead and back into ourselves among the living. At best, this might have figured in Teo's concession. Isidra's last bid to have Pedro share power that night sagged like the very roof of the Manaquita house, and she withdrew from contesting the much more experienced Pedro.

The markings Pedro made, firmas, *tratados* as they are sometimes called, are inscriptions by which a prenda-nganga-enquiso is worked, controlled, and ultimately fought if need be. *Firma* in Spanish means "signature," and *tratado* means "pact" or "deal." Such compacts, laid down in writing, are attempts to fix the protean flux of the dead so that it can be worked. Paleros who know much about firmas admit they are often inscrutable, prone to unstable interpretation and effect. After a cauldron has been cooled in agua ngongoro to receive the firmas, marking them on a cauldron is the first affirmative change the cauldron undergoes on its path to becoming a prenda-nganga-enquiso. Firmas are powerful versions of the dead and to write them, or "throw" them, establishes a point where the simultaneity of living and dead is made felt.[4] Manipulated by the living, firmas also help establish the will of the living over the dead and are the substrate into which all other powers of the dead to be packed into a cauldron will root.

Firmas are hard to describe, if only because they have been made trite in the literature that deals with African-inspired inscription. This is especially the case with Haitian vèvès, with which Palo firmas have much in common.[5] Firmas are made with chalk, usually complex overlappings of lines, arrows, cruciforms, circles, and other shapes. They are drawn on a variety of surfaces, most commonly the floor, but also on walls and objects—like the knife before a sacrifice. In Palo, firmas are also drawn on the body in the form of the wounds ngueyos receive when they are initiated.

As far as I could discern, Palo teaching does not recognize an origin for firmas, as it does not recognize origins for many rituals. Partly because of this and partly because of their simultaneous power to fix and blur forms of the dead, firmas have exquisite power and are held very dear by the men and women who collect them and use them in their work. One learns to draw them from elders, but rarely are firmas accompanied by knowledge about them. There was much wisdom about firmas that neither Teodoro nor Isidra ever taught me. Teodoro, especially, was secretive about his own. It was a terrible privilege to be in the room when they were used, and making prendas-ngangas-enquisos was one such moment. At the same time, Pedro and Teodoro reminded us that paleros should never throw a whole firma, not even when teaching it to a trusted initiate, for fear that it will be copied and, in some unforeseeable future, used in sorcery against one. As such, each time a firma is taught it would seem to be diminished, which would surely be the case were it not for the substantial improvisation that accompanies their use.

Firmas are often credited to the responsive dead. When a tata or yayi teaches a firma to a padre or madre (ngueyos are never taught firmas), it is the dead that are cited to authorize their use. In the case of Isidra and Teodoro, the firmas they taught came from Tata Emilio and his mother, among others. Recollections of the dead and the affective force of their memory cling to firmas, as they do to anything once held dear by the dead. In this, firmas are much like precious jewelry, or clothing, that gathers the dead around their survivors. However, one significant difference separates firmas from these kinds of objects and from signatures in the West, for that matter, which also invoke the dead: the living can reproduce and improvise firmas without losing their authority.

Authorized and inspired by the dead, firmas are felt versions of the dead, which is to say, forceful manifestations of them. Firmas, though they are attributed to specific individuals among one's responsive dead, are used more often to invoke specific powers among the ambient dead that suffuse those who throw. Firmas catalyze what force inheres in the ambient dead immediately around those throwing them, helping to create atmospheres favorable to the craft of the palero or palera who is using them. If used skillfully, one or many firmas can condense the surrounding dead into a generalized atmosphere of possibility and potential, which the author of the firma then appropriates, usually to better work his or her prenda-nganga-enquiso. Firmas are used to create zones wherein the intimate co-permeation of living and dead is made explicit, at times for protracted periods of time, so that new versions of the dead can be manufactured or made to work by the living. Generating this atmosphere is critical to prenda making and Palo craft.

Written on a cauldron, the firmas become the basic premise of a prenda's potential. They guarantee that materials placed therein, each of them versions of the dead, will not just retain their force of influence when brought under the control of the living but ensure it will be stable and malleable. Firmas, more than anything, guarantee the accumulation and sedimentation of the dead inhering to materials, so they can later be drawn out by the prenda's keeper.

Pedro was well along the marking of the little cauldron when Isidra interrupted him to let him know she would be copying his work. Perdo looked up with the same stare he had previously used to repel Teodoro, but Isidra was determined. "If I don't know what you have worked there, the prenda will be out of my control. You must let us copy them; it is your duty. This prenda will be our problem, not yours." Pedro thought for a second, then nodded his assent. Once we were actively writing he seemed more than happy to aid us in our work. The only way to have access to the full range of powers in the prenda was to know its firmas. One of the prendas we were making was to be hers, as were the two we were to refurbish, and when our work was finished she had in her Palo notebook the firmas guaranteeing the stability of each one.

Cradling the heavy cauldron in his lap and using a little ball of cascarilla, he marked its exterior sides. With small equilateral crosses he established the four principal coordinates of Lucero. He then chose which of these directions would be its face, the direction by which it would be approached and addressed by its keeper and other callers. In most cases this decision is either arbitrary or based on how the prenda-nganga-enquiso sits on its legs. With the little red cauldron, however, it was clear that its little spout should distinguish its face, or mouth, and Pedro located a mark directly below this. Mirroring the cardinal points on the outside of the cauldron, he marked the four inside points of the cauldron and the bottom. His firmas were considerably more complex on the inside, and because cascarilla marks in such thick lines, it was hard to discern the points of intersection and continuity of the arrows, circles, and crosses as these were piled one atop another in compound inscriptions. Isidra and I did our best to keep up, but despite his patience our renditions of his firmas were at best approximations.

Compound firmas are extremely complicated. Smaller firmas are set off as clauses within a larger drawing, which contains them and mobilizes their potential. When he turned the cauldron over to mark the bottom, the last of the firmas he drew, he again worked out a compound inscription. That firma was set inside what looked like the outline of a crescent moon.[6] Within it he drew a tree, a bird, and waves of water, and over these a bewildering series of bent arrows, cruciforms, and circles. This done, he placed it firmly on its three little feet, and then looked around the room at each of us for our approval. He received it without hesitation, and in that moment seemed more calm than he had all night, as if his persistent doubts about unwanted powers of the dead insinuating themselves around us were receding. In working the cauldron he had reclaimed it from its prior commitments and contacts and replaced them with his own. Only then did he call for the nfumbe.

We were tested, more from the tension that had pervaded the interactions around the little cauldron than from any physical exertion. Pedro had emerged from the first phase of prenda making as the authority in command of our work, the winner of a low-frequency match of Palo he and Isidra and Teodoro had engaged in. Having submitted now to his lead, we were elated to have him ask for the most volatile of the substances to be introduced into the kettle. Finally, we would begin using the materials we had so painstakingly collected in the countryside, on the streets of Havana, in the cemetery, and from the underground market. We were all barefoot, and, except for Isidra, the three of us were shirtless, as paleros should be when working with powerful agglutinations of Kalunga's force. We were each marked with cascarilla and vouchsafed by charms and necklaces containing substantial powers to cool, slow, and otherwise calm the flows of the dead around us. These precautions were necessary throughout the process of prenda making, and never was this more felt than when the nfumbe was brought into the room and its presence added to the already substantial density of the dead that surrounded us.

14. Nfumbe

Having purged the cauldron of capacities that were not firmly understood and having marked it with firmas to cool and root the currents of the dead that would traverse Lucero, Pedro was impatient to get the nfumbe into the room. *Nfumbe* is a Palo Kikongo word that means "dead one."[1] It is an ambiguous term within Palo's language of the dead and means as much "dead person" as "force of the dead." It is also the term used to refer to human bones.

All prendas-ngangas-enquisos made by the rules of Palo Briyumba contain nfumbe—a skull and finger and foot flanges, at the least.[2] Teodoro described unpacking the contents of prendas-ngangas-enquisos he had refurbished only to find no nfumbe inside. "What's the point of an enquiso," he said, "if there is no nfumbe?" The nfumbe orient the dead around their cauldrons and help condense them into a workable density. If the nfumbe can be settled in the cauldron, a difficult task in itself, it acts as a coagulant for the various potentials of the dead that paleras and paleros introduce into their cauldrons, or move into relevance around them. So worked, the nfumbe brings a limited stability to the multitude of the dead moving around and through prendas-ngangas-enquisos. Palo's claims to efficacy in fate-transforming works rest to a great degree on avowals of singular access to the dead and their powers of revaluation, and for this paleras and paleros must accomplish solidifications, however gelatinous, of Kalunga, which courses around and through their prendas. Those who approach Palo healers for help assume that some version of the dead "resides" within the prendas they consult, and that by virtue of tending to such obvious versions of the dead these healers are able to reshape their fates. Those who make and tend prendas have more complex renderings of the nfumbe, but such understandings are always personal, idiosyncratic, and not codified;

they are affirmed in the practice of making and working prendas-ngangas-enquisos.

Prendas-ngangas-enquisos cannot share nfumbe. Each type—in this case Lucero—requires specific classes of nfumbe. This means that paleros and paleras must personally visit cemeteries to ensure they are acquiring the nfumbe specified for the prenda they seek to build. To introduce the wrong nfumbe would be disastrous. In the case of the Lucero, what was needed was a "nfumbe nani," or the bones of a boy. This was consistent with the understanding of Lucero as a capricious, irreverent, and curious prenda-nganga-enquiso, said to resemble a mischievous boy. Again, this is a likeness to Eleguá, the Ocha/Santo sovereign of chance and playful contingency, who in turn shares a kinship with the popular Spanish Catholic icon El Niño de Atocha.

It was my impression that the use of a boy's remains for the Lucero was true to this affinity with Eleguá. The gender of prendas-ngangas-enquisos, and the gender of the nfumbe they contain, corresponds directly with the gender of the Ocha/Santo sovereigns they are said to share a likeness with. Mama Chola Nkengue, for example, requires the bones of a woman and is gendered feminine, as is Ochún, the Ocha/Santo sovereign of love, sweetness, and feminine charm.[3] However, Ocha/Santo sovereigns do not contain nfumbe, so the influence of west African notions of divinity on Cuban-Kongo prendas-ngangas-enquisos must be restricted to those of metaphoric affinity.

The nfumbe intended for the little cauldron was in a dirty plastic bag in Isidra's patio. She was afraid to keep it and the other nfumbe inside her house. At any moment, the dead organized around the bones of the two nfumbe might dissolve their coagulation and begin to spread indifferent and disordered force through our gathering, bringing havoc to our work. The dead made coherent in the form of the nfumbe could spread in countless unfavorable directions, the most difficult of which would turn the dead infusing our bodies into a shadow of the dead [muerto oscuro], which would proceed to scatter or destroy the materials gathered for our work. Teodoro had experienced such possession before, where an assistant in prenda making was overcome by the force of the nfumbe, which had to be subdued before it damaged the work in progress. Less severely, a disorganized nfumbe could take the form of a series of persistent errors in our work, thus blighting the prendas we made. Our goal was to keep the two nfumbe neutral without losing any of their potential during the hours they spent out of their prendas.

It fell on me to fetch the nfumbe. From the moment we acquired them it had fallen on me to handle them. I assumed this was because I was the padre of least hierarchy, and therefore the most expendable should the nfumbe seek a victim to torment. I was also the most obligated by Palo hierarchy to do what I was told, and in the case of the nfumbe no one else wanted to be near them. Thinking about this later, I have sometimes wondered if I wasn't asked to handle the nfumbe because Isidra and Teodoro knew that of the three of us I was the least likely to surrender to them. I had never been possessed, nor shown any signs that I ever would be, which meant that my affinity with the dead was less than theirs and I was thus the least subject to harm and harassment. Out back, I found them in their plastic bags, resting quietly. The bags were marked with different knots to distinguish them.

We had brought the two nfumbe to Isidra's late the day before, and they had spent the night and the better part of the next day fenced in her patio. One of the brown beeswax candles was lit there. As in the room where we were working, the candle lit into the flows of Kalunga, which soothes the dead greatly. It was important that the candle never falter, even in daylight, to keep the nfumbe from seeping through the flimsy bags holding them, as they are prone to do. It was my task to check the candle every few hours, especially during the long first night they spent at Isidra's. Pedro's candles were so true I needed only one the whole night. Still, I worried about the candle going out and decided to stay awake. While the others slept I sat with the nfumbe, writing by their candlelight.

I don't need to look back on those notes to remember that I felt strange about the plastic bags, but even more so about the profound differences that separated me from Isidra, Teodoro, and Pedro. As a materialist, to me the nfumbe were but bones. Years earlier I had taken Marx at his word in the *Eighteenth Brumaire* and left the dead to be buried by the dead.[4] The future was ours to make. Had I feared them more I would have been closer to my three teachers, and many times that night I wished I was. What little fear I could have mustered would have drawn on the ghost stories that terrified me as a child in the Michigan woods. The nfumbe would have then assumed truer proportions, as shadows come to life from cemeteries in the forest. Such thoughts were long behind me, and I had no interest in rekindling that kind of surrender. Strangely, I felt that if I allowed myself those specters the consequences would be uncontainable, as uncontainable as the nfumbe themselves.

Other thoughts perturbed me in my vigil, but none more than my impulse to harshly judge my teachers for having participated in the bone trade in the first place. At times I was overcome by a compunction that said it was wrong to do anything with the bones except bury them and forget them. The prohibition on being too close to human remains was at work in me then, and I tried to understand it at the visceral level at which it was moving in me. Coming to grips with it, I felt that the transgression I experienced in that moment was as close as I would get to the admiration, and fear, my teachers felt toward the nfumbe. Working through this, I came to appreciate the constraints Palo placed around the nfumbe, elaborate and intense prohibitions, though very different from my own. It was these prohibitions that transformed the bones into the felt power called nfumbe. In exhuming the bones and bringing them into the heart of their craft, my teachers brought to them a terrific vitality that exalted them.

The night was full of fruitful struggles for me, and when I managed to finally put aside childhood visions and subjective compunctions that passed as judgment, I was met with yet another reservation. As I sat with the nfumbe and shared their light I wondered how something so powerful and vibrant, so profoundly revered and respected in Palo, could be left all night in a plastic bag. For a minute I let my mind wander and asked myself if the nfumbe wouldn't be more comfortable if I opened their bags a little. I admit to a prejudice against plastic that had me thinking they would prefer something more dignified, like paper. I then recognized myself giving all too much life to lifeless things and, considering they'd had such a rough several hours, I let the nfumbe rest as they were.

It is worth recounting how we acquired the nfumbe, because it tells much about the state of Palo at the turn of the twenty-first century, the forty to fifty years since the beginning of the Cuban Revolution. Though it is hard to distinguish absolute importance among Palo materials and substances, few compare with nfumbe in their importance for prenda-nganga-enquiso making. Only blood is as powerful a version of Kalunga. Nfumbe are not easy to come by and have always demanded much of those who wish to engage them.

According to La Regla de Congo paleras and paleros must exhume the nfumbe they seek.[5] Trekking to the cemetery to dig up one or two nfumbe is considerably easier in the countryside, where cemeteries are unguarded. This is different in the city, where guards keep all sorts of intruders out. To address this, the market in Palo wares extends deep into Havana's cemeteries, to the groundskeepers and administrators who source the nfumbe trade.[6]

The illicit markets that thrive in the cemeteries of Havana are worthy of in-depth, complex study, and the nfumbe trade must be only one of many informal types of income earned by the people who work there. The guards and diggers sell skulls and other bones, while the administration sells access to better plots, or longer stays in a grave before the state-mandated exhumation and removal of remains to a wall niche. These men and women find that protecting the cemetery is good for their pocketbooks, and as in most other jobs in Cuba they have turned what little authority they have in their workplace into control of a good, service, or right of access, which is then traded on an informal market for income many times their official earnings. Prices vary slightly from nfumbe to nfumbe, from cemetery to cemetery, but three hundred Cuban pesos has remained a steady price for more than twenty years. This amount equaled a month and a half of an average Cuban's wage in 2000; those entering the hierarchy of padre spend a good while saving for their nfumbe. Adding the tata's fee (which is less than the nfumbe), the animals to be sacrificed (together more than twice the price of the nfumbe), and all feast costs, receiving a prenda-nganga-enquiso in Havana today requires diligent savings, or lucrative underground market work.

Teodoro said that Emilio had six or seven initiates working in the cemeteries of Guanabacoa when he died. By his account, everyone employed at the cemetery was involved in Palo. Grave diggers and groundskeepers watch graves and mortuary niches for signs of neglect. When a request for an nfumbe comes along, they check with someone in the office, who will verify the grave has not been visited in many years. Administrators take their cut from an nfumbe sale for this information, which diminishes the risk to all involved. They also provide the grave digger with the nfumbe's full name, which is imperative for packing a prenda successfully. In 1997, according to Teodoro, there was a dragnet in the various Guanabacoa cemeteries that led to the arrests of a network of grave diggers, guards, and administrators. It was revealed that more than forty nfumbe were sold from one Guanabacoa cemetery in that year alone.

Our nfumbe were gathered in Guanabacoa, where they were delivered to the Quita Manaquita house. Whenever nfumbe are contracted the unexpected is prone to happen, and trips to the cemetery are especially uneasy. In response to Isidra's considerable apprehension, Teodoro had set up the delivery; he was considerably more at ease than Isidra or I. As we waited, Teodoro revealed that he did not know the people who were coming with the nfumbe. He didn't need to. Underground markets in Cuba are not only about exchanges of goods but also about exchanges of confidence: networks of friends, family, and associates who trust one another by word of mouth. The market we were a part of was as much about the circulation of confidences as it was about the circulation of nfumbe. It was a matter of knowing how to generate trust within the network, which Teodoro did well. Still, because we weren't going to the cemetery he was afraid of getting ripped off or of getting stung by the police. Fraud and the police, like trust, are part of the fuel of any illicit trade in Cuba.

What apprehension or impatience Teodoro might have felt as we waited emerged as a mumbled tirade against the Revolution. He must have been tense, or he would never have said what he did in front of Isidra. "It is crazy we have to buy the nfumbe at all," he said. "The Revolution has made exhumation totally impossible. Who exhumes anymore in Palo? The police, the control around the cemetery, of course the price of nfumbe is up around three hundred pesos. Next they'll ask for it in dollars! Putting a prenda together is starting to look like receiving a Santo, at least as far as cost. It interferes with teaching Palo. The Revolution guarantees textbooks to the children to teach them Revolution, Che Guevara, Yankee Imperialism, but do they teach Palo? What they do with all this control over people is guarantee that a tata won't have a prenda to teach with! Imagine if schoolbooks cost as much as a single nfumbe! You would be illiterate!"

He was almost talking to himself as he went on, with Isidra trying to ignore him. "You lose so much. . . . Many things are lost at the graveside, too. You lose important time with the nfumbe. How am I supposed to ask the nfumbe if it wants to leave the grave and come with me if it is already dug up, delivered to my porch? That's not good. It is not a good shortcut. So then you have to ask the nfumbe that shows up on your porch if it wants to come, with half the neighborhood watching. But the grave diggers, they know, so they turn their head, because they want you to get the nfumbe off their back. No one wants to have to carry a nfumbe back, so they let you throw the chamalongo without them looking. But what a difference! In the past you went to the grave, lit a candle, threw down your firmas, blew aguardiente around, talked to the nfumbe, worked the chamalongo. The way things are now you can't help but have trouble with the nfumbe. Palo suffers for this; more and more prendas are hard to control because their nfumbe aren't with the deal. And the dirt! You lose the dirt from the grave if you don't do the digging yourself. How are you going to put an enquiso together without earth from the grave? There is too much handling of the nfumbe, too much changing hands; you risk agitating it. These things are not good." Teodoro then went into a long complaint about the charlatans and the hucksters who he said were springing up everywhere, selling lousy wares and engaging in plain fraud. Slowly he sank deeper into despondent mumbling. Isidra listened quietly. She did not interrupt him as she usually did when he blamed the Revolution for his hardship.

The nfumbe finally arrived, and in a word the price was settled. Teo had a candle, cigar, cane liquor, and cascarilla ready to consult the nfumbe. He quickly improvised a Palo "exhumation," lighting the candle and drawing a firma on the ground in front of the plastic bags. We freshened them with aguardiente and cigar smoke. With his chamalongo he made the necessary throws to discern each nfumbe's will. He wasn't afraid to throw so that everyone there could see, and his negotiations with the dead were efficient and easy. One agreed to come along without the slightest hesitation, such that Teodoro joked that it was jumping out of its bag to join us.

But the other nfumbe, the one we needed to make Lucero Mundo, rejected Teodoro's initial proposition and said through the chamalongo that it would not join us. This flummoxed Isidra, but she kept quiet, waiting to see how Teodoro would entice it to change its mind. Teodoro was not one to take inconvenient outcomes of his throws as definitive, and he prepared to throw again. This action was in contrast to Isidra, who let the dead dictate to her through the chamalongo. Teo usually settled matters in his favor by skillful use of Palo Kikongo speech, to ask for clarifications and adjustments that would garner new throws. He eventually negotiated a deal with the nfumbe, promising it plentiful libations of alcohol and a generous course of animal offerings after it was settled into its cauldron. It would have gotten these offerings anyway, so his dealings with the dead seemed brusque and not exactly sincere. Isidra did not like the initial negative reply and later would have reason to argue that much more should have been done to placate this nfumbe. Nonetheless, she was eager to close the deal and did not openly challenge Teodoro's throws and terms. For his part, Teodoro explained that the nfumbe's reluctance was to be expected and argued that the nfumbe would be great for Lucero Mundo because it displayed the qualities of restlessness and independence for which Lucero is known. Matters with the nfumbe were settled more or less, and without further delay the couriers who had delivered the nfumbe withdrew into the network that had brought us together.

Our walk to catch a ride to Isidra's in the dim of early night was uneventful, except for the marvel of evening, when the world is cast in slate and sounds ring with distant, liquid tones. We were soon at the outskirts of town and Isidra commented on the fact that we had met no police. This was because the little nfumbe was already acting as a true Lucero, opening our path and guiding us through crossings unhindered. She was happy to leave Guanabacoa behind. In that instant we were picked up by a metallic blue '56 Oldsmobile, which, to our surprise, was empty except for the driver. Inside, the car was a grotto of navy blue vinyl upholstery and blue shag carpeting, which covered the floors, ceiling, interior panels, and dashboard. The windows were tinted, and little blue lights poked out of the shag here and there like phosphorescent life nestled in an undersea bed. A mix of Rolling Stones and rueful Mexican boleros poured out of the tape deck. The driver was tiny, skeletal and withered, and the wheel was enormous in his hands. The back seat swallowed us into a reclining position, and Teo stretched out to strike a pose, as if he were the diva of some New York City lounge. The giant ride, with its sunken atmosphere, glided along like a submarine on an underwater approach across the harbor to Havana. Teodoro recognized the fortuitous conjunction of our easy pick-up and the obviousness of our subaquatic ride and exclaimed with all due admiration, "Kalunga, *asere*, Kalunga!"[7]

Once at Isidra's, the nfumbe were left outside, protected from sight by the awning in her patio and a fence covered in creeping vines. Some tatas and yayis insist that initiates into the hierarchy of madre and padre sleep curled at the foot of the first prenda-nganga-enquiso they receive, and Teodoro said that in the past a palero seeking a nfumbe would sleep on the grave before exhuming it. Knowing this, Isidra seemed reassured the couple of times she woke to check on the nfumbe only to find me sitting, keeping vigil with my notebook at my side. Nonetheless, she was never really at ease with those bags, and lay back down only because she knew we would go sleepless for several nights once our work on the prendas began.

15. Insinuation and Artifice

That night passed, as did the following day, and as evening settled on El Cerro, Pedro sent me to the patio for the nfumbe. When I returned the door was closed, and I was required to identify myself by my initiation name before entering. When the door opened, I was hit in the face with blasts of aguardiente and white wine from Teodoro's lips, which were meant to cool the dead coursing through me before I stepped into our work space. Teodoro abstained from using chamba in these aspirations because it was used to liven the dead and alert them, something we wanted to avoid. Before taking the bag, he shrouded me in cigar smoke. These were the basic precautions that surrounded the handling of the nfumbe—libations of aguardiente and white wine, and plenty of cigar smoke, repeated each time the bones were handled. The nfumbe was treated with utmost care to keep its heat subdued. Isidra would not touch either the bag or the dead therein.

Given this, it surprised me that once safe inside the room the nfumbe was plopped on the floor, just one white plastic bag among others. Pedro was organizing what he would need in the process of packing the prenda and shuffled the nfumbe to the side with his foot. During the next three days this mix of extreme precaution and casual familiarity would pervade. Lucero was the first of two new prendas and then there would be the refurbishments. In hindsight, it was put together with relative calm compared to all the work that followed.

Before the nfumbe could be settled into the little cauldron, Pedro positioned a small piece of broken mirror atop the white chalk drawing he had made in the bottom of the vessel. Holding the cauldron in his hand, Pedro stared into the bottom and contemplated the mirror glimmering from its depths. He took a moment to drown it in aspirations of aguardiente and white wine. He moved slowly and took his time, looking down at the mirror after each soaking. He then filled the little cauldron with smoke by blowing through his inverted cigar. He was deliberate in studying the tendrils, watching them flow and twist around one another. He said, "The cauldron no longer has a bottom [esta cazuela ya no tiene fondo]. Now it opens onto the world of truth [el mundo de la verdad], which is the dead [que es el muerto]." The smoke had dissipated and he smiled into the cauldron's depths. "Now," he said, "all you see is the sky. Look in, see the sky. Wherever the prenda goes it will always be close to the sun, and the moon, and the stars [los astros]."

Pedro asked for the nfumbe. Teodoro repeated the aspirations and fumigations. Unlike Pedro, Teodoro rarely took the time to study the wafts of smoke. But this time he took care and he read the smoke carefully. He opened the bag and reached in. What emerged in his hands were fragments of crushed bones. The little nfumbe had been destroyed somehow and there was no easily discernable skull, which is the most cherished part of the nfumbe. Teo looked at Isidra disappointed, and within seconds he was overcome by doubt. He sifted through the bag and soon a look of resignation spread across his brow. Before he could speak Isidra moved to disqualify the nfumbe, and before Pedro or I could look up the two were sunk in bitter recriminations. Isidra reminded Teodoro that this particular nfumbe had been hesitant to come with us and accused him of malpractice for not having opened the bag, let alone discerned the situation with his chamalongo throws. Teodoro's promises to appease the nfumbe had been shallow and futile; he had not seen the gravity of things, and now we were facing the consequences. In that moment Teodoro was overcome by an uncharacteristic agressivity, and he started back against her, shouting in his defense.

But Pedro spoke, interrupting them, saying, "Tondele kwame, pañame, 'mano mio, 'mano prenda, 'mano nganga, tondele kwame. Cool it, friends," he said, "we are all siblings of the same prenda, the same nganga, so let's cool it." Then he said, "There is no need for a whole skull [kriyumba]. That would be ideal. But who says this nfumbe isn't powerful? Isidra is right; this nfumbe is unhappy. I can see how it is unsettling you, but that is exactly what a Lucero should do. It is shaking things up and turning them inside out. That's why Lucero is called Vira Mundo [Turn the World Upside Down]. The nfumbe is perfect." He paused, looking at them. "Don't forget, Briyumba Kongo introduced the use of the skull [kriyumba] to Palo, and if anyone can tell you if a skull is good it is us briyumberos. So take it slow, madrina, I have dealt with this problem before. All we need is a little piece of the gourd [jicara], not the whole thing."

Pedro's words settled matters, and before Isidra could find new doubts to set against the nfumbe he set me to work sifting through the fragments.

This I did until I found a modest piece with a bit of curve. It was no bigger than the chamalongo made from coconut shell. In my hurry I took
none of the precautions of aspirating or fumigating the bones, but no one
seemed to notice. Pedro studied the little piece just an instant before declaring
that it would do. Isidra and Teodoro seemed to accept his words, and we again
focused on our work.

Nfumbe have names. Each nfumbe has a name and it must be known
for each prenda. In the bag I came across a piece of paper with the name of
the boy whose bones we now worked with. Though the grave diggers may
have sold us a shattered skull, the network had kept its word and provided
us with this crucial note.

Pedro placed the little cauldron on the floor and had me read the name
aloud. He had Isidra write it down and had me copy it too. On a separate piece
of brown paper, we wrote the nfumbe's name seven times and then over each
name wrote the name seven more times. We gave to him this piece of paper,
and he folded it and placed it in the bottom of the cauldron, on top of the
mirror. He said, "This is the anchor. When we want the nfumbe we'll call it by
name, and, like that, pull it out."

More materials go in the very bottom of the cauldron before the
nfumbe's skull: bits of silver and gold, stones fused from lightning strikes
[*piedra de rayo, matari*], and little sheets of paper with printed Catholic
prayers.[1] There is infinite variety among Palo branches and societies when it
comes to the order and placement of these contents. I was most struck by the
fourteen Catholic prayers for El Niño de Atocha, La Virgen de Regla, La Virgen de la Caridad del Cobre, La Virgen de la Merced, and many others.

Pedro now took earth from an open grave, which we had gathered in the
countryside, and poured it on top of the mirror and the prayers. Then he
patted it down to make a low bed for the nfumbe. This was not earth from
the nfumbe's own grave, which would have been ideal. Grave earth is a
powerful material that orients the dead and settles it by reproducing its
resting place, so that it can repose. It is meant to encourage the nfumbe's
stillness.[2] Any grave earth will do, and both Isidra and Teodoro said there
were times when just regular earth is used, when no other sources availed
themselves to urban paleras and paleros.

Taking a bunch of bone fragments, Pedro aspirated them and surrounded
them in smoke while he held them in his hand. He did this for three small
handfuls, until a small mound of bones rested in the bottom of the red cauldron. He covered this pile with a small disk. It covered the nfumbe like a little cap. The entire mound was then aspirated with white wine, aguardiente,
and fumigations of cigar smoke. The nfumbe was in place, and Pedro

quickly buried it beneath more grave earth until another flattened bed was made. He followed with aspirations and cigar fumigations.

We had just finished this step when Pedro, who by candlelight was nearly blind and worked almost exclusively by touch, stopped us. "I've forgotten something," he said. "Something is missing." His voice was quiet and careful. The dead were moving through him. Our hearts sank. The care we were taking with the nfumbe was costing us time and we had so much work yet to do. Teo asked sharply and without patience, "What is it?"

Teo didn't wait for a reply, didn't wait for Pedro to describe what he felt, which was an affront to his uncle and to the dead, who were in a moment of visceral contact. When a tata or yayi speaks of a sense or image they are picking up [recogiendo] from the dead, those around should pay heed. Teo had no patience for it and sent me tearing through the sea of plastic bags looking for the forgotten element. We kept a list of prenda materials, and he started going through it to see if mentioning one thing or another would help his uncle home in. The list was exhaustive, and Teo and I finished our searches at the same time, turning up nothing. Pedro seemed to ignore us and held his hand to his closed eyes as if trying to discern something far off. Finally, he spoke, "We forgot the coins. Look for the coins."

When we found them—they were under Isidra's little bench—Pedro reached into the cauldron and dug into the earth with his long finger nails, until he found the little cap and lifted it, leaving the rest of the earth intact. Carefully, he lifted out the brittle bones, having me hold them in my cupped hands while the cap piece rested on his knee. He dug further until he exposed the prayers and the nfumbe's name and placed the coins there without ado. Pedro returned the bones and earth to their place and sealed them again, returning the cap with the thin layer of earth that covered it still intact. A little more grave earth, again, aspirations and fumigations, and he was done.

The episode left a wake of uncertainty in the room, to which Isidra succumbed. "Too many things are amiss," she said. "The nfumbe was crushed, and now we forgot something as simple as the coins. Isn't it possible that something more is going on here? I can feel the dead, and there are disturbances. Pedro, tell us, is it the muerto oscuro you felt before, or something else bringing hardship to our work?"

Pedro discounted Isidra's suggestion. He was tired of her misgivings and her propensity to introduce doubt into our gathering. He was offended that she did not approve of his fix with the coins and chose to invoke the muerto oscuro to express her misgivings. He was especially insulted that Isidra questioned the integrity of the prenda we were making and that she insisted on actualizing fears about an unruly Lucero or other forces among the dead coming to harm us. Pushing her doubts to the limit, Isidra said, "Let's check. Let's check to see what is in the room with us." Frustrated, Pedro moved to dispel her doubts. He picked up his set of chamalongo, which he kept in a little gourd full of water under his bench, and, as he threw them, asked the dead at large, all the dead that churned around us, if we could go on. "Kalunga, Kalunga, which saturates, has everything until now been done to the satisfaction of the dead?"

He threw the four shells with a dismissive flick of the wrist. *Alafia* landed, four shells face up.[3] Alafia responds to a question with indisputable affirmation. It is sought after and wished for when questions are asked of the dead. When it is received, those present touch the ground with both hands where the shells lie, then bring their fingertips to their lips for a kiss. Alafia is the opposite of the four shells falling face down, *muerto parado* [dead afoot or dead at a stop], which expresses the displeasure of the dead and announces the will of one among the dead to speak, usually in admonishing terms. Pedro's question was to the point, and the whole of the dead replied in kind: Kalunga was satisfied with our work, among the flows that held us and made us, nothing objected to the choices we had made, including the little nfumbe now interred in the cauldron.

To throw the chamalongo in the midst of building a prenda-nganga-enquiso is risky, and only a very experienced palera or palero would try it. Too many variables come into play if word comes back from the dead that something is off, that the nfumbe is unhappy, or something else is out of order. An experienced palera or palero, however, will know how to appease an unhappy power or correct for an ill omen. Pedro's four open shells required no corrective, his alafia was utter confidence to continue and lifted any doubt that his choice to use the broken nfumbe was fine.

Isidra was immediately settled, for no further questions could be raised in the near or distant future about the will of the nfumbe to be contained in the cauldron. Isidra was rarely settled, but a throw of alafia was as close as she ever got. Pedro's throw established that the nfumbe was settled, comfortable, and prepared to become a part of Lucero. Isidra was thrilled, and days later said that Pedro had impressed her greatly with the throw. "Pedro has given us a prenda we will never doubt!" she said. Then she remembered Enrique Estévez Jiménez, the kimbisero from Oriente and, mocking him, said, "Only someone afraid to throw the chamalongo could think up a prenda so disobedient that it needed a bridle! If you know what you are doing in Palo, all you need is the chamalongo." And Isidra was right. There was incontrovertible confidence to be drawn from knowing how to handle the coconut shells, which really meant knowing how to handle the dead, negotiate with them, and interpret their emanations with subtlety. This was exactly the reason we had Pedro with us.

Isidra was now ready to go forward, and her change of heart lifted us. Where before shadows of doubt hung low, at times growing into the shape of hostile dead, suddenly a horizon could be seen in our work. It was as if the prenda had begun to assert its sovereignty over the reaches in which we labored and opened a path through what had until then been the murky waters of Kalunga.

With our energy redoubled, we turned our attention to the materials waiting to be included in the cauldron. Many contents follow the nfumbe into a prenda-nganga-enquiso, and they have been written about and cited in existing writing on prendas and Palo.[4] Some of the materials we had brought back from Sierra Morena—including feathers, ashes, cotton, mercury, and a humming bird—were combined in little packets madé of corn husks, called *masangó*.[5] Each husk was loaded with a different combination proscribed by Palo Briyumba custom. Before added to the corn husk, each material received aspirations and generous breaths of cigar smoke. Then, holding the husks one at a time in our hands, we would twist each one closed by winding the ends in a movement away from the body. As the winding became tighter, the husks would bind down into a tight knot. Then we wound them each with a different color of thread. We sang as we worked:

Pedro:	¡Nkanga yo nkanga!	Load, I load![6]
	¡Yo nkanga masangó!	I knot masangó!
Chorus:	¡Nkanga yo nkanga!	Load, I load!
	¡Yo nkanga masangó!	I knot masangó!
Pedro:	¡Nkanga yo nkanga!	Load, I load!
	¡Yo nkanga masangó!	I knot masangó!
Chorus:	¡Nkanga yo nkanga!	Load, I load!
	¡Yo nkanga masangó!	I knot masangó!
Pedro:	¡Nkanga yo nkanga!	Load, I load!
	¡Yo nkanga masangó!	I knot masangó!
Chorus:	¡Nkanga yo nkanga!	Load, I load!
	¡Yo nkanga masangó!	I knot masangó!

The song was sung quickly and with energy, and we repeated it over and over as a kind of joyful work song.

Seven masangó were made, each with specific properties and values that could be invoked later while working with Lucero. Each was aspirated with aguardiente and white wine and fumigated with cigar smoke. They were then sealed in a layer of wax, which was dripped, drop by drop, from Pedro's precious candles. They were finished with the indispensable aspirations and fumigations.

The importance of the masangó for a prenda-nganga-enquiso cannot be underestimated in Palo Briyumba. Their respective charges, their loads so to speak, establish the capacities of the prenda. The packets detail the prenda's force in the world. The materials they hold are turns of the dead, each with tendrils extending into Kalunga. Each has a particular relation of heat, density, and tension within the prenda. By virtue of having been handled and considered, sung over, worked, and turned, these materials become substances, and as substances exude the dead inhering in them in intense concentrations. They are volatile, active, and rife with potential. From these substances the nfumbe, and the prenda by extension, draw much of their speed, efficacy, and potential to transform fate and life.

The multicolored bundles of substances were placed in the kettle on the bed of earth covering the nfumbe. Pedro began filling all around them with grave dirt, and it was clear the elderly palero favored this kind of earth in the initial phases of prenda making, though he would soon use others. We had collected a variety of soils for our work, and it was important that each prenda contain a full complement of them. When materials for a prenda are collected, earth is sought from forests, fields, hillsides, riverbanks, and the crossing points of lonely roads. In the city, earth is taken from the corners of the property that houses hospitals, prisons, universities, airports, railroad tracks, and police stations, among other places. Each is valued for being saturated with the influence of the dead that determines such places, which allows a palera or palero access to the activities they control. These influences are considered immanent in the natural world, and soil is considered the base element of nature.

Earth is prenda material par excellence. Other than bones and blood, it is the privileged matter of the dead. In Palo's vision of powerful substances, earth [ntoto] is the basic element, the common denominator of all Palo craft.[7] It has strong affinities with Kalunga in its ubiquity and indeterminate potential. It is porous, plastic, and generic. Each anonymous grain lends itself to transformation, as it has throughout the history of human kind. Dirt underwrites the contagious in unique ways, being a workable, receptive surface, permeable and penetrable.

Relative to the quantity in which we had the various and different soils, Pedro set to work filling up the cauldron. First he used *ntoto de bibijagua*, which is red clay churned into little balls by ants as they dig their nests, then expelled to the surface where they dry in the sun, like thousands of tiny bricks. This red dirt is esteemed for having come from deep in the ground and for bearing within it the efficaciousness of the thousands of ants that have handled it. We had gathered it in Sierra Morena, and Pedro was thrilled to have several bags of it on hand. At a certain moment, Pedro turned his attention to the other soils. By handfuls and little pinches, Pedro then added these to the cauldron, which was nearly full. He took special pause with the *ntoto de carcoma* and the *ntoto de jaguey*. The first was a mass of darkened tree trunk that had become a termite nest. When abandoned by its makers, ntoto de carcoma looks like a charred sponge, complete with pores and tunnels. It is fragile, but sharp and difficult to break apart with the hands.

Ntoto de jaguey, by contrast, is the finest of powders, produced by wasps burrowing deep in the folds of great jaguey trees. Dangerous and inassimilable loads or bundles are left at the foot of these trees, which are prodigious at dissipating these otherwise unmanageable forces. This dust is not easy to gather, because wasps build their nests in the creases of the jaguey where its roots and branches meet and fuse with the trunk. What remains from their gnawing at the bones of the great trees are plumes of sawdust that cascade downward over little ledges and outcroppings and accumulate atop the wasp nests. Of these two soils, and of the others as well, Pedro used but a pinch or two. After adding each soil to the cauldron, he aspirated and blew cigar smoke.

The masangó bundles were covered, and before proceeding further Pedro took a moment to pin them and the nfumbe into place. For this he used three horseshoes, which he hammered into place, forming a triangle inscribed by the prenda's rim, with the bones gathered in the center of the cauldron. Horseshoes, by virtue of having two ends, were excellent for bracing more or less rounded shapes like masangó and the pile of bones. In the prenda we would build later, the horseshoes were excellent for bracing the kriyumba. Bones are more plastic than one might imagine. This plasticity can lend a spring-like quality to the tension of a horseshoe pounded correctly. Pedro and Teodoro called the process of bracing the contents of the prenda "shoeing" it [calzar la prenda]. Satisfied with the tension effected by three crisscrossed horseshoes, Pedro then lifted the bucket of agua ngongoro to pour a hefty amount into the cauldron, saturating everything in it.

All that remained to complete the prenda was the sticks of wood [palos] and the railroad spikes, which Pedro called kaboyo.[8] Lucero is bound by Kongo Law to include twenty-one sticks, which we placed in the prenda after everything else was settled. Briyumba prendas-ngangas-enquisos are characterized by a ring of sticks extending beyond their rim, which dissipate and concentrate potentials of the dead, much like the great jaguey trees. After years of use, the sticks blacken and fuse together, the spaces between them filled with dried blood, feathers, pieces of paper, folded money, little bundles of substances, packets, and earth. As the prenda is used and grows, the ring is filled in with the skulls of animal offerings and objects stacked atop it. The ring of sticks thus extends the volume of the prenda significantly. This also makes it possible to retrieve elements, like prepared bundles, from its uppermost layers.

The sticks each have different qualities and purposes of effect, many of which can be discerned in the name of the tree or bush. There is no uniformity across Palo praise houses as to which sticks are used, except that all prendas-ngangas-enquisos in Palo Briyumba are obligated to contain at least *palo yaya* and *palo tengue*, which Isidra called the mother and father of the forest. Lucero Mundo required so many sticks that one could chose among many powers. Each stick was a minor form of the dead, able to influence the actions of the living if worked correctly. Lucero, which commands over crossings, portals, and paths, contained sticks from bushes with names such as *cambia rumbo* [change of course], *abre camino* [path opener], *vence batalla* [battle winner], *palo justicia* [justice], and *cambia voz* [voice changer] and included, among many others, ceiba, *palo malambo, palo aroma, jibá, jocú*, and *paramí* [for me], each with a different kind or form of effect. Lucero could assume a complement of twenty-one of these effects. Prendas that contain only five or seven sticks give one trouble in choosing powers. Mama Chola Nkengue, for example, called for no more than five sticks by Teo's reckoning and had to include at least yaya and tengue. Furthermore, as Mama Chola would be used to address issues of love, sex, and desire, she was obligated to contain paramí and vence batalla, which left room for just one other. Among prendas-ngangas-enquisos, those gendered feminine carry the fewest sticks, which diminishes their use.

The effects of each stick, which Teodoro and Pedro called *nkunia*, can be used to heal or harm, and their wood dust is used in offensive and defensive Palo craft.[9] Occasionally, when the need is great, dust from one or more of the sticks that compose a prenda-nganga-enquiso will be used in the fabrication of a sorcery bundle. This is rare, however, because an active prenda-nganga-enquiso generates countless bundles over the lifetime of its keeper, and soon its sticks would be used up. Instead, the properties of each stick are reflected in their corresponding bushes and trees in the forest, the branches and twigs of which are sought out and ground up for use in Palo craft.

Not all the sticks are nailed into the prenda at once. A few of the harder woods are left for last, to act as pins and braces, along with railroad spikes.

Yaya and tengue are both hardwoods, especially tengue, which rings like a bell when two pieces of it are struck together. Teodoro liked to finish with tengue, which he positioned in the center of what would be the prenda's face. The sticks introduced into Lucero were sharpened into stakes, and Pedro and Teo took turns pounding them into the cauldron with a mallet. It was hard work and done in such a way as to preserve maximum tension within the cauldron. As they pounded, Pedro sang a counting song, rifting on the number seven. This was one of Emilio's songs, which brags about a powerful prenda with only seven sticks:

Pedro:	Siete con siete,	Seven and seven,
	Siete, na' más,	Seven, not more,
	Siete con siete,	Seven and seven,
	Siete, na' más,	Seven, not more!
	Siete nkunia tiene mi nganga.	My nganga has seven stakes.
	¡Siete, na' más!	Seven, not more!
Chorus:	Siete con siete,	Seven and seven,
	Siete, na' más,	Seven, not more,
	Siete con siete,	Seven and seven,
	Siete, na' más,	Seven, not more!
	Siete nkunia tiene mi nganga.	My nganga has seven stakes.
	¡Siete, na' más!	Seven, not more![10]

Once the sticks were in place, a thin layer of black ash from a charcoal fire was added to bring the contents flush with the rim of the cauldron. When a prenda-nganga-enquiso is built, careful attention must be given to the distribution of earth and bones and stones, horseshoes and railroad spikes, or it can end up off balance, prone to tipping one way or another. The heavy railroad spikes are the last wedges in a prenda, the final elements guaranteeing the integrity and permanence of the substances collected inside. The spikes, which are driven to protrude from the rim of the prenda, are also placed with aesthetic considerations in mind.[11]

We were now near the end of our work with Lucero. Pedro and Teodoro still pounded. As they added the spikes, the earth and bones in the center of the Lucero bulged unexpectedly, threatening to explode outward. Each new mallet blow, instead of fixing the contents of the prenda, shook and displaced them. Despite the horseshoes binding them, the contents in the middle of Lucero were not solidly enough pressed, one to another. The fact of the shattered nfumbe continued to plague us. When an intact kriyumba sits in the center of a cauldron, the spikes are pounded in with more confidence and force, pinning everything into place. Our hammering disturbed all the work we had done before. The fear of a catastrophic mistake that had dissipated with Pedro's chamalongo throw began to creep back. Isidra knotted up, staring in dismay as the nfumbe in the center of Lucero stirred with each blow.

It was with skill, and more than anything with defiant aplomb, that Pedro moved to still the specter emerging in the room. His mallet strikes were unflinching and precise. After each one he stared around him undaunted, challenging each of us to ask him to stop. He struck and struck, each blow distributing considerable force throughout the cauldron. Despite it being inadvisable to sink more than three, Pedro placed all seven spikes.

Pedro was proud of his prenda making and showed it with a subtle and not immodest flair. He knew there was grave doubt in Isidra and Teodoro about placing the last spike, but he moved to finish Lucero anyway. Reaching into the bucket of fetid agua ngongoro, where all the iron and metal pieces for the prenda had been soaking, he pulled out a chain and one last spike. The chain was iron, found a few days before at one of the unauthorized sidewalk markets that sprout along Matadero Street flanking the Cuatro Caminos market and that specialize in bolts, nails, tools, and old butcher's knives. It was an old dog chain that still had flakes from its chrome finish. Pedro took one end of it, pinned it to the earth with the last spike, and drove it in. He then wrapped the chain twice around the ring of sticks and began to pull it tight. The sticks bent toward the center of the prenda, raising the pressure throughout the cauldron. As he tightened the chain he struck at the spike, crushing and pressing everything inside. The horseshoes and the sticks held, bound and pressed into higher and higher tension.

With nothing left to add, Pedro invited Teo to crown Lucero with a small seashell. All prendas have last minute aesthetic touches and this was homage to Tata Emilio's Lucero and to Teodoro's Lucero, both of which had a conch shell protruding from their center.

Around us the floor was awash in reddish mud from the baths of swampy agua ngongoro and aspirations of aguardiente and white wine. Everything that was to go into the next prendas was mired. The white bags and walls of the room, our little benches and our bodies, were streaked with muddy handprints. The room smelled of the countryside after rain, except more sour because of the cane liquor and dry wine we blew almost constantly. We had one prenda yet to build and two to refurbish, each more work than the Lucero had been. At least now we had Lucero Mundo to guide our efforts, and the longer we spent among the dead the more we appreciated his aid.

In all we spent three full days, with only short rests, working on the prendas. Never were the dead absent from our work, nor was the fear of failing and bringing misery upon us ever dispelled, despite the little Lucero lighting our way. It seemed as if the invocation of uncertainty, and our proximity to the unpredictable influences of the dead, were proportionate to the future power of each prenda. It was ultimately this power that we pursued and that bound us sleepless to our labors.

PART IV

Palo Craft

· · · · ·

Our movements among the dead in the process of building our prendas left us exhausted. The privilege of having helped to make Lucero for myself followed many months of dutiful work with both Isidra and Teodoro after my initiation as padre nganga. Learning how to make a prenda-nganga-enquiso is the first step in being able to confidently fashion Palo works, and that lesson is quickly followed by the realization that the prenda one has now committed to care for is a force of its own, forever reaching for greater power against its keeper. Cultivating struggle against a prenda is a refined way of ensuring that the craft worked through it is effective (chapter 16). Palo includes works of cleansing, protection, and attack, crafted with so-called prendas cristianas [Christian prendas] (chapter 17). These prendas are capacious versions of the dead; they are labored agglomerations of Kalunga and capable of accomplishing most healing commissions. But they alone do not guarantee the sovereignty of Kongo Law in Cuba, and for this paleras and paleros rely on the power of the much maligned prenda judía [Jewish prenda]. The prenda judía alone vouchsafes Palo's claim to equal participation in Cuba's Creole cosmos since the nineteenth century (chapter 18). Prendas judías are rare, but Teodoro kept one and together we worked with it on one occasion (chapters 19 and 20). One does not work with the prenda judía inconsequentially; it takes the intellectual and practical capacities of its keeper to the limits, and the world is never the same afterward.

16.   Struggle Is Praise

The prendas we built were feasted a few days after they were finished. Prendas should not sit around without having Palo played for them because the nfumbe inside become impatient and unruly. They are coaxed into their kettles and urns with promises of lavish tribute that must be met expediently. Our delay was due to our inability to find animals Isidra could afford, and it took time for our combined networks of underground exchange to bring the animals into our hands at a fair price. Ocha/Santo and Palo blossomed in the midnineties after the economic liberalization in 1994 and the visit of Pope John Paul II in 1998, and Havana's licit and illicit markets in sacrificial animals have been overwhelmed by demand since, with prices climbing exorbitantly. The presence of Ocha/Santo pilgrims from the United States, Spain, Venezuela, and Nigeria, among other places, who come with rushed initiation schedules and more dollars than most Cubans hope to see in a lifetime, has sent prices even higher the last several years, especially in the summer months.

Teodoro Tocayo, who in the end put a prenda together from the materials we didn't use in our work, was by training a rural veterinary technician, and it was through an informal economy of debt and service barter that bound him to farmers in Havana's immediate outskirts that we eventually got many of our animals. What Tocayo couldn't provide for his prenda, which were good materials from the countryside, he was able to provide in animal offerings. Each prenda we made and refurbished was feasted with a full complement of its preferred offerings. Lucero feasted on the blood of a young black goat and two young black roosters. Chola delighted in the blood of a yellow chicken. Isidra, always frugal, and always wary that envy would take root between her prendas, invited her existing prendas to share in the offerings of the new and refurbished ones, thus satiating every one. Her Siete

Rayos was fed the special offering of a large snapping turtle, a reddish ram, and two of the black and orange roosters in which this prenda delights. After the feast, which included invited members from the Manaquita house matching knowledge and testing wills—a contest Teodoro won—the prendas were left to sit, soaking in the offered blood for seven days.

The vital organs of each animal—heart, liver, kidneys—including those of the turtle, were sautéed and placed in little gourds at the foot of the prenda to which they had been offered. Atop each prenda as a crown of glory and death were the heads, and wing and tail feathers, of the animals it had consumed. The legs of the goats and rams flanked the prendas. Thus displayed, the prendas took on jarring animal likenesses, dressed as they were in the dismembered bodies of their sacrifices. Three days into their repose the blood and organs putrefied as the prendas wallowed in the decomposing majesty of the animals' spent lives. The smell of decayed flesh and the buzz of countless flies filled the air, and made the room where the prendas rested impossible to bear. Maggots covered the prendas and animal remains in teeming layers. Isidra was nearly driven out of her house by them and wanted badly to clean the prendas, especially when a neighbor across the alley threatened to call the police about the stench. But Teodoro mocked her and instead praised the flies and maggots. He insisted that we not disavow them but rather revel in their feast because they, too, oriented and capacitated the prendas. When the last thing we wanted to do was be near them, Teodoro urged us to fight our repulsion and make obeisance by sitting with the prendas for hours. During one such vigil he drew us nearer yet and, seemingly unmoved by the sight, pointed out the circular paths the thousands of maggots made as their bodies moved around the rim of each kettle or urn. "The dance of *chichi-bilongo,*" he said. He also demonstrated how the maggots shaved the hair off the heads and legs of the animals as they gnawed. "The hair falls into the prenda," he said, "just like the hair of the ngueyo. Chichi-bilongo are of the dead *[son cosa de muerto].* They wriggle *[menean]* between the living and the dead. When we die, the earth eats us *[ntoto uria nkombo],* and chichi-bilongo dances us along on our way to the dead. *Chichi-bilongo, mukango bacheche*—maggots are good for a prenda. They keep a prenda close to the dead, they are a blessing we Manaquitas don't discount."

Satiated with first offerings and fully vitalized, prendas assert their will. Palo elders like Pedro and Isidra say that new prendas want only the obedience and disciplined servitude of the padres and madres who keep them. They want only to be respected, praised, and fed. The real weight of this arrangement doesn't become evident until later, when a prenda makes demands that are difficult to meet. Prendas are inflexible and do not yield, even when their keepers have been meticulous. Prendas do not like stasis, and they seek blood to grow and become powerful. They desire to swell with offerings and, one day, with the blood of initiates. They often ask for more than their keepers can, or want, to give. Enrique Estévez Jiménez, the kimbisero from Oriente, spoke truthfully in this regard. When an offering cannot be made, regardless of circumstances, an air of uncertainty develops around a prenda.

Kongo Law stipulates the amount of attention prendas must receive. A full complement of animal offerings should be made to them once a year, on the anniversary of their making—their "birthday." Likewise, another day each year is set aside to honor each prenda with full offerings, the date of this feast corresponding with the feast day of the Ocha/Santo sovereign with which the prenda shares a likeness and into whose sovereignty they incur. Zarabanda, for example, will feast on the anniversary of its making, and also on June 29, which is the feast day of the Ocha/Santo sovereign Ogún and the Catholic San Pedro. A thoughtful and conservative godmother or godfather in Palo will understand the trouble of gathering the resources for such feasts and coordinate the birth of a prenda with its annual feast day, which is not only propitious but also lessens the burden carried by their initiate to one feast a year.

Prendas-ngangas-enquisos are also fed when they are worked, the offering provided by a palero's or palera's client. When prendas are used in crafting Palo, at least one rooster, if not two, should be offered to them, depending on the gravity of the case for which the work is being undertaken.[1] Serious cases of misfortune that require intricate Palo work may require the offerings of a four-legged animal, but this is rare. Palo maintains a great deal of prestige among Cubans because it fashions less costly "works" than Ocha/Santo or Ifá. In practice, the different kinds of offerings, which are the basis of prenda care, are often forgiven or discounted when crafting Palo because a client cannot afford them. The result is that Palo offerings are more ad hoc and incomplete than Kongo Law requires. Prendas and those who keep them manage nonetheless, and, as was evident in Teodoro's case, prendas are often worked with no offering at all and can go years with hardly any nourishment and still be effective. This, of course, depends on a prenda's caregiver, and his or her skill at keeping a hungry prenda subdued.

As a matter of course, a good part of becoming a madre or padre nganga is learning how to negotiate flexibly and intrepidly with a prenda for offerings and obeisance. The relationships of madres or padres with their prendas are lifelong. The better care prendas receive, the stronger they become and the better protection they offer their keepers from Palo attacks by others.

Well-kept prendas-ngangas-enquisos become indispensable guarantors of good fortune, health, and success in their keeper's ventures. At the same time, the more powerful prendas become, the more likely they are to overcome the will of their keepers and subject them to their whims. It is a careful arrangement of strength and will, obeisance and mastery, that paleras and paleros must achieve so that their prendas are as strong as possible, yet not so strong that they strip their keepers of their command.

The search for uninterrupted good fortune and peace can convert those who keep them into willful servants of their prendas, wholly subservient to them and never daring to command them in the working of Palo craft.[2] Many prendas sit in the homes of their keepers, who maintain them as powerful sentinels but hardly use them to craft Palo works. Isidra, it seemed to me, was close to this mode of prenda keeping. She served hers meticulously and exceeded by far the acts of obeisance stipulated by Kongo Law, a habit evident in the health of her prendas, which were moist, odorous, and vibrant. At the same time, she took hardly any clients and rarely worked her prendas. The harmony of her relationship with her prendas was, in fact, rooted in anxious respect. Isidra did not challenge their authority or sovereignty over her, even if the cost was dear. This was evident to me on many occasions, including numerous days when she would not leave her house because one of her prendas forbade it, regardless of her appointments.

Teodoro was also bound to the prendas of the Quita Manaquita house. Though he mostly refused to obey their demands to feast, and failed miserably in his other commitments to them, he was unable to free himself from their vice of obligation. Teodoro's posture toward his prendas vacillated between careless insubordination and guilt-ridden resentment. His relationship with them seemed shaped mostly by fateful acceptance of the fact that regardless of his diligence and whatever surrender he could muster, his burden would never become bearable.

A struggle of wills marks all relations between prendas and paleros, and this is evident from the first prenda that a madre or padre receives. Initiates to the status of madre and padre are normally forbidden from participating in the making of their first prenda, just as they are prohibited from sacrificing animals to it.[3] The result is that the new prenda, the power of which is incontestable by its recipient, harbors numerous mysteries the initiate fears probing. The initiates are dependent on the tata or yayi from whom they received their first prenda for the wisdom that unlocks the secrets to the prenda's handling and command. New padres and madres will spend years in obedient service to their tatas and yayis to slowly draw from them the knowledge necessary to negotiate successfully with their prendas. Until this is learned, a new prenda has a great advantage over its keeper and rules a palera's or palero's house as an inscrutable and terrifying ally. Tatas and yayis take advantage of this ignorance, adroitly withholding their teachings to keep an initiate subordinated as long as possible. The last thing a new madre or padre wants is to mishandle her or his prenda, for if it is not cared for to the letter of the version of Kongo Law taught by their tata or yayi, the prenda may cease protecting them. Worse yet, a neglected prenda might actively introduce ill fortune into its keeper's life.

The way to gain one's independence from a domineering yayi or tata and thus truly begin to benefit from a prenda's guarantee of safety and release, is to become a diligent student of Palo's teachings. These teachings are in songs, gleaned from listening carefully to senior tatas and yayis, and madres and padres, as they spar with sung riddles at Palo feasts. Lessons are culled from the movements of a madrina's or padrino's body when handling their prendas-ngangas-enquisos. Senior tatas and yayis teach the craft of command over prendas, and over the dead, only reluctantly and then only to their most loyal initiates. They always hide bits of wisdom from their students, and the learning is slow. One must know how to ask oblique questions wound in respect and subordination and in such a way begin to learn the first things about handling a prenda. Not until one is invited to help in the making of a prenda, however, does one truly begin to understand these entities and turn the tables of command.

Negotiations between a keeper and his or her prenda are often, though not always, mediated and modified by chamalongo queries. The back and forth in negotiating command is often sung on the part of the palera or palero, who discerns the prenda's potentials as pulses in Kalunga, the ambient dead. What is picked up [recogido] is verified and fixed by throws of the chamalongo. The contours of subordination and control assumed by person and prenda are functions of a person's skill at devising for oneself new throws of the chamalongo. This is a Palo virtue, but not easily accomplished. It requires a command of Palo Kikongo songs and speech, but more than anything, it demands endurance on the part of the keeper when confronting the fear and doubt involved in tarrying long with an unsatisfied and unpredictable prenda.

Considering the many obstacles that stand between padres and madres and the eventual command of their prendas, the easiest posture to assume when confronted with the captivating promises of their prendas and their equally powerful shapes of dread is one of subordination. Bowing to the will of the prenda is the most conservative and prudent arrangement. This means that day in and day out it is usually prendas that enjoy the deference of their keepers and makers. Learning to overcome submission to prendas, if only momentarily, so that the finest benefits of commanding them can be had, remains the goal of all who acquire them.

Like Isidra, most keepers of prendas-ngangas-enquisos manage a workable submission. The ambient and responsive dead are invoked to counter the prendas, in a delicate balance of power that begins to emerge between prendas and keeper. Isidra triumphed over her prendas only with the help of her dear responsive dead, which she would gather near and which would help her interpret the will of her formidable Siete Rayos, Madre de Agua, and other prendas. Her dead, and her keen attunement with the ambiance in which they and her prendas subsisted, were her ultimate protection from the various prendas she kept, if ever these turned and harmed her.

In fact, Isidra's mother and aunts and other responsive dead would never have allowed her to receive her prendas without their consent. It is always one's dead that lead one to Palo, give permission for initiations, and stand with one when commitments to prendas are made.[4] One's dead are prepared for the challenge of dealing with a prenda. It is they who have called a prenda forth from out of the ambient dead. Why this is so I cannot say for sure; for though I was surrounded by responsive dead throughout my fieldwork, they were rarely forthcoming with their motives. I can only assume one's responsive dead recognize the precariousness of what it means for the living to drift aimlessly amid the indifferent flows of Kalunga and so seek allies for them. The nfumbe that are sought for prendas are as much versions of the ambient dead as are one's responsive dead, and they share significant affinities with the living, like having bodies and names. However, the nfumbe are also strangely anonymous, in that they are drawn almost at random from the generic multitude of the dead. The nfumbe serve as a kind of hinge between the living and ambient dead. They are a form of both and serve in a capacity unimaginable for the responsive dead. These qualities lend the nfumbe particular importance, and lead one's responsive dead to seek them out to be made into a prenda.

Speculations about the motivations of the responsive dead aside, it is ultimately the nfumbe that makes a prenda forceful. Every palera and palero desires their nfumbe to rest placated, but not diminished, inside their prenda. During their move from grave to cauldron, the nfumbe are disturbed and every effort is made to cool and settle them. Once the cauldrons and urns have been packed and finished, they are bathed in the heat and force of an animal's blood. Offerings of blood fortify and bring the nfumbe back to contentious volatility, just as they fuse the nfumbe with the other contents packed with them. The more they are fed, the more animated and vibrant prendas become.

Having a vivacious nfumbe animating one's prenda brings hardships on its keeper, but paleras and paleros would prefer nothing more. Energetic nfumbe are sought for the making of powerful prendas, and paleros and paleras often boast about the impositions and unreasonable demands of their most powerful ones. It is better to have a prenda known for being overbearing in its dominance, and rebellious in its submission, than for its benevolence or passivity. Palo loves speed, strength, and clever decisiveness and attributes these qualities to its most precious prendas. The profound respect, and even foreboding, paleras and paleros feel toward the dead drives them to wish for vigorous and mercurial nfumbe. This bolsters and elevates prendas—as sentinels, armaments, and rivals.

Built, vitalized, and engaged in a struggle for command, prendas are worked. They are worked in a labor of will and fearful love that casts paleros headlong into the flows of the ambient dead. With the same heave of one's fate into the surges and currents of Kalunga that one makes when prendas are built, paleras and paleros seek out the ambient dead to craft its immanent flows into an instrument of their will. They craft the dead in intimacy, through audacious turns of its many forms, many of which are packed and concentrated in a prenda. Out of respect for prendas, the rules of Kongo Law are followed in these manipulations and the responsive dead are always invoked to assist.

Even Teodoro's prendas, which languished unattended in the decaying Manaquita praise house, were treated according to Kongo Law when he worked with them. Teo principally used his Lucero, though many *tratados*, or "works," required him to employ a combination of prendas, including Mama Chola, Centella Ndoki, and Ma're Lango. When he worked Palo, Teo would speak and sing to his prendas in Palo Kikongo. He would praise the prendas with songs that called them by name and elevated them, and he promised them specific offerings within improvised verses. Sometimes he would apologize plaintively for not making sufficient offerings, and when he broached the topic of his neglect, he begged them pitifully to tolerate him a little longer. Dusty and dry, hardly vital at all, Teodoro's prendas were often sluggish in answering him or responded to his throws of the chamalongo in diffuse, unenthusiastic terms. However disappointing, this was an obstacle the knowledgeable Teodoro could surmount, and he used his understanding of the creases and folds of Palo command until he eventually won over his despondent prendas. When he needed to, he would use harsh language and threats with them, raising his voice and commanding his prendas to work for him.

Standing over his prendas he would shout at them and insult them, if need be, to make them come to life and ready themselves to be worked.

Teodoro's aggressive posturing when working his prendas is hardly rare for those who work Palo.[5] Isidra did not address her prendas in this way, but she did not call on her prendas to obey her very often. My sense is that Teodoro's mode of addressing his prendas is the more common among paleros when they work their craft. I think this if only because Teodoro's attitude toward his prendas was codified in the very language with which prendas are addressed. Exemplary of this was Teodoro's use of the word *arrear* to mean the working of Palo against an enemy. He would say with anticipation and energy before getting down to business with his prendas, "*¡Vamo' a arrear!*" In Spanish, arrear means to drive, as in to drive mules or cattle forward. The image of powerful, reluctant animals rustled and forced forward is the correct one.[6] In the case of Teodoro's prendas, the idea of powerful and displeased beasts prodded to move was appropriate. The prodding is also a reference to the enemy about to be stung with Palo craft. But there is a second definition of the verb *arrear* that points to the prendas as the recipient of the action. *Arrear* in Spanish also means "to adorn," as in a prized animal before it is displayed, which is fitting to the way one engages with one's prendas. Despite pushing and struggling against them so they would meet his demands and resenting them when they punished him, Teodoro always accorded his prendas great respect and went to lengths to honor and elevate them when working with them.

Struggle returns again and again. To raise one's relationship with a prenda to the level of a struggle is the greatest compliment a prenda can receive. It is a prenda's most lavish adornment. Publicly stated relations of contention with a prenda ground its prestige, potential, and force and require sumptuous expenditures of energy and time on behalf of its keeper to sustain. The attention of its keeper is what a prenda wants more than anything, and there is nothing like the attention lavished on a needed rival. Prendas and keepers alike revel in the stories of a prenda's stubbornness, rebelliousness, and ruthless despotism. Such anecdotes maintain the prestige of prendas in the minds of those privileged enough to have relations with them. Requiring punishment or coercion and having the fame of being strong enough to resist its keeper's prods, becomes part of a prenda's air of autonomy and vigor. Teodoro's Lucero, which he blamed for the unfortunate situation in which the Manaquitas found themselves, was surrounded with just such a narrative of strength and struggle, coercion, treachery, and surrender.

17. Cristianas

No prenda in Teodoro's house was revered like his Lucero. That prenda had once been second to those collected and cared for by Emilio at the Quita Manaquita house. Emilio's Zarabanda was always the most exalted and, as the center of Manaquita praise, received effusive offerings. With Emilio's death, Teodoro's Lucero recognized in its keeper an opening for itself, and it began to claim attention and priority over the others. Even if Teodoro had wanted to keep Emilio's Zarabanda central to the Manaquita house, he could not have. Day by day his Lucero weighed on him. There was not a mishap or an unexpected turn of good fortune that Teodoro didn't attribute to that prenda and to his obedience or defiance of it. Soon, Teodoro's Lucero came to rule the Manaquita house, its mirrored eye surveying the world from under the conch shell's rim. Lucero wants to be first, above all.

When I was introduced to it in 1999 Lucero was the only Manaquita prenda to have feasted in a long time. Teo used it for his day-to-day consultations and healing, and by this labor it managed to squeeze from Teodoro an occasional sacrifice. Lucero was laden with packets and bundles and folded pieces of paper. People came to see Teodoro from all over, some from distant places, like Pinar Del Rio in western Cuba, where Teo had traveled a lot in his father's day. His clients were often people with some connection of initiation or otherwise fictive kinship to the Quita Manaquita house or were referred to Teodoro on the strength of the lingering Manaquita prestige. But most of Teodoro's clientele was from Guanabacoa, and many of his regular visitors were people from his neighborhood.

The people who consulted with Teodoro sought, among other things, limpiezas [cleansings]. Also called *despojos* [clearings], these are the first order of Palo intervention against misfortune. They brush ill-boding dead out of an afflicted person, then distance them into the indifferent flows of

Kalunga, where it is hoped they will be dispersed. Limpiezas are performed in both Palo and Ocha/Santo. Often a person comes looking for help with a bad turn of luck and in consultation with her or his dead a limpieza is prescribed. Almost always the ill-will of a client's rival is perceived to be disturbing the calm of the dead surrounding and permeating the person. Both Teodoro and Isidra detected such disturbances and instabilities regularly around people who consulted with them. Telltale symptoms of people afflicted thus were sleeplessness, nervousness, anxiety, feelings of dread, persistent unhappiness, and bad dreams. The symptoms are physical, and those who keep prendas-ngangas-enquisos understand them as turbulent turns of the dead saturating the afflicted. At the same time, they appreciate that what they are healing is *fate*, and thus the life that is suspended in it.

Limpiezas involve different combinations of fresh herbs, sometimes seven, sometimes fourteen different kinds, sometimes more, each combination having different strengths or qualities to turn the dead. The cool vitality of the herbs is drawn from the prodigiously indifferent force of the ambient dead as this is actualized in profligate nature. This coolness is used as a counter to the ill-portending heat and turbulent currents provoked by hostile intentions, which are sent through Kalunga, to press close to and afflict a person. A wilting plant is considered evidence that ill and woe have passed through the surrounding dead and been absorbed by the plant.

To free a person of a foul future the herbs are bundled into hand brooms that are cooled with aspirations of aguardiente and fumigations of cigar smoke. They are then used to sweep out the hot and unstable dead permeating and surrounding the body of the afflicted. In Palo, limpiezas usually call for the client to come dressed in an old T-shirt soiled with his or her sweat. Before the limpieza begins, the afflicted is asked to speak aloud the names of his or her dead, as these must be among those consulted for direction during the cleansing. After sweeping and swatting the body with the broom, amid songs to focus the intention of the cleansing, the shirt is torn from the client's body by the attending palera or palero, who casts it to the ground. Having twisted and broken the herbs now laden with the ill-portending dead, these are wrapped in the torn shirt and the whole bundle is set ablaze, or not, and finally sent out of the house, depending on where the responsive dead, or the prenda—letting their intentions be known through throws of the chamalongo—want them sent. They are usually wrapped in a plastic bag and dumped where the dangerous charge they carry will disperse, places Palo and Ocha/Santo recognize for their great power to dissipate ill will back into the ambient dead—forests, open plains, fields gone wild, cemeteries, railroad tracks, and the enormous roots of ceibas and jagueyes are common places.

Isidra was good at limpiezas and specialized in them. But limpiezas alone could hardly meet all the needs of the clients she admitted, most of whom she would refer to Teodoro when further work was required to straighten their fate. Misfortune is so oppressive that rarely are people convinced that a swatting with herbs will improve their lot, and many undergo limpiezas only as a preliminary step in pursuit of a calm horizon.

Palo and Ocha/Santo are often interwoven in an afflicted person's pursuit of healing, and it is usually after exhausting resources in Ocha/Santo that one approaches Palo in search of relief from hard luck. Ocha/Santo interventions include divination with cowry shells that indicate herbal prescriptions and acts of obeisance for attending to one's allies among the dead and purifying one's grace with Ocha/Santo sovereigns. They include cleansings such as limpiezas and may include a visit to the oracle of Ifá, kept by babalawos. The oracle of Ifá prescribes offerings and acts of obeisance directed toward the entire assemblage of Ocha/Santo sovereigns, who are entreated to intervene on behalf of the afflicted to set things right with his or her fate according to their command over different realms of human affairs.[1]

Ocha/Santo and Ifá combat an unpropitious fate by drawing on the vigilance of one's responsive dead and the sovereign justice of the Orichas as their principal means of healing. Often, what they are said to combat is the envy and ill will of others. Santeros will say that when all is well with one's dead and when one's Ocha/Santo sovereigns are pleased with their subject, then if affliction remains it must be caused by the ill wishes of another. Such ill wishes are made vital and dangerous through Palo craft, which fashions them into potent versions of the dead. Paleros, too, for that matter, say Palo craft is the means by which ill will is given force and turned toward actuality among the dead. Once ill will is thus churned up, it becomes a shadow portending misfortune as it spreads through the ambient dead like a toxin. It seeks to afflict with disease, loss, humiliation, and death. Ocha/Santo combats these by rallying one's responsive dead and the sovereigns of Ocha/Santo to defend the afflicted and ward off the attack, thus dissipating the shadow of dread back into the ambient dead whence it was drawn. Ocha/Santo and Ifá tend to fear and pour scorn on Palo, though many santeros and adepts Ifá are initiates in Palo and attribute to Palo great power as a remedy of last resort. Ocha/Santo and Ifá do not, by and large, reply to an aggressor with aggressive craft of their own. That is Palo's privilege and the source of its prestige and disdain. Where Ocha/Santo and Ifá cease in their efforts to produce much-needed relief from affliction, Palo picks up. It does so with wisdom and knowledge of its craft, gleaned from bending close to the dead.

After a limpieza, sometimes along with it, Palo has one principal defensive work, called a resguardo. Making resguardos was among Teodoro's specialties. Resguardos are combinations of Palo substances valued for their protective effects. Tiny pieces of nfumbe left over from prenda making, offensive and defensive branches shaved or grated into dust, and tiny pinches of earth from a grave and from an anthill are usually included. Resguardos often include many substances besides, from coins to little bits of silver; feathers are important, as are other animal remains. Pervasive in Palo bundles is kimbansa, a prolific grass that grows everywhere like a weed, in cracks in the sidewalk, empty lots, and the deep forest, where a clearing lets in the sun. Kimbansa is lavish nature condensed into its humblest, most ubiquitous form. Isidra said kimbansa had a compact with the dead because "it is everywhere and born of itself."

Once the materials are collected, they are tied into tiny bundles with corn husks as wrappers.[2] These are then sewn into little cloth packets that can be carried on the body at all times. A good resguardo can be no bigger than a bottle cap. As the resguardos are worked, they are sung over to bring their substances into relation with one another and to focus the intention of their making. Depending on the quality of the aggression one seeks to counter, the little packets are then sung into relation with the prenda best suited to help the client: Siete Rayos to defend against furtive attack; Zarabanda against open aggression; Ma're Lango for struggles against women, sorcery against one's children, and misfortune with fertility; Mama Chola against jealousy, sexual manipulation, and other affronts to one's love. Other prendas protect in other matters. Lucero, for example, shields against misfortune in one's trajectory through life, including one's travels and attempts to enter or exit different social strata.

Once sung into affinity with a chosen prenda, tuned to it, the resguardo should be offered the blood of that prenda's preferred meal of fowl. The blood of the animal vitalizes the substances in the resguardo and places prenda and resguardo within the same currents of Kalunga. When the sacrificial bird can't be had, usually because the client cannot afford it, paleras and paleros will use prepared blood they keep bottled for making resguardos. Once fed and brought into affinity with a prenda, the resguardo acts as a warning to any offensive dead that all the power of the prenda stands behind its bearer.

Limpiezas and resguardos sometimes have only limited effect, and when a person's horizons do not clear or misfortune compounds, Palo craft becomes more aggressive and seeks to address directly those suspected of causing affliction. Palo, in its conceptions of misfortune, attributes it principally to the ill will and actions of other people. Paleras and paleros seek out the aggressors, who are usually motivated by envy or bitterness. They identify these antagonists in the anecdotes, doubts, and intuitions of their clients, who usually have a sense of those in their lives who do not wish them well. Paleras and paleros recognize that in their doubts and subtle fears their clients are actualizing the dead around them, and so they seek to verify and nuance these intuitions with chamalongo queries. The chamalongo, which actualize the will of the prenda and the dead surrounding the afflicted, indicate without failure those responsible for a client's troubles. The name of the aggressor is quickly discerned and, with this in hand—and the client's consent to begin work—paleras and paleros will pursue the offending party and cut them down, fighting misfortune with misfortune.

Palo's wisdom comprehends what it means to suffer misfortune. It understands how misfortune circulates and sickens the atmosphere around an afflicted person. Those who work Palo understand that a sense of dread hardly dissipates of its own accord, and when the ill-meaning person who is the source of hardship is discovered, Palo teaches that what has been sent must be returned. When an aggressor persists in perturbing a person time and again, so that neither limpieza nor resguardo has succeeded in relieving a client, then the cure is a counterattack. Whereas Ocha/Santo and its priesthood of Ifá attempt to dissuade those aggressed from counterattacking by dissipating their fear and anger with rites meant to cool their head and purify their relation with the dead and the sovereigns of Ocha/Santo, Palo guards another teaching. It studies envy as a force with a will of its own. Palo knows envy lurks in all people and that those who are overcome by it will not cease to wish dread on those whom they resent. Palo knows that regardless of the healing prowess of Ocha/Santo and Ifá (the efficiency of which paleras and paleros by and large do not doubt), there will always be cases where the victim of misfortune must reply with force. The afflicted are driven to Palo when they are struck with misfortune again and again. Isidra said, "At the end of the day, when your enemies won't let up, it's at the foot of a prenda nganga that you'll find a solution to your pain."

Teodoro understood how desperate the desire to be rid of misfortune could become. He understood from his own experience the depths of despondence, and he received those who suffer foreboding unto despair so that if they must strike back to feel hope they could do so. Teo understood the limit where the harm of one and the freedom of another—from fear or subordination—were bound inextricably together. He understood the point when one must act, or sink into desolation. He harbored the wisdom of the emphatic reply to ill will and knew attack as his most reliable mode of healing.

Palo teaches that misfortune and the dead are bound together. It understands how the living are immersed in, and saturated by, the oceanic mass of Kalunga. Its teaching is that this mass can protect and heal the living, just as it can be turned against the living to become a conduit of harm. Palo is the art of communicating an atmosphere of hope or dread across the expanses of the ambient dead, to change the fates of the living. With experience, a practitioner of Palo can detect when misfortune has been worked against a person and determine what form a reply must assume. Usually, the response involves works of misfortune, too. In the service of protecting and healing a client, practitioners of Palo negotiate the multifarious surfaces of harm to create an acrid atmosphere around an aggressor. This is done by appropriating the great fluid vastness of Kalunga to send a counterstrike of misfortune with the speed and clarity of sound passing through water. The capacity to produce such transformations in the atmosphere of the dead around a person is Palo's pride. It is effective and unsentimental.

To paleras and paleros, their work takes on many names. To refer to Palo in general, Teodoro used the noun *brujo* [witch]. To refer to Palo strikes of misfortune crafted with Palo, he used the nouns *kindiambazo* [prenda hit] and *cazuelazo* [cauldron blow]. To refer to the crafting of these strikes, he used the verbs *brujear* [witch-ify], *arrear* [goad], and *guerrear* [to war, battle]. Among Cubans in general, it is *brujería* [witchcraft] that is most commonly used to refer to the work of paleras and paleros; though the word carries negative connotations in Spanish (as do the English "witchery" or "witchcraft"), it is not a word from which practitioners of Palo shy away. Certainly Teodoro was proud to refer to himself as a brujo and to work brujo *[trabajar el brujo]*. To brujear, he would tell you, was his life's passion. *"¡Que lindo es el brujo!"* I heard him exclaim time and again. "Witchcraft," he would say, "is lovely."

But among paleros, by far the most popular term for their works of emphatic reply is *bilongo*. In Palo Kikongo, *bilongo* means "a work," and Cabrera and Díaz Fabelo, in their respective dictionaries of Palo terms, recognize it as "witchcraft."[3] The word is commonly enough used by paleros, and persuasive enough in its sound and intimations that it has slipped into popular usage; perhaps among people in Havana's poor neighborhoods it is as common as *brujería*. Famous salsa pieces have been written about bilongos, especially in reference to their use in love magic.[4]

Its popular currency aside, for paleros who know its workings the bilongo carries all of the weight of laboring with the dead. To work a bilongo, the ambient dead is agitated and its anonymous flows gathered and engaged through manipulations of matter, which are made important with words and songs. The most common bilongo Teodoro worked took the shape of a bundle or packet, which had wrapped inside many of the same substances he used in resguardos: ground nfumbe and pinches of the principal earths that constitute prendas, especially grave dirt and dirt from hospitals, jails, police stations, crossings, and workplaces. Just what earth was included in a specific bilongo depended on the wishes of the aggrieved and on the strategy Teodoro devised for the counterstrike. Wishing illness to befall an aggressor meant adding earth from a grave and from a hospital. Sulfur and different colored powders were added depending on the intention of the work. Black was an important color. When Teodoro spied hairy spiders or lizards, he would catch them and toast them over a burner until they could be crumbled into dust. He would add these to his bilongos. He said these pests [bichos] would travel with the dead at his command and would drive inside his victims, then bite and sting from the inside to herald illness, just as they do in life.[5]

A word is due on the use of pests in Palo craft. That hairy spiders and centipedes and lizards and scorpions are ground up and added to the contents of bilongos may sound cliché, being too strong an echo of medieval European images of witchcraft. That slaves in Cuba could have picked up this imagery from the Spanish is hardly impossible and that they would have appropriated it is also not difficult to imagine, because they would have found it so persuasive over their oppressors. In fact, such turns of European specters are at the heart of Palo craft. This said, Cabrera records another source for the power of pests in Palo craft. By the reckoning of some of her oldest informants, who in turn evoked their dead in their thinking, when pests—*bichilingos, vitilingos,* or *la soyanga* in the Palo Kikongo of Cabrera's day—begin to overtake the house of an old person, they do so as heralds of the old one's death.[6] Lizards soon follow to prey on the insects. When these come it is understood that death is inevitable. That a progressing infestation accompanies the weakening of an old person would seem obvious and that bugs and lizards are thus considered privileged associates of death, its heralds and its avatars, makes practical sense. These animals are then sought for Palo craft, so that they might, by virtue of their intimacy with the dead, afflict the intended recipient of a bilongo.

Teodoro's bilongos also included shavings or pinches of sawdust from palos, like those in his prendas-ngangas-enquisos, chosen for their effects within unencumbered nature. Different trees actualize different turns of the dead in their hardness or smell or the pattern of their knots, so the choice of stick depended on the particular effect he sought to fashion in the ambient dead churning in the recipient of his bilongos. Teodoro also liked to use the feathers of owls, vultures, woodpeckers, and other birds when these were available.

Once the dirt, sawdust, crushed bones, feathers, and pests were ground together, the name of the party to be assailed was included among the contents of Teodoro's bilongos. If his clients managed to bring materials that belonged to the person they sought to assail—hair, scraps of clothing, a cigarette butt, a photograph—these were added. The whole of the contents were placed into a moist corn husk, which became their casing. Before the husk was closed, Teo would take a few pinches of the dusty contents, which he would set aside for later use. The cornhusk was then twisted and knotted and further wrapped in black cloth, then bound with black thread. Once the heart of the bilongo was fabricated and packed away, Teodoro would have his clients, if they were present, do the winding with the thread, always in cycles away from their body, while repeating to themselves the name of the person they sought to overpower.

Bilongos assume other forms than the simple packet. These are dictated by the conventions of the craft—Palo Briyumba, Palo Mayombe, Palo Monte, or Palo Kimbisa—by the teachings of a particular house and by the intentions of the palera or palero making them. Around the roots of ceibas in Havana one can occasionally see a sour orange, cut in half and sandwiching coffee grounds, salt, and a piece of paper with the name of the person the fate of which the bilongo is meant to sour and embitter (in Spanish, *salar*, to salt). A variation on the common bilongo is to tie the bundle just under the head of a railroad spike by winding it with black thread. Bilongos can also take the shape of jars and bottles containing all those substances meant to salt or poison the ambient dead around one and thus bring mournful days to the bilongo's intended recipient. Bilongos made in jars are by far the most interesting and beautiful of Palo's works of emphatic reply. Other forms are available, and there is much room for inspired customization in bilongo craft. Teodoro was a skilled bilongo craftsperson and sometimes could spend a whole afternoon assembling a packet or two and bringing them into relation with his prendas, especially with his Lucero, by working with blood from a sacrifice.

Material turns of the dead are directly incorporated into bilongo craft, with the intention of catalyzing the emergence of other versions of the dead in and around the bilongo's intended recipient. A well-crafted bilongo should inspire unexpected intuitions, fragments of memories, old fears, and insidious rumors that, together, poison the recipient's sense of security. Bilongos have their greatest efficacy in these registers, which are simultaneously worked to subtly reveal the bilongo to the intended recipient.

Most bilongos are buried in the ground close to the home of their target, if possible in their backyard or close to their front door. Teodoro said that a buried bilongo was more powerful because it would "root" and begin to turn the dead that permeated the earth toward the intentions folded into the bilongo. Prendas, it is said, are sometimes buried for this purpose, and the practice of burying bilongos is a further reflection of Palo's confidence in earth as a substrate of and for the dead. The pinch of dust Teodoro took from the bilongo in the moment before it was tied he carried folded in brown paper. He either took this with him when he went to bury the bilongo or gave it to his client, often a spouse or family member of the bilongo's intended recipient, whom he entrusted to place the bilongo. The pinch of dust was then placed in the palm and blown on the threshold of the recipient's home or, in the case of bilongos intended to turn lovers or spouses, blown into their closets or their bed. The dead in the prenda with which the bilongo has been brought into relation will then go to it "like a bloodhound," said Teodoro. Across the boundless expanses of Kalunga the bilongo draws the nfumbe inside the prenda, which, when sent on an errand of attack, Teodoro called *nfuiri* or *ndoki*.[7] A properly crafted bilongo, correctly bundled and sung over, praised and charged, will draw a ndoki without fail, as a force traveling between fixed points.

This is the moment of a bilongo's action, the moment when it is revealed to be working against a person who takes notice of the dust or of the upturned earth where the bilongo is buried. Sometimes, a palero or palera is caught off guard burying a bilongo, and the work is left exposed where it can be seen and retrieved by the intended recipient. When it is detected, the bilongo remands its recipient to the domain of murmurs and whispers and unleashes the unlimited potentials of intuitive guesses, to which the recipient succumbs to discover who, and what exactly, is arrayed against her or him. Suspicion becomes a question, which is whispered to and fro, and as it circulates it increases until it becomes fear, usually working in favor of the bilongo's sender. This, of course, depends much on the skill of the palera or palero who, along with her or his client, must be good weavers of insinuation if the work is to have utmost effect. It is not surprising that José Lazaro, among Cabrera's dear informants, referred to Palo craft as *murumba*, which I take to be a Palo Kikongo pun on the Spanish *murmurar*, to whisper.[8]

Tidings of ill will travel through everyday whispers and unattributed mumblings, which are turned by the bilongo. This is the vehicle whereby ill will is made to proliferate around a person, through the viral appropriation of allusions and insinuations. Bilongos are crafted with this in mind and leave multiple traces, as much in words as in sprinkles of dust on bed sheets, so that in the very instant they are revealed they give rise to the anticipation of the strike. Thus they compound reality.[9] Bilongos are the material form secreted by ill will, which then exudes allusions that inspire fear and turn the imagination dark and fearful. Bilongos are so successful at inspiring gloomy interpretations that people often imagine them to be at work where they are not, seeing in earth upturned by an animal or in dust collected on a windowsill the bad intentions of some enemy. Well-made and well-placed bilongos embed in the ambient dead surrounding a person and quickly transform it to dread. Thus, the bilongo begins to darken the recipient's course. Without strong connections to the dead to defend against the bilongo and determine the quality of the ambient dead around one in a positive manner, and without having the confidence and coolness from the protection of an Ocha/Santo sovereign or having a prenda of one's own to receive the blow, then the recipient of the bilongo will feel his or her life turn sour. This is why Palo is sought to respond, again and again.

A bilongo is worthless in the eyes of the palera or palero who makes it if it isn't bound through blood to one prenda or another. In Havana, the prendas Lucero, Zarabanda, Siete Rayos, Ma' Kalunga, Mama Chola, Centella Ndoki, and Tiembla Tierra are the generative powers of Palo craft. In a practice like Teodoro's, these prendas are used every day for the production of resguardos and bilongos, and the ill that is received by them, and channeled out again, is great. Each has different specialties of action and is employed according to its keeper's strategy of response. These prendas, which are the principal agents Palo Briyumba builds and keeps, are known collectively as prendas cristianas [Christian prendas]. They are called cristianas because they contain holy water from a Catholic Church and are thus considered baptized. A baptized prenda is also supposed to contain a Christian nfumbe, taken from a cemetery where one can assume the host of the dead gathered there are baptized. Teodoro considered most cemeteries Christian, and in Havana the only exceptions were Guanabacoa's Jewish cemetery, and the city's Chinese cemetery. Correspondingly, almost all prendas used today are cristianas.

The importance of a prenda being cristiana, or not, has to do with the range of action it is said to possess. Prendas cristianas, because of the nfumbe they contain, said Isidra, have a pact with the Christian God, made at the moment of their baptism. They are thus, as Christians, excluded from killing. Their intended use is to protect their keepers and their clients from malicious Palo craft and to reply to damage done to fate by striking against rivals. With a prenda cristiana, Palo works counterstrikes against the sender of ill will and emphatically demonstrates the dangers of persisting in harming the afflicted. But with a prenda cristiana one does not seek to kill.

By Isidra's reckoning, one who sends ill will and then receives it in return will usually desist, because shadows come to worry their fortunes, and once troubled they realize the mistake they have made in seeking to harm. Isidra trusted a counterstrike crafted with a prenda cristiana and considered it sufficient in most cases of affliction. In fact, she was a teacher of moderation when it came to crafting a reply to an aggressor. She was sure they would desist if the message was clear. Palo craft did not have to be brutal, in her eyes. Teodoro was more jaded about the motives of others and tended to craft his responses to a person's aggression with the firmest strikes a prenda cristiana could muster. He was partial to working with his Lucero Mundo but was just as comfortable engaging his Zarabanda or crafting bilongos that involved bringing two prendas into relation, so that the aggrieved would have a bilongo that benefited from the powers of each. He did not think that an aggressor's will was easily bent, and he preferred that his work be decisive. This was a Palo virtue.

Even so, Teodoro knew there was no end to the back and forth of Palo craft. Unlike Isidra, he did not expect even his finest bilongos to go unanswered. He knew well enough that his work would likely draw a response from his clients' rivals. A good part of his task as a healer was to absorb such replies himself, so that his clients needn't. Thus it was hoped the hardships of the aggrieved would come to an end, with Teodoro serving as the firewall against the back blow. For this he had his prendas, which as a collective assemblage were a formidable barrier to fend off most kinds of strikes and counterstrikes.

Teo saw his world clearly enough—for him Palo was about strength and cunning, and the only guarantee one could have against the envy and hatred of others was more strength, more knowledge, and more courage. This is why he appreciated the craft of prendas cristianas, because their work was not of a deadly sort. Prendas cristianas are used to frighten, sicken, intimidate, and coerce—but not kill. This made working with them sustainable and, at the level of strategy and subtlety of craft, exquisitely challenging. "A Christian," said Teodoro, "cannot kill. That is practically mathematical. Christians can't kill; God forbids them."

Isidra, however, was unconvinced. She believed prendas cristianas could kill if not properly handled. She said that she had seen deadly Palo worked only with cristianas and that the issue was keeping the prenda under control.

There was also the matter of how long a victim would survive with a poisoned fate. If a prenda is being worked against someone and they aren't properly protected, eventually, she said, a blow that would have otherwise glanced off will strike squarely, and the person will be killed. "It is a matter of seconds when stepping into the street," she said. "You may just step in front of a truck one second too soon. That's bad luck; you were rushing; you were distracted, but that's what bilongos are about."

Isidra used her prendas cristianas sparingly and tended to them meticulously; for these reasons she felt she had complete control over their strikes and blows when she chose to send them. Isidra had a friend, a militant in the party like herself, whose daughter, Belén, consulted with her occasionally. Belén was a young woman in her early twenties, crazy to leave Cuba no matter what. She was a dreamer, a young woman lost in fantasies of wealth and glamour that supposedly waited for her in another country. She was not a person who spent much time in the present, and her daydreams about the life she would have, if she could only get out, were her passion. She was not unlike many young people in Cuba today. With the help of a friend from Spain, she joined an Internet matchmaking service and in no time was swamped with letters from Spanish men jumping on the next flight to Havana. One offer materialized, and the eager Spaniard arrived brimming with money to show his newfound girlfriend a good time.

In his letters and telephone calls the man had been perfectly decent, but as the visit unfolded, Belén grew disenchanted. He was more than twice her age and spent most of his time drunk and propositioning other women. As a matter of course, he developed a crush on a friend of Belén's who didn't seem to mind his drinking and carrying on. Before long it was rumored that the Spaniard was going to leave Cuba with her. Belén couldn't imagine that her friend would steal away her hope of getting off the island. Her disappointment sank Belén into a terrible depression, which kept her from doing anything to confront the situation, and it seemed obvious to her mother that Belén should see Isidra to figure out exactly what was going on. In short time it was discerned with the help of Belen's dead and Isidra's Siete Rayos that in fact her friend was working Palo against her.

Despite her anger and further disappointment, Belén wanted nothing terrible to befall the couple. When she handed Isidra photographs of each of them, out of which Isidra was to fashion a bilongo to respond to her friend's deceits, she pleaded with Isidra that her work not be deadly. She just wanted them separated. She wanted the man to leave Cuba alone. Isidra was confident, not only that she could accomplish what Belén wanted, but also that the couple, besides their dashed hopes, would not be harmed. She put Belén through a limpieza to lift her depression, then took responsibility for the rest. Because she had only prendas cristianas with which to work and because her prendas were satiated with generous offerings, they would not overreach their objective. The bilongo Isidra fashioned for Belén was a "beautiful" work employing a small jar made of brown glass, the photographs Belén gave her, and two tiny dolls, which were packed along with powder made of grave earth, salt, coffee grounds, the rind of a sour orange, and shavings directly from sticks protruding from her Siete Rayos. Belén's involvement with the work seemed to lift her spirits.

Not all people are as benign as Belén and Isidra. For some hurt and anger grow to consume their lives. For having lost her ticket off the island and a good friend in the same instant, Belén's disappointment hardly bore any ill will, except for wanting the Spaniard to leave Cuba as unlucky as she had been. In other instances, ill wishes do not cease at wanting bad luck to befall another. Enmities run deep in people and sometimes their pain does not relent until the fantasy of having a rival die overtakes them. Wishing someone would die is hardly a rare sentiment, especially among those subjected mercilessly to the will of another. Cornered by anguish, envy, or hatred, a person's fantasies can assume distorted dimensions of cruelty and simultaneous emancipation. The relationship between the two is ancient, and the wish of death can become so persuasive that it is nurtured with affection until it settles into a person's depths. There it can become baroque in its designs, such that people are capable of imagining all kinds of suffering and humiliation befalling their adversaries before they perish.

Great pleasure is derived from such imaginings, but they sicken too. Like a narcotic, the consuming desire to be rid of a feared enemy grips one in a deadly, loving vice. The pleasure of such desires corresponds to visions of release from a relationship of asphyxiating subordination, which are unfortunately impossible to imagine without first passing through the tainted fantasies. Such lethal imaginings often involve long, dreadful tangents, with little to offer except to further sink one into self-loathing, knowing that one should not want to kill another. Ugly pits of disconsolation come to pock the self.

Palo foresees this affliction and can help lift a person from such dead ends. Palo gives form and flight to such wishes and recruits the dead to such ends as one's dreams of woe envision, so that in ubiquitous anonymity the dead bring despair, pain, and death upon another. It proposes a cure to the hatred and the ill-wishing that make people feel so miserable. The simple prospect of effecting another's death through skillful manipulation of the dead is enough to alleviate, for some, the awful burden of harboring envy, hatred, and unrelenting ill will. Turning the fantasy of killing from consumptive misery into felt liberty is specialized work in Palo, but none of its prendas cristianas are suited for it. Rather, Palo cultivates a different prenda for this work, and in the handling and reverence of this entity is contained much of what is frightening and great about Palo and its craft. It is called prenda judía, and through it those who work Palo seek to kill.

18. Judías

Prenda judía means "Jewish prenda." The chapters that follow address the extraordinary role of this prenda in Palo craft. In its intellectual conception, the prenda judía offers singular insights into the creative transformations by slaves of the cosmos of their Catholic masters in Cuba, just as it reveals the degree to which such transformations were calculated within the incessant struggle for power and control that was Cuban slave society.

The use of the terms *cristiana* and *judía* is an open adoption of nineteenth-century Spanish Catholic ideas concerning good and evil in an ethnocosmic register. These ideas were elaborated and constantly renewed through the difference marked by the term "Jew" in Spain from the medieval through the colonial period, if not to the present.[1] What is less obvious is how slaves, particularly Kongo slaves, redefined this difference in search of power against their Spanish slavers. The newly redefined Cuban-Kongo Jew was instrumental in organizing fate-changing forces, not only against the politically, economically, and cosmologically dominant Spanish, but also against the emergent Cuban-Yoruba cosmos that appears to have prevailed among slaves and their descendants during the second half of the nineteenth century, especially in Havana. In the process of this revaluation of Catholic ideas, which were themselves organized by Catholic fear, Kongo slaves and those they inspired redeemed their cultural and political marginality.[2] In the process, it appears they may have redeemed the utter marginality of the Jew of Spanish Catholicism, though surely not in a way the Europeans named by this Jew could endorse. But Kongo slaves and their cosmological descendants transformed Catholic ideas about Jewish people into a precious resource for religious sovereignty in Cuba's rivalrous religious melange. The revaluation they achieved in the nineteenth century, and still cultivate to this day, affirms rather than refutes the prevalent value judgments of Catholic anti-Semitism, while simultaneously mocking these judgments by elevating what is considered Jewish to a position of exquisite praise within Cuban-Kongo understandings of power and healing.

Teodoro kept a prenda judía but rarely used it. This was not because he didn't have occasion for it, or clients who begged him to use it in their cases. Teodoro did not lack for clients so desperate to be rid of antagonists that they concretely wished them dead. But wanting death to befall someone is easier dreamed than done, and Havana can be thankful for the limitations that Kongo Law places on the prenda judía. In fact, of the hours and days Teodoro spent working Palo craft against those perceived of using it against his initiates and clients, hardly any time was dedicated to his practice with his prenda judía. Teodoro preferred to use his prendas cristianas; they were easier to handle and demanded less costly offerings. Another practical consideration was more important yet: prendas cristianas were much more effective. Teodoro said that the dead oriented by prendas judías fear the dead oriented by prendas cristianas. Teo said the judías hide from the cristianas if they are encountered amid the flows of the dead that pervade the streets of Havana. And it is taken for granted that on any ordinary day the streets and homes of Cuba are not only filled with, but composed by, such Christian dead moving to and fro. So it made no sense to work judía [trabajar judía].

With one exception. On one occasion Kongo Law stipulates the use of the prenda judía, and all other Laws of Cuba's Creole cosmos yield before it. On this occasion, once a year, the Christian dead are neutralized and the dead oriented by the prenda judía, which are Kongo dead, course through Havana uncontested. On this occasion Teodoro worked deadly bilongos to heal his most despairing clients. "Judía" [the Jewish One, fem.]—as Teodoro called it—was used only when the protective force of the "benevolent" Catholic divine was annulled. On this occasion not only is the Catholic divine rendered void, but so is Yoruba-inspired divinity diminished. On Good Friday, by Palo's reckoning, all those entities and works that draw resources from European divinity lay dormant and useless, including the sovereign Orichas of Ocha/Santo and Palo's own prendas cristianas. Despite drawing principally upon the dead, each are powered greatly by their association with the "Law of Whites"—Catholicism. And on the weekend of Good Friday, with Catholic divinity dying on its cross, the bearers and keepers of such substances and entities as are vouchsafed by association with this dying God are abandoned in the world and left defenseless against misfortune. During these hours, the dead condensed by a prenda judía stir to new intensity and seep forth from their cauldrons to spread through Kalunga.

While Christendom groans under the grief of the death of its God on Good Friday, the prenda judía, because it partakes of the Catholic divine only as a specter, survives this death undiminished. Occurring but once per year, the days when the prenda judía are worked have the feel of a carnival for those fortunate enough to associate with one. Basic prohibitions are suspended and a distinct, yet undefined, order emerges. An air of possibility and excitement marks the days, compounded by fear and a sense of danger. On the weekend of Good Friday, knowing paleras and paleros, santeras and santeros, cover their prendas cristianas and Ocha/Santo sovereigns with white sheets to keep them cool and protect them in their defenselessness. Isidra and Teodoro both did this. Isidra also shuttered her windows and insisted the days be a time of stillness and calm, until Sunday, when God and the Orichas would be back, renewed. Until then her prendas cristianas and her Orichas would be unable to protect us from what was coming. "One should stay indoors," she said, "and if you must go out, do so only during the day."

One of the few writers to have written about the prenda judía with any grace is Lydia Cabrera, who does this prenda, and all of Palo, a great service when she invokes the voices of her informants from the 1940s. Those voices—all male in the case of Cabrera's informants—tell us there are many drawbacks to keeping this prenda, and they are unequivocal about the danger this prenda condenses. The bad thing about a prenda judía, says Basilio, a grave digger of Cabrera's acquaintance, is that often the nfumbe in a prenda judía will behave as if it were still alive, won't leave the side of its keeper, and then wants to get mixed up in everything the keeper does. A prenda judía can get jealous of its keeper, until one day the prenda kills him. Another informant, Castro Baró, says that a prenda judía must be kept separated from the others; best would be to keep it outdoors. Baró continues, warning that if it is kept in the house it perturbs its keeper and will not let him sleep until he heeds the prenda's call and curls up at the prenda's feet like an obedient dog.[3] The prenda expects other doglike qualities from its keeper, such as being watchful and keeping strangers away, especially women and children.[4] Another of Cabrera's acquaintances tells her the prenda judía is stubborn to the point that it provokes headaches and will drive its keeper to do things that can land him in trouble with the police, like entering a cemetery.[5] Cabrera's teachers also suggest to her, and some explicitly state, that the prenda judía has a taste for Christian blood.

The prenda judía's troubles only begin where they seem worst: Judía is not only Palo's most useless prenda but also its most powerful one—that by which Palo kills. It is also the entity to which ritual homicide in the past was popularly attributed, especially in the decades following Cuban independence. Cuban whites for many years at the turn of the twentieth century accused blacks of sacrificing Christian children, especially white girls, to their prendas, most likely to their prendas judías.[6]

The allegations date at least to the first decade of the twentieth century, if not before, when a series of sensationalized murders solidified the fear of ritual homicide by newly freed blacks in the minds of Cuban whites.[7] Coming on the tail of Cuba's independence in 1899, and happening in the midst of more than two decades of radical change in the legal status of blacks and people of color since emancipation in 1886, the trial and execution of blacks accused in the killing of a little girl in 1904 made racist fears of black savagery, especially the powerful image of human sacrifice in the service of African sorcery, seemingly real.[8] Drawn as it was from medieval European Catholic nightmares of blood rites performed on children, this image coalesced, and further inspired, racist violence in the first decades of Cuban independence. It continues to mark Palo today. Forty-five years into the Revolution, and a hundred years after the 1904 accusations, I have heard parents of different skin tones and class positions in Cuba frighten their children by telling them to behave or a "black man with a sack" [*un negro con un saco*] will carry them off to feed his cauldron. Popular stories teach Cuban children to fear being "stuffed in a cauldron" [*¡Cuidado, o te van meter en cazuela!*].

That the spectral Jew of European Catholicism haunted Cuban whites in the nineteenth century is not so astonishing considering the crucial role the image of Jews had in defining Catholicism since the eleventh century.[9] Unexpected is that Cuban Catholics redirected this specter by transforming it into specific allegations of ritual murder by blacks. The atmosphere of civil transformation and the concrete reconfiguration of political power that gripped Cuba at the time were without doubt a potent substrate wherein such a transformation could occur. More surprising yet is the way this specter had already been taken hold of by blacks, who had appropriated it to powerful means. Today, frightening stories told by Cubans of all backgrounds keep vibrant the apparition of the black witch who hunts children for their blood. Paleras and paleros tell the stories, too, and cultivate the insinuation of ritual murder in the less salutary comments they make about the prenda judía. Teodoro did this with cautious skill, but no less delight, and he was hardly alone. Cabrera's informants are likewise cautious but precise on this topic. They tell her that a prenda judía is prone to betray its keeper and will someday clamor for the keeper's blood. If the prenda judía doesn't receive the blood, it will continue to seek it until it is spilled somehow—by an accident in the street or by a stray bullet. By that means the prenda judía will attain what it hungers for. An unspecified informant tells Cabrera that certain prendas demand the blood of a woman and that her menstrual blood is offered to the prenda so that, once primed, it can little by little claim the rest of her blood until she dies. One of her "old ones," as Cabrera calls some of her informants, says that what the prenda judía seeks specifically is Christian blood, but since that is prohibited tricks must be used to make the prenda desist its craving. Ciriaco and T., the latter of which Cabrera considers a good source, tell her that with or without tricks, one day the prenda judía will demand "the blood of a little angel."[10]

Teo, for his part, doubted that children were ever offered to a prenda in Cuba. "No," he said, "sacrifices of children occurred in *tiempo ndile*, in *tierra naombre*, back in Africa." He said it was a lie that Palo, let alone Ocha/ Santo, had anything to do with killing children. Teo, who could be adamant on this point, nonetheless held open the possibility that in Cuba's far eastern mountains Haitians sacrificed their own children to their prendas judías. Since the Haitian Revolution, the figure of "the Haitian" has served as the most abject and frightening mask Cuban whites could paint over African society and culture. This applied to Teodoro, too, who considered any excess possible where Haitians were concerned and feared mightily their crafts of the dead.[11]

Teodoro's thinking about the whispers of ritual murder that surround the prenda judía, and the consequences of heeding them, included an opinion on the infamous case of the toddler Zoyla Díaz, one of at least two 1904 child murders that were used to brand blacks with the mark of savagery. I was surprised he knew the case at all, as the murder of Zoyla Díaz took place some forty-five years before Teo was born. I had imagined it a topic dear only to historians and other students of turn-of-the-century Cuba.

I first read about the case of Zoyla Díaz's murder in Fernando Ortiz's *Los Negros Brujos*, an early foray by Cuban social science into the topic of African-inspired culture and religion on the island. The assumptions and conclusions of the book are profoundly flawed, as is its fieldwork and ethnographic interpretation. Nonetheless, it is a document of precious historical value, one that shows us the hall of mirrors that was, and continues to be, the writing on Cuban religion, with whites looking at blacks, looking at whites, looking back again.[12]

As Ortiz tells the story, in the month of October 1904, a group of "brujos" got together to heal a member of their praise house, who suffered from "sterility."[13] According to another account of the case, the authorities came to understand the affliction the woman suffered as an "illness caused by whites before emancipation," which led to the death of six of her nine children.[14] The treatment devised by the "Congos" required the sacrifice of a white child, whose heart and blood were needed to effect a cure. Several first-generation Africans and Creole blacks were accused of the murder and convicted.[15] Two of them, Domingo Bocourt, who was African, and Juan Molina, who was Creole, were ultimately garroted for homicide. The case electrified Cuban society at the time, led to white vigilantism, and harshly divided the country along black and white lines for the next twenty years.[16]

In the midnineties, I followed the Zoyla Díaz murder and the ensuing trials at Cuba's national library, looking into news accounts from the first decade of the twentieth century until I was convinced, like most sensitive and politically engaged people would be, that the Zoyla affair was paradigmatic of white racist fantasy and persecution, precisely in a moment when full political participation was contested by blacks. For me, the case of Zoyla Díaz recalled the worst of lynch mobs and racist injustice in the U.S. South during Reconstruction and up through the civil rights movement.

Then one afternoon in 1999, in Guanabacoa at a Briyumba feast at the Quita Manaquita praise house, I heard the following mambo begun with energy and delight:

Caller:	¡Ni-ni-niña! ¡Ni-ni-niña!	G-g-girl! G-g-girl!
	¡Niña no baila mi Kubayende!	Girl doesn't dance my Kubayende!
	¡Niña no baila mi Kubayende!	Girl doesn't dance my Kubayende![17]
Chorus:	¡Ni-ni-niña! ¡Ni-ni-niña!	G-g-girl! G-g-girl!
	¡Niña no baila mi Kubayende!	Girl doesn't dance my Kubayende!
	¡Niña no baila mi Kubayende!	Girl doesn't dance my Kubayende![18]

Then the singer, a middle-aged man who previously had been silent as a caller during the feast, and whom I didn't recognize from the Manaquita house, changed the verse:

Caller:	¡A la niña Zoyla,	The girl Zoyla,
	¡Se la llevaron de noche,	They took her at night,
	Se la llevaron en coche!	They carried her off in a hearse![19]
Chorus:	¡Eh! ¡A la niña Zoyla,	Ah! The girl Zoyla,
	¡Se la llevaron de noche,	They took her at night,
	Se la llevaron en coche!	They carried her off in a hearse!

The chorus rallied around this verse, driving their voices enthusiastically, and the caller kept it going back and forth several times, then changed again:

Caller:	¡Saura, saura!	Vulture, vulture!
	¡Ndoki mayombe saura,	Mayombe's fighting vulture,
	Ndoki mayombe saura!	Mayombe's fighting vulture![20]
Chorus:	¡Aye-e, saura!	Aye-e, vulture!
	¡Ndoki mayombe saura!	Mayombe's fighting vulture!

Caller and chorus bounced the words back and forth several times, then the caller changed again:

Caller:	¡Menga va correr!	Blood will run![21]
	¡Como tintorera,	Like dye,
	Menga va corer!	Blood will run!
Chorus:	¡Menga va correr!	Blood will run!
	¡Como tintorera,	Like dye,
	Menga va corer!	Blood will run!

I was struck by the change, because at first it seemed incongruous. It was the same mambo used just before a sacrifice, just before the knife draws the blood of the offering. Caller and chorus passed it back and forth for a minute or two before returning to the story:

Caller:	¡Ni-ni-niña! ¡Ni-ni-niña!	G-g-girl! G-g-girl!
	¡Niña no baila mi Kubayende!	Girl doesn't dance my Kubayende!
	¡Niña no baila mi Kubayende!	Girl doesn't dance my Kubayende!
	¡Eh! ¡A la niña Zoyla,	Ah! The girl Zoyla,
	¡Se la llevaron de noche,	They took her at night,
	Se la llevaron en coche!	They carried her off in a hearse!
Chorus:	¡Ni-ni-niña! ¡Ni-ni-niña!	G-g-girl! G-g-girl!
	¡Niña no baila mi Kubayende!	Girl doesn't dance my Kubayende!
	¡Niña no baila mi Kubayende!	Girl doesn't dance my Kubayende!
	¡Eh! ¡A la niña Zoyla,	Ah! The girl Zoyla,
	¡Se la llevaron de noche,	They took her at night,
	Se la llevaron en coche!	They carried her off in a hearse!

Caller and chorus worked the mambo with renewed energy, so that the feast, which had been lagging, was momentarily revived. A concise version of the story told in the combination of Palo songs reads, "They took little Zoyla by night. They carried her off to her grave. Oh! Ndoki! Palo's fighting vulture! Her blood will run! Like dye runs! The girl isn't dancing now! She doesn't dance like Kubayende! Not like Kubayende!"

Until I heard the verses, I hadn't asked Teodoro about the case of Zoyla Díaz. But the mambo opened a space, because Teo was always pleased to interpret Palo songs for me. The very fact of the mambo, and his comments about it, established that today the case continues to be one of terrific contention for people of color in Cuba, especially for those who love Palo, whose knowledge of the murder is linked by uncertain connections to the lore of the prenda judía.

Teodoro, for example, didn't know many details about the case but was sure about the outcome. He knew the accused, whom he called "El brujo Bocú" and identified as a great palero, and referred to Domingo Bocourt, the African man garroted for the murder of Zoyla Díaz.[22] Interestingly, Teodoro said Bocú had an associate named "Tín-Tán," likewise a great palero.[23] Teo was sure Bocú and Tín-Tán were innocent and that a white killer, using racist fantasies as his alibi, had forced the two blacks to pay for his crime.

Then again, Teodoro harbored another interpretation of the murder, and with time it emerged. After hearing the mambo, the murder of Zoyla Díaz came up now and again, Zoyla having become a vaguely discernible shadow quavering in the ambient dead that surrounded us. She was hardly mentioned by name but rather took the form of allusions that lodged in the silences between words, and from time to time she haunted the atmosphere of the Quita Manaquita house. My task was to sift through the allusions with as much tact as they were cast, and little by little I discerned that Teodoro thought Zoyla's murderer could have been, in fact, a brujo, a witch, maybe a Haitian, who used Zoyla's blood to feed his prenda judía, then used this newly charged prenda to lead the police to Bocú and Tín Tán, who under all circumstances were falsely accused. Bocú and Tín Tán were unable to counter the Haitian's sorcery, and the true brujo escaped. Teo asked, "Do you think anyone with the balls [cojones] to kidnap and murder a little girl to feed his prenda judía would actually get caught? Any prenda fed the blood of a little girl," he said, "would be invincible. Think about it."

Therein lies the power of the prenda judía; it emanates from the prestige bestowed by the right to kill, from the silence that surrounds its keeping, and in the insinuations this silence exudes. Despite disavowals as to sacrifices it may have demanded in times past and secrecy around the offerings that have substituted for it, Palo, in its varied and ambivalent discourse on the prenda judía, very much keeps alive its forbidding mystique.

Why is the term *judía* used to qualify this most malefic of Palo's prendas? Common Palo wisdom maintains that two types of prendas are kept, cristianas and judías. People outside Palo know that a "bad" prenda, or a prenda that does "bad things," is a prenda judía.[24] Paleras and paleros, too, will say the prenda judía is "bad." This, however, is not so much because it kills, as because it has "no relationship with God." In fact, paleras and paleros will say judía, as they call this prenda for short, is bad because it has a "compact with the devil." Such statements were vexing to me, because my experience of working judía with Teodoro and Isidra taught me that not only was the prenda judía considered bad, it was also profoundly revered. This respect pointed to a more complex consideration, for which the terms "good" and "bad" were simultaneously shorthand and a veil for a relationship of considerable subtlety.

It is too simple to think that Kongo slaves and those they inspired chose the qualifier "Jewish" because the Spanish adjective *judía* was synonymous with "bad." In fact, the designation of a prenda as *judía* appears to carry no specific anti-Semitic connotations for those who actually keep and work these prendas. The judía's first order of difference from the others was obvious: it is made with a nfumbe, said Teodoro, that wasn't baptized. This allows the nfumbe to kill, because it has no pact sealed in baptism with the Catholic God that prohibits it from doing so. The prohibition on killing, then, acquires a specifically Christian attribution. Finding, gathering, and cultivating nfumbe with no such limitation leads prenda makers to seek nfumbe in Jewish cemeteries, where by virtue of tradition the dead interred wouldn't have been baptized. It seems obvious, then, that the designation of *judía* is due to the bones contained in the prenda.[25]

"But a Chinese nfumbe is better," contradicted Teodoro, who maintained that the sorcery of the Chinese was yet more difficult to counter than that of Haitians. "The Chinese," he said, "weren't baptized either. To have a Chinese nfumbe makes for the finest prenda judía. Then again, if you had the nfumbe of a murderer, baptized or not, that would be best of all, especially if the killer had been executed." Such an nfumbe would have already flouted the law of God and be a guaranteed messenger and executor of Palo's deadliest bilongos. "You see," he said, "prenda judía doesn't mean Jewish nfumbe."

Teodoro's statements, echoed by Cabrera's informants of fifty years ago, make evident that to better understand the prenda judía it is necessary to look beyond simple attributions of good and bad within an implicit Spanish Catholic connotation and also beyond a metonymy of content in the kind of bones the prenda judía is said to contain. The prenda judía merits a broader social context—the same context usually afforded other African-inspired forms and entities in Cuba.

Historical speculation and cosmological intuition grounded in ethnographic experience are necessary for this task. The story of the prenda judía is rooted in the story of the reconquest of Iberia by Castile and Aragon in the fifteenth century and the ensuing persecution by the Holy Inquisition of the Jews and Muslims who remained and attempted to hide.[26] This story was for its part never separate from the zealous and fearful images of Jewish spectrality nurtured by European Catholicism at least since the twelfth century, images Spanish Catholics communicated to the people under their rule in the Americas.[27] So, the story of the prenda judía is also that of the European exploitation of Africa and of the bondage and traffic of slaves that began even before the appearance of the Americas on European maps.

As Spanish networks of Atlantic slavery developed in the sixteenth and seventeenth centuries, so did the power of the Holy Roman Empire, which was tied to the fortunes of the Spanish monarchy. Just as Spain's power declined in the eighteenth and nineteenth centuries, so did Rome's power in Europe. As Catholic power fell in tandem in Madrid and Rome, Catholic anti-Semitism and accusations of Jewish ritual homicide began to rise.[28] Rarely, if ever, in the last five hundred years was the Catholic world free of the figure of the Christ-murdering Jew; in all the centuries of Spanish Catholic contact with Africa, hardly were the fears and accusations of ritual murder by Jews more detailed and widely diffused than in the nineteenth century, when tens of thousands of slaves were brought to Spanish Cuba.[29]

The racist fantasy of ritual murder that erupted in Cuba at the turn of the twentieth century not only reiterated ingrained European fears of African savagery and cannibalism, but did so while invoking the spectral Jew of Iberian Catholic anti-Semitism. Catholic fantasies about Jewish blood rites date to the twelfth century at least; official church sanction of the accusations can be fixed in the late fifteenth century.[30] Popes, priests, and popular Catholic theology promulgated nightmare images of Jewish blood rites throughout the age of Spanish colonialism, principally through the Franciscan and Dominican orders and the Roman Catholic press.[31] Elaborately labored fears of ritual homicide of Christians by Jews did not disappear from Catholics' minds during the nineteenth century.[32] At this time large numbers of Cuba's slaves came under Spanish dominion and their understanding of the Catholic cosmos would have become starkly concrete, if it wasn't made so already by Catholic missionaries in their native lands. In fact, the nineteenth century, which from all other indications was a period of remarkable secularization and revolt in Europe and the Americas, saw Catholic accusations of Jewish ritual homicide, and the interminable Inquisition that acted on these, return with medieval force. Other than during the fifteenth century, never had European Catholicism made anti-Jewish zeal the hallmark of its missionary and colonial projects.[33] This fervor was no less evident in the last decade of the nineteenth century, precisely when Spanish dominion was slipping from Cuba and the prospect of new rights for slaves and free people of color was shaking Cuba's white Catholic political order.[34]

It is remarkable that unrestrained images of ritual homicide promulgated by the Catholic press could have fueled an already ardent racism against newly emancipated blacks in Cuba and passed from the figure of the Jew to the makers and keepers of prendas judías. Such a jump likely happened well before Cuba won its independence from Spain in 1899 and came under U.S. domination. Following independence, Cuban blacks suffered decades-long campaigns of lies against their African-inspired practices, of which the accusations of ritual homicide in the murder of Zoyla Díaz were among the "strangest fruit." Campaigns continued throughout the first decade of the century, culminating in the massacre by whites of blacks organizing to fight for their political rights in 1912.[35] Persecutions continued throughout the second decade, including "witch hunts" that ended in lynchings.[36] The next decades saw a decrease in whites' publicly stated fears, and by the fifties, ritual homicide of white children by blacks was discredited as a motive for murder.[37] The Revolution has hardly been more generous to Cuba's African-inspired praise houses than any of its predecessor regimes, but at least it did not revive blood libel in its disdain for Palo, Ocha/Santo, and the Abakuá societies.

This nineteenth-century context, in which slaves were forced aboard European ships and onto Catholic plantation expanses in Cuba, at the same moment the Vatican and the Catholic press painted the Catholic cosmos as wracked anew by the spectral power of Jews, seems crucial to any consideration of the inspiration for the prenda judía. Prior to this, the Catholic cosmos was imposed on central and west Africans for more than three hundred years, enough for correspondences to grow up between Catholic powers of fate and those of African slaves. Elizabeth MacAlister, in describing the protean role of the spectral Jew in the Haitian Lent-period popular music and ritual scene known as Rara, makes a strong argument for the place of Easter Week passion plays in communicating the spectral image of the Jew to an enslaved African population.[38] Similar liturgical dramas most likely played an important role in sourcing Cuban-Kongo ideas about Jewish power in the Catholic cosmos. Along with the profligate and protean power of the Virgin Mother, and the piety and martyrdom of the saints celebrated in the Catholic calendar (that Africans and their descendants in Cuba recombined with their own powers of fate in what is dominantly called "syncretism"), Africans would have received the true-to-life tales carried by priests, sailors, plantation owners, and whites of all stripes, of the monstrous beings that unsettled Catholics and drove them to despair. These figures, ancient participants in the Catholic cosmos and as powerful as any others in founding Christian self-understanding, were the devil, the witch, and, concretely for the Spanish Catholic Church in the nineteenth century, the Jew.

Taking into account the broad diffusion of blood libel against Jews by the Catholic Church in the nineteenth century, one can safely assume that slaves received tales of devils and blood rites, just as they received exhortations to surrender to the cult of the Virgin Mother and perhaps much more than they received formal catechism. However, the existence and practice of the prenda judía suggests that slaves, especially Kongo slaves and their Creole descendants, took up these spectral figures in a very different way from which they were conveyed. Along with fearing Catholicism's demons, which slaves surely did, the prenda judía suggests that slaves also studied them for the secrets to their power. After all, nineteenth-century Catholic anti-Semitism attributed to Jews the torment and murder of Christ.[39] This was the murder of a God that to slaves, particularly Kongo slaves it seems, was the God of their misery, and one from whom salvation could hardly be expected. To lay claim to the dreaded killing of that God and affirm this death in the creative manufacture of the prenda judía so that it could be manipulated in favor of Kongo-inspired healers was an astonishing feat of spectral appropriation and improvisation. To make such a claim, of course, would come with the onerous liability of goading fears and hatreds already harbored by Catholics confronted with the supposed murder of Christ on Good Friday. Considering the allegations already arrayed against blacks in the racist imaginary of white Cubans, it seems to have been a burden some slaves and those they inspired chose to assume.

The spectrality of Jews in the Catholic universe since the Middle Ages, and the history of nineteenth-century Catholic anti-Semitism, only begins to suggest the cosmological and historical inspirations of the prenda judía. To better understand the cultivation of this prenda it might do well to speculate a little on the merging of cosmologies that happened when large numbers of slaves from widely varied groups and geographically separated regions of Africa were brought together under conditions of duress, humiliation, and the raw fight for life. After all, it was only certain slaves and their descendants who conceived the prenda judía, probably in Havana during the nineteenth century, and these slaves called themselves, in Spanish, "Congos."

It is my contention that far from collaborating in a harmonious solidarity, central and west African healers, each with their ethnically particular modes of engaging and changing fate, pitted their crafts of healing against one another. Just as central and west African inspirations would have been in conversation with each other, their practitioners would have been contentious, fighting for life in circumstances that made bondage, illness, misfortune, and death all too common.

Together, but also each in their own particular and autonomous way, central African and west African peoples and their descendants confronted Catholicism. This rule had every intention of supplanting African ideas about fate, life, and transformation and had the formidable advantage of being the religion of the dominant people and their political regime. The struggle that ensued between Catholic ideas and those of central and west African peoples concerning fate, its manipulation, and its repercussions is visible in the contours of all African-inspired practice in Cuba. It continues to this day. Central and west African modes of turning and healing fate and life were established as Creole forms, taking a measure of each style. In Havana, La Regla de Congo/Palo and La Regla de Ocha emerged. The lines of a new cosmos were etched, a Creole cosmos, where distinct sovereignties, each to different degrees grounded in the dead and in divinity, vied—and continue to vie—for the confidence and willful surrender of the living.

In their historical negotiation against one another for dominance—not only among those afflicted by slavery but also among those who ruled—it is no surprise that Kongo and Yoruba cosmologies would each have made claims of access to the power vested in the Rule of Whites. The power of divine grace and benign absolution from misfortune is the hallmark of Christian goodwill, and west African slaves seemed to have established predominant claims to this power, for reasons that may forever remain mysteries.[40]

Yet contemporary ethnographic observation suggests that Yoruba divinity narratives had finely tuned affinities with Catholic notions of divinity. Because of this, Kongo ideas of the dead, and of crafting matter saturated with the dead to transform fate, would have relegated Kongo healers and slaves to a place of marginality within an emerging Creole cosmos, dominated by Catholic narratives but accepting (at least popularly) combinations of Yoruba and Catholic elements. Skillful improvisation and recombinations of Yoruba and Catholic narratives of the divine likely gave west African healing and divination practices the upper hand against fellow central African slaves in the claim to the Christian God's poise and forgiveness—and thus a prominent place in the emerging popular cosmology. This forgiveness and goodwill, grounded in a vibrant notion of divinity, was not eschewed completely by central African healers, as the overwhelming popularity of prendas cristianas attests. But if contemporary Palo is any indication, central African healers did find themselves relegated to a secondary distance from the powers of purification and release of the Catholic God, which west African modes of inspiration appropriated in the founding of the Law of the Oricha. Recognizing the significant affinities between west African and Catholic modes of ordering the world through the concept of divinity, central African men and women appear to have devised their sovereignty in the newly emergent cosmos through the conjuring of the prenda judía and the affirmation of what was abject, frightening, but no less powerful, in the Catholic cosmos. The witch, the devil, and the Jew became them.

So, it was a fear-bound paradox within the narrative of Catholic divinity, namely the mortality of God at the hands of Jews and the Catholic fear of Jewish spectrality, that Kongo slaves, and those they inspired, appear to have cultivated in their bid for self-determination within the uniquely Cuban cosmos that emerged during the nineteenth century. Kongo wisdom affirms the dead before all else, and surely those inspired by it recognized keen similarities between certain classes of the Kongo dead and European figures of spirits and devils. Out of the fold where the Kongo dead and minkisi inspiration overlap with Catholic images of devils and witches, Kongo-inspired slaves and healers drew the idea for the prenda judía in all of its ignoble, despised, and contingent majesty. Looking today at the division of healing labor between Palo and Ocha/Santo, it appears that west African–inspired practice ceded the ground of the Jew, the devil, and the witch to central African–inspired practice without contest. Perhaps it found the Kongo-inspired appropriation too alien, perhaps too risky, and perhaps too contradictory to the cosmological terrain it was staking closer to the Catholic-like principles of purity, hierarchical spiritual mediation, and divine absolution.

Perhaps west African inspirations, which would become Ocha/Santo, ceded this territory strategically, to have the powerful devilishness of death-wielding sovereignty reside yet with blacks. In this way, it would be held in reserve by Kongo inspiration, by Palo, which was more or less safely marginalized by Yoruba-inspired practice in Havana. In the folds where Palo and Ocha/Santo meet in Havana, one such fold being the weekend of Good Friday, the prenda judía is powerful enough to dominate those who do not work it, but also limited so that Ocha/Santo is eclipsed only momentarily. West African-inspired Ocha/Santo thus occupies a position between Cuban-Kongo sorcery and Spanish-Catholic fear as the principal form of healing able to mediate between these two.

Africans brought to Cuba do not seem to have fleshed out their understanding of things "Jewish" from any relevant contact with Jews themselves. In this sense the Jews of Cuban-Kongo praise are spectral indeed, having always been absent except as characters in Spanish Catholic stories, and all the more powerful because of this.[41] Cuba had no significant Jewish population until after its independence from Spain. Until 1834, the Spanish monarchy, which was true to Rome's anti-Semitism, persecuted Jews by means of the Holy Inquisition. Spain also maintained "blood purity laws," which forbade Jews from traveling to its colonies.[42] Unlike the rest of the Spanish territories in Latin America, which gained their independence from Spain between 1819 and 1825 and soon became havens for Spanish Jews, Cuba remained under direct Spanish control until 1899. According to Ortiz, during the first centuries of colonial rule in America the Spanish Crown enforced more laws that tried to limit access to Cuba strictly to Castilians and opened up its colonies to other Europeans only on the cusp of the nineteenth century.[43] Jews were not allowed to travel to Cuba until 1881, and then only in the smallest numbers. In 1899 Cuba had fewer than a thousand Europeans living on the Island who were not Spanish Catholic. A Jewish community of any substance did not exist in Cuba until after the turn of the century, when the U.S. occupation opened a lasting place for one.[44] There were exceptions, of this there can be no doubt, but it appears certain that the Jew encountered by Africans and their descendants in Cuba in the nineteenth century was more virtual than actual, more spectral than concrete.[45] Actualizing this Jew would be the work of Cuban-Kongo healers.

The prenda judía, then, became that power over life and fate created by Kongo and Kongo-inspired peoples, who worked it out of the storied folds of three cosmologies. Without it, there would be no Kongo Law. In affirming the figures of the devil, the witch, and the Jew in a creative act of cosmological innovation, Kongo peoples devised a power that could wield death against the protections of all other sovereignty, be this west African or Catholic. By effectively rendering void Spanish Catholic and west African power over life once per year, on Good Friday, the prenda judía continues to be that force which grounds the autonomy of Kongo Law in Cuba. In the world of tumult, bondage, and misfortune that was the nineteenth century in Cuba, this new power guaranteed the importance of Kongo inspiration in the emerging order, and that is what mattered.

Thus, "bad," as Teodoro and Isidra used the word in reference to the prenda judía, did not mean "evil," despite the miasma of ritual homicide and deadly sorcery. In fact, when they called the prenda judía "bad," they were far from affirming an explicit link between evil and Jews in Palo's understanding of itself. "Bad" in their usage meant, rather, "not Catholic," "not white," not that which partakes of the divine. Inversely, it meant that which partakes exclusively of the dead. To some degree, for Teodoro and Isidra, "bad" meant that which aroused the ire of dominant divinity by momentarily destroying it on Good Friday, then acting in its absence. Palo prendas often have second or middle names that allude to a capacity to radically transform, such as *desbarata compone* [takes apart and puts together, or destroys and creates] or *vira mundo* [turns the world, world changer, or, less literally, flip the world upside-down]. Judía is shorthand for just such a notion of complete transformation as is involved in killing a God. Judía here means sovereignty on par with greater forces than the universe of whites. "Bad" in Palo means that Palo dares to invoke its dead to overthrow divinity itself. Thus, it earns simultaneous regard and disdain, as much within Palo as outside of it. In the case of Palo, notions of "bad" or "Jewish" refer to an affirmative, creative, audacious, overcoming of all things divine and oppressive, be these Catholic or Yoruba-inspired. That "bad" can mean "prestigious" or "good" should be familiar enough, as African-American slang has long established the "badness" of things great.

In Palo, midnight of Good Friday marks the climax of the moment of transformation that begins with the nailing of God to the cross. God's protection and the confidence this inspires are lost and forever changed upon God's death, and even on the Sunday of God's resurrection the world does not return to what it was. Perhaps this is why practitioners of Palo and Ocha/Santo, who on Good Friday cover their prendas cristianas and Ocha/Santo sovereigns, on Sunday expose them again without a feast at all, and without comment. There is no celebration, no playing of drums, and no calling of the Orichas. There is only a complict silence. Easter Sunday, Christianity's greatest feast day, is without proportionate reflection in Palo and Ocha/Santo. This is all the more remarkable considering the travail those who practice Palo have passed the two nights prior.

19. Tormenta Ndoki

Prendas cristianas are perpetually tended with routines of obeisance—aspirations of cane liquor and cigar smoke fumigations, as well as daily consultations and routine animal offerings. Prendas judías spend most of the year neglected, in "slumber." Just as all Palo entities are distinct from one another in their appearance—Zarabanda being distinguishable from Siete Rayos, Tiembla Tierra from Mama Chola, and so on—a prenda judía is easily recognizable. As all prendas are kept at a distance from Ocha/Santo sovereigns, so is the prenda judía kept apart from prendas cristianas. This distance, said Isidra, allows it to "rest."

"When you enter a room where prendas are kept," she said, "the one that is kept off to the side, that will almost always be a prenda judía." She also mentioned that the prenda judía is kept apart because the cristianas won't abide it and will act out against their keeper until the judía is removed. "You see," she said, "judía corrupts the others, and you will always incite the cristianas when you work her, except on Good Friday. Anyway, the prenda judía wants nothing to do with the others; judía is afraid of them and would rather keep to herself." Teodoro concurred, saying, "Prendas judías and prendas cristianas are like cats and dogs, or two roosters. Keep them apart! You can't have judía next to prendas cristianas because they war against one another and make your life a wreck. You must also please God," he said, "and putting a prenda judía near a prenda cristiana would offend God. If you are going to keep a prenda judía, it must be allowed to rest."

I was introduced to Teodoro's prendas cristianas long before I met his prenda judía. He kept his judía, to which he referred with feminine articles and pronouns, under a window framed by two tall shelves that made a niche for her. When we would greet Lucero, Zarabanda, Mama Chola, Siete Rayos, Centella Ndoki, Tiembla Tierra, and Ma're Lango, along with all their aides and helpers, the prenda judía was always at our backs, covered with a burlap sack that shed flakes of black paint. For months I was aware the prenda was behind us, but I was reprimanded for looking directly at her. Occasionally, Teodoro and Isidra would greet her to my exclusion, making a fuss over her. Not until after my initiation as ngueyo in the Quita Manaquita house was the burlap sack drawn back and a formal introduction made. It was considered a privilege to greet her—one asked her permission, which Teodoro did on my behalf—and the few times I knelt before her I followed Isidra and Teodoro in calling her by name and singing praise songs composed exclusively for her.

Her proper name was Tormenta Ndoki. Teodoro called her Tormenta [storm, tempest] for short and Tormentíca [little storm, sweet storm, dear storm] when he let his affection for her show. She was smaller than his Zarabanda, akin in size and color to his Lucero Mundo, though even smaller. If setting her apart and covering her wasn't enough to distinguish her, she was also different in that her nfumbe was plainly visible. To my knowledge, all other skulls in Palo Briyumba prendas-ngangas-enquisos are buried beneath the earth packed into the cauldron, but Tormenta Ndoki's was only half buried, so the eye sockets and the crown of the head obtruded. The sticks that extended significantly from most of Teo's other prendas were, in Tormenta's case, a low ring of wooden stubs lining the inside rim of her cauldron, so that nothing obstructed her line of sight.

"*Kriyumba 'fuera, vititi ndoki,*" said Teodoro. "With the skull out, Ndoki watches; it sees." The skull also allowed us to have a direct engagement with her, so that it could be touched and offerings let fall directly onto the crown of her head. Keepers of a prenda judía establish an intimacy with them unlike other prendas, because they engage the head and face of the nfumbe. Such an interaction is considered extremely hot, as hot as anything in Palo.[1]

Even with her repose taken into account, like the other prendas in the Manaquita house Tormenta Ndoki suffered from neglect. After I was introduced to her I would visit Teo to greet and praise his prendas, and we would ignore Tormenta Ndoki. There was a sense that Tormenta did not want to be bothered and also a sense that we did not really want to rouse her. Most of the time, Isidra gave Tormenta Ndoki wide birth, especially because she was neglected; she argued that the disrespect would be compounded if we greeted her without the intention of making an animal offering.

There are few Palo or Ocha/Santo feast days in the weeks and months preceding the Catholic Easter holiday. Most of the calendar feast days for Ocha/Santo's sovereigns (when Palo feasts its dead too) are in the second half of the calendar year. The accelerated pace of life between September and the end of December—when not only are Ocha/Santo sovereigns feasted but also many initiations held, along with elaborate acts of obeisance and divination—tapers off in January. This leaves Ocha/Santo's divine appeased and the dead refreshed, such that the coolness they inspire in people matches that of Cuba's sun-dappled winters.[2] With the exception of Oyá, whose festival day is in February, the feasts for the principal Orichas don't begin again until June, first with Eleguá and then Ogún's, just in time for the return of the heat of summer. The frenzy of the Catholic calendar in the months and days preceding the crucifixion of Christ, especially the liturgically intense Lenten season, has no correspondence—as do saints' festivals in the summer and autumn—in Palo or Ocha/Santo. This says much about the choices Africans and their descendents made in Cuba as they assimilated the Catholic narrative of Christ's divinity. In fact, the only homage paid to the great Christian procession through the first quarter of the year, until the resurrection of Christ near the spring equinox, is the working of the prenda judía, which is a celebration not of the Christian God's rebirth, but of his death.[3]

What most struck me about the weeks just before Good Friday of 2000 was the way enemies seemed to multiply around Teodoro, Isidra, and their initiates. In late February, a client of Isidra's died, a man she was helping to win his wife back from a younger lover. She attributed the death to a palero from San Miguel del Padrón, outside of Havana, with whom she had an old rivalry, and who she was sure was in league with her client's rival. About the same time, a brother of Teodoro's had his prison sentence extended, which Teo attributed to the mischievous work of old enemies of his father's. All around, Teo's clients started to come down with serious problems.

Reflecting on the trend, Teodoro said it was due to the season, which he called in weather terms *tiempo cuaresma*, the turbulence of Lent. March and April, when winter turns to spring, is a time of winds and storms in Cuba. They are less severe than those of October, but just as unpredictable. During tiempo cuaresma, clouds pile up in columns, nights are darker and temperatures shift abruptly. People should be cautious when they go out, said Isidra. Sunny days become downpours, just as friends become enemies. Teodoro considered the tumult of the winds and clouds to be a shape of Kalunga, the sea of the dead, and the atmosphere of uncertainty it inspired during this time of year. "The storms of Lent," said Teodoro, "are due to the dead *[tiempo cuaresma se debe al muerto]*."

As the turbulence around us mounted, the most severely afflicted of Teodoro and Isidra's kin and clients were channeled toward the prenda judía.

With crises and misfortune multiplying, we agreed to gather at the Quita Manaquita house on the night of Good Friday. Teo would prepare Tormenta Ndoki, and we would bring the offering, among other gifts, for her.

The walk from Independencia to the Manaquita House that night was as lonely as any in Guanabacoa. The sidewalks were empty, while above the crowns of royal palms, mango trees, ceibas, and jagueyes shook, buffeted by cold winds. The full moon was just beginning to wane but still cast dull shadows. On the bus coming over, Isidra had expressed reservations about working the prenda judía, which she said would have unforeseen repercussions for each of us. She also had doubts about Teodoro's ability to maintain his composure with Tormenta Ndoki. She hadn't feasted in a long time, and Isidra predicted she would be especially difficult to handle. Her doubts rested not with Teodoro's know-how but with his discipline. "If Tormenta tests him and he doesn't remain in control," said Isidra, "we're out of there. We would all be served by having old Pedro with us. You saw how helpful he was when we made the Lucero and the others."

By her guess, Tormenta Ndoki was easily more powerful than Teodoro and her together. Behind her mood were second and third thoughts about the animal we carried for Tormenta Ndoki. Isidra's doubts that Teodoro would keep his end of the bargain and work the prenda judía led her to lowball the animal offering, and we had bought only a spindly young rooster. Now she feared it would hardly have enough blood to appease Tormenta after so long a fast. She voiced her doubts the whole way up the hill. "If she turns on us," Isidra said, "I'm going to be the first one out the door, and you'll be right behind me! This has to be done right, and if it isn't, we will all face the consequences." She stiffened as we turned the corner and, with a stern gesture of her hand, suspended all conversation.

Teodoro Tocayo answered our call on the sagging door of the Manaquita house. For some time now, a warm connection had developed between him and Teodoro. He had been spending more and more time in Guanabacoa, days at a time. To some degree, he was living with Teodoro. And since his initiation as padre, Teodoro had taken to referring to Tocayo as his mayordomo, calling him *bakofula*—his steward in Palo craft. Now Teo had help with his prendas, which gave hope to the society members who still cared about the state of the Quita Manaquita house.

There was only so much Teodoro Tocayo could do for the house, however. He had too little expertise in Palo, and far too little self-confidence, to move Teodoro out of his intractable funk. Tocayo did have certain gifts, though, one of which was a graceful and conscientious manner in attending those clients and friends of the Manaquitas who would pay a visit to the house. He brought a welcome routine to Teodoro's life and was a pleasant presence to all of us who visited there. His growing role in Teodoro's affairs pleased Isidra greatly.

Teodoro Tocayo's good judgment and hospitality were amply demonstrated when he greeted us. Before letting us in, he marked my forehead and cheeks with white cascarilla chalk. He had the tact to ask Isidra for permission to mark her, because he knew she had surrendered her head to Ocha/Santo and that touching her there was likely prohibited by her initiations. Isidra marked herself, but for a time afterward she commented on the thoroughness Tocayo demonstrated in this gesture. He let us pass into the darkened house, and we moved quickly through the living room to where the prendas were, only to find their room locked. This was out of the ordinary, but Isidra immediately understood that Teo was imposing a ritual knock on our gathering. She gave the required three knocks, and Teodoro answered, "*¡¿Kinani?!*" This was his command that we speak our initiation names. This we did, Isidra proudly and emphatically, me haltingly despite practice. We were let swiftly through, with Tocayo at our heels.

A single candle lit the room, casting long, dim shadows. We turned to regard the prendas as we were in the habit of doing but found them covered with a white sheet, which appeared to float above them like a pale, broken plane receding into the corner. Above, the shelf where Tiembla Tierra and many of Teo's materials for working Palo were kept was also covered. The shrouds were the sheets from Teodoro's bed, which Tocayo had washed and which Teo would do without until Sunday.

Looking back at the candle, the only point of reference in the dark, I could see that it lit Tormenta Ndoki, opposite our normal orientation in the room. She had been brought forward slightly from out of her niche under the window. The bench that normally hid her was placed off to the side. Four squat stools were placed in front of her, in semicircle. Tormenta's cauldron had been freshly painted black, and an occasional glimmer could be seen on the gloss of the paint. Weapons flanked her, a thin rapier on the left and a sword on the right, both glistening with new black paint. The candle was at Tormenta's feet next to a glass of water. Teodoro's Cuatro Vientos, a little wooden statue with four faces, was there too, freshly painted. An iron ingot that normally rested in the cauldron next to Tormenta's skull, and also a four-inch segment of railroad track, each newly painted, were among the things on the floor. Perhaps it was the obtuse angle of the candlelight, but to my eye Tormenta Ndoki's nfumbe seemed to protrude more that night. The ridge of her brow was above the earth, and it was possible to peer into the darkness of her eye sockets. Flat shadows there captured the looker in a feeling of inscrutable depth. The effect was much like the uncertain feeling of being apprehended by the twinkling mirror that flashed out of Teodoro's Lucero Mundo.

To Tormenta Ndoki's array of weapons and shadows we added our gifts and offerings, with which we asked if we could sit with her. We presented her with candles, aguardiente, plenty of cigars, and a little bottle of chamba. The chamba was from a batch Isidra made some months back. It was strong and dank, and a small amount was a special gift. A modest offering of flowers, daisies, and marigolds stood out for its frailty against the arresting appearance of the prenda judía. As a gift of freshness and unspoiled vitality it seemed to me no less an offering of color itself, prized for its kinship with ineffable sensation, which is always an intimately felt version of the dead. The rooster we carried was laid at her feet, still in the canvas bag. Teo was pleased with the gifts, but Tormenta's brooding was palpable.

The sight before us was not without shame for me, and even more for Isidra. Taking in the care with which her keepers had readied Tormenta Ndoki made us dreadfully aware that, when compared with their efforts, we had hardly kept our part of the deal. The thought of the spindly rooster now at Tormenta's feet filled us both with chagrin. Pulling it out, it was clear the rooster was too small. Teo saw it and raised his eyebrows in disapproval.

All our gifts, regardless of how lovely, paled in importance to the rooster. Had we brought Tormenta Ndoki a hundred candles and all the flowers of Pinar del Rio, they would not have compensated for that spindly bird. Its meek chirps did little to bolster its candidacy as an adequate sacrifice for Tormenta, who already counted Teo significantly in her debt. Even had the rooster been robust and full of life, Tormenta might still have accepted it only grudgingly; the ideal offering would have been a black dog or a black cat. In the reading of one's fate that is conducted during initiation into Ocha/Santo, Isidra was forbidden from killing dogs or cats. Teodoro, despite a lifetime of Palo sacrifices, disdained killing animals and often asked others to do it for him. He completely excused himself from the idea of offering a dog or a cat. In fact, Teodoro asked me if I would do it for Tormenta, because I was padre nganga and had earned the right to sacrifice, but I would not. Considering everyone else had an excuse for not sacrificing, I felt I could refuse. Tocayo hadn't yet earned the right to kill and I think he was relieved.

Given our reluctance to offer a dog or a cat, Teodoro said it would be fine to substitute a big black rooster. Isidra and I had fallen short. This was especially troubling for Teodoro, who was making the offering only to wash down her principal meal, which was to be his own blood. For this was the prenda judía's true delight, "menga cristiana," he said, "Christian blood," given from her keeper's own body to appease her deepest craving. Teodoro was prepared to give her this, as he was every time he worked Tormenta Ndoki, but was concerned the rooster would give too little to wash down his blood. A taste of him would be left with her.

Teo expected another person to arrive, but midnight rolled around and he decided to start. Looking us over, he began to distrust the cascarilla marks made by Teodoro Tocayo and passed around a little ball of the chalk so that we could each mark ourselves again. The simple slashes and tiny cruciforms on our faces, hands, and feet were meant to keep ourselves, and the dead that coursed through us, cool and impervious to any ill astray in the night. Our heads were covered with white caps, though Isidra wore her customary aquamarine turban in deference to Yemayá, whose sovereignty over her head was uncontested. We were meant to be wearing white clothes, too, though few of us were. Tocayo had no head covering, and Isidra would not let us begin without this, so Teo fetched him the last of his bed linens— a pillowcase to tie tightly around his head. Teo was wearing a white satin cap with a voluminous crown that hung down over his forehead and left ear. He was shirtless and barefoot, with his pants rolled up around his calves. Putting aside the cigarettes that were ever lit in his crooked hands, Teo took up one of the cigars and handed around the rest. The cigars, as well as their smoke, he called *nsunga*. We lit up, even Isidra, who normally avoided cigars, and before long the room was filled with smoke, its curls turning the atmosphere to a pungent earthiness akin to the dead and pleasing to them.

Around us was silence, except for the television next door, which was blaring the Friday movie, as if by that means to keep the storms of that night at bay. During weekdays, the Revolution's two channels were finished with their programming by midnight, with the exception of special events—the rebroadcast of a speech by Fidel was by far the most common. Weekends brought relief from the tedium of the workaday television in the form of Hollywood movies. Friday's films were usually better because they paid homage to the history of cinema and, with luck, sometimes showed films by filmmakers such as John Huston and Billy Wilder. On Saturdays, however, even if earlier in the day the "supreme leader" had kept ten thousand workers rallying under a punishing sun for six hours while he explained the perils of globalization and cultural imperialism, revolutionary television careened into frivolity and the twilight strata of state paradox with the broadcast of Tom Cruise action flicks and early J-Lo vehicles. I don't know what film the Revolution was playing that Good Friday, but it could well have been Fritz Lang or Orson Welles rolling in the background.

Teodoro arranged us on the little benches facing the prenda. Smoking his cigar, he began his work by taking up a piece of plywood that could have been the seat of a chair. He drew a compound firma on it, which he said was Kubayende. The cascarilla was thick and powdery and did not mark with definition. Nonetheless, when he was finished he presented us with Kubayende— kin to the beggar Lazarus, chief among the poor, the ill, and the dead. He aspirated aguardiente over it, then dry sherry and a sip of chamba, which he rolled over his tongue before expelling it as a fine mist. The firma ran and became indecipherable. Still, he studied it as it dissolved against the grain of the plywood, and in the trails Teodoro discerned many things. He placed it on the floor at Tormenta's feet. He used the plywood to avoid writing the firma on the cement floor of the room, because entities densely populated by the dead, such as prendas and firmas, should never rest on cement or tile.

The chamba lit the room on fire. The actions we had taken to cool our immediate environment were suddenly tested by the burst of blistering vapor from Teo's cheeks. Chamba is made to burn, to agitate the dead out of doldrums. The chamba burned our eyes, noses, and throats and left us choking. When the air cleared, our attention was turned wholly on Tormenta, as if she had slapped us. We paid her utter heed, and the room fell into a long silence.

In time Teodoro broke the quiet and spoke. "I'm thinking about my father," he said. "The way Emilio used to make this room *sing* when we worked judía!" Teodoro was then gripped by something that drew him away and he let his head sink, looking down at the firma he had made. After a while he looked up as if unsure of the time he had spent withdrawn. He pinched the bridge of his nose and shook his head. "Kalunga," he said. Then he composed himself and spoke again: "You knew Emilio, didn't you, Isidra?" His question was meant to draw her out, to have her join him in his uncertain encounter with Emilio and thereby confirm the shapes his father had taken in his mind. But she was reluctant to give up any images of her beloved tata, even to his son, and kept her thoughts to herself, except to say simply, "I was his initiate." For a moment there was silence again, and nothing moved except Emilio in the bodies of those who knew him, and even in those who didn't.

The silence this time was harder to break, but Teodoro did it again, as if it were his burden to do. "This is how we worked judía," he said, "just a few of us, like this—Emilio, me, Julio, who's dead, and his little brother, Enrique. You know Enrique and that prenda of his at the end of the block. Emilio kept our work with Tormentíca close. We would go back and forth, singing and calling to her, making bilongo after bilongo, and fucking over our enemies.

¡Bin-ban! ¡Bin-ban! We would work without distraction—no screwing around. It was an important night, Tormenta Ndoki's night! Speaking of the old times, listen to this. Tocayo and I were out back chopping the grass yesterday, cleaning up around the house. It's been twenty-five years since my yayi, my dear mother, stepped foot into this house, and she is the true keeper of Tormenta Ndoki. This prenda that you see here belongs to her. She doesn't have it with her now because she's married to a babalawo, and Ifá doesn't allow for the keeping of judía. Not even if it's kept outside the house. Her husband says she can't keep it. I hope some day she takes it, because it is hers, not mine."

Teo paused, his eyes again focusing past the floor. Then he went on, "Twenty-five years since she's set foot here, twenty five years, and yesterday she shows up. We were out back when a knock came. *¡Tun-tun-tun!* Who is it? I open the door, and it's her. Imagine! She comes by sometimes, says hello, but never comes in the house. Yesterday she just marched right in and went straight for Tormenta, sat down with her and had me pull up a stool. 'Get me this,' she said, 'get me that.' In no time we were working up a bilongo, singing, and getting Tormentíca fired up. You see my mother's bilongo there. This is her prenda, Tormenta Ndoki. She was initiated, first as ngueyo, then as madre. She received Tormenta Ndoki as madre, in a ceremony with twenty-one tatas in the forest! There was no one else at her initiation, just her, Emilio, and twenty-one tatas! It's never been done since! When Emilio put Tormenta Ndoki together he made her so that only he could work her in my mother's absence, and before he died he taught me. I work with Tormenta only by my mother's permission, and if she needs something done, I do it for her. She has given permission for us to use Tormenta tonight. But she said to me, 'Paint her Teodoro! You can't have her so dusty and ignored!' So you see the paint now. Blessings, my yayi! Blessings, Tormenta Ndoki!"

Then his manner shifted, and he stood up and set his hips square, facing the prenda, and called out an invocation common in his house, to which we replied in chorus:

Teodoro:	¡Cuna Nzambi!
Chorus:	¡Dios!
Teodoro:	¡Cuna Nzambi!
Chorus:	¡Dios!
Teodoro:	¡Salam Alekkun!
Chorus:	¡Alekkun Salam!
Teodoro:	¡Salam Alekkun!
Chorus:	¡Alekkun Salam!

Then Teodoro began to sing to Tormenta, a sad, lyrical mambo, which to me seemed an entreaty of some kind that spoke of the restricted quality of Briyumba feasts. Palo mambos of appeal are slow and moving, and their melodies are full of longing. Unlike the buoyant feast mambos, which have a beat that races ahead of the words, mambos of appeal are accompanied only by a rolling of fingers across the head of the drum, so that a sound like distant thunder backs the rising and falling melody. The song was sung in the first-person voice of someone left out of a feast:

Teodoro:	Aye-e, la kimbambula,	Greetings to the feast,
	Aye-e, la kimbambula,	Greetings to the feast,
	Todo mundo tiene paso, paso Briyumba,	Everyone dances Briyumba's step,
	Menos yo.	But me.
	¡Aye-e, a la kimbambula!	Greetings to the feast![4]
Chorus:	Aye-e, la kimbambula,	Greetings to the feast,
	Aye-e, la kimbambula,	Greetings to the feast,
	Todo mundo tiene paso, paso Briyumba,	Everyone dances Briyumba's step,
	Menos yo.	But me.
	¡Aye-e, a la kimbambula!	Greetings to the feast!
Teodoro:	¡Eh! ¡Kimbambula, kimbambula!	Ah! Feast, feast!
	¡La buena noche!	Good evening!
	¡Kimbambula, kimbambula!	Feast, feast!
	¡La santa noche!	Blessed evening!
	¡Kimbambula, kimbambula!	Feast, feast!
	¡Tormenta Ndoki!	For Tormenta Ndoki!
	¡Kimbambula kimbambula!	Feast, feast!
	¡La buena noche!	Good evening!

Each verse was passed back and forth between Teodoro and the rest of us five or six times, though sometimes it was many more. At his discretion, Teo switched to other mambos. As he sang to Tormentíca, he would occasionally crouch down close to her and tap her forehead with his middle finger. He would run his hand down the side of the skull, across the brows, as if caressing the face. As he received the verse from the chorus he would point to her, so that there could be no mistake his address was meant for her. He touched her kettle, knocking gently. Little by little he woke her by singing and nudging her to wakefulness. When he had exhausted all of one mambo's possibilities within convention and improvisation, he was very quick to move to another, so there was never a break. Teodoro Tocayo followed him on the drum, and when the mambo called for a beat rather than a roll, he knew almost ahead of his tata. As Tocayo shifted to the basic Briyumba beat, Teodoro took to supplicating Tormenta Ndoki, beginning in earnest the process of calling her out:

Teodoro:	Ya buen señor, tié-tié, Ya tierra Congo, tié-tié.	Already, dear Lord, tié-tié, Already, Kongo lands, tié-tié.[5]
Chorus:	Ya buen señor, tié-tié, Ya tierra Congo, tié-tié.	Already, dear Lord, tié-tié, Already, Kongo lands, tié-tié.
Teodoro:	Ya buen señor, tié-tié, Tormenta Ndoki, tié-tié.	Already, dear Lord, tié-tié, Tormenta Ndoki, tié-tié.
Chorus:	Ya buen señor, tié-tié, Tormenta Ndoki, tié-tié.	Already, dear Lord, tié-tié, Tormenta Ndoki, tié-tié.
Teodoro:	Palo, ya buen señor, tié-tié, Buena noche, nganga ndoki, tié-tié.	Palo, already, dear Lord, tié-tié, Good evening, nganga ndoki, tié-tié.
Chorus:	Ya buen señor, tié-tié, Buena noche, nganga ndoki, tié-tié.	Already, dear Lord, tié-tié, Good evening, nganga ndoki, tié-tié.
Teodoro:	Ya buen señor, tié-tié, Ya tierra Congo, tié-tié.	Already, dear Lord, tié-tié, Already, Kongo lands, tié-tié.
Chorus:	Ya buen señor, tié-tié, Ya tierra Congo, tié-tié.	Already, dear Lord, tié-tié, Already, Kongo lands, tié-tie.

Again we went back and forth many times until Teo called us down, invoking Nzambi Npungu, calling that force among the dead, that it might aid Tormenta Ndoki in her waking. As he sang, Teo also attended to Tormenta by directing us with hand gestures to aspirate her with aguardiente or surround her in cigar smoke. He also kept up his own contact with Tormenta, knocking her harder and stamping on the floor in front of her, calling her. He continued his entreaties and his mambos of appeal:

Teodoro:	Ñao, ay dios, nganga ndoki,	Ay, dear God, nganga ndoki,
Chorus:	Ñao.	Ñao.[6]
Teodoro:	Ñao, ay dios, nganga ndoki,	Ay, dear God, nganga ndoki,
Chorus:	Ñao.	Ñao.
Teodoro:	Buenas noches, Tormenta Ndoki,	Good evening, Tormenta Ndoki,
Chorus:	Ñao.	Ñao.
Teodoro	Ay dios, pati fuera,	Dear God, the father is gone,
Chorus:	Ñao.	Ñao.

Teodoro:	Buenas noches, ya pati bien,	Good evening, now father is well,
Chorus:	Ñao.	Ñao.
Teodoro:	Ay dios, nsila ngoya,	Dear God, the crossroads,
Chorus:	Ñao.	Ñao.
Teodoro:	Buenas noches, nganga ndoki,	Good evening, nganga ndoki,
Chorus:	Ñao.	Ñao.
Teodoro:	Ay dios, munansambi,	Dear God, house of God,
Chorus:	Ñao.	Ñao.
Teodoro:	Nzambi nganga son bendito,	Nzambi's ngangas are blessed,
Chorus:	Ñao.	Ñao.
Teodoro:	Maximene, ya son maldito,	The dead, they are accursed,[7]
Chorus:	Ñao.	Ñao.
Teodoro:	Cambia juicio, komulwenda,	Judgments change, komulwenda,
Chorus:	Ñao.	Ñao.
Teodoro:	Nkieto palo, mayimbe vuela,	Palo is still; the vulture flies,
Chorus:	Ñao.	Ñao.
Teodoro:	Tata golpe choqua naombre,	Tata's blows shake Kongo lands,[8]
Chorus:	Ñao.	Ñao.
Teodoro:	Tu toca ngunga, yo nsala ndoki,	You ring the bell; I'll work ndoki,[9]
Chorus:	Ñao.	Ñao.
Teodoro:	Chakolomene, buena nfinda,	Chakolomene, good lands of the dead,
Chorus:	Ñao.	Ñao.
Teodoro:	Buena noche, mi Campo Lemba,	Good evening, my cemetery,
Chorus:	Ñao.	Ñao.
Teodoro:	Ay dios, sabana ngombe,	Dear God, a bull loose on fields,
Chorus:	Ñao.	Ñao.
Teodoro:	Ay dios, sabana nkumbe,	Dear God, like a drum on fields,[10]
Chorus:	Ñao.	Ñao.
Teodoro:	Teremene, ndiato Congo,	Teremene, ndiato Kongo,
Chorus:	Ñao.	Ñao.

Teodoro:	Dios, bendición mi padrino,	Blessings on my godfather,
Chorus:	Ñao.	Ñao.
Teodoro:	Ay dios, la kwenda nfuiri,	Dear God, the march of the dead,[11]
Chorus:	Ñao.	Ñao.
Teodoro:	Bendición mi madrina,	Blessings on my godmother,
Chorus:	Ñao.	Ñao.
Teodoro:	Ay nganga, la kwenda nfuiri,	Dear nganga, march of the dead,
Chorus:	Ñao.	Ñao.
Teodoro:	Ay dios, 'manonganga,	Dear God, nganga's siblings,
Chorus:	Ñao.	Ñao.
Teodoro:	To' lo hermanos a pie kindembo,	Siblings, at the prenda's feet,
Chorus:	Ñao.	Ñao.
Teodoro:	Buena noche, ngembo Palo,	Good evening, Palo's bat,[12]
Chorus:	Ñao.	Ñao.
Teodoro:	Ay dios, ngembo yaya,	Dear God, the she-bat,
Chorus:	Ñao.	Ñao.
Teodoro:	Nganga ndoki está lambrono,	Nganga ndoki is happy,
Chorus:	Ñao.	Ñao.
Teodoro:	¡Nganga ndoki está la'brono!	Nganga ndoki is happy!
Chorus:	Ñao.	Ñao.
Teodoro:	Mira ngona ya está la nsulo,	Look, the moon is already in the sky,
Chorus:	Ñao.	Ñao.
Teodoro:	¡Mira ngona está la nsulo!	Look, the moon is in the sky!
Chorus:	Ñao.	Ñao.
Teodoro:	'Lumbra pemba lo sakariri,	Devils light the land of the dead,
Chorus:	Ñao.	Ñao.
Teodoro:	¡Lumbra pemba sakariri!	Devils light the land of the dead!
Chorus:	Ñao.	Ñao.
Teodoro:	Sakariri munandiako,	Devils, in their house,
Chorus:	Ñao.	Ñao.
Teodoro:	¡Sakariri munandiako!	Devils, in their house!
Chorus:	Ñao.	Ñao.

Teodoro's words were an invocation of Tormenta Ndoki as much as they were an invocation of the dead in each of us. His song was drawn from the heart of the Quita Manaquita repertoire and, true to the ancient sense of the Quita Manaquita society, he sang us into being as *devils among the dead*. He gathered us, Tormenta Ndoki and her "devil" children—the dead and the Children of the Dead [Quita Manaquita]—into the most intimate sense of Palo society

Teodoro's mambos had been slow and plaintive, but gradually his demeanor toward Tormenta Ndoki grew more aggressive. Each mambo lasted several minutes, as Teodoro passed it to us with much improvisation and then received it again. As he sang, Teo paid close attention to any sense he got from Tormenta Ndoki as to her disposition. What Tormenta felt was perceived by no one but him, who knew from what he picked up in the dead around him just how much he would have to push the prenda judía. Though Tormenta may have remained inscrutable to her, Isidra was nonetheless a keen reader of exchanges between the living and the dead, and she could tell from studying Teodoro that Tormenta was not responding well. Even as he beseeched her, Teodoro became impatient with her, as if he knew he would have to be more forceful. Later, Teodoro referred to his prayers and songs of entreaty as tempering [*templar*] or heating the dead.[13] It seemed to me that in singing to Tormenta as he did, little by little increasing his insistence and his physical presence, himself getting hotter and hotter, he was tempering not only Tormenta but all the dead within and around him. We could feel the air charged with uncertainty and the attention of everyone in the room fixed on Teodoro and his engagement with the prenda. He never stopped singing in the first half hour of our session with Tormenta; he only became more and more impatient with her.

He added another entreaty to the many he had already sung, bringing his invocation of Tormenta Ndoki into tune. As his manner became more insistent with her, the lyrics became more confident and aggressive, celebrating Palo's power to defend itself with lethal workings of the dead. This mambo was a little faster than the others, and Teodoro was increasing his momentum:

Teodoro:	¡Ngangara que estoy!	I'm ready!
	¡Ay, Dios! ¡Nganga ndoki!	Dear God! Nganga ndoki!
Chorus:	¡Ngangara que estoy!	I'm ready![14]
Teodoro:	¡Ay, Dios! ¡Tormenta Ndoki!	Dear God! Tormenta Ndoki!
Chorus:	¡Ngangara que estoy!	I'm ready!

Teodoro:	¡Buenas noches, mi burukuame!	Good evening, my brothers!
Chorus:	¡Ngangara que estoy!	I'm ready!
Teodoro	¡Ay, Dios! ¡Burukuame!	Dear God! My siblings!
Chorus:	¡Ngangara que estoy!	I'm ready!
Teodoro:	¡Nganga congo ya son primero!	Kongo ngangas are now first!
Chorus:	¡Ngangara que estoy!	I'm ready!
Teodoro:	¡Buenas noches, mi nganga ndoki!	Good evening, my nganga ndoki!
Chorus:	¡Ngangara que estoy!	I'm ready!
Teodoro:	¡Nganga ndoki que nunca tesia¡	Nganga ndoki never dies!
Chorus:	¡Ngangara que estoy!	I'm ready!
Teodoro:	¡Ya que tesia, mundo llora!	If she dies, the world cries!
Chorus:	¡Ngangara que estoy!	I'm ready!
Teodoro:	¡Si mundo llora, mundo acaba!	If the world cries, the world ends!
Chorus:	¡Ngangara que estoy!	I'm ready!
Teodoro:	¡Arriba truena los patipemba!	Fathers of the dead thunder above!
Chorus:	¡Ngangara que estoy!	I'm ready!
Teodoro:	¡Los patipemba, los chamalongo!	The dead, the chamalongo!
Chorus:	¡Ngangara que estoy!	I'm ready!
Teodoro:	¡Chakolomene la buena finda!	Chakolomene, good lands of the dead!
Chorus:	¡Ngangara que estoy!	I'm ready!
Teodoro:	¡Finda Kongo, nfinda ndilanda!	Kongo lands of lamentation!
Chorus:	¡Ngangara que estoy!	I'm ready!
Teodoro:	¡Buke, buke yo suala kongo!	I searched, searched for Kongo lands!
Chorus:	¡Ngangara que estoy!	I'm ready!
Teodoro:	¡Chakolomene, la buena finda!	Chakolomene, good lands of the dead!
Chorus:	¡Ngangara que estoy!	I'm ready!
Teodoro:	¡La finda kongo, pemba nganga!	Land of the dead, land of the nganga!
Chorus:	¡Ngangara que estoy!	I'm ready!

Teodoro:	¡Ya mañana, pemba nganga!	Now tomorrow, nganga's land!
Chorus:	¡Ngangara que estoy!	I'm ready!
Teodoro:	¡Buena noche, ma'rina naganga!	Good evening, madrina of my nganga!
Chorus:	¡Ngangara que estoy!	I'm ready!
Teodoro:	¡Buena noche, 'mano menga!	Good evening, blood brothers!
Chorus:	¡Ngangara que estoy!	I'm ready!
Teodoro:	¡Da licencia Kubayende!	Kubayende grants permission!
Chorus:	¡Ngangara que estoy!	I'm ready!
Teodoro:	¡Tumbando cojo, ya Kubayende!	Crippled, goes Kubayende!
Chorus:	¡Ngangara que estoy!	I'm ready!
Teodoro:	¡Palo, que son cosa de tierra Kongo!	This is the stuff of Kongo lands!
Chorus:	¡Ngangara que estoy!	I'm ready!
Teodoro:	¡Tierra Kongo nunca tesia!	Kongo lands will never die!
Chorus:	¡Ngangara que estoy!	I'm ready!
Teodoro:	¡Ya que tesia, mundo acaba!	And if they die, the world will end!
Chorus:	¡Ngangara que estoy!	I'm ready!
Teodoro:	¡Palo, si mundo acaba, mundo llora!	Palo, if the world ends, the world cries!
Chorus:	¡Ngangara que estoy!	I'm ready!
Teodoro:	¡Palo, el que debe culpa, paga culpa!	Palo, who is to blame pays with blame!
Chorus:	¡Ngangara que estoy!	I'm ready!
Teodoro:	¡Ay Dios! ¡Mi nganga ndoki!	Dear God! My nganga ndoki!
Chorus:	¡Ngangara que estoy!	I'm ready!
Teodoro:	¡Palo, los sentimientos que me llevan!	Palo! The things I feel move me!
Chorus:	¡Ngangara que estoy!	I'm ready!
Teodoro:	¡Palo, los sentimientos de kuna nsila!	Feelings from the crossing, my cradle!
Chorus:	¡Ngangara que estoy!	I'm ready!
Teodoro:	¡Ay Dios! ¡Buena noche!	Dear God! Good evening!
Chorus:	¡Ngangara que estoy!	I'm ready!

Teodoro:	¡Buena noche, mi Tormenta!	Good evening, Tormenta!
Chorus:	¡Ngangara que estoy!	I'm ready!
Teodoro:	¡Buena mecha, Tormenta Ndoki!	Tormenta Ndoki is the fuse!
Chorus:	¡Ngangara que estoy!	I'm ready!
Teodoro:	¡Ay Dios! ¡Ndoki malo!	Dear God! Bad Ndoki!
Chorus:	¡Ngangara que estoy!	I'm ready!
Teodoro:	¡Mundele kwama, ndoki bueno!	Set fire to white folks, good ndoki![15]
Chorus:	¡Ngangara que estoy!	I'm ready!
Teodoro:	¡Saca cuenta los sikanakua!	Devils will settle accounts!
Chorus:	¡Ngangara que estoy!	I'm ready!
Teodoro:	¡Hecha humo pa' la loma!	Blow smoke at the hills!
Chorus:	¡Ngangara que estoy!	I'm ready!

Teodoro sang of the dead and Kongo dominance and asserted Palo's force to destroy its oppressors. At the same time he was developing his call of Tormenta into something more intense, becoming more belligerent with her, rapping her kettle with more resolve. As he sang of Tormenta being the fuse that would light the world of whites ablaze, he directed Tocayo to hit Tormenta with blasts of chamba, which burned. "Get it in her eyes!" shouted Teodoro. Tocayo also blew plumes of chamba into the air, giving the room an acrid bite, so that we were all choking. "¡Camina, Nganga!" cried Teodoro "¡Hecha! ¡Carajo! ¡Camina! Get up, Nganga! Move!"

Plumes of cigar smoke joined the chamba in the air, and the drums intensified until the atmosphere of the room was transformed into a world of smoke and fire and rolling thunder, a land of proud devils, the whole of it punctuated by our shouts prodding Tormenta. Our cheeks were tear streaked from the chamba, and at times I felt as if I couldn't breathe and would have to leave the room or I would vomit. Leaving would be an offense against Tormenta Ndoki, and when I tried to get up Isidra held me in my place with a stern hand. Between the chamba and my cigar I was sick, and I struggled to keep it together. Isidra watched me closely, knowing that the episode could be evidence of my having been attacked with sorcery.

When I recovered, I was sitting on my little bench. Teo and Isidra were shaking and prodding me. Isidra was laughing and complimenting her chamba, because it had reduced me to a vomiting mess and challenged any harmful flow of the dead that might have been at work inside me. Teo, for his part, was sure the chamba had finally worked on Tormenta Ndoki, whose first clear signal of being roused was trying to take me, to "mount" me. Teodoro was delighted and seemed as if he couldn't make up his mind as to what he wanted more: my swift recovery or my full possession by his prenda judía. Either way, my surrender was evidence that Tormentíca was riled and ready to step out and mount one of us. I recovered quickly enough, but my teachers have never let me forget the moment of my submission to Tormenta Ndoki, becoming part of her mythology, and part of mine.

20. Storms of Lent

As I cleared my head the room erupted into sound. We had Emilio's old drum with us, and Teodoro Tocayo took it up with an energetic Briyumba rhythm as we switched away from verses of appeal into feast mambos. Emilio's drum was crafted from the top quarter of an old tumbadora, hand-made from narrow slats of wood that had for decades been dry-rotting from the ground up, and which Teo called *"el tambor de brujo,"* "the witch's drum" or "witchcraft's drum." Teodoro had left it in the sun all day, so that the goatskin would tighten and "tune." It made a high, melodic sound. We also had a small *cajón*, a compact plywood box built to sound percussively. We used a pair of railroad spikes as a clave, to set the root relationships between the percussion and the voice. Before long, the atmosphere we generated was agitated, with the dead stirred up into choking, acrid exhalations veiled in smoke and trembling with thunder and earth-moving reverberations. Such turbulent reaches are precisely what Teodoro sought; they were the privileged space of Tormenta Ndoki, the territory from which her spectral devilry is worked.

In the midst of our playing and singing, a knock came to the door of the house. Teodoro had us pause and sent Tocayo to answer. Within seconds he escorted a man back to the room. When he saw the gathering he stepped back, coughing shortly from the chamba that hung in the air. Then he greeted Tormenta with reluctance and caution; he was breathing hard when he approached her. He kneeled, then knocked on the ground three times with his knuckles before mumbling her name. He tarried with her but a moment, then turned to Teodoro and spoke to him in sentences of strung-together Palo Kikongo to say they were "playing" Palo on the hilltop over, that the work with judía was getting good and hot across the way. Did we want to come over to play devil *[jugar diablo]*? It seemed all of Guanabacoa was wrapped up in judías, and those feasts were sure to be exceptional, but we were on our way to having Tormenta ready and we determined to stay put and tend to the work at hand. The man left without hesitation. He was not the person Teodoro had been expecting, and with a shrug of uncertainty he returned to the drums and songs.

As we played and sang we not only woke Tormenta Ndoki but also tried to provoke her. The idea was to incite her. That was dangerous, but Tormenta's usefulness depended on excesses of rage. Then she would be cruel. Every sting she received, she would then pass to her intended victims. This is one reason Isidra feared Teodoro's indiscipline, because commanding Tormenta Ndoki would require every bit of stamina once she was ablaze. Only by dominating the prenda thoroughly could Teodoro guarantee that the ill we conjured would be directed outward, reach its mark, and not go astray or come back to cause us harm.

Rousing a prenda is no small task, and though choking on chamba made us all very optimistic, in Teodoro's judgment she was not yet ready. The ritual abuse he proceeded to inflict upon the prenda, which is to some degree inflicted on all prendas, but especially on judías, is worthy of attention. The word *arrear* again shines important, as does the word *ngombe*, which means "bull" or "ox" and is a term by which the nfumbe, and sometimes the person possessed by the nfumbe, is sometimes called in Palo Kikongo. The term *ngombe* is consistent with the verb *arrear*, meaning to prod a beast forward. Teodoro's insults of Tormenta Ndoki, and his reference to her as ngombe, were hardly severe compared to some cases of ritual offense that are recorded. Cabrera's great informant, Calzán, tells her that prendas judías need to be insulted and cursed into acting. Cabrera records him cursing his prenda in the harshest terms: "You son of a . . . , you do what I say. You aren't stronger than me! Fuck! You don't like being covered with a black rag? Well, that is exactly why I use it—it's blacker than the skin of the whore mother that aborted you without knowing who your father was!" Calzán then tells his prenda that he wishes she would go to hell for not obeying him.[1]

If Tormenta's verbal treatment was gentler than the treatment received by Calzán's judía, her physical abuse was no less. Teo did not whip her or hit her with a broom, as prendas sometimes are.[2] But he did follow through with tempering her, and his incitements and the violence he used against her were significant. His words moved from pleading invocations to songs of command as he sang:

Teodoro:	¡Kwenda ndokita, kwenda ndoki!	Go forth, sweet ndoki, go forth!
	¡Kwenda ndokita, kwenda ndoki!	Go forth, sweet ndoki, go forth!
	Ndoki bueno, ndoki malo.	Good ndoki, bad ndoki.
	¡Cuando yo vira cara,	When I turn to look,
	yo vira pa' ti na más!	I look only at you!

The song was one of authority, explicitly calling the ndoki to get up and go. The mambo wasn't without its sweetness and tenderness, however, despite anchoring a growing assault of physical abuse. Using the diminutive *ndokita* was an attempt to settle her in the same moment he assailed her. Furthermore, the last line of each verse was an appeal to his loyalty and devotion to her, promising he had eyes only for her. All prendas are said to be exceptionally possessive and jealous of their keepers, but especially prendas judías.

Sweetness and appeals to tender dedication included, in the middle of the mambo Teo took a bottle of 90 proof alcohol from among the many things he had prepared to work with that night and poured it on the ground under the prenda. As we bounced the mambo back and forth, Teodoro improvising above us, he struck a match and set her ablaze. The room, already choking, filled with the light from the fire and new shadows of smoke. The ring of flames around Tormenta rose to her rim, but she was forever emergent above them. Despite the firelight, her eye sockets never betrayed their shadows. We continued singing, verse after verse, each time more agitated and loud, until the fire began to die:

Teodoro:	¡Kwenda ndokita, kwenda ndoki!	Go forth, sweet ndoki, go forth!
	¡Kwenda ndokita, kwenda ndoki!	Go forth, sweet ndoki, go forth!
	Ndoki bueno, ndoki malo.	Good ndoki, bad ndoki.
	¡Cuando yo vira cara,	When I turn to look,
	yo vira pa' ti na más!	I look only at you!
Chorus:	¡Kwenda ndokita, kwenda ndoki,	Go forth, sweet ndoki, go forth!
	¡Kwenda ndokita, kwenda ndoki!	Go forth, sweet ndoki, go forth!
	Ndoki bueno, ndoki malo.	Good ndoki, bad ndoki.
	¡Cuando yo vira cara,	When I turn to look,
	yo vira pa' ti na más!	I look only at you!

Teo let Tormentica burn until the alcohol was spent, and Tormenta was at last brought to the wakeful vitality he sought. In fact, as he progressed in his treatment of her, he seemed to be enjoying himself more and more, but not without concerns. As we kept the chorus going, he laughed, saying, "Fuck! She has my attention all year long, and all I ask for is one day of the year and she has to be so stubborn! Do you think I *want* to catch her on fire? No! How else will she listen? You can't he sentimental when you work Palo, and less yet when you work judía!"

After the prodding, tempering, and maltreatment, Teo felt he could begin to work her. He felt he had Tormenta's attention, and that his dominion over her was established. The atmosphere around her was thick with fear and agitation, and Teodoro let it grow a little stronger before bringing it down to a sudden stillness, calling off the drums and singing. He surveyed the scene, as much the newly fired judía as his obedient vassals [*vasallos*], drumming and singing and doing what he commanded us to do.

With the basic invocations sung and called, and with Tormenta Ndoki woken to his call, Teodoro softened his tone and politely asked her if she would agree to be taken outside. Just as he had mastered her, Teodoro once again became the supplicant; his demeanor shifted, and he suddenly sounded consoling, entreating her so as not to irritate her. He asked her if she didn't want to be outside, at the foot of the ceiba in the back patio. After all, prendas judías love the outdoors and are more insistent about being taken outside than the others. After she was set on fire we figured she might want some fresh air. We couldn't, however, just take Tormenta from her resting place without consent, and Teo began to gather his chamalongo. After a mumbled appeal by which he displayed his respect for her, he asked her in a pleading tone, "Tormenta Ndoki, my brilliant nganga, my sweet ndoki, you've been inside all year. Would you come outside now, to sit a little under the ceiba [*ndundo*] and receive the blessings of the moon [*ngona*]? Look out the window, Nganga Ndoki. See the moon? Tormenta Ndoki, sweet Tormenta, can I work you under its light?"

Teodoro liked to work his chamalongo in Palo Kikongo. After a few moments of invocations and displays of obeisance, the words of which he guarded jealously under mumbles, Teodoro threw the chamalongo into the air while stepping back. He said stepping back protected you from the ill judgments of the dead, when they were so rendered. No, said Tormentíca, she would not go outside. Teo was surprised by her reply, as we all were. There was no reason she wouldn't want to be outside, unless she was simply being stubborn on a whim. He picked up the chamalongo from where they had fallen and with them in his hands he rephrased the question, adding that she would enjoy her feast meal better outdoors. No, she said again. Isidra sank into herself, her shoulders slumped into her belly as she let out a hiss of exasperation. Her disappointment spread across the room. Tormentíca was putting up resistance to the least of our requests, to the sweetest and most comfortable suggestion. A conversation nearly erupted between Isidra and Teo then, as she mumbled something about the general neglect of the prenda and his indiscipline. He cut her short before she could finish, silenced her with a sharp hiss, which was the only time I ever saw him surmount her so succinctly in a clash of wills.

There was nothing to do but keep working. To take Tormenta outside against her wishes would have been folly. What remained to be seen was whether she would assent to being worked at all. To ask the question directly seemed imprudent, so we turned our attention back to the reason we had gathered, which was to craft Palo that would kill our most reviled antagonists. By the rules of the Quita Manaquita house, no one present could be there without a "work" to place with Tormenta Ndoki. The works took the form of wrapped bundles, bilongos, most of which had been prepared beforehand. Each bilongo was stitched up in black cloth and sealed with black thread and candle wax. We each placed ours on the plywood Teodoro had decorated with the firma of Kubayende, next to his mother's bilongo. Teo had two bilongos yet to fashion for clients before we could begin in earnest. There were people who were prohibited by Kongo Law from being there, the uninitiated, menstruating women, and students of Ifá, and he was finishing bilongos for two of these. We waited for him while he made them quickly.

Each of us had made our bilongo packet alone so as to guard the confidence of our deed. After all, we meant to kill those whose names were included among the substances in our bilongo. We watched Teo make the two packets, which were hardly different from the masangó we had made when we built the Lucero Mundo and the other prendas a while back, nor noticeably different from other masangó we had loaded when working with prendas cristianas. One of Teodoro's new bilongos was ready to be stitched up, and Isidra took up the task with efficient skill. The other, like most bilongos, had a corn husk for its principal casing. Normally this was soaked for a few minutes in water, or agua ngóngoro, before loading it up, so that it would be pliable. Grave earth was the principal ingredient in his last bilongo, to which he added bibijagua anthill dirt, which he kept in a jar. He also added little chips from several branches he had on hand, and a powder he called "black precipitate" [precipitado negro]. A single sprig of kimbansa weed was laid into the husk cupped in his hand, as was a single strand of a vulture's feather. He had me hold it while he finished the contents of the bilongo with pencil and paper.

Isidra had brought the pencils and a large sheet of *papel de traza,* the unbleached, brown paper that is valued in Palo and Ocha/Santo craft. Papel de traza is not easy to find in Cuba—no paper is. But Isidra got hers by paying a few pesos to her local bodeguero, who saved her the sheet or two that came in each box of powdered milk the Cuban state subsidized for all children under six. It was nice paper, thick, like construction paper. Teo tore a small piece, about the size of a playing card. On this he spent a little time drawing a firma. He then turned it over and wrote the intended victim's name many times. When he had finished, he folded the paper seven times and placed it in the corn husk with the other things. Taking the bilongo back, he closed the husk and began twisting it with both hands, careful to be winding the husk in turns away from his body.

When he had finished twisting the masangó into a tight knot, he wrapped it in a small piece of black cloth. This he bound with black thread, which he wound in counterclockwise cycles away from his body, always holding the packet in his left hand. With the packet thoroughly bound, he dripped candle wax on it, something that was tiresome and which he eventually had me finish. He did not stop singing, however. With a little patience, the last bundle was sealed. Teodoro had me place it next to the others, so that finally Tormenta could be sent out.

Before the rooster could be given, Teodoro first had to offer his own blood. That Tormenta Ndoki had a taste for people's blood established her as residing at the limits of voraciousness within Palo values of force and substance. Palo lore accords different degrees of heat to blood, and it is the blood of people that is considered the hottest, most powerful, and most forbidden. The offering of a keeper's blood is reserved for the prenda judía; none of the other prendas partake of human blood, except during initiations, when the blood of initiates is offered to the prenda cristiana that receives them into Palo society. The difference between the two offerings is that the prenda judía demands the blood of a Christian every time she is worked; it is her preferred nourishment, without which she would not allow herself to be handled.

In keeping with the ritual order of heat and force, Teodoro fed Tormenta his blood first. It follows that a person's blood, hot beyond all of Palo's substances, would be the final addition to Tormenta Ndoki's heating and tempering, before she began to refresh with the rooster. Among the little hoard of materials and substances Teo had gathered for working that night was a small razor blade, a Sputnik razor like the ones he used to cut in Palo initiations. Teo was expert at making the kinds of incisions that draw blood but leave no scar, and as he turned his arm over to contemplate its underside he started us singing:

Teodoro:	Mbele, mbele,	Knife, knife,
	¡Mama quiere menga!	Mama wants blood!
	¡Mama quiere menga,	Mama wants blood,
	¡Mama quiere menga!	Mama wants blood!
Chorus:	Mbele, mbele,	Knife, knife,
	¡Mama quiere menga!	Mama wants blood!
	¡Mama quiere menga,	Mama wants blood,
	¡Mama quiere menga!	Mama wants blood!

As he continued the song, he made a small incision, a single cut on the underside of his arm where the base of the thumb meets the wrist bone. He studied it closely, singing while he waited for the blood, and as a drop started across his wrist he changed mambos and took us with him:

Teodoro:	¡Menga va correr!	Blood will run!
	Como tintorera,	Like dye,
	Menga va correr!	Blood will run!
	¡Eh! ¡Menga va correr!	Ah! Blood will run!
	¡Como guarilanga,	Like dye,
	Menga va correr!	Blood will run!
Chorus:	¡Menga va correr!	Blood will run!
	¡Como tintorera,	Like dye,
	Menga va correr!	Blood will run!
	¡Eh! ¡Menga va correr!	Ah! Blood will run,
	¡Como guarilanga,	Like dye,
	Menga va correr!	Blood will run!

His wound was barely visible in the candlelight, but the trickle of blood that came from it cut across his arm like ink. He held his arm just over Tormenta's skull, singing his offering to her. Several drops fell, but soon the wound was dry. He finished by blowing aguardiente over his wound, and let the blood-stained alcohol fall on the ingot at Tormenta's feet. "Just like that," he said.

Such is the offering of Christian blood to the prenda judía today in Cuba. As Teo told me earlier, he was baptized, as all paleros and santeros should be. Sometimes baptisms are official, done in the church with a priest when the person is an infant. Other times, especially because of the suppression of religion during forty years of Revolution, baptisms are done informally, in ceremonies at home, with holy water taken from the church.

With his offering done, Teodoro explained in subdued tones that Tormenta Ndoki was bound by a promise to accept blood only from her keepers. The iron ingot he kept with her was the evidence and test of that secret agreement, made long ago with Emilio. This was the reason he also gave a bit of his blood to the ingot every time he worked her. So long as the ingot remained intact, and feeding it a little blood seemed a good way of guaranteeing this, Tormenta Ndoki would have to settle for her keeper's blood, badly as she might long for another's. Cabrera records a similar story, with more detail than Teo could give. In her version, a palero informs Cabrera that if she were to keep a prenda judía and it became fixated on her child and demanded her child's blood, she would have to trick it to get it to desist. The prescribed trick is to promise the child to the prenda, but only if first the dead coursing through the prenda mounts a person and eats whatever its keeper presents it with. Thinking it is going to get a chicken or a goat as a prelude to the child, the prenda agrees. It then takes possession of someone, maybe its very keeper, but what the ndoki finds it must eat prior to the child is a piece of iron, an ingot or a file. Says Cabrera's informant, "If it can't eat the iron, it can't eat the child. That's the deal."[3] Whether or not it is the same deal Emilio made, or the same trick played, the ingot there with Tormenta Ndoki served the same purpose and likewise bound her by trickery to her keeper's will.

The ingot is the material exuded by a subtle play at the intersection of the dead and the theater of possession. In it, the ruinous extremes of the prenda judía's narrative were contained. With the trick of the inedible iron, the nineteenth-century Catholic nightmares of Jewish blood rites and the racist fantasies of child sacrifice in early twentieth-century Cuba, were at once contained and, in the form of the ingot, affirmed. The ingot was the material reservoir where unsustainable excesses from the creative condensation of different cosmological themes were deposited and held. Teodoro's blood was in the same category—a materialization, a *substantiation*, or actualization of cosmological excess. Our very gathering that night was predicated on these excesses.

Having given his blood with little pomp, Teodoro turned his attention to the rooster laying among so many other things now at Tormenta's feet. He returned to the second blood mambo. Without pausing he picked up the bird and whispered a few words into the rooster's mouth. Within a second, Teodoro tore out its tongue with his teeth. Holding the rooster's mouth open, he let a few drops of blood from its mouth fall on the ingot. Then, keeping with the pace of the sacrifice, he forsook the knife and simply tore the rooster's head off with his hands. This is the preferred mode of killing birds in Palo, if not made impossible by the strength or size of the animal. Teodoro placed the animal's head next to Tormenta Ndoki's skull, as he let the blood pour from its neck onto the prenda judía. Soon it was bathed in the animal's blood. To our relief, the rooster had more blood than we might have guessed and Isidra thanked the dead. Besides refreshing her after the heaviness of his blood, Teodoro said, the rooster's blood would put Tormenta off his trail so that she wouldn't crave him. The last few drops of the rooster's life he directed haphazardly toward the bilongo bundles at Tormenta's feet, and each packet, of which there were nine, and the firma beneath them received a little.

As is customary in Palo, Teodoro placed the rooster on the ground in front of Tormenta and knelt down to press on it with his hands, squeezing from it any life that may have remained behind. The bird let go of its last breath with a faint croak somewhere in its throat. With that, Teo changed the song, which he had not let falter through the bird's ordeal. It was a mambo he had already used that night, but the repetition of mambos is not uncommon in Palo practice. Again he bid Tormenta Ndoki move, this time sending her forward on her night's mission:

Teodoro:	¡Kwenda ndokita, kwenda ndoki!	Go forth, sweet ndoki, go forth!
	¡Kwenda ndokita, kwenda ndoki!	Go forth, sweet ndoki, go forth!
	Ndoki bueno, ndoki malo.	Good ndoki, bad ndoki.
	¡Cuando yo vira cara,	When I turn to look,
	yo vira pa' ti na más!	I look only at you!

Teo sent her off, encouraging her forward with verse after verse, quickly, without pause or hesitation.

We sent her on our words and wishes, riding the songs we sang for her, so she would travel with fury and speed like a wave through Kalunga to our intended victims. It was well past midnight on Good Friday when Tormenta Ndoki was set free into the flows and condensations of the dead that are collectively Havana, its streets, its homes, and its people. She was free to roam because the Christian dead who normally impeded her, and whom she would normally shy away from, were subdued and powerless because their God hung dead on his cross. Tonight, Tormenta would find lonely stretches of Kalunga traversed only by ndoki like her, coming and going on their gloomy errands. As she went, Teodoro captured the image of her flight in song. He pictured Tormenta Ndoki first as a bird of prey, then as a host of dead multiplying by the hundreds, then dissipating and condensing again into a devilish force, then transforming into whistling winds and thunderstrikes across the anonymous atmosphere of the dead. In the protean shifts described in his song, she was also a tiger and a bull ox loose on the open plain, heralded by the clash of its horns against a foe. Regardless of the form she assumed, Tormenta was always at the same time a raptor, a hawk at his command:

Teodoro:	¡Doce la noche, ngavilán voló!	Midnight, and the hawk flew!
	¡Doce la noche, ngavilán voló!	Midnight, and the hawk flew!
Chorus:	¡Doce la noche, ngavilán voló!	Midnight, and the hawk flew!
Teodoro:	¡Palo! ¡Las doce la noche, ngavilán voló!	Palo! Midnight, and the hawk flew!
Chorus:	¡Doce la noche, ngavilán voló!	Midnight, and the hawk flew!
Teodoro:	¡Palo! ¡A las doce la noche, ngavilán voló!	Palo! Midnight, and the hawk flew!
Chorus:	¡Doce la noche, ngavilán voló!	Midnight, and the hawk flew!
Teodoro	¡Palo! ¡A las doce la noche, ngavilán voló!	Palo! Midnight, and the hawk flew!
Chorus:	¡Doce la noche, ngavilán voló!	Midnight, and the hawk flew!
Teodoro:	¡Nfuiri cientos, nacen ceintos!	From hundreds dead, are born hundreds more!
	¡Ngavilán voló!	And the hawk flew!
Chorus:	¡Doce la noche, ngavilán voló!	Midnight, and the hawk flew!
Teodoro:	¡Saca la cuenta, sikanakua!	Devil, settles scores!
	¡Ngavilán voló!	And the hawk flew!
Chorus:	¡Doce la noche, ngavilán voló!	Midnight, and the hawk flew!
Teodoro:	¡Palo! ¡Doce la noche, ngavilán voló!	Palo! Midnight, and the hawk flew!
	¡Ngavilán voló!	And the hawk flew!
Chorus:	¡Doce la noche, ngavilán voló!	Midnight, and the hawk flew!
Teodoro:	¡Palo! ¡Doce la noche, ngavilán voló!	Palo! Midnight, and the hawk flew!
	¡Ngavilán voló!	And the hawk flew!
Chorus:	¡Doce la noche, ngavilán voló!	Midnight, and the hawk flew!
Teodoro:	¡Chifla, chifla, la tormenta!	The storm sings and whistles!
	¡Ngavilán voló!	And the hawk flew!
Chorus:	¡Doce la noche, ngavilán voló!	Midnight, and the hawk flew!

Teodoro:	¡Truena, truena, como nbrono!	Thunder, Thunder, so good!
	¡Ngavilán voló!	And the hawk flew!
Chorus:	¡Doce la noche, ngavilán voló!	Midnight, and the hawk flew!
Teodoro:	¡Mpaka, mensu, layi-laya!	Mpaka, mensu, layi-laya![4]
	¡Ngavilán voló!	And the hawk flew!
Chorus:	¡Doce la noche, ngavilán voló!	Midnight, and the hawk flew!
Teodoro:	¡Ya se que, se que manda!	Now I know, what commands!
	¡Ngavilán voló!	And the hawk flew!
Chorus:	¡Doce la noche, ngavilán voló!	Midnight, and the hawk flew!
Teodoro:	¡Chakolomene, Buena nfinda!	Chakolomene, Good lands of the dead!
	¡Ngavilán voló!	And the hawk flew!
Chorus:	¡Doce la noche, ngavilán voló!	Midnight, and the hawk flew!
Teodoro:	¡Nfinda congo, ngo bilanga!	In Kongo lands, a tiger prowls!
	¡Ngavilán voló!	And the hawk flew!
Chorus:	¡Doce la noche, ngavilán voló!	Midnight, and the hawk flew!
Teodoro:	¡Da vuelta nganga, munansambi!	The nganga runs circles, 'round the house of God!
	¡Ngavilán voló!	And the hawk flew!
Chorus:	¡Doce la noche, ngavilán voló!	Midnight, and the hawk flew!
Teodoro:	¡Buena noche, mi taona!	Good evening, my horned one!
	¡Ngavilán voló!	And the hawk flew!
Chorus:	¡Doce la noche, ngavilán voló!	Midnight, and the hawk flew!
Teodoro:	¡Bendición, mi padrino!	Blessings on my padrino!
	¡Ngavilán voló!	And the hawk flew!
Chorus:	¡Doce la noche, ngavilán voló!	Midnight, and the hawk flew!
Teodoro:	¡Bendición, mi madrina!	Blessings on my madrina!
	¡Ngavilán voló!	And the hawk flew!
Chorus:	¡Doce la noche, ngavilán voló!	Midnight, and the hawk flew!

Teodoro:	¡Oficio congo, cosa grande! ¡Ngavilán voló!	Kongo craft is a great thing! And the hawk flew!
Chorus:	¡Doce la noche, ngavilán voló!	Midnight, and the hawk flew!
Teodoro:	¡Buena noche, Tormenta Ndoki! ¡Ngavilán voló!	Greetings, Tormenta Ndoki! And the hawk flew!
Chorus:	¡Doce la noche, ngavilán voló!	Midnight, and the hawk flew!
Teodoro:	¡Ngombe suelto la sabana! ¡Ngavilán voló!	The bull is loose on the plain! And the hawk flew!
Chorus:	¡Doce la noche, ngavilán voló!	Midnight, and the hawk flew!
Teodoro:	¡Tarro ngombe, chocará! ¡Ngavilán voló!	Hear the bull's horns clash! And the hawk flew!
Chorus:	¡Doce la noche, ngavilán voló!	Midnight, and the hawk flew!
Teodoro:	¡Juegará Sesekinfula! ¡Ngavilán voló!	The devil will play! And the hawk flew!
Chorus:	¡Doce la noche, ngavilán voló!	Midnight, and the hawk flew!
Teodoro:	¡Respeta nfumbi, munansambi! ¡Ngavilán voló!	House of God, respect the dead! And the hawk flew!
Chorus:	¡Doce la noche, ngavilán voló!	Midnight, and the hawk flew!
Teodoro:	¡Jura nganga, e'ta clarita! ¡Ngavilán voló!	Swear to the nganga, but of course! And the hawk flew!
Chorus:	¡Doce la noche, ngavilán voló!	Midnight, and the hawk flew!
Teodoro:	¡Ay Palo! ¡Layi-laya! ¡Ngavilán voló!	Oh, Palo, Layi-laya! And the hawk flew!
Chorus:	¡Doce la noche, ngavilán voló!	Midnight, and the hawk flew!
Teodoro:	¡Yo makuto, Palo tengue! ¡Ngavilán voló!	I make a bundle, from Palo tengue! And the hawk flew!
Chorus:	¡Doce la noche, ngavilán voló!	Midnight, and the hawk flew!
Teodoro:	¡Palo Yaya, buena noche! ¡Ngavilán voló!	Greetings, Yaya, mother Palo And the hawk flew!

Chorus:	¡Doce la noche, ngavilán voló!	Midnight, and the hawk flew!
Teodoro:	¡Este Briyumba ndiambo cuaba! ¡Ngavilán voló!	This Briyumba, ndiambo cuaba! And the hawk flew!
Chorus:	¡Doce la noche, ngavilán voló!	Midnight, and the hawk flew!
Teodoro:	¡Ngando cheche, buena noche! ¡Ngavilán voló!	Great feathers, greetings! And the hawk flew!
Chorus:	¡Doce la noche, ngavilán voló!	Midnight, and the hawk flew!
Teodoro:	¡Canto ligueña, No se amarra! ¡Ngavilán voló!	The chameleon's song, Can't be tied down! And the hawk flew!
Chorus:	¡Doce la noche, ngavilán voló!	Midnight, and the hawk flew!
Teodoro:	¡Palo! ¡Ngando cubre ngando! ¡Ngavilán voló!	Palo! Feathers, cover feathers! And the hawk flew!
Chorus:	¡Doce la noche, ngavilán voló!	Midnight, and the hawk flew!
Teodoro:	¡No más ngando, Que batalla! ¡Ngavilán voló!	There are no more feathers, Than there are battles! And the hawk flew!
Chorus:	¡Doce la noche, ngavilán voló!	Midnight, and the hawk flew!
Teodoro:	¡Buena noche, Kubayende! ¡Ngavilán voló!	Greetings, Kubayende! And the hawk flew!
Chorus:	¡Doce la noche, ngavilán voló!	Midnight, and the hawk flew!
Teodoro:	¡Bendiciones, Manaquita! ¡Ngavilán voló!	Blessings, Manaquita! And the hawk flew!
Chorus:	¡Doce la noche, ngavilán voló!	Midnight, and the hawk flew!
Teodoro:	¡Tiempo ndile, ngangulero! ¡Ngavilán voló!	Like the old days, prenda keeper! And the hawk flew!
Chorus:	¡Doce la noche, ngavilán voló!	Midnight, and the hawk flew!
Teodoro:	¡Buena noche, 'spanto sueño! ¡Ngavilán voló!	Greetings, nightmare! And the hawk flew!

Chorus:	¡Doce la noche, ngavilán voló!	Midnight, and the hawk flew!
Teodoro:	¡Espanta la mula, como tata!	Frighten a mule, like a tata!
	¡Ngavilán voló!	And the hawk flew!
Chorus:	¡Doce la noche, ngavilán voló!	Midnight, and the hawk flew!
Teodoro:	¡Doce la noche, ngavilán voló!	Midnight, and the hawk flew!
	¡Ngavilán voló!	And the hawk flew!
Chorus:	¡Doce la noche, ngavilán voló!	Midnight, and the hawk flew!
Teodoro:	¡Doce la noche, ngavilán voló!	At midnight, the hawk flew!
	¡Ngavilán voló!	And the hawk flew!
Chorus:	¡Doce la noche, ngavilán voló!	Midnight, and the hawk flew!

The song went on, exalting Tormenta Ndoki, the power of Briyumba, Palo, and the preeminence of Kongo Rule. As Tormenta spread out of her cauldron, she did so in the shapes of Teodoro's imagining, pushing through the ambient dead with terrible force. As she went, Teo saw her transformed into forms drawn from European nightmares: devils, apocalyptic storms, and predators on a hunt. In the form that was convenient for her, perhaps all of them at once, Tormenta assailed her victims and laid them low. If Palo's prenda judía is a turn of Catholicism's spectral Jew, in this moment she was also a turn on the Passover angel, bringing destruction where she would.

We kept Tormentíca company on her errand by singing to her, driving her on, praising her volition and dangerousness. Isidra occasionally took the song from Teodoro, interrupting him at the calling point and replacing his melody and lyrics with her own. The rhythm and beat remained the same. The many songs Isidra sang to Tormenta that night were mostly from her home in the countryside, more Spanish than Palo Kikongo, but Cuban Kongo nonetheless, at its most austere:

Isidra:	¡No se viene pa' juga',	Don't come to play,
	No se viene pa' juga',	Don't come to play,
	A pie de mi Tormenta,	You don't kneel before my Tormenta,
	No se viene pa' juga'!	If you think you're going to play!
Chorus:	¡No se viene pa' juga',	Don't come to play,
	No se viene pa' juga',	Don't come to play,

	A pie de mi Tormenta,	You don't kneel before my Tormenta,
	No se viene pa' juga'!	If you think you're going to play!
Isidra:	¡No se viene pa' juga',	Don't come to play,
	No se viene pa' juga',	Don't come to play,
	A pie de nganga ndoki,	You don't kneel with nganga ndoki,
	No se viene pa' juga'!	If you think you're going to play!
Chorus:	¡No se viene pa' juga',	Don't come to play,
	No se viene pa' juga',	Don't come to play,
	A pie de nganga ndoki,	You don't kneel with nganga ndoki,
	No se viene pa' juga'!	If you think you're going to play!

Isidra then shifted to a mambo of obeisance and respect:

Isidra:	¡Eh-eh-eh-aeh! A pie de mi nganga,	I am at your feet, my nganga,
	Que tú me mandas!	That you command me!
	¡Yo a pie de mi nganga,	I am at your feet, my nganga,
	Que tú me mandas!	That you command me!
	¡Saluda ndoki, que tú me mandas!	Regards, ndoki, you command me!
Chorus:	¡Eh-eh-eh-aeh! A pie de mi nganga,	I am at your feet, my nganga,
	Que tú me mandas!	That you command me!
Isidra:	¡Eh! ¡A pie de mi nganga,	Ah! I am at your feet, my nganga,
	Que tú me mandas!	That you command me!
	¡Saluda Tormenta, que tu me mandas!	Regards, Tormenta, you command me!
Chorus:	¡Eh-eh-eh-aeh! A pie de mi nganga,	I am at your feet, my nganga,
	Que tú me mandas!	That you command me!

The mambos seemed countless, and between Teodoro and Isidra their variety was great. We sang into the night, waiting for word from Tormenta Ndoki. It would be a few hours before she was back, and we would sing until she announced her arrival. We sang and sang until we got tired and wanted desperately for the long night of judía's reign to end. We could do nothing but keep singing, because even when Tormenta returned we would not be allowed to leave, not unless the moon was down in the sky and dawn was near. As Teo said, "the devil's in the street; Good Friday isn't for strolling around. After the moon goes down you can go, but not until then. Right now Nkuyo are at the nsila ngoya [crossroads]; Kataka, Horonda, and Ntundo are on the loose.[5] You don't want to go out now."

After a while our singing began to lag, and we struggled to stave off exhaustion and sleep. We talked a little and tried to keep singing, though not without long pauses where anecdotes were told and questions asked. Slowly silence grew in the room. We sat and waited. Occasionally, Teodoro would take a small white saucer from between the squat legs of his stool and hold it to the candle. He would pass it through the fire until it was black. He turned the plate over and looked at the shapes left by the soot, which took the form of curls and wisps of gray. He read these for news of Tormenta's movements, but he kept his insights to himself. He simply looked up from the plate and said, "She's still out there [todavía camina]."

This is what Teodoro said about the use of the plate. "When you work judía, you work the plate and candle. The plate is more sure when you work judía, because the mpaka and mensu partake of God, and they aren't so good tonight. The chamalongo I use tonight, too. The chamalongo are of the dead. I use the plate to receive transmissions from the dead, which come through the candle. It lights the dead and heats them, and knows more about them than you or me. The plate makes the transmissions visible. Then I use the chamalongo to check them out and verify them. But I could verify them with anything. I once saw a great brujo use four pieces of bread to talk with the dead, just like you or I would use the chamalongo. You always check the plate against the chamalongo. The plate gives me sight [vista] into the dead, but it isn't perfect. I have vision until I begin to doubt what I see, and then I lose my sight. That's how it works. Now I won't use the chamalongo until Tormenta is back, which will be soon enough. I'll keep looking and looking. You see?"

I thought I did, but at that time I didn't understand the degree to which the plate, the flame, the soot, and the dead were, in Teodoro's world, each forms of one another. They were each versions of the same vast ambiance by which we were all permeated—Kalunga. Tormenta Ndoki was the same, and she was out there moving amid the measureless dead, pushing and hunting as a rogue wave pushing through the infinite sea that is Kalunga. As a wave she was discrete, separate, and moved against the worst fears of the living. Yet without the vastness of Kalunga, through which she coursed, she was powerless. Kalunga, the ambient dead, allowed her to pass through as an incorporeal force, and with great speed she was at the side of her intended victims. She was hardly impeded by the limits of their bodies, as these were but densities of the same fluid through which she traveled. Instantly she was inside them, into their uncertainty, and by means of fear and doubt she laid waste to their fates and thus to their lives. Tormenta Ndoki had terrible rounds to make that night, and it would be a mistake to imagine that she visited grief upon her victims one by one. Nine bilongo were gathered at her feet, and she could just as well have multiplied into nine lines of intention, or hundreds as the mambo said, simultaneously extending out from her cauldron. In his singing, Teodoro imagined her as one and many at once, and the forms she took needn't be linear transformations of one another. Tormenta went as a hawk, a bull, wind, thunder, fire, and a host of devils all *at once*. We would have to sing and drum into the night until we received word that she, as one and many, was back home.

Each time Teodoro checked the plate we picked up our singing on cue. I cannot say how many songs we sang, or how many times we fell into silence, or how long we waited. Teodoro must have checked the plate three or four times, but he was in no hurry. He enjoyed the singing and going back and forth with Isidra, learning songs from her and she from him. In the act of singing, songs were drawn out that neither of them previously remembered, and we all marveled at how our singing seemed driven by some other power. The songs, said Isidra, came from the dead. "*Canto saca canto*," she said, "songs recall songs." Hers were drawn from the dead of Sierra Morena, with some in her repertoire from Emilio. Teodoro's were owed entirely to Emilio, inspired by Havana Palo.

At some point, whether it was a waver in the candle's flame, a change in the chill of the night, or some other sense he tuned into, Teodoro picked up the white plate and held it face down over the candle. He passed it back and forth, and back again, occasionally glancing under the rim. When it was properly sooty, he looked at it carefully, raising his eyebrows now and then, contemplating the things he discerned. "Tormenta Ndoki is back," he said, "her work is done. Get up!" Then he sang:

Teodoro:	¡Kiangalanga, llegó la hora!	The hour is come![6]
	¡Kiangalanga, llegó la hora!	The time is come!
Chorus:	¡Kiangalanga, llegó la hora!	The hour is come!
	¡Kiangalanga, llegó la hora!	The time is come!
Teodoro:	¡Kiangalanga, llegó la hora!	The hour is come!
	¡Kiangalanga, llegó la hora!	The time is come!
Chorus:	¡Kiangalanga, llegó la hora!	The hour is come!
	¡Kiangalanga, llegó la hora!	The time is come!

Teodoro:	¡Kiangalanga, llegó la hora!	The hour is come!
	¡Kiangalanga, llegó la hora!	The time is come!
Chorus:	¡Kiangalanga, llegó la hora!	The hour is come!
	¡Kiangalanga, llegó la hora!	The time is come!

We sang with him a minute or two, and then he spoke to Tormenta Ndoki in Palo Kikongo and Spanish. "Tormenta Ndoki, my nganga, look, your candle is lit, waiting for you. I'm here. Yayi Nganga, Tata Nganga, Padre Nganga are all here waiting for you. My nganga, the moon is low in the sky, and you're back now from your stroll. I have some aguardiente for you, and some wine, too. Let me give you some smoke, to settle you. Oh, little nganga! You can rest now, rest the year, you've gone and come and now we won't ask you anything for a while. Tomorrow we'll take these bilongo to the cemetery, where we hope our enemies, thanks to you, will soon join them. Tell me, Nganga Ndoki, Tormenta, my thunder, my fire, is there anything left to do, anything you need or want? Has everything been done for you?"

He was feeling good, and rather than throw the chamalongo, Teodoro remembered a small vial of gunpowder he had in his pocket. I had found it for him a while back while plying one of Havana's markets where Palo and Ocha/Santo wares are sold. Gunpowder is illegal in Cuba, as is anything perceived as materiel for making weapons. It is sold under the table to paleros in utterly minute quantities. Teo prized gunpowder and saved it for occasions like this, because as a medium to determine a prenda's will or mood it was unsurpassed.[7] Gunpowder was also used in tests of the dead when they possessed members of his house. Pushing the bilongo packets to the side, he made seven little piles of the powder on the plywood firma, in a straight line. His cigar had died a short stub in his mouth, but he relit it, and after working its tip to a bright orange nub he held it to the first pile of gunpowder. In the blink of an eye the seven little mounds erupted, the spark of one jumping to the next, almost instantaneously. In the low light, the flash blinded us all, and for a few seconds we saw nothing but blue-pink after-images where the piles had been. No bit of gunpowder remained—a resounding affirmative from Tormenta. She was pleased. Teo, looking around the room in a fit of confidence, said he would check with her once more with the chamalongo to make sure, and he threw two up, two down—a strong yes. "That's it," he said, "she's pleased; she's done!"

With that, he broke into another song. After a few minutes we sang less and less, choosing rather to talk until Teo released us at dawn, after he was sure the street was free from the dead he and others had sent forth that night. We left Tormenta that morning with our darkest wishes laid at her feet and a confidence that our world would be different as a result. Despite the exhaustion, Isidra was cheerfully high. She wanted only to get home, where we would spend the rest of the weekend in calm repose, guarding against the judía that was surely being worked against us. We left Teodoro and Tocayo with the task of carrying the bilongos to the cemetery that morning, where they would summon by name those we had consigned to Tormenta. Before we left, we said farewell to Tormenta Ndoki and sent greetings with her for the dead to where she was withdrawing. Tocayo drummed and Teo sang:

Teodoro:	¡Ay! ¡Dimo adiós la guira!	Oh! Let's say good-bye to the prenda![8]
	¡Hasta el año venidero, la guira!	Until next year, prenda!
Chorus:	¡Ay! ¡Dimo adiós la guira!	Oh! Let's say good-bye to the prenda!
Teodoro:	¡Nganga ndoki venidero, la guira!	Next year, nganga ndoki, prenda!
Chorus:	¡Ay! ¡Dimo adiós la guira!	Oh! Let's say good-bye to the prenda!
Teodoro:	¡Hasta el año venidero, la guira!	Until next year, prenda!
Chorus:	¡Ay! ¡Dimo adiós la guira!	Oh! Let's say good-bye to the prenda!
Teodoro:	¡Tormenta Ndoki maleko, la guira!	Mischievous Tormenta Ndoki, prenda!
Chorus:	¡Ay! ¡Dimo adiós la guira!	Oh! Let's say good-bye to the prenda!
Teodoro:	¡Quita malo trae bueno, la guira!	Get rid of the bad and you get the good, prenda!
Chorus:	¡Ay! ¡Dimo adiós la guira!	Oh! Let's say good-bye to the prenda!
Teodoro:	¡Kandango palo kandango yaya, la guira!	Male prenda, female prenda, prenda!
Chorus:	¡Ay! ¡Dimo adiós la guira!	Oh! Let's say good-bye to the prenda!
Teodoro:	¡Ya va chieto como chieto, la guira!	She also goes well, the prenda!
Chorus:	¡Ay! ¡Dimo adiós la guira!	Oh! Let's say good-bye to the prenda!

Teodoro:	¡Hasta el año venidero, la guira!	Until next year, prenda!
Chorus:	¡Ay! ¡Dimo adiós la guira!	Oh! Let's say good-bye to the prenda!
Teodoro:	¡Si yo me acuerda, yo me llora, la guira!	If I think of you, I'll cry, prenda!
Chorus:	¡Ay! ¡Dimo adiós la guira!	Oh! Let's say good-bye to the prenda!

Then Teodoro changed the song slightly and closed:

Teodoro:	¡Adiós, mi Colorado, ¡Memoria por allá,	Good-bye, my fiery one, Remember me where you are going,
	Memoria por allá!	Remember me over there!
Chorus:	¡Adiós, mi Colorado, ¡Memoria por allá,	Good-bye, my fiery one, Remember me where you are going,
	Memoria por allá!	Remember me over there!
Teodoro:	¡Adiós mi Colorado, ¡Memoria por allá,	Good-bye, my fiery one, Remember me where you are going,
	Memoria por allá!	Remember me over there!
Chorus:	¡Adiós mi Colorado, ¡Memoria por allá,	Good-bye, my fiery one, Remember me where you are going,
	Memoria por allá!	Remember me over there!

Conclusion

The Easter weekend passed. The death of God on Good Friday was celebrated throughout Havana in those Palo houses that worked a prenda judía. The dead condensed by these prendas were sent out as ndoki, hunting cats, birds of prey, devils, and angels of death against a diminished Catholic world. Not only was the world of Catholicism vulnerable to the powers of judía, so was the world vouchsafed by the powers of Ocha/Santo sovereigns. All divinity was surpassed on that night by the multitude of the Palo dead. The powers of these dead were framed by the Catholic construction of Jewish difference as devil and witch and drew considerable energy from the fear and uncertainty these spectral entities inspired. As ndoki, this spectral Jew organized the very possibility of Palo sovereignty in Cuba's unsettled religious panorama. The resurrection of Easter Sunday went without a feast in either Palo or Ocha/Santo. At home, Isidra removed the bedsheet she had used to cover her Ocha/Santo sovereigns, and without explicit comment expressed that she was happy to have them back in the game of fate.

The storms of Lent dissipated, as Teodoro said they would, and the coming of spring could be felt more surely. The days ahead seemed strange—brighter, but also more uncertain. Each of us had sought to kill on Good Friday, each of us had sent Tormenta Ndoki on a bitter errand, and now we faced the repercussions of those acts. Days later, Teodoro claimed his victim was killed the very night of our gathering, by a massive stroke while watching the Friday movie. This was impossible to confirm, because only he knew his victim, just as each of us guarded the identities of ours. Isidra never again spoke of the work we did that night, nor hinted at her outcome. My bilongo had no effect whatsoever.

Though Tormenta Ndoki might not have been successful in killing on our behalf, the act of gathering on Good Friday to rouse the prenda judía and send her against our antagonists was not without consequences for each of us. In this regard, the prenda judía was triumphant—each of us knew that our coming together as witches [brujos] in the company of the devil and the Jew under Tormenta's cloud meant crossing inviolate lines. Doing so gained us command within the worlds of African inspiration in Cuba, until Sunday, when Tormenta faded to her cheerless repose, shrinking from the return of divinity to its throne. Then a restive sense of vulnerability overtook us, as our adversaries began fashioning their replies.

We had visited the limits of fate-changing force within African inspiration in Cuba, and the limits of sociality, and crossed them audaciously. The decisive transformative potential of the divine—of God and the orishas—was for a few days transferred to us, just as the sacredness of the sacrificial victim is suddenly transferred to the killer, in inverted form.[1] The ambiguous feeling of power and vulnerability that developed around each of us as outlaws among the dead, against the order guaranteed by Ocha/Santo sovereigns and Catholic divinity, was what I imagine Bataille and his colleagues in the College of Sociology described as the "left hand," or "negative sacred."[2] This we inhabited gloriously, as if each of us had suddenly become uniquely relevant to the reigning Ocha/Santo and Catholic rules of fate. For a few days we were healed of these rules and the injustices they engender; we were free of what is inexorable in a world ruled by divinity. Even after, when things seemed fixed again, the fateful world of divinity was changed, because we had defied it by affirming the sovereign importance of the dead within it. For that we thanked Tormenta Ndoki.

In working Tormenta Ndoki I found condensed in her care and keeping what makes Palo great in Cuba. Through the prenda judía, Palo's beauty emerges like a morning star shimmering alone against the inky sky of divinity's rule.[3] In the form of all its prendas, but especially the prenda judía, Palo is a cultivated form of defiance. It is a craft that refines the practice of transgressing against divine power, to make fates that have withered and petrified in the shadow of God fluid and visceral again. It is a practice that values revolt, risk, and change, because they reveal limits that are implicit and promise to introduce within their boundaries the unknown, and the new. Palo's mode of contestation is to linger insistently with the dead—which saturates matter as water comingles with water—while seeking the "immediacy of being" that is known only in transgression.[4]

I have written the greater part of the preceding ethnography as a preface to the transgression of keeping and working a prenda, especially a prenda judía. The craft of prenda keeping, especially the making of works meant to kill, can be grasped only through an understanding of Kalunga, the ambient dead, el muerto. On this Isidra and Teodoro concurred; it was the heart of their teaching. Kalunga is a plane of immanence from which Palo and its myriad forms of the dead emerge and the limit of explanation regarding the dead, prendas, and the healing/harming they effect. Not by coincidence, Kalunga reflects across its undulating surface and in its countless permutations in matter what is exceptional about Palo—its creative potential, its love of the base and the abject, and its love of speed and unsentimental decision taken to transform staid and oppressive fates. Kalunga is the fluid of immediate becoming that paleras and paleros seek to actualize in prendas; it is a foreshadow of inspiration and Palo's anticipation of creating new forms of the dead, new forces, new fates, and new lives.

Kalunga, in its indeterminacy, in its evasiveness of form and place, has allowed Palo to step out of dominant west African–inspired and European codes of influence, at least since the end of the nineteenth century, if not since Kongo slaves arrived on Cuban shores. Kalunga's immanence does not judge identities or states; it does not seek to fix bodies or ideas. Rather, it allows for simultaneous affirmation of disparate concepts—it assumes paradox as one of its modes of becoming. This embrace of paradox makes an ally of the unexpected and places substantial bets on what is unstable in a world defined by the stark verticality of divine sovereignty. Only affirmed paradox allows Palo to claim access to such unstable powers as the devil, the witch, and the Jew as Catholicism imagines these. And only Palo has chosen to actualize these specters through a studied practice that combines earth, bones, blood, sticks, and other material versions of Kalunga into meaningful works of fate.

In Teodoro's Quita Manaquita house, Palo was taught to me as an engagement with the dead immanent in matter. I see this teaching as a form of materialism that posits a complicity between matter and fate, as these are each suffused by Kalunga. Isidra, speaking from her own university education in Marxist dialectics, insisted that Palo, in its love of substances and its insistence on addressing events in the realm of matter, was a form of materialism. What Palo society taught me through its hierarchy, and always in practice, was the immanence of living and dead in matter, to such a degree that the living were forms of the dead, versions of the dead in the matter of living bodies. Palo seeks to alter the "giveness" of those bodies, what is fated in them and the lives they sustain, through artful manipulations of Kalunga, of which these bodies are but condensations and by which they are permeated. This is healing, harming, and sorcery.

The complicity between matter and fate, posited most plainly in the practice of keeping a prenda, I discerned everywhere in Palo. I had recognized it before in the writings of Hegel, Marx, Adorno, Benjamin, and even in Bataille, who felt that in matter lay the secret to what is human and to what humanity might become. Matter, conceived as the negation of what is divine in human life, promised a way out of a metaphysics guaranteed by the image of God. Palo's materiality comes close to conceptions of the object advanced by Benjamin and Adorno. Benjamin, especially, believes that in the object (the commodity for him) lies the potential to create and transform the fate of modern life. My interpretation of prendas, above all the prenda judía, found a kindred materialism in Bataille, too, because of his certainty that in the baseness of matter all idealism (itself guaranteed by the image of God), including that idealism secretly ensconced in most kinds of materialism, would dissolve into more relevant forms of life. Because I had read Bataille, I was able to love the prenda judía perhaps as he would have loved it—as the despised, the bloody, and the abject that undoes the vertical dignity of a divine order.

Yet my education in Palo asked more from my thinking, because Kalunga demanded an apprehension of matter that did not operate exclusively through the awesome power of negation and of the subject-object dialectic. The particular complicity of matter and fate Palo emphasized found too much potential in indeterminate shapes of matter. During the second half of the nineties, an interest in affirmation had begun to take hold in me, from reading Nietzsche and Deleuze and then from getting acquainted with Palo, and these lines of thought and experience have come together in this text. In this way, I have been able to appreciate Isidra and Teodoro's embrace of events so minor they were barely distinguishable amid the immanence of Kalunga and to affirm such occurrences even at the risk of appearing to dwell too long with the insignificant. Thus, I have found connections to thinking and action that rest not on the identity and regularity of concepts but in their instability and inconsistency.

Nietzsche and Deleuze became conceptual bridges to my understanding of Kalunga and thus of Palo. Nietzsche's irreverent disdain for negation and dialectics freed me from a Hegelian *fatefulness* that places matter below concepts, because Nietzsche found a language to affirm material surfaces over conceptual depths through a confessed love of Heraclitean fluidity and fragmentation. Nietzsche also insists on a love of the body and that the earthly life of the body is the basis of thinking. And Deleuze I thank for his playful couplings of dialectical opposites—his mutual affirmation of substances and entities that should negate and subsume one another—and his willingness to explore immanence. Deleuze, I thank also, for his sensual empiricism, for his insistence that action is a form of grace all its own, that in action what is given and naturalized will be tested and the new will emerge. In this, Deleuze's thought (Nietzsche's too) shares an irrevocable intimacy with Palo: their mutual love of taking action for the sake of seeing what comes, of seeing what is fortuitously destroyed and what is unexpectedly made new. Thus the material world is remade, and the screens of naturalized existence parted.

Deleuze's empiricism connects me back to the project of ethnographic writing. This text is an empirical writing project in two ways. First, it communicates Palo not through explicit abstraction or elaborate confections of theoretical content and encyclopedic collection but rather through sinking into the material of my study—people's fascination with the dead in matter. I have remained close to what became important as my study opened up in the course of fieldwork, refusing habits of thought (such as the "symbol" or the "sign") I might have automatically employed in translating what people say and what they mean. I chose to express form in the content of content and sought a way forward for ethnography by finding inspiration therein. I have taken people literally in their explanations and then conformed my thinking to their literality, which requires thinking within impossible constraints. Perhaps this is what we call experimentation.

And in this is found the second empiricism of this writing. In the course of this work, I have often been at a loss for what direction to take and, in the very midst of writerly disorientation, searched for a way forward always by lingering with Kalunga, Palo, and prendas, until my language and my thought were transformed by some ungraspable event. I valued pragmatic openness as I pursued solutions to impasses in this text, solutions not in concepts I had at the ready but in actions taken in the moment, in engagements with the matter of content in a pinch, which is what Palo does so beautifully. This was a pragmatism that placed great hope in action and affirmed that ethnographic creation emerges as a step taken without utilitarian justifications, with nothing but the desire to take the step. In choosing to write about Palo I have wanted to find clues to ethnography's potential, clues as to the futures that lie within the writing that composes its present and past forms. What can ethnography be? What do its past forms inspire? What might it give birth to? These questions I sought not to resolve but simply to ask during the many choices made in the course of writing. Ethnography is not a static form, despite its unavoidable institutionalization and the heartbreaking discipline necessary for its teaching. It must be written again and again, and in the event of this writing, which is in every line indeterminate and in every word new, ethnography forever seeks the eternal return of its potential and its future.

Notes

1. Following the convention of scholars of Africa, I employ an uppercase "K" ("Kongo") when referring in English to central African cultures that exist and existed along the lower Congo River in what are now the countries of Congo and the Democratic Republic of Congo. This is to distinguish the BaKongo people, their languages, and their cultures, from the nation states. Because Cuban scholars do not follow this convention, I employ the uppercase "C" ("Congo") when citing Spanish sources that refer to the BaKongo people and those they inspired in Cuba. For example, I translate "La Regla de Congo" as "Kongo Law" and "Kongo Rule." Readers of Victor Turner will recognize the term "society of affliction" as indebted to his *Drums of Affliction*.

2. *Ocha*, the word used by practitioners of Yoruba inspirations [Santería] in Cuba to formally describe their lives, is a contraction of the Yoruba Oricha, which names the sovereign powers of fate in Yoruba-inspired praise in Cuba— the heads, so to speak, of realms of fate. See Abraham, *Dictionary of Modern Yoruba*, 479 (*orí*) and 483 (*òrìṣà* = *òòṣà*). La Regla de Ocha, the Rule of Ocha, is thus the rule of the Oricha, of the sovereign heads. In Havana, *ocha* is also used as shorthand for *santos* [saints], the sovereigns at the exceptional pinnacle of a pyramid of transformative potential rising from the broad base of profane, material life. La Regla de Ocha is popularly referred to as Santo—the Rule of the Saints, of the brilliantly transformative.

3. Deleuze, *Logic of Sense*, 1990, pp. 66–73.

4. Hegel, *Phenomenology of Spirit*, 17–20.

5. Ibid., 115. See also Marx, *Capital*, 76–87, and Lukács, *History and Class Consciousness*, 83–89, 92–95.

6. Adorno contends with the theory of the object and its reifying quality in *Negative Dialectics*, 11–12, 31–33, 174–76, 183–92. Benjamin's concern with the capacity of the object to overtake the imagination is most evident in his sustained inquiry into commodity fetishism, perhaps most accessible in his Paris oeuvre. See, for example, "Paris Capital" and "On Some Motifs."

7. Hegel, *Phenomenology of Spirit*, 104–6, 115–16.

8. Gilróy, in *The Black Atlantic*, characterized "the new" in terms of a "politics of transfiguration" that "strives in pursuit of the sublime, struggling to repeat the unrepeatable, to represent the unrepresentable" (38). Gilroy's Nietzsche-inspired theme of transfiguration, or transvaluation, is important for my study of Palo. My use of the term *Creole* is indebted to Glissant's *Caribbean Discourse* and suggests a "power formation" wherein disparate resources (such as those termed "Spanish" and "Kongo") are affirmed in relatively unstable couplings rather than synthesized into static identities through dialectical negation.

9. Turner, *Drums of Affliction*, 15–16; Janzen, *Ngoma*, 1–7. *Ngoma* means "drum" throughout much of central and southern Africa and names rites or feasts marked by the playing of drums and acts of healing.

10. Janzen, *Lemba*, 273–92. For an exceptional account of Lemba, see Janzen, *Lemba*.

11. Janzen, *Ngoma*, 11–14, quote on 103.

12. MacGaffey describes the indigenous institution of slavery among the BaKongo in a variety of instances; see *Religion and Society*, 9–11, 25–39, and *Kongo Political Culture*, 32, 71–72, 152–59.

13. For estimates that give some indication of the numbers of slaves brought to Cuba during these years, see Curtin, *Atlantic Slave Trade*, 265–73. See also Ortiz, *Negros esclavos*, 37–66.

14. A historical account of African and Creole social and aid societies during this period can be found in Howard, *Changing History*. See also Brandon, *Santeria from Africa*, 69–76.

15. The term *munanso congo* is from Palo Kikongo—Creole speech based on Kikongo and Spanish—and translates, literally, as "Kongo house." I render this as "praise house." Throughout the text I provide translations or references to translations from Kikongo from two dictionaries. Bentley's *Dictionary and Grammar of the Kongo Language* was published the year after emancipation in Cuba and is thus a good record of the language spoken by the enslaved Kikongo speakers who would inspire Palo. Laman's *Dictionnaire kikongo-français*, which draws generously from Bentley, is a more comprehensive text based on thirty years of missionary work in Lower Congo beginning in 1891. In his *Dictionary and Grammar*, Bentley cites *muna* as "those who are enclosed" (310, 358) and *nzo* as "house" (407). *Muna-nzo* would thus be "those who are enclosed in the house" and *Munanso Congo* "those who belong to the Kongo house or Kongo community." See also Laman, *Dictionnaire*, 829–39. I borrow the term "praise house" from Creel, "Gullah Attitudes," 71, 93n14.

16. Recent examples include Palmié, *Wizards and Scientists*; Bólivar Arostegui and González Días de Villegas, *Ta makuende yaya*; and Barnet, *Cultos afrocubanos*.

17. Hertz's elaboration of right and left regarding the use of hands is well known. The left is that which is "repressed and kept inactive, its development methodically thwarted." The left, in the body and the social alike, is the illegitimate, impure, unstable, maleficent and dreaded (*Right Hand*, 92, 100).

18. I am grateful to Andrew Apter and Donald J. Cosentino for a 2007 conversation regarding the etymology of *Ocha*.

19. The ritual vocabulary of Palo is inspired principally by Kikongo. The linguistic anthropologist Armin Schwegler has argued recently that Palo speech is the result of a "direct transmission and tight preservation" of Kikongo in Cuba from the earliest moments of slavery on the island. I expand this definition to include nominally Spanish words as well as one-time Kikongo words ("Vocabulario (ritual) bantú," 101–94). For *nganga* as "sorcerer" or "healer," see Bentley, *Dictionary and Grammar*, 371, and Laman, *Dictionnaire*, 683.

20. Janzen, *Ngoma*, 12, 72, 108.

21. For a more detailed treatment of prendas-ngangas-enquisos in these terms, see Ochoa, "Prendas-Ngangas-Enquisos." For my treatment of prendas as agents, entities, or actors, I am indebted to Bruno Latour (*Reassembling the Social*, 63–86).

22. In stating that Palo affirms "immediacy and the object," I am contradicting the epistemological limits that had framed my initial approach to Palo, which viewed prendas-ngangas-enquisos as "objects" distinguishable from subjects or other socially potentiated entities. In suggesting that the dead and matter are immediately connected what I am rejecting is the Hegelian premise that objects necessarily interrupt immediate experience.

23. MacGaffey, in his outstanding study of BaKongo thought, refers to this proliferation as a "series" of the dead. Unlike his series, however, the proliferation I suggest for the Cuban Kongo dead is more resistant to the categorizations MacGaffey proposes for the dead among the BaKongo (*Religion and Society*, 76).

24. My use of a logic of affirmation, propagation, and paradox in describing Palo's dead is indebted to Deleuze, *Logic of Sense*, 1–41, 253–64. For propagation and proliferation as modes of understanding and experience, see Bataille, *Accursed Share*, 19–40. See also Bataille, "Notion of Expenditure," 116–29.

25. People familiar with Kongo cosmology, or with Palo's dead, will immediately suggest Nzambi Mpungu as such an authority, because Nzambi Mpungu is often offered as a likeness to God. These readers will also recognize that the status of Nzambi Mpungu as a singular authority over the dead is much in doubt. See, for example, Laman, *Kongo III*, 1, 53, where Nzambi and the dead are coterminous, and MacGaffey, *Religion and Society*, 6, 73–76. Nzambi Mpungu in Cuban Palo is the power in matter that pushes back against human manipulation and imposes itself against a person's will and, I propose, another version of the dead. Like any version in Cuban Palo, Nzambi Mpungu is in practice no higher or more sovereign than any other form.

26. Adorno, *Negative Dialectics*, 31–33, 37–40, 140–43.

27. "We are not to philosophize about concrete things; we are to philosophize, rather, out of these things" (Adorno, *Negative Dialectics*, 33).

CHAPTER TWO

1. Deleuze and Guattari, *What Is Philosophy?* 15–36.

2. MacGaffey, *Religion and Society,* 43. See also Bentley, *Dictionary and Grammar,* 288, and Laman, *Dictionnaire,* 207.

3. MacGaffey, *Religion and Society,* 63–88.

4. Bataille, *Theory of Religion,* 23–25. For a characterization of immanence in relation to subjects and objects, see Deleuze, *Pure Immanence,* 26.

5. Canetti calls this fluid mass "the invisible crowd" and writes, "It could be argued that religions *begin* with invisible crowds. They may be differently grouped, and in each faith a different balance between them has developed. It would be both possible and fruitful to classify religions according to the way in which they manipulate their invisible crowds." Canetti later depicts the opposition of the crowds of the dead to the crowd of the living as essential not only for social cohesion but for despotism as well: "The two crowds keep each other alive" (*Crowds and Power,* 45, 63, 265–69).

6. "Plane of immanence," "sense," "rhizome," and "war machine" are among a series of terms that run throughout Deleuze's work to speak the "zone" from which subjects and objects emerge, from which imagination—which is prior to valuation and beyond good and evil—appears as event. See *Logic of Sense,* 66–73; *Pure Immanence,* 25–33; and Deleuze and Guattari, *What Is Philosophy?* 37.

7. I am reminded in this last assertion of Nietzsche's enigmatic phrase: "Let us beware of saying death is opposed to life. The living is merely a type of what is dead, and a very rare type" (*Gay Science,* 168).

8. Bascom, *Yoruba,* 71. See also MacGaffey, *Religion and Society,* 43, 54–55.

9. Castellanos and Castellanos, *Cultura afrocubana,* 63 (my translation).

10. "*Will and wave.*—How greedily this wave approaches, as if it were after something. How it crawls with terrifying haste into the inmost nooks of this labyrinthine cliff! It seems that it is trying to anticipate someone" (Nietzsche, *Gay Science,* 247–48). Nietzsche's invocation of Heraclitus to describe a world of the senses outside of Platonic valuation can be found in "Twilight of the Idols," 247–48.

11. Bataille, *Theory of Religion,* 23–25; Deleuze and Guattari, *What Is Philosophy?* 15–36.

12. I owe this last translation to a private conversation with Robert Farris Thompson, October 2001.

13. Teresa M. (Muñoz), better known in Cabrera's writings by her Ocha/Santo initiation name, Omí Tomí, was especially forthcoming in knowledge. Born in Havana the daughter of a Mina slave, she was emancipated at birth by a pair of spinsters who were her mother's owners. Their love for the little girl was such that they raised her, said Omí Tomí proudly, "in the living room." They also made her their sole heir. Cabrera's father—a young and brilliant lawyer at the time, according to Cabrera—met Omí Tomí when she came to him desperate for help with whites trying to steal her inheritance. In Cabrera's words,

"Everything had been set up. She had been legally stripped of her right [to inheritance] and to sue would have been useless." Omí Tomí became a tailor for Cabrera's grandmother and mother and later introduced Cabrera to her other great informant, Claixta Morales, also known by her Ocha/Santo initiation name, Oddedei (Cabrera, *El Monte*, 26–27).

14. "[E]l Muerto, en todas las reglas, pare al Santo. Antes de saludar a los Santos, se saluda a los Muertos" (Cabrera, *Monte*, 62; my translation).

15. Cabrera, *El Monte*, 62.

16. The term *íku* is in *Dictionary of Yoruba*, 115; *bi-* is in Delano, *Yoruba Monosyllabic Verbs*, 39.

17. Deleuze, *Pure Immanence*, 29, 31.

18. Deleuze, *Logic of Sense*, 66–81.

19. Ochoa, "Versions of the Dead," pp. 484–88.

20. Deleuze, in his description of what he calls "pure becoming," affirms the indifferent and at times paradoxical possibilities of "sense." It is from his discussion of sense and non-sense that I owe the characterization of the dead as generic and indifferent: "The stoics said it all: neither word nor body, neither sensible representation nor *rational representation*. Better yet, perhaps sense would be 'neutral,' altogether indifferent to both particular and general, singular and universal, personal and impersonal. It would be of an entirely different nature" (*Logic of Sense*, 19).

CHAPTER THREE

1. Cabrera, *El Monte*, 63 (my translation). Robert Farris Thompson has suggested that the little corners are kept in outhouses or bathrooms because these spaces share contiguity with the earth and water, both of which are subsumed within Kalunga in Palo and Kongo thought (private conversation with Thompson, October 2001).

2. The radically minor status of the dead is reflected in some recent academic works on Santería altars and aesthetics, which overlook the little corners and the dead almost entirely. See Flores-Peña and Evanchuk, *Santería Garments and Altars;* Lindsay, *Santería Aesthetics;* and Brown, *Santería Enthroned.*

3. Thompson has shown the importance of the equilateral cross in Kongo cosmology among the BaKongo and in Cuba, in which the cross marks the intersection, or point of contact, between living and dead (*Flash of the Spirit*, 108–11). I would like to suggest that the number nine is a Catholic inspiration, as nine is important in Catholic death rituals, of which the *novena*, or nine-day burial rites for the dead, is the clearest example.

CHAPTER FOUR

1. Kardec-inspired espiritistas in Cuba use the word "spirit," but in my experience this use is not usually picked up in Palo or Ocha/Santo discourse.

2. I am thinking here of Nietzsche's pairing of Apollo with Dionysus *(Birth of Tragedy)*.

3. Committees for the Defense of the Revolution (CDRs) were initiated in 1961. They are present in every block of Havana and the provincial capitals. In the countryside there can be one or more per town. They are charged with a broad array of civilian defense tasks, including nighttime watches. In many predominantly black communities like Sierra Morena the CDRs simply neglected the role of policing Ocha/Santo and Palo feasts. In other communities CDRs were rejected altogether, as with the remote communities of Haitian inspiration that practice a variety of vodoun in the highlands around Santiago de Cuba.

4. For a late iteration of the singularity-individuality coupling in Deleuze, see *Pure Immanence*, 29; for an early iteration, see Deleuze, *Logic of Sense*, 177–80.

5. Francisca Siete Sayas is a common form of the Kongo dead that appears in espiritista masses. The alliance between Cuban Espiritismo and Kongo inspirations deserves close study.

6. See Taussig, *Magic of the State*. In 1954 Cabrera writes that among the spirits possessing mediums in espiritista masses were Cuban independence leader José Martí and the famous liberation hero and physician Juan Bruno Zayas. "Many of the higher [spirits] are so political that they come from the beyond to support a candidacy with the same impassioned interest as the living and with the same apocalyptic fury that in Cuba defines the deafening political oratory of politicians of flesh and bone." Cabrera adds that these spirits demand of the living votes for one political party or another *(El Monte, 30; my translation)*.

7. For a treatment of rumors surrounding the participation of Fidel Castro in Yoruba-inspired Ocha/Santo, see Miller, "Belief and Power," 149–85.

CHAPTER FIVE

1. In Sierra Morena, as elsewhere in the Cuban countryside, the admixture of central and west African inspirations practiced by many people is known by the name of its musical form, which is called Bembé. I am consciously adopting Bembé to propose this rural amalgam of central and west African (principally old Dahomey Goravodu) forms be considered a distinct tradition of African inspiration in Cuba. Bembé is more akin to Haitian vodoun, which mutually harbors Rada (old Dahomey-inspired) and Petro (central African–inspired) forms, than to Havana Palo and Havana Ocha/Santo, which exist as separate laws. Rural Cuban Bembé is quite distinct and gloriously original enough to merit its own careful consideration.

2. The Revolution's Conjunto Folklórico Nacional has become the object of recent scholarly studies; important among them is Hagedorn, *Divine Utterances*.

3. Argeliers León was a pupil of Fernando Ortiz. León published works on African inspiration in Cuba throughout the sixties and then again in the eight-

ies. For a treatment of Leon's involvement with the Conjunto Folklórico Nacional, see Hagedorn, *Divine Utterances*, 138–68.

4. Emilio O'Farril's participation in the Conjunto Folklórico Nacional is documented in Hagedorn, *Divine Utterances*, 86, 140, 155.

5. The pun on the Spanish "bomba" [bomb] should not be missed. Cabrera argues that the boumba preceded the prenda-nganga-enquiso form of Kongo-inspired substances in Cuba and records an account of a boumba suspended from a ceiling. Coincidentally, she cites among her informants on this point a man named Juan O'Farril. I was unable to elicit from Teodoro any connection between Cabrera and his family (*El Monte*, 124, 127–29). MacGaffey cites examples of multiple Kongo minkisi contained in cloth bundles and one particular nkisi called Mbundu, which was used to divine the truth in the case of serious disputes. "[Mbundu] is kept hung-up in the house, in the roof by the wall where it may have heat from the fire so that the medicine will not congeal from the cold"(*Art and Healing*, 17). See the entry for mbumba in Cabrera, *Vocabulario Congo*, 226, and *Reglas de Congo*, 178–79.

6. Teodoro's translation of the Palo Kikongo term *munanso congo* into Spanish was *casa templo*, which translates literally as "temple house" and which I render as "praise house." Teodoro preferred *munanso congo*, and I employ "praise house" and "praise community" as synonyms for it. When asked, Teodoro would only offer the cryptic reply, "Quita Manaquita means that just as I can give to you, so can I take away." Cabrera cites Nkita as "espiritus de muertos," which is to say, the dead. She goes on to say, "Of ones who died violently. Old folks kept them in gourds. [Nkita] are to be sought in the forest or the river" (*Vocabulario Congo*, 71). Cabrera also translates Nkita as "the dead," "water spirit," "forest spirit," and, curiously, "boumba" (*Reglas de Congo*, 121, 128, 178). I take Mana to be a contraction of Mw-ána, which Laman notes as "child, descendant, progeny . . . drum played loud" (*Dictionnaire*, 645). Keeping in mind the organization of Palo society into a hierarchy based on fictive kinship, Quita Manaquita, by my rendering, means "The Dead and the Children of the Dead." Janzen refers to Nkita as an ancient "drum of affliction," or a healing society, which was powerful in the Congo River basin in the eighteenth and nineteenth centuries and still active in Kinshasa at the end of the twentieth century. Nkita, according to Janzen, concentrates on healing lineage affliction by remanding the living to the dead to reconstitute community authority (*Ngoma*, 11–14). Bakongo power objects (minkisi) bearing "Nkita" as a part of their name are cited by MacGaffey, *Art and Healing*, 160, 167, 171, 182.

7. Regla was the site of one of Havana's slave barracks, where newly arrived slaves were concentrated before being sold. See Ortiz, *Negros esclavos*, 166, 174n13. To this day, Guanabacoa and Regla remain predominantly black enclaves the Revolution has been unable to integrate. Similar, though smaller, enclaves exist in the Marianao and La Lisa sections of Havana, which were famous before the Revolution for their poverty and intensity of African inspiration. With names like Puente Negro, El Palenque, and Palo Quema'o, communities still line both sides of the Quibú River separating Marianao from La Lisa and continue to

shelter the poorest people of color, now usually immigrants from Santiago and Oriente Province to the far east of the island.

8. The organization of black Atlantic praise houses has been an abiding interest of ethnographers and historians. Palo praise houses have rarely been represented, however. The first serious attempt can be found in Cabrera, *Reglas de Congo*, 130–38. More recent descriptions can be found in Bólivar Arostegui and González Días de Villegas, *Ta makuende yaya*, and Argyriadis, *Religión à la Havane*, 145–213. See also Palmié, *Wizards and Scientists*, 181–89.

9. Brandon, *Santeria from Africa*, 69–76.

10. The police figure prominently in early Cuban writings about Palo and Ocha/Santo. Cabrera's first ethnographic notes, made in the summer of 1930, include the appearance of the police and the need for a permit to hold Palo and Ocha/Santo feasts (*Páginas sueltas*, 209). A notable chapter of Ortiz's *Negros brujos* is composed entirely of press clippings about arrests and police actions against African-inspired practices in Cuba (151–79). A permit for African-inspired feasts is still needed in Cuba, and a curfew of 10 P.M. is imposed.

11. Prendas-ngangas-enquisos, like the Kongo minkisi that inspired them, each have names that distinguish them as individual entities and according to type. See MacGaffey, *Art and Healing*. I suggest Zarabanda comes from the Kikongo words: *nsala* [a manner of working] and *-wanda* [strike, blow, or slap]. Zarabanda would thus be "that with which a blow is fashioned." See Bentley, *Dictionary and Grammar*, 390, 460, and *Appendix*, 817. MacGaffey cites the Kikongo *nsala* as "soul" (*Religion and Society*, 124). Combining Bentley's and MacGaffey's suggestions, *nsala-wanda* would thus become "soul-striker," a name consistent with Palo craft, but an imprecise translation (at least of Palo Kikongo) because in my experience "soul" was not a word or concept employed in Palo. Thompson, commenting specifically on Zarabanda prendas-ngangas-enquisos in Cuba, suggests the Kikongo etymology "*nsala-banda*, a charm-making kind of cloth" (*Flash of the Spirit*, 110).

CHAPTER SIX

1. Much of what is described as Palo ritual life in this book attempts to maintain riddles such as Teodoro's and, like his instruction, is invariably incomplete. I follow not only Teodoro's style but also Palo aesthetics in general, which in the very moment of concealing knowledge plays with its revelation. If there is an aesthetics of "the secret" in Palo it is of secret making, instead of secret keeping, and invariably built on the movement of disclosure. For a discussion on the social power of concealment and revelation, see Simmel, *Sociology of Georg Simmel*, 307–75, and Taussig, *Defacement*, 47–98.

2. In the early nineties, in an attempt to address spiking street crime in an economy crumbling after the fall of the Soviet Bloc, the Cuban regime reissued a law to address what it called "dangerousness" [*la peligrosidad*]. It was used against the unemployed to fight all forms of petty crime, from prostitu-

tion to numbers running. To this day, dangerousness is a charge brought against countless youth to control poor neighborhoods in Havana.

3. By Palo Kikongo I mean a Creole speech based on Kikongo and Spanish and not by any means Kikongo proper, neither nineteenth-century Kikongo nor contemporary Kikongo. Palo Kikongo is a prestige tongue spoken between those who practice Palo. Though Palo Kikongo includes many words that are directly Kikongo, their meanings are often uniquely Creole and their spellings are Hispanicized. When songs or prayers are sung or spoken in Palo Kikongo, Spanish sometimes dominates despite a proliferation of Kikongo words. By my definition, Palo Kikongo includes words that are etymologically Spanish but carry meanings or connotations specific to Kongo Law.

4. Ortiz argues that the term *bozal* was one among a series used to describe an African slave's proficiency with Spanish. Bozal was used to refer to Africans who could speak no Spanish, whereas *ladino* was used to refer to those who had some command of their master's tongue. Criollo, or Creole, was used to designate slaves born in Cuba. Not surprisingly, the terms carried an implicit commentary on a slave's intelligence, ladino coming to designate intelligence and quick learning, while bozal meaning slow or awkward (*Negros esclavos*, 168, 175n21). Knight, in his influential study of Cuban slavery, refers to bozales as "raw Africans who could not speak Spanish." He provides no further translation of the word (*Slave Society in Cuba*, 63).

5. Ortiz's *Glosario de afronegrismos* is a first approach to understanding the connections between Palo and Ocha/Santo ritual speech and popular speech. Attempts at cataloging ritual use of Kikongo can be found in Cabrera, *Vocabulario Congo*, and Díaz Fabelo, *Lengua Conga residual*. Castellanos and Castellanos repeat much of Cabrera's material in their *Cultura afrocubana*. Fuentes Guerra and Schwegler, *Lengua y ritos*, is a welcome contribution.

6. *Fula* has no etymology in standard Spanish. Bentley cites, "Mfula, 2, *n*. (P[ortuguese]. polvora = pulfula = fula), gunpowder" (*Dictionary and Grammar*, 100, 348).

7. My translations of Teodoro's voice derive from webs of Palo Kikongo, Spanish, and English. Palo Kikongo, like all languages, is ultimately an assemblage of the translatable and the untranslatable.

8. Bentley, *Dictionary and Grammar*, 342.

CHAPTER SEVEN

1. See, for example, Ortiz, *Negros brujos*; Cabrera, *El Monte* and *Reglas de Congo*; Barnet, *Cultos afrocubanos*; Argyriadis, *Religión à la Havane*; Palmié, *Wizards and Scientists*; and Brown, "Garden in the Machine."

2. Cabrera cites an informant: "In a Kongo praise house that is well grounded in order and consensus there is no one who doesn't benefit. Whether the house follows a Kongo line or a Lucumí [Ocha/Santo] line, this is well worked out [*En una casa de Mayombe bien fomentada, de orden y concierto, no hay quien no se beneficie, ya sea la casa de línea conga o lucumí, eso está*

muy bien calculado]." At the same time, quoting another informant she asserts, "I hope this last assertion doesn't confuse previous statements: we maintain that the principal thing in Palo is the dead *[Espero que esta última explicación no embrolle las anteriores: retengamos que lo principal en Mayombe es el Muerto]."* (*Reglas de Congo,* 129, 132; my translations).

3. Ngangulera is the feminine form of "a person who works a nganga." Ngangulera is a Creole figuration emerged from the tense circulation of words between Kikongo and Spanish. It is a word used by whites to disparage blacks, equivalent to "witch." Like the word "witch," however, paleras and paleros take it up with pride and relish the fear it generates in those outside Palo.

4. Díaz Fabelo affirms that in some instances menstruating women have received prendas-ngangas-enquisos but have been denied the privilege of sacrificing to them until after their menstruation ceases. Without the right to sacrifice, the keeper has limited autonomy to use the prenda-nganga-enquiso to its fullest potential (*Lengua Conga residual,* 127).

5. Among the best books to emerge on Cuba in recent years is Sublette, *Cuba and Its Music.* Sublette's indisputably well-informed history does what practitioners of Palo insist any account of Rumba do: correctly position Congo music as generative and determinant of Rumba (258).

CHAPTER EIGHT

1. Bentley, *Dictionary and Grammar,* 346.

2. A similar correspondence appears in Haitian vodoun, where Petro's Kongo spirits are deemed to be hot and "fiery," while Rada's west African spirits are deemed to be "cool" (Thompson, *Flash of the Spirit,* 12–16, 180–83).

CHAPTER NINE

1. Rayamiento, from the Spanish verb *rayar,* means to mark in a line, with a pencil, knife, or other means. *Rayar* in Cuba also means "to shred." *Un rayamiento,* a noun, designates a gathering of a Palo praise society at which a person (or persons) is marked with lines cut into the skin as part of her or his initiation into Palo society. I have heard English-speaking initiates of Palo houses in New Jersey and Oakland refer to the verb *rayar* as "to scratch." I find this translation mild, somehow trying to do away with cutting and "shredding," the marking of a person explicit to Palo life.

2. I have changed the name of this Palo Monte praise house.

3. According to Teodoro, Campo Lemba is "the cemetery at night, the realm of the dead," Campo Santo is "the cemetery during the day," and Campo Finda is simply "the cemetery."

4. "**Aki,** a prefix applied to the name of a person when he is spoken of and all who are with him. . . . **Akinani** (a combination of **aki** . . . and *nani,* interrogative personal pronoun), who are they?" (Bentley, *Dictionary and Grammar,* 246). "**Nani,** *pron. inter.* (pl. **akinani,** *see* **aki** *under* **A**), who?" (366). See also

Laman, *Dictionnaire,* 658. For a misinterpretation of *kinani,* which nonetheless has relevance for interpreting the use of this word in contemporary Palo, see Cabrera, *Vocabulario Congo,* 198.

5. I have altered the initiation names.

6. *Mi lemba* is very likely a reference to the Lemba society, as described by Janzen in *Lemba.* For Teodoro, lemba was the dead, like Kalunga. Janzen cites the etymological basis of lemba in *lembikisa,* a word meaning "to calm" (*Lemba,* 3). See also Bentley's definition in *Dictionary and Grammar:* "**Lemba,** *v.,* to make gentle, to tame, civilize; soothe, ally, appease, assuage; cut, castrate, geld" and "**Lembeka,** *v.t.,* to tame, make calm, soothe, allay, pacify, appease, civilize, break in, to cool (by adding cold water)" (321, 322). I find more relevance in Laman, who writes, "**lemba** (S), pl. **ma-,** sortilege, ensorcellement, v. **lémba,** calmer" (*Dictionnaire,* 391). In short, Lemba is a society/gathering of the dead where sorcery/healing is effected.

7. The word *carile* (*karile, carire, karire*) remains a mystery to me. Teodoro once said *carire* was an ancient form of prenda [*fundamento muy antiguo*]. Cabrera translates *karire* as "devil" [*diablo*] (*Vocabulario Congo,* 194). In her *Reglas de Congo,* Cabrera cites "old informants" who extol the virtues of eating eel [*anguila*], which among other things fortifies the mind and defends the body against illness. One tells her that eel eaten with peppercorns and tiny shrimp or crab, "of the kind that are found at times inside oysters" "defends the body along the path of *Ndundu Karire,* which is the Devil, master of the *Nsila,* of a crossing" (158; italics added).

8. Campana Luisa is the name of a storied prenda.

9. Cabrera cites the use of *fimba* to refer to *firma* (*Reglas de Congo,* 147). This usage opens the way to a possible Palo Kikongo pun on the Spanish *firma,* which means "signature" and alone offers strong possibilities for understanding this practice. Laman suggests, "**fímba,** chercher, fouiller, suivre le piste; flairer; renifler; rechecher; examiner; questioner; [to search, follow, trace, to sniff, to examine, to question]" (*Dictionnaire,* 149). The practice of using firmas to look into, invoke, and draw insight from the dead comes to mind. BaKongo used olfactory terms such as "smelling out" to talk about clairvoyance with a nkisi (Laman, *Kongo III,* 71). Thompson comments that present-day Kongo minkisi used for apprehending what is not immediately evident often take the shape of carvings of dogs, prodigious embodiments of the olfactory (*Flash of the Spirit,* 121).

CHAPTER TEN

1. Laman records the writing of designs in chalk during initiation into a Kongo society, of affliction on which the initiates are made to lie (*Kongo III,* 247).

2. *Nzambi* is universally translated as "God." See Cabrera, *Vocabulario Congo,* 271; Bentley, *Dictionary and Grammar,* 96, 406; Laman, *Dictionnaire,* 821; Turner, *Drums of Affliction,* 14; Turner, *Forest of Symbols,* 107, 294; and Janzen, *Lemba,* 192. I maintain that the translation of "God" does not exclude

some kinship with Kalunga, as I have defined this term in chapter 2, and that Nzambi, in the context of Cuban-Kongo inspiration, must be considered as an enigmatic version of the dead, as generic force in matter and relations. Laman, in his chapter on Nzambi, writes, "Nzambi is identical with Chambi, the name which the ancestors of the Kongo retained when they left their country Chari in Southern Sudan." "Departed close relations are often called nzambi. A dead father is spoken of as: 'Nzambi, my late father'" (*Kongo III*, 53, 58).

3. I have changed Virtudes's surnames.

4. *Mbele* means knife; *Mbele bobo*, razor blade. See Cabrera, *Vocabulario Congo*, 224, and Laman, *Dictionnaire*, 526. Díaz Fabelo translates *makondo* as "plantain" [*platano*] in *Lengua Conga residual*, 51. Also see Cabrera, *Vocabulario Congo*, 114, and Bentley, "[p]lantain, n., dinkondo," *Dictionary and Grammar*, 161.

5. Ochoa, "Prendas-Ngangas-Enquisos," p. 405.

6. Cabrera, *Consejos, pensamientos y notas*, 26.

7. For *menga*, see Cabrera, *Vocabulario Congo*, 227, and Laman, *Dictionnaire*, 549.

8. Dog-likeness is not demeaning in Palo as it might be in Catholic or Yoruba-inspired understandings. Kongo inspiration locates dogs as having a privileged proximity to the dead and therefore powers of seeing or smelling out those events that evade understanding or lie in the future. See, for example, Thompson, *Flash of the Spirit*, 121, and Laman, *Kongo III*, 75–76. The term *perro de prenda* is derived not only from the extreme submission implied by being possessed by the dead around a prenda but, just as importantly, from the powers of divination (smelling out) attributed to those possessed during Palo feasts.

9. I am unable to find a definition or etymology for *guarilanga*.

10. Blood will run! Like dye, blood will run! This is the second great Palo praise song for blood, the first being the song praising the knife.

11. In newspapers from the nineteenth century, it is common to run across advertisements offering slaves for sale or asking for assistance in finding a runaway slave. Such announcements normally described the slave by name, sex, skin color, Spanish proficiency, and any marks such as ritual scarifications. See, for example, *Diario de la Marina*, October, 16, 1852.

12. "Malekun, Sala!" is from Arabic.

CHAPTER TWELVE

1. Siete Rayos is also known as Nsasi. Laman cites, "**Nsànsi,** du préc., nkisi qui protège, élève l'enfant et le preserve de tout maléfice" and "nsasi (My [Mayombe]), cimetière pour les chef" [cemetery, burial place for chiefs] (*Dictionnaire*, 758, 759).

2. Hearn has recently written a book, *Cuba: Religion, Social Capital, and Development*, about Atarés and Ocha/Santo.

3. Wirtz, *Ritual, Discourse, and Community;* Dodson, *Sacred Spaces;* and James, *Brujería cubana* all provide valuable portraits of African-inspired praise forms in Oriente.

4. See Cabrera, *Kimbisa,* and Muzio, *Andres Quimbisa.*

CHAPTER THIRTEEN

1. *Agua ngongoro,* says Cabrera in *Reglas de Congo,* is bound-up with the ceiba and lends powers of "vision" (144). Both Cabrera and Bentley cite *ngongoro* and *ngongolo* as "centipede" or "millipede" (*Vocabulario Congo,* 248; *Dictionary and Grammar,* 374). Laman gives this definition but adds a variety of possibilities, including "**ngongolo** (O [Ouest]), griffe, ongle. [claw or nail]; **ngongongo**, chute, eau qui tombe (rivière) [water fall]; **ngongongo** (O [Ouest]), mante religieuse [praying mantis]; **ngongongo**, corbeau [crow, raven] (*Dictionnaire,* 692). An etymological connection to Pedro's "cooling water" is too weak to imply.

2. The song lays claim to the healing powers of agua ngongoro, or so it would seem. The Spanish allows for a second reading, however, which is sadder but consistent with the sometimes plaintive tone of Palo songs: Agua ngongoro is a cure / Agua ngongoro why *doesn't* it heal me? Though the melody of the song is slow, it has an affirmative energy, and my sense is that the first of my two renderings is the correct one. I highlight this ambiguity simply to mention that a blues underlies many Palo songs and can never be discounted when interpreting its meanings.

3. Pedro explained this song as a riddle: Lucero [the prenda-nganga-enquiso] doesn't light the depths of night [Lucero the star does that]. What then does Lucero [the prenda-nganga-enquiso] light? Lucero lights the depths of the earth and the sea, which is where the dead concentrated in the prenda-nganga-enquiso draw their force.

4. A similar formulation can be found in Thompson, who describes firmas as "points" where the realms of the living and the dead meet (*Flash of the Spirit,* 108–11).

5. Thompson's work is an exception to this, as is McArthy Brown's dissertation on Haitian vèvè. See Thompson, "Translating the World," and McArthy Brown, "Vèvè of Haitian Vodou."

6. "Sun, moon and clouds may all be incorporated into minkisi" (Laman, *Kongo III,* 65).

CHAPTER FOURTEEN

1. The term *nfumbe* is derived from the Kikongo word *mvumbi.* Cabrera defines *fumbi* as "spirits active inside ngangas which are handled by the Padre Nganga," nfumbe as the "spirit of the dead" or the "dead one," and *mbumbi* as "dead one, cadaver" (*Vocabulario Congo,* 180, 226, 245). Laman gives the

following definitions: "**mvumbi** (Be, pl. **ba-**), cadaver, per. morte" and "**mfumbi** (NE [Nord Est]), diverses médecines qui tiennent au **nkisi Matompa**" (*Dictionnaire*, 683, 556). Other possible Kikongo attributions from Laman include "**mfùmbi**, de **fùmba**, meurtier, homicide; brigand, assassin; bourreau; intermédiaire, créature payee pour faire le mal" and "**mfùmbi** (NE), albinos dont les cheveux sont employés pour **nkisi**" (556).

2. Laman records the use of bones in Kongo minkisi: "Attempts have also been made to make use of the magic power exercised by bandoki [witches] by taking a finger, a piece of bone or the like from a ndoki [witch] and incorporating it with nkisi" (*Kongo III*, 69). See also MacGaffey, *Art and Healing*, 12.

3. Siete Rayos, Zarabanda, and Lucero are gendered masculine, as are Changó, Ogún, and Eleguá, with whom they are connected, respectively. Likewise, Mama Chola Nkengue, Ma're Lango, and Centella Ndoki are gendered feminine, as are their Ocha/Santo affinities Ochún, Yemayá, and Oyá. Palo also proposes androgynous powers with Tiembla Tierra, like Ocha/Santo proposes them with Obbatalá.

4. Marx, *Eighteenth Brumaire*, 18.

5. The visits paleros make to cemeteries for nfumbe have been described by Cabrera in *El Monte*, 121, and others. Discussing the fabrication of nkisi among the Bakongo, Laman communicates that "Usually a nkuyu [aggressive, mischievous dead] must be captured and incorporated into the nkisi, as it is the nkuyu's power, in combination with the medicine and the magic prectised [*sic*] by the ngnanga, which makes the nkisi effective. The bankuyu [pl. nkuyu] are found in the burial ground, especially by the grave of a powerful chief or great nganga. All sorts of tricks are resorted to in order to soften the heart of the nkuyu and entice it, such as putting out appetizing food and palm wine so that a piece of raffia cloth may be thrown over the nkuyu. Thus caught, it can be incorporated into the image or the nkisi" (*Kongo III*, 74, cited in Palmié, *Wizards and Scientists*, 333n25).

6. The nfumbe trade is popularly acknowledged in Cuba, from jokes to mass media allusions. An obvious example is in Tomás Gutierrez Alea's famous 1968 comedy, *Death of a Bureaucrat*. When the protagonist pays a team of grave diggers to raid Havana's Colón cemetery in search of his recently deceased uncle's Communist Party card, which was interred with his remains, the men set out under the cover of darkness. As they approach the cemetery gate their leader says, "Let's go boys; we've done this before!"

7. *Asere* is common slang for "friend," akin to "dude" in contemporary U.S. English. It is popularly believed to have emerged into common usage from Havana's Abakuá men's societies.

CHAPTER FIFTEEN

1. *Matari* is defined by Cabrera as "**Matari, Mataria:** Stone" (*Vocabulario Congo*, 222; *Reglas de Congo*, 147); by Díaz Fabelo as "Mataria: Stone, rock" (*Lengua Conga residual*, 110); and by Laman as "**Matádi**, du sing., des pierres, des rochers, des récifs [stones, rocks, corals]" (*Dictionnaire*, 506).

2. Cemetery or grave earth is important in Kongo-inspired healing throughout the Black Atlantic (Thompson, *Flash of the Spirit*, 105, 128).

3. The word *alafia* is borrowed from the terminology of Yoruba-inspired divination with coconut shells (Cabrera, *El Monte*, 380–91).

4. See, especially, Cabrera, *El Monte*, 123. See also Brown, "Garden in the Machine," 302, 371–76. For Kongo minkisi and their contents, see Laman, *Kongo III*, 74, and MacGaffey, *Art and Healing*.

5. The term *masangó* is possibly a conjunction of "**mása,** pron. **ma-,** mais, millet [corn]," for the corn husks used in wrapping Palo packets, and "ngo," meaning "leopard," in short, a diminutive "corn husk leopard," in reference to the perceived power of the packets (Laman, *Dictionnaire*, 503, 689). See Thompson on *nkangue* charms for leopard imagery in charm making in northern Kongo today (*Flash of the Spirit*, 128).

6. Laman defines *nkanga* as "**nkànga,** de **kànga,** action de lier [to tie]" (*Dictionnaire*, 709). Bentley translates it as "to tie," *Dictionary and Grammar*, 289. Cabrera states, "**Nkanga:** Amarrar, ligadura mágica; amarre [to tie down, a magical tie, a binding]" (*Vocabulario Congo*, 251, 103). Thompson identifies the word *nkangue* as a noun, meaning "one who arrests" (*Flash of the Spirit*, 128). Because what is being accomplished is the "loading" of the masangó, an affinity emerged with the Spanish verb *cargar*, "to load." Conjugated into Palo Kikongo, *cargar* becomes *nkarga* or *nkanga*.

7. See Cabrera, *Vocabulario Congo*, 260. Laman defines *ntoto* as "terre, terrain" (*Dictionnaire*, 799).

8. I am unable to find this use of Palo Kikongo in any dictionary.

9. Laman lists *nkunia* as "**nkúni,** pl. de **lukúni,** bois de chauffage [firewood]" (*Dictionnaire*, 735), Bentley as "**Nkuni,** n., firewood, fuel" (*Dictionary and Grammar*, 386), and Cabrera as "Nkunia: Tree. Stick. *Algarrobo*" (*Vocabulario Congo*, 254). Taking this etymology into consideration it is possible to advance an argument that the sticks, or stakes, incorporated into all prendas-ngangas-enquisos are fuel for a fire. Much of Palo lore dealing with attacks by a prenda-nganga-enquiso employs a terminology of heat and fire (see chapter 16). MacGaffey records a nkisi called Nkondi (hunter nkisi—"one who lies in wait") that employs firewood against its enemies. Citing Laman, he suggests the bundle of firewood once carried by the nkisi figurine was used to crush its opponents (*Art and Healing*, 141–42). I suggest the wood carried by this hunting nkisi is used to flush out game with fire—a tested technique for hunting in the bush—while Nkondi waits to seize its prey. Likewise, nfumbe on a hunt may use their nkunia to light fires around the enemies of their keeper to flush them out of hiding and into the nfumbe's clutches. I am reminded of the well-known Palo Kikongo recitation that goes, "¡*Sopla guira, llama ñoka, ñunga, ñunga, saca mundele!* [Aspirate the prenda; call the serpent; fire, fire, burn out the whites!]."

10. Like so many Palo verses, the lyrics can be read as a blues, where prestige and loss combine.

11. Brown suggests the spikes act as goads, which makers drive into their prendas-ngangas-enquisos to force their action. Brown draws a connection to

the nails driven into Kongo minkisi figurines. This is an entirely plausible connection, though in building the prendas, Pedro did not explicitly drive the spikes as goads ("Garden in the Machine," 375).

CHAPTER SIXTEEN

1. See Palmié, *Wizards and Scientists,* 173. I differ with Palmié's argument that Palo offerings adhere to a commodity logic rather than one of gift exchange. This position ignores the ritual context of Palo craft and prenda keeping, where offerings, despite their repetitive quality, are always singular and specific and therefore far from the reified state of commodities. Palmié disregards the uniqueness of every healing context, as well as the irreducible particularity of each offering presented to a prenda. In this way, sacrificial offerings elude the logic of equivalence that necessarily underlies the commodity form. Palmié's analogy of payments in Palo and gifts in Ocha/Santo furthermore elides the considerable contractual ambiguity that so often underlies sacrifice, whether in Palo or Ocha/Santo.

2. See Cabrera, *Reglas de Congo,* 148.

3. This restriction is true for Palo in Havana. In the central Cuban countryside paleros on occasion make their own prendas and sacrifice to them at will without initiation of any kind.

4. The will of the responsive dead to have a prenda made, and their consent at the moment of initiation, is usually discerned in espiritista-led "masses" that are arranged once an initiation has been decided on.

5. Cabrera recounts several forms of ritual abuse inflicted on prendas (*Reglas de Congo,* 148, 187–88).

6. The force inside a prenda, the prenda itself, or the dead the prenda sends forth to possess its servants, is often referred to as *ngombe,* or ox bull. See chapter 20; Cabrera, *Vocabulario Congo,* 247; and Laman, *Dictionnaire,* 690.

CHAPTER SEVENTEEN

1. For a fine description of Ocha/Santo– and Ifá-centered healing, see Brown, "Garden in the Machine," 304–10. He includes a description of despojos that combine Ocha/Santo and Palo elements.

2. Thompson, *Flash of the Spirit,* 128. Thompson, who is otherwise excellent in his treatment of African-inspired arts in Cuba, misses the corn-husk wrapper in his description of Cuban-Kongo *nkangue* charms, suggesting instead the use of raffia cloth. The tiny ridges of the corn husk are clearly distinguishable in the image he includes (262n5 and 263n6).

3. Cabrera, *Vocabulario Congo,* 162, and Díaz Fabelo, *Lengua Conga residual,* 105. Laman observes, "**bi-lóngo (N)**, v. **lóngo**, remède magique de **nkisi**; remède en général; offrande à **nkisi**; **(O)**, qqch de vivant dont on absorbe du sang (= **nkita**)" (*Dictionnaire,* 38). Bentley cites, "**Bi**, 12, *n.,* evil, badness, vice,

wickedness, depravity, sinfulness, naughtiness" and "**Nlongo,** 4, *n.*, medicine, drug, fetish, poison" (*Dictionary and Grammar*, 253, 389).

4. Cabrera records what she calls an old burlesque melody: "*Unos dicen que a la una/ otros dicen que a las dos / y yo digo que a las tres / bilongo mató a Mercé* [Some say it was at one / others say at two / I say it was at three / that a bilongo killed Mercé]" (*Vocabulario Congo,* 35). Mercé is short for Mercedes, a common woman's name. There are several other renditions of the bilongo's powers in the lyrics of Cuban popular music.

5. See Cabrera, *Reglas de Congo,* 144, for a similar formulation.

6. Ibid., 192.

7. See Cabrera for the term *nfuiri* (*Vocabulario Congo,* 245). For *ndoki,* Cabrera cites, "Devil, witch. Spirit, imp, maleficium. Useful for poisoning at a distance. Blind enemies. Vampire. Witch, sorcerer" (244). Laman adds, "**Ndòki,** de **lòka,** auteur presume d'un sortilege, d'un maléfice; sorcier, ensorceleur, qui par ensorcellement ôte là à qqn" (*Dictionnaire,* 671). See also *Kongo III,* 72.

8. Cabrera, *Reglas de Congo,* 133, 224n. Cabrera at times uses the construction *se murmuraba* to establish the atmosphere of fear and doubt that surrounds those who suspect Palo craft is being worked against them; for example, see *Reglas de Congo,* 185. See also page 196 for the term *murumberos* [paleros].

9. Taussig, *Defacement,* and Simmel, *Sociology of Georg Simmel.*

CHAPTER EIGHTEEN

1. I am greatly indebted to Kruger's *Spectral Jew* for helping me texture things "Jewish" in Palo. Kruger's discussion of spectrality (8–17), through Derrida's well-known formulation of absence-presence, has allowed me to rephrase the terms with which I take up European Catholic fantasies and nightmares of Jewish otherness. The spectral, by my understanding, speaks to the fictive (absent) yet socially real (present) powers attributed to Jews by European Catholics, and to the felt consequences of these powers on all sides of the relationship. I appreciate Kruger's turn on Jewish spectrality through the concept of embodiment but do not work with that part of his argument in what follows.

2. My sense for revaluation is beholden to Nietzsche, *Genealogy of Morals.*

3. Cabrera dedicates several pages of *Reglas de Congo* to the prenda judía and its lore (181–88). For Basilio's testimony, see pages 186–87; for Castro Baró's, see page 181 and its note.

4. Laman in several instances describes nkisi-inspired divination as having olfactory qualities, like those of a dog (*Kongo III,* 75–76, 82–83). Kongo "smell-diviners" enter an ecstatic state to discern particular diseases afflicting an individual and also those responsible for sending the illness. See also Cabrera, *Reglas de Congo,* 181.

5. Cabrera quotes an unspecified informant: *"es muy caprichosa y da dolores de cabeza como cuando se empeña en que la lleven a pasear al cementario y puede uno tropezarse con la policía o con quien no convenga"* (*Reglas de Congo*, 185). For the prenda's blood preferences, see page 181.

6. Ibid., 181–82. For a fine account of Cuban politics and race relations in the years following emancipation and independence from Spain, including detailed accounts of campaigns of racial persecution that employed accusations of witchcraft and ritual homicide, see Helg, *Our Rightful Share*, 108–9, 130–31.

7. Helg, *Our Rightful Share*, 109–16.

8. Ibid.; Palmié, *Wizards and Scientists*, 212.

9. Kruger, *Spectral Jew*, xxvi, 4.

10. Cabrera, *Reglas de Congo*, 181–85, quote on 185.

11. Teodoro's knowledge about Haitians and their descendants in the eastern mountains of Cuba was sketchy. By all accounts the descendants of Haitians in Oriente Province do not practice Havana versions of African inspiration, nor do they keep prendas. Their practice is largely inspired by Haitian vodoun. At the same time, contemporary researchers of Cuban vodoun detail rites dedicated to propitiating devils, which are much storied among their informants. See James, Millet, and Alarcón, *Vodu en Cuba*, 248–67.

12. See Ortiz, *Negros brujos*, 83–84, 126–27. Ortiz is unable, in *Negros brujos*, to distinguish central African from west African practices in Cuba though he knows the geographic and ethnic differences are important on the island. As a result, he lumps both forms of African-inspired knowledge into one category he calls *brujería* [witchcraft]. His model, where at best Kongo elements are assimilated into a largely west African practice, is vaguely reminiscent of vodoun. He draws largely on a 1900 description of African forms in Brazil as well as missionary and other accounts of west African peoples for his interpretations. Ortiz then passes this interpretation through the lens of nineteenth-century positivist criminology, in which as a younger man he was trained by the Italian criminologist Cesare Lambroso. Ortiz's book has been recently treated by Helg, *Our Rightful Share*; Hagedorn, *Divine Utterances*; and Palmié, *Wizards and Scientists*, among others.

13. Ortiz, *Negros brujos*, 83. Historians Aline Helg and Stephan Palmié have treated the specific events of the case of Zoyla Díaz concisely, including interpretations of the facts of the case that differ from Ortiz's. See Helg, *Our Rightful Share*, 109–13, and Palmié, *Wizards and Scientists*, 211. See also Hagedorn, *Divine Utterances*, 190.

14. Helg, *Our Rightful Share*, 110; Palmié, *Wizards and Scientists*, 211.

15. Helg, *Our Rightful Share*, 111.

16. The aftermath included the 1912 War of the Races, which to this day epitomizes white atrocities against blacks in the history of Cuba. See Helg, *Our Rightful Share*, 194–226. Racist attitudes persist in Cuba today, and to some extent the image of early twentieth-century ritual homicide still fuels them.

17. Kubayende, also noted as Cobayende or Kuballende, is an exalted figure among the Palo dead because "he was the only one ever to return to life." As a

consequence, he is considered a privileged arbiter of the fine line between life and death. Kubayende shares a likeness with the biblical figures of Lazarus the resurrected and Lazarus the beggar (San Lázaro) and the Ocha/Santo sovereign Babalu Ayé. To sing "the girl doesn't dance my Kubayende" is to mock her irrevocable death. Kubayende's dance is that of the dead vibrating with life.

18. My translations of Palo Kikongo mambo lyrics rely on Teodoro's and Isidra's interpretations, unless otherwise noted. When possible, I have compared their interpretations of Palo Kikongo to recorded Palo Kikongo usages in Cabrera and Díaz Fabelo, as well as with Laman's and Bentley's Kongo dictionaries. Where discrepancies have arisen I have used the interpretation of my informants. Some text has been left untranslated. My transcriptions employ verse repetition to convey a sense of rhythm and alternation in Palo song.

19. *Coche* means "a car" in much of Latin America. In Cuba it still carries the meaning of horse-drawn cart, as Cubans call the automobile *la maquina* [machine/engine]. Kubayende is pictured by paleros, as San Lázaro sometimes is by santeros, as the driver of a horse-drawn funerary cart.

20. Once out of their cauldrons, ndoki take on many forms. Common among them are predatory birds, like vultures and hawks.

21. This song is one of Palo's classic blood mambos, the same as discussed in chapter 10.

22. Ortiz refers to Domingo Bocourt as "brujo Bocú" (*Negros brujos*, 84).

23. Tín-Tán was the nickname of a black man named Sebastián Fernández, accused of raping and killing a ten-year-old girl in the months before the murder of Zoyla Díaz. His trial and subsequent hanging under uncertain circumstances while awaiting execution established much of the social atmosphere in which the murder of Zoyla Díaz was received. Though Teodoro collapsed the two cases, Tín Tán personally had no part in the events leading to the arrest, trial, and murder of Bocourt. See Helg, *Our Rightful Share*, 109.

24. For example, see Palmié, whose treatment of prendas as Creolized Kongo minkisi is thorough, except on this point (*Wizards and Scientists*, 254n346).

25. Brown cites Jewish bones as the prenda judía's defining characteristic ("Garden in the Machine," 299n67).

26. The Vatican opened the archives of the Holy Office of the Inquisition for the first time in 1988, and thus a new source of information on the Catholic Church's history of relations with Jews became available. Historian David Kertzer's *Popes against the Jews*, a work dealing largely with nineteenth-century church doctrine and propaganda—and thus of great aid in elaborating an image of Catholic-Jewish relations during the years many slaves came to Cuba—is among the first scholarly works to emerge from these archives.

27. See, for example, Cervantes, *Devil*; Harris, *Aztecs, Moors and Christians*; and Boyarin, *Unconverted Self*.

28. Kertzer, *Popes against the Jews*, 28–37.

29. Kertzer provides a wealth of material on nineteenth-century Catholic anti-Semitism. See *Popes against the Jews*, especially, 61–151.

30. Ibid., 152.

31. Ibid., 75, 133–51, 153.
32. Ibid., 60–130.
33. Ibid., 153–65.
34. Ibid., 213–36. See also Helg, *Our Rightful Share*, 55–90, and Palmié, *Wizards and Scientists*, 217–25.
35. See Helg, *Our Rightful Share*, 204–11, 220–26.
36. Helg, *Our Rightful Share*, 221, and Palmié, *Wizards and Scientists*, 240.
37. Cabrera, *Reglas de Congo*, 182. Ortiz suggests that ritual homicide was rare in Cuba and has doubts about it occurring at all. Nonetheless, he affirms that ritual motives could have been involved in the Zoyla Díaz murder (*Negros brujos*, 130).
38. McAlister, *Rara!* 117–19.
39. Kertzer, *Popes against the Jews*, 11, 93.
40. Palmié, *Wizards and Scientists*, 195.
41. Kruger, *Spectral Jew*, xxvii, 8–17.
42. See Levine, *Tropical Diaspora*, 2, 9, 1.
43. Ortiz, *Negros brujos*, 10.
44. Levine, *Tropical Diaspora*, 2, 6.
45. The English occupation of Cuba for eight months in 1762 is the most relevant example, when Jewish merchants helped boost the Cuban sugar industry and during which time thousands of African slaves were imported. See Levine, *Tropical Diaspora*, 10.

CHAPTER NINETEEN

1. Such an engagement is also more akin to working with a boumba, an early form of prenda much akin to Kongo minkisi bundles. Cuban boumbas made the nfumbe's bones available to the healer along with the other materials. See Cabrera, *El Monte*, 124.
2. For a comprehensive calendar of Ocha/Santo feast days, see Brown, *Santería Enthroned*, 305.
3. There may be rites practiced in Ifá divination on or around Easter Sunday, but of these I am not aware.
4. The translation of *kimbambula* as "Palo feast" was Teodoro's *[fiesta de Palo]*. Cabrera cites *kimba* as an initiation (*Vocabulario Congo*, 196–97). See also "Nkimba," in Bentley, *Dictionary and Grammar*, 383. Bentley elaborates on the secret society of Nkimba, which he believes to be spreading inland from the coast and which supposedly grants the power to catch witches. Members learn a ritual vocabulary, which Nkimba initiates call *kimbwamvu* (*Appendix*, 507). Laman defines nkimba as "une société secrète" (*Dictionnaire*, 719).
5. Cabrera identifies *tié tié* as the *bijiríta*, a bird powerful in Palo craft (*Vocabulario Congo*, 282). This mambo cannot be translated well without knowing for sure how the bijiríta or its remains is used in Palo works, and here it is being invoked metaphorically. I have left it untranslated. The song here is also partial, as I do not present all of Teodoro's improvisations over the chorus.

6. I have not been able to ascertain a meaning for Ñao.

7. *Maximene* is "el muerto," the inscrutable, or ambient dead, as well as the future (Teodoro's translation).

8. *Tierra Naombre* was the term Teodoro used to refer to Kongo lands in Africa.

9. For *ngunga*, see Cabrera, *Vocabulario Congo*, 250. Also see Bentley, who specifies *ngunga* as a bell in the European form (*Dictionary and Grammar*, 20, 375). For *nsala*, see Cabrera, *Vocabulario Congo*, 255. Bentley cites *nsala* as a "manner of working" (*Dictionary and Grammar*, 390). This could also be the source of *salar*, to "salt" or "work against." Paleros often greet and say good-bye with the exclamation *¡Buen sala! [nsala]*, which could mean "good works!" "May your works go well!"

10. "**Nkumbi**, 4, *n.*, a drum used when libations of blood are being poured out at the grave of a great hunter" (Bentley, *Dictionary and Grammar*, 385).

11. In Palo Kikongo, *kwenda* means "to go." Bentley defines kwenda as "a going" and "an advance" (*Dictionary and Grammar*, 317).

12. *Nguembo* is translated as bat in Cabrera, *Vocabulario Congo*, 249; Bentley, *Dictionary and Grammar*, 372; and Laman, *Dictionnaire*, 686.

13. The Spanish word *templar* literally means "to temper." The heat employed in the process of tempering is what has stuck with the word in Cuba, which in vulgar but everyday Cuban Spanish acts as a verb meaning "to fuck." There is a vocabulary of sexual aggression around working with all prendas regardless of their gender. Getting the prenda ready for action, heating it, can be read as "fucking" it. Similarly, Cabrera's informants refer to those possessed by a prenda as "getting fucked" by the dead. They also use the word *simbó*, which is an easy variation on the third-person past tense of the verb *zingar* [*zingó*], which in Cuban Spanish means "to fuck" (*Reglas de Congo*, 186).

14. Bentley translates *ngangara* as "an embrace" (*Dictionary and Grammar*, 371). In Palo Kikongo this could refer to feeling secure or strong with a prenda at one's side. I suggest *ngangara que estoy* to mean something like "I'm *ngangafied!*" or "I'm embraced by my prenda!"

15. Bentley and Laman define *kwama* as "fire" and *mundele* as "whites" (*Dictionary and Grammar*, 316, 358; Laman, *Dictionnaire*, 350, 609).

CHAPTER TWENTY

1. Cabrera, *Reglas de Congo*, 187; Ortiz, *Los Negros Brujos*, 65.

2. See Cabrera, *Reglas de Congo*, 188.

3. Ibid., 183.

4. *Mpaka* and *mensu* are a set of goat's horns packed and sealed with charges that give their user the power to see into the dead. One of the two, the mensu, has a little mirror set into its seal. Bentley translates *mpaka* as "horn" (*Dictionary and Grammar*, 352).

5. These are Palo entities I had not heard Teo name before. MacGaffey defines *n'kuyu* as a "ghost" (*Religion and Society*, 73). Cabrera cites *nkuyo* as a

little wooden doll that makes mischief at its keeper's bidding (*Vocabulario Congo*, 255). Díaz Fabelo records *enkuyo* as a dangerous form of the Ocha/Santo sovereign Eleguá (Eshu) for Palo Kimbisa (*Lengua Conga residual*, 140).

6. I propose that *kiangalanga* is a Palo Kikongo onomatopoeia, a likeness to ringing bells.

7. For the use of gunpowder to vitalize and discern the will of minkisi in nineteenth-century Kongo, see Laman, *Kongo III*, 65, 75.

8. The word *guira* refers to a gourd, which, according to Teodoro, prendas-ngangas-enquisos were built into in the past. First clay vessels and then iron kettles replaced the gourds. *Guira* refers to a historical, antique image of Kongo minkisi.

CONCLUSION

1. Hubert and Mauss, *Sacrifice*, 33, 127n186.

2. Bataille, "Attraction and Repulsion I," and Leiris "Sacred in Everyday Life," 25, 111.

3. "Perhaps it is like a flash of lightning in the night which, from the beginning of time, gives a dense and black intensity to the night it denies, which lights up the night from the inside, from top to bottom, and yet owes to the dark the stark clarity of its manifestation, its harrowing and poised singularity" (Foucault, "Preface to Transgression," 35).

4. Ibid., 37n16.

Bibliography

Abraham, R. C. *Dictionary of Modern Yoruba*. London: University of London, 1958.

Adorno, Theodor. *Negative Dialectics*. New York: Continuum, 1973.

Argyriadis, Kali. *La religión à la Havane: Actualité des représentations et des pratiques cultuelles havanaises*. Amsterdam: Overseas Publishers Association, 1999.

Barnet, Miguel. *Cultos afrocubanos: La regla de Ocha, la regla de Palo Monte*. Havana: Unión, 1995.

Barrera, Florentino. *Resumen analítico de las obras de Allan Kardec*. Buenos Aires: Vida Infinita, 2000.

Bascom, William. *The Yoruba of South Western Nigeria*. Prospect Heights, IL: Waveland, 1984.

Bataille, Georges. *The Accursed Share: An Essay on General Economy*, Vol. I: *Consumption*. Trans. Robert Hurley. New York: Zone Books, 1988.

———. "Attraction and Repulsion I." Trans. Betsy Wing. In *The College of Sociology (1937–39)*, edited by Dennis Hollier, 103–12. Minneapolis: University of Minnesota Press, 1988.

———. "The Notion of Expenditure." Trans. Allan Stoekl, Carl R. Lovitt, and Donald M. Leslie Jr. In *Visions of Excess: Selected Writings*, edited by Allan Stoekl, 116–29. Minneapolis: University of Minnesota Press, 1993.

———. *Theory of Religion*. Trans. Robert Hurley. New York: Zone Books, 1989.

Benjamin, Walter. "On Some Motifs in Baudelaire." Trans. Harry Zohn. In *Illuminations*, edited by Hannah Arendt, 186–92. New York: Schocken Books, 1969.

———. "Paris Capital of the Nineteenth Century." Trans. Edmund Jephcott. In *Reflections*, edited by Peter Demetz, 146–62. New York: Schocken Books, 1986.

Bentley, W. Holman. *Appendix to the Dictionary and Grammar of the Kongo Language as Spoken at San Salvador, the Ancient Capital of the Old Kongo Empire, West Africa*. London: Baptist Missionary Society / Kegan Paul, Trench, Trübner, 1895.

———. *Dictionary and Grammar of the Kongo Language as Spoken at San Salvador, the Ancient Capital of the Old Kongo Empire, West Africa*. London: Baptist Missionary Society / Trübner, 1887.

Bólivar Arostegui, Natalia, and Carmen González Días de Villegas. *Ta makuende yaya y las reglas de Palo Monte: Mayombe, brillumba, kimbisa, shamalongo*. Havana: Unión, 1998.

Boyarin, Jonathan. *The Unconverted Self: Jews, Indians, and the Identity of Christian Europe*. Chicago: University of Chicago Press, 2009.

Brandon, George. *Santeria from Africa to the New World: The Dead Sell Memories*. Bloomington: Indiana University Press, 1993.

Brown, David Hilary. "The Garden in the Machine: Afro-Cuban Sacred Art in Urban New Jersey and New York." Diss. Yale University, 1989.

———. *Santería Enthroned: Art, Ritual, and Innovation in an Afro-Cuban Religion*. Chicago: University of Chicago Press, 2003.

Cabrera, Lydia. *Consejos, pensamientos y notas de Lydia E. Pinbán, copiados por P. Guayaba para la Benemérita Amérika Villarbínbín*. Ed. Isabel Castellanos. Miami: Universal, 1993.

———. *El Monte*. 1954. Reprint, Miami: Universal, 1983.

———. *Páginas sueltas*. Miami: Universal, 1994.

———. *La regla del Kimbisa del Santo Cristo del Buen Viaje*. Miami: Universal, 1977.

———. *Reglas de Congo: Palo Monte, Mayombe*. Miami: Peninsular, 1979.

———. *Vocabulario Congo (El Bantú que se habla en Cuba)*. Ed. Isabel Castellanos. 2nd ed. Miami: Universal, 2001.

Canetti, Elias. *Crowds and Power*. Trans. Carol Stewart. New York: Seabury, 1978.

Castellanos, Jorge, and Elizabeth Castellanos. *Cultura afrocubana*, Vol. 3: *Las religiones y las lenguas*. Miami: Universal, 1992.

Cervantes, Fernando. *The Devil in the New World: The Impact of Diabolism in New Spain*. New Haven, CT: Yale University Press, 1994.

Creel, Margaret Washington. "Gullah Attitudes toward Life and Death." In *Africanisms in American Culture*, edited by Joseph E. Holloway, 152–86. Bloomington: Indiana University Press, 1990.

Curtin, Philip D. *The Atlantic Slave Trade: A Census*. Madison: University of Wisconsin Press, 1969.

Delano, Isaac O. *A Dictionary of Yoruba Monosyllabic Verbs*. Ibadan, Nigeria: University Press, 1969.

Deleuze, Gilles. *The Logic of Sense*. Trans. Mark Lester with Charles Stivale. New York: Columbia University Press, 1990.

———. *Pure Immanence: Essays on a Life*. Trans. Anne Boyman. New York: Zone Books, 2001.

Deleuze, Gilles, and Felix Guattari. *What Is Philosophy?* Trans. Hugh Tomlinson and Graham Burchell. New York: Columbia University Press, 1994.

Díaz Fabelo, Teodoro. *Diccionario de la lengua Conga residual en Cuba*. Santiago de Cuba: Casa del Caribe, 1999.

A Dictionary of the Yoruba Language. Ibadan, Nigeria: University Press, 1979.

Dodson, Jualynne E. *Sacred Spaces and Religious Traditions in Oriente Cuba.* Albuquerque: University of New Mexico Press, 2008.

Echeruo, Michael J. C. *Igbo-English Dictionary: A Comprehensive Dictionary of the Igbo Language with an English-Igbo Index.* New Haven, CT: Yale University Press, 1998.

Flores-Peña, Yasmur, and Roberta J. Evanchuk. *Santería Garments and Altars: Speaking without a Voice.* Jackson: University Press of Mississippi, 1994.

Foucault, Michel. "Preface to Transgression." Trans. Donald F. Bouchard and Shery Simon. In *Language, Counter Memory, Practice,* edited by Donald F. Bouchard, 29–52. Ithaca, NY: Cornell University Press, 1977.

Fuentes Guerra, Jesús, and Armin Schwegler. *Lengua y ritos del Palo Monte Mayombe: Dioses cubanos y sus fuentes africanas.* Madrid: Iberoamericana, 2005.

Gilroy, Paul. *The Black Atlantic: Modernity and Double Consciousness.* Cambridge, MA: Harvard University Press, 1993.

Glissant, Edouard. *Caribbean Discourse: Selected Essays.* Charlottesville: University Press of Virginia, 1992.

Hagedorn, Katherine. *Divine Utterances: The Performance of Afro-Cuban Santería.* Washington, DC: Smithsonian University Press, 2001.

Harris, Max. *Aztecs, Moors and Christians: Festivals of Reconquest in Mexico and Spain.* Austin: University of Texas Press, 2000.

Hearn, Adrian H. *Cuba: Religion, Social Capital, and Development.* Durham, NC: Duke University Press, 2008.

Hegel, G. W. F. *Phenomenology of Spirit.* Trans. A. V. Miller. Oxford: Oxford University Press, 1977.

Helg, Aline. *Our Rightful Share: The Afro-Cuban Struggle for Equality, 1866–1912.* Chapel Hill: University of North Carolina Press, 1995.

Hertz, Robert. *Death and the Right Hand.* Trans. Rodney Needham and Claudia Needham. Glencoe, IL: Free Press, 1960.

Howard, Philip A. *Changing History: Afro-Cuban Cabildos and Societies of Color in the Nineteenth Century.* Baton Rouge: Louisiana State University Press, 1998.

Hubert, Henri, and Marcel Mauss. *Sacrifice, Its Nature and Functions.* Trans. W. D. Halls. Chicago: University of Chicago Press, 1964.

Igwe, G. Egemba. *Igbo-English Dictionary.* Ibadan, Nigeria: University Press, 1999.

James, Joel. *La brujería cubana: El Palo Monte.* Santiago de Cuba: Oriente, 2006.

James, Joel, José Millet, and Alexis Alarcón. *El vodu en Cuba.* Madrid: Oriente, 1998.

Janzen, John M. *Lemba, 1650–1930: A Drum of Affliction in Africa and the New World.* New York: Garland, 1982.

———. *Ngoma: Discourses of Healing in Central and Southern Africa.* Berkeley: University of California Press, 1992.

Kertzer, David I. *The Popes against the Jews: The Vatican's Role in the Rise of Modern Anti-Semitism.* New York: Knopf, 2001.

Knight, Franklin. *Slave Society in Cuba*. Madison: University of Wisconsin Press, 1970.

Kruger, Steven F. *The Spectral Jew: Conversion and Embodiment in Medieval Europe*. Minneapolis: University of Minnesota Press, 2006.

Laman, Karl. E. *Dictionnaire kikongo-français: Avec un étude phonétique décrivant les dialectes les plus importants de la langue dite kikongo*. Ridgewood, NJ: Gregg, 1964.

———. *The Kongo III*. Upsala, Sweden: Studia Ethnographica Upsaliensia, 1962.

Latour, Bruno. *Reassembling the Social: An Introduction to Actor-Network-Theory*. Oxford: Oxford University Press, 2005.

Leiris, Michel. "The Sacred in Everyday Life." Trans. Betsy Wing. In *The College of Sociology (1937–39)*, edited by Dennis Hollier, 98–102. Minneapolis: University of Minnesota Press, 1988.

Levine, Robert M. *Tropical Diaspora: The Jewish Experience in Cuba*. Gainesville: University Press of Florida, 1993.

Lindsay, Arturo, ed. *Santería Aesthetics in Contemporary Latin American Art*. Washington, DC: Smithsonian Institution Press, 1996.

Lukács, Georg. *History and Class Consciousness: Studies in Marxist Dialectics*. Cambridge, MA: MIT Press, 1971.

MacGaffey, Wyatt. *Art and Healing of the Bakongo Commented by Themselves: Minkisi from the Laman Collection*. Stokholm: Folkens Museum-Etnografiska, 1991.

———. "Complexity, Astonishment and Power: The Visual Vocabulary of Kongo Minkisi." *Journal of Southern African Studies* 14, no. 2 (January 1988): 188–203.

———. *Kongo Political Culture: The Conceptual Limit of the Particular*. Bloomington: Indiana University Press, 2000.

———. *Religion and Society in Central Africa: The BaKongo of Lower Zaire*. Chicago: University of Chicago Press, 1986.

Marx, Karl. *Capital*. Vol 1. New York: International Publishers, 1967.

———. *The Eighteenth Brumaire of Louis Bonaparte*. New York: International Publishers, 1964.

McAlister, Elizabeth. *Rara! Vodou, Power, and Performance in Haiti and Its Diaspora*. Berkeley: University of California Press, 2002.

McCarthy Brown, Karen. "The Vèvè of Haitian Vodou: A Structural Analysis of Visual Imagery." Diss. Temple University, 1975.

Miller, Ivor Lynn. "Belief and Power in Contemporary Cuba: The Dialogue between Santería Practitioners and Revolutionary Leaders." Diss. Northwestern University, 1995.

Muzio, Maria del Carmen. *Andres Quimbisa*. Havana: Union, 2001.

Nietzsche, Friedrich. *The Birth of Tragedy*. Trans. Walter Kaufmann. New York: Vintage Books, 1967.

———. *The Gay Science*. Trans. Walter Kaufmann. New York: Vintage Books, 1974.

———. *The Genealogy of Morals.* Trans. Walter Kaufmann. New York: Vintage Books, 1989.

———. "Twilight of the Idols." In *The Portable Nietzsche,* edited and translated by Walter Kaufmann, 463–563. New York: Penguin Books, 1982.

Ochoa, Todd Ramón. "Prendas-Ngangas-Enquisos: Turbulence and the Influence of the Dead in Cuban-Kongo Material Culture." *Cultural Anthropology* 25, no. 3 (August 2010): 387–420.

———. "Versions of the Dead: Kalunga, Cuban-Kongo Materiality and Ethnography." *Cultural Anthropology* 22, no. 4 (November 2007): 473–500.

Ortiz, Fernando. *Glosario de afronegrismos.* Havana: Siglo XX, 1924.

———. *Los negros brujos.* Havana: Ciencias Sociales, 1995.

———. *Los negros esclavos.* Havana: Ciencias Sociales, 1975.

Palmié, Stephan. *Wizards and Scientists: Explorations in Afro-Cuban Modernity and Tradition.* Durham, NC: Duke University Press, 2002.

Schwegler, Armin. "El vocabulario (ritual) bantú de Cuba. Parte I: Acerca de la matriz africana de la 'lengua congo' en El Monte y Vocabulario Congo de Lydia Cabrera." In *La Romania Americana: Procesos lingüísticos en situaciones de contacto,* edited by Norma Díaz, Ralph Ludwig, and Stefan Pfänder, 97–194. Madrid: Iberoamericana, 2002.

Simmel, Georg. *The Sociology of Georg Simmel.* Trans. Kurt H. Wolff. Glencoe, IL: Free Press, 1950.

Sublette, Ned. *Cuba and Its Music: From the First Drums to the Mambo.* Chicago: Chicago Review Press, 2004.

Taussig, Michael. *Defacement: Public Secrecy and the Labor of the Negative.* Stanford, CA: Stanford University Press, 1999.

———. *The Magic of the State.* New York: Routledge, 1994.

Thompson, Robert Farris. *Flash of the Spirit: African and Afro-American Art and Philosophy.* New York: Vintage Books, 1984.

———. "Translating the World into Generousness: Remarks on Haitian Vèvè." *Res* 32 (Autumn 1997): 19–36.

Turner, Victor W. *The Drums of Affliction: A Study of Religious Processes among the Ndembu of Zambia.* Oxford: Clarendon, 1968.

———. *The Forest of Symbols: Aspects of Ndembu Ritual.* Ithaca, NY: Cornell University Press, 1970.

Williamson, Kay. *Igbo-English Dictionary Based on the Ontisha Dialect.* Benin City, Nigeria: Ethiope, 1972.

Wirtz, Kristina. *Ritual, Discourse, and Community in Cuban Santería: Speaking a Sacred World.* Gainesville: University of Florida Press, 2007.

Index

Abakuá men's societies, 6, 106, 215, 278n7
accumulation, 14, 156
actualization of Kalunga: fear and, 195; ill will and, 193; the living and, 30, 37, 45, 80; the object and, 37, 45, 107–8, 192, 197; prenda and, 261; specters and, 219, 261. *See also* Kalunga (ambient dead/the dead)
Adorno, Theodor, 7, 16, 262, 265n6
affirmation, mutual, 32, 33, 71, 206, 207
affirmation of matter, 13–15
Africa, cultures of west, 34–35, 83, 145, 159, 215, 217–19, 270n1, 274n2, 282n12. *See also* Kongo cultures
African-inspired society/societies, 8. *See also specific societies*
aides, 74, 88, 93, 116–17, 121, 123–26, 224, 225
ambient dead, use of term, 37. *See also* Kalunga (ambient dead/the dead)
ancestors (eggun), 24, 35. *See also* Kalunga (ambient dead/the dead); responsive dead
animal blood (menga): bilongo and, 247; cooling characteristics of, 108; Kalunga, and hot vitality of, 107–8; prenda, and hot vitality of, 107–8, 119–20, 188, 244; prenda care and, 75, 91, 108–9, 119, 139, 183–85, 226, 246–47; resguardo and, 194; songs and, 117; as version of Kalunga, 114–15; visceral force of, 115. *See also* animals; animal sacrifices
animals: eating, 108–9, 128; as generic, 81; ndoki as, 247–52, 255, 259, 283n20; organ offerings and, 184; prenda making and, 134; skulls of, 87, 135–36, 141, 174. *See also* animal blood (menga); animal sacrifices; feathers; matter/materiality; *specific animals*
animal sacrifices: killing animals for, 111, 118–19, 226, 246; prenda care and, 75, 91, 108–9, 119, 139, 183–85, 226, 246–47; rayamiento and, 108–9, 128; songs and, 75, 117. *See also* animal blood (menga); animals
anonymous dead, 24, 188. *See also* Kalunga (ambient dead/the dead)
astros, los (stars), 137–38, 142, 167, 277n6
authorities in praise houses, 58, 76–77, 85–86, 94, 147–48
autonomy, 41, 190, 219, 274n4

babalawo (devotee of Ifá sovereign Orula), 41, 95, 193, 229
bakofula, 74, 116–17, 121, 123–26, 224

Text: 10/13 Aldus
Display: Aldus
Indexer: Naomi Linzer
Compositor: Westchester Book Group

CPSIA information can be obtained
at www.ICGtesting.com
Printed in the USA
FSOW02n0959010217
30271FS